Vegetables

CHRISTOPHER KIMBALL'S
MILK STREET

Vegetables

250 BOLD, SIMPLE RECIPES FOR EVERY SEASON

CHRISTOPHER KIMBALL

WRITING AND EDITING BY
J. M. Hirsch and Michelle Locke

RECIPES BY
Matthew Card, Diane Unger and the Cooks at Milk Street

ART DIRECTION BY
Jennifer Baldino Cox and Brianna Coleman

PHOTOGRAPHY BY
Connie Miller of CB Creative

FOOD STYLING BY
Christine Tobin

VORACIOUS

LITTLE, BROWN AND COMPANY
NEW YORK   BOSTON   LONDON

Hachette Book Group supports the right to free expression and the
value of copyright. The purpose of copyright is to encourage writers
and artists to produce the creative works that enrich our culture.

The scanning, uploading, and distribution of this book without permission
is a theft of the author's intellectual property. If you would like permission
to use material from the book (other than for review purposes), please
contact permissions@hbgusa.com. Thank you for your support of the
author's rights.

Little, Brown and Company
Hachette Book Group
1290 Avenue of the Americas, New York, NY 10104
littlebrown.com

First edition: October 2021

Voracious is an imprint of Little, Brown and Company, a division of
Hachette Book Group, Inc. The Voracious name and logo are trademarks
of Hachette Book Group, Inc. The publisher is not responsible for websites
(or their content) that are not owned by the publisher.

The Hachette Speakers Bureau provides a wide range of authors for
speaking events. To find out more, go to hachettespeakersbureau.com
or call (866) 376-6591.

Photography by Connie Miller of CB Creative
Food Styling by Christine Tobin
Prop Styling by Brianna Coleman

ISBN 978-0-316-70598-1
LCCN 2021938173

10 9 8 7 6 5 4 3 2 1

IM

Print book interior design by Gary Tooth / Empire Design Studio
Printed in China

RECIPES BY VEGETABLE

INTRODUCTION

Chili-spiked carrots. Skillet-charred Brussels sprouts. Hearty, roasted cauliflower steaks. Crisp and browned potatoes brightened with harissa and herbs. Vegetables at the center of the plate. Wonderfully so.

For much of history, most people around the world treated meat as an accent or flavoring, not the main event. The exception, of course, has been Britain and the U.S., generally awash in cheap meat (hence the 18th century ballad, "The Roast Beef of Old England").

The Middle East, for example, offers mostly vegetarian cuisines, whether you live in Tel Aviv or Beirut. In this tradition, we are not afraid to add just a bit of ground meat to a vegetable stir-fry or anchovies to add savory depth to skillet-charred Brussels sprouts. This is not a vegetarian cookbook; it's a modern guide to preparing vegetables.

It's not a matter of inventing anything new. The rest of the world is way ahead of us in taking vegetables to heart because grains, legumes and produce already were at the center of their diets. Given, however, that supermarket vegetables often lack in flavor what they deliver in visual appeal, the modern cook no longer can rely on the inherent flavor of, say, celery or cucumbers to get the culinary job done.

We need to look to the global pantry and the wisdom of other cultures to rescue the sad history of vegetables here in the U.S. (In an early edition of "The Boston Cooking School Cookbook," vegetables garnered just 42 pages out of 757. And a typical offering was "Carrots Huntington" — 4 cups of carrots cooked with ½ cup butter and ½ cup cream. Yikes!)

To up our game in the vegetable department, we had to get on the road to spend time with home cooks who could show us the way. We traveled to Athens to learn why winter vegetable stews should taste lighter and brighter, not heartier and heavier. In Cairo, we tasted eggplant that got not just flavor, but also bold pops of texture from whole spices. And in Puglia, Italy, we had a revelatory bite of zucchini enriched by ricotta cheese and lemon.

The results speak for themselves. With one head of cauliflower you might choose Cauliflower Shawarma; Smothered Cauliflower with Tomatoes, Capers and Raisins; Sichuan Dry-Fried Cauliflower; Pasta with Cauliflower, Garlic and Toasted Breadcrumbs; or Curried Cauliflower Rice with Peas and Cashews. Ease up on the butter and cream.

One final note. We have started with recipes that have provenance and history. Bắp xào tôm khô, for example, is the starting point for Corn with Shrimp, Chilies and Scallions. But this book does not offer authentic recipes per se; adaptations are necessary to make recipes work in an American kitchen. (And the notion of perfectly replicating a recipe from, say, Oaxaca, is a hopeless endeavor. You can get across the fundamental concept but not the heart and soul of a recipe in a kitchen thousands of miles away. Even the water is different.)

The premise is simple. It's high time that vegetables move to the center of the plate so that meat can, more often, take a secondary role, a source of flavor rather than the main attraction. But that does not mean that here at Milk Street we do not love whole hog barbecue or a steaming bowl of Taiwanese Beef Noodle Soup.

All things in moderation. Including moderation.

1

MEZE

Tomato Tart
with Olives and Gruyère

A sheet of frozen puff pastry, thawed and rolled into a slightly larger rectangle, is the crust for this simple but impressive savory tart. We toss the sliced tomatoes and onion with salt and pepper to season the vegetables while also allowing them to release some of their moisture for both better texture and flavor after baking. Using the tines of a fork to poke holes in the rolled-out pastry prevents the center from becoming too puffy, but leave a 1-inch border around the edges so the pastry forms a light, crisp outer crust.

START TO FINISH: 40 MINUTES
SERVINGS: 4 TO 6

1 pound plum tomatoes, cored and cut crosswise into ¼-inch slices

½ small red onion, thinly sliced

Kosher salt and ground black pepper

1 sheet frozen puff pastry, thawed

2 tablespoons Dijon mustard

4 ounces Gruyère **OR** provolone cheese, shredded (1 cup)

½ cup pitted black olives **OR** green olives **OR** a combination, chopped

1 tablespoon extra-virgin olive oil, plus more to serve

Don't use regular round tomatoes in this recipe. Plum tomatoes, which are relatively firm and dry, work best.

1. **Heat the oven to 450°F** with a rack in the middle position. Line a rimmed baking sheet with kitchen parchment. In a large bowl, toss together the tomatoes, onion and ½ teaspoon each salt and pepper; set aside. With a rolling pin, roll the pastry into a 10-by-14-inch rectangle, then place on the prepared baking sheet. Using a paring knife, score a 1-inch frame around the edge of the pastry, then poke holes in the pastry with a fork, avoiding the border. Spread the mustard on the pastry, avoiding the border, then sprinkle with the cheese.

2. **Using a slotted spoon,** distribute the tomato-onion mixture in an even layer on top; discard the liquid remaining in the bowl. Sprinkle with the olives and drizzle with the oil. Bake until the pastry is golden brown, 15 to 20 minutes. Cool for 5 to 10 minutes before slicing. Serve drizzled with additional oil.

Optional garnish: Chopped fresh oregano **OR** torn fresh basil **OR** chopped drained capers **OR** a combination

Savory Fresh Corn Pancakes

START TO FINISH: 40 MINUTES
MAKES TWELVE 4-INCH PANCAKES

These savory pancakes are best made with corn kernels freshly cut from the cob. Out of season, 4 cups frozen corn kernels, thawed and patted dry, are a reasonably good alternative. The batter can be made with either buttermilk or whole milk, so use whichever you have or prefer. The pancakes are great alongside bowls of chili or grilled pork chops or seafood. To serve as a light main, top them with sour cream or crème fraîche, plus flaked smoked trout or slices of smoked salmon, with a salad to accompany. Leftover pancakes reheat well on a wire rack in a 250°F oven.

¾ cup plus 1 tablespoon all-purpose flour

1½ teaspoons baking powder

1 tablespoon white sugar

Kosher salt and ground black pepper

2 large eggs

4 cups corn kernels (from about 5 ears corn)

1 cup buttermilk **OR** whole milk

3 scallions, thinly sliced **OR** ½ cup lightly packed fresh cilantro, chopped

1 chipotle chili in adobo sauce, minced, plus 1 teaspoon adobo sauce

8 tablespoons grapeseed or other neutral oil, divided

Don't crank up the heat to brown the pancakes more quickly. Steady, medium heat helps ensure that the batter as well as the corn kernels fully cook through by the time the exteriors are nicely browned.

1. In a small bowl, whisk together the flour, baking powder, sugar, 1 teaspoon salt and ¼ teaspoon pepper. In a large bowl, whisk the eggs, then stir in the corn, buttermilk, scallions, chipotle chili and adobo sauce. Add the dry ingredients and fold until just combined.

2. In a 12-inch nonstick skillet over medium, heat 2 tablespoons of oil until shimmering. Using a ⅓-cup measuring cup, drop 3 portions of batter, evenly spaced, into the skillet. Use the back of a spoon to spread into 3½- to 4-inch pancakes, then cook until the pancakes are golden brown on the bottoms, 2 to 3 minutes. Using a metal spatula, flip the pancakes and cook until the second sides are golden brown, 2 to 3 minutes; transfer to a wire rack. Wipe out the skillet and heat 2 tablespoons of the remaining oil until shimmering. Cook the remaining batter in the same way, wiping out and adding 2 tablespoons oil to the skillet after each batch.

Optional garnish: Chopped pickled peppers

Roasted Tomato Bruschetta with Taleggio and Herbs

Pumpernickel bread offers much more flavor than the average crusty white wheat loaf for this take on a delicious finger food from Italy. Purchase a presliced loaf or buy a whole one and slice it ½ inch thick. We take plum tomatoes, which are drier and firmer than standard round tomatoes, and roast them in the oven to soften their texture and concentrate their flavor. Taleggio is a rich, semisoft northern Italian cheese that has a pungent aroma but a mild, subtly nutty flavor. If it's not available, brie is a great alternative. We top the bruschetta just before serving with a tangle of chopped fresh herbs and greens.

START TO FINISH: 35 MINUTES
SERVINGS: 4

———

4 large slices pumpernickel bread, each about ½ inch thick (see headnote)

4 tablespoons extra-virgin olive oil, divided, plus more for brushing

3 medium garlic cloves, minced

1 pound ripe plum tomatoes, cored and sliced crosswise into ¼-inch rounds

Kosher salt and ground black pepper

¾ cup lightly packed fresh basil OR mint, roughly chopped

¾ cup lightly packed fresh flat-leaf parsley OR dill, roughly chopped

1 cup lightly packed baby arugula OR baby watercress, roughly chopped

1 tablespoon balsamic vinegar, plus more to serve

6 ounces Taleggio cheese OR brie cheese

Don't remove the rind from the cheese. The rind is edible on both Taleggio and brie, and offers a contrast in texture from the creamy center.

1. **Heat the oven to 450°F** with a rack in the middle position. Brush both sides of the bread slices with oil, then place in a single layer on a rimmed baking sheet. Bake until the bread is toasted on both sides, 5 to 6 minutes total, flipping the slices once about halfway through. Transfer the bread to a wire rack; reserve the baking sheet.

2. **In a small bowl,** stir together 2 tablespoons of the remaining oil and the garlic. Brush the reserved baking sheet with 1 tablespoon of the remaining oil, then place the tomato slices on top, arranging them in a single layer. Brush the slices with the oil-garlic mixture and sprinkle with ¼ teaspoon salt. Roast until the tomatoes are softened and beginning to brown, 12 to 15 minutes. Remove from the oven and set aside.

3. **In a medium bowl,** toss the herbs and greens with the remaining 1 tablespoon oil, the vinegar and ¼ teaspoon each salt and pepper. Divide the cheese among the bread slices, spreading it to cover the surface. Using a wide metal spatula, place the tomatoes on top of the cheese, dividing them evenly. Top the bruschetta with the herb-greens mixture and drizzle with additional vinegar.

Muhammara

Muhammara is a spicy-tart dip for flatbread made from walnuts and roasted red peppers. The name comes from the Arabic word for reddened, and the dish originated in Syria, where it often is served alongside hummus and baba ganoush. Aleppo pepper is made from ground dried Halaby chilies; it tastes subtly of cumin and fruit, with only mild heat. Look for it in well-stocked markets and spice shops, but if you cannot find it, simply leave it out—the muhammara still will be delicious. Serve with flatbread or vegetables for dipping or use as a sandwich spread.

4 teaspoons ground cumin

7-inch pita bread, torn into rough pieces

1 cup walnuts

Two 12-ounce jars roasted red peppers, drained and patted dry (2 cups)

1 teaspoon Aleppo pepper (optional; see headnote)

½ teaspoon red pepper flakes

Kosher salt and ground black pepper

3 tablespoons pomegranate molasses, plus more to serve

2 tablespoons lemon juice

6 tablespoons extra-virgin olive oil, plus more to serve

Chopped fresh flat-leaf parsley, to serve

Don't forget to pat the roasted peppers dry after draining them. *Excess moisture will make the muhammara watery in both flavor and consistency.*

1. **In a small skillet over medium,** toast the cumin, stirring, until fragrant, about 30 seconds. Remove from the heat and set aside.

2. **In a food processor,** process the pita bread and walnuts until finely ground, about 45 seconds. Add the cumin, roasted peppers, Aleppo pepper (if using), pepper flakes and 1 teaspoon each salt and black pepper. Process until smooth, about 45 seconds, scraping the bowl as needed.

3. **Add the pomegranate molasses** and lemon juice and process until combined, about 10 seconds. With the machine running, drizzle in the oil. Taste and season with salt and pepper, then transfer to a serving bowl. Drizzle with additional pomegranate molasses and oil, then sprinkle with parsley.

Turkish Tomato and Red Pepper Dip

There are countless variations on this fresh, flavorful Turkish meze known as ezme. In general, most are combinations of raw vegetables—finely chopped tomatoes, sweet peppers and onions, drained to rid the mixture of excess moisture, then seasoned. Seasoning varies, but we found that adding chilies and paprika, fresh parsley, a drizzle of thick pomegranate molasses and some lemon juice gave us a balanced, full-flavored dip. Serve with toasted pita or lavash, alone or as an element of a meze platter.

START TO FINISH: 35 MINUTES
SERVINGS: 4 TO 6

1 pound ripe tomatoes, cored, halved crosswise and seeded

1 medium yellow onion, quartered

1 medium red bell pepper, stemmed, seeded and quartered

Kosher salt

1 teaspoon sweet paprika

1 teaspoon ground sumac (optional)

1 serrano chili, stemmed, seeded and minced

¼ cup finely chopped fresh flat-leaf parsley

1 tablespoon pomegranate molasses, plus more to serve

1 tablespoon lemon juice

Extra-virgin olive oil, to serve

Don't forget to seed the tomatoes to remove some of their moisture. Also, don't try to process all of the vegetables at once. Processing in batches results in more evenly sized pieces. And pulsing, rather than letting the machine run, helps ensure the vegetables are chopped, not processed to a puree.

1. In a food processor, combine half of the tomatoes, half of the onion, half of the bell pepper and 1½ teaspoons salt. Pulse until the vegetables are chopped into rough ⅛-inch pieces, 10 to 12 pulses; do not puree them. Transfer to a fine-mesh strainer set over a medium bowl. Repeat with the remaining tomatoes, onion and bell pepper and 1½ teaspoons salt, then add to the first batch in the strainer. Let drain, stirring occasionally, for about 15 minutes.

2. Discard the liquid collected in the bowl, then transfer the vegetables to the bowl. Add the paprika, sumac (if using), chili, parsley, molasses and lemon juice, then stir to combine. Taste and season with salt. Using a slotted spoon, transfer to a serving dish. Drizzle with oil and additional pomegranate molasses.

Zucchini with Lemon, Za'atar and Tahini Yogurt

Silky, supple broiled zucchini slices are paired with tangy, tahini-enriched yogurt and finished with toasted walnuts for this simple side or starter. Bracing lemon, both zest and juice, along with pungent garlic, za'atar (a Levantine spice, seed and herb blend) and fresh herbs provide bold flavor accents. Serve this with warmed flatbread for dipping into the tahini-yogurt sauce.

START TO FINISH: 35 MINUTES
SERVINGS: 4 TO 6

¼ cup extra-virgin olive oil

1 tablespoon grated lemon zest, plus ¼ cup lemon juice

1 tablespoon za'atar

2 medium garlic cloves, finely grated

Kosher salt and ground black pepper

3 medium zucchini (about 1½ pounds total), sliced into ¼-inch rounds

1 cup plain whole-milk yogurt

3 tablespoons tahini

½ cup walnuts, toasted and roughly chopped

½ cup chopped fresh mint **OR** basil

Don't overcook the zucchini. *Lightly charred slices have the best flavor and appearance, but broilers vary in heat output, so monitor their progress. It's better to err on the side of scant browning and just tender texture than to char the zucchini to the point of being overcooked, as the slices will become mushy and lifeless.*

1. **Heat the broiler** with a rack about 4 inches from the element. In a large bowl, whisk together the oil, lemon juice, za'atar, garlic, ¼ teaspoon salt and ½ teaspoon pepper. Measure 3 tablespoons of the mixture into a small bowl and set aside.

2. **To the oil-lemon juice mixture** remaining in the large bowl, add the zucchini and toss. Distribute the slices in an even layer on a broiler-safe rimmed baking sheet, then broil until tender and lightly charred on both sides, 10 to 15 minutes, flipping the slices with a wide metal spatula about halfway through. Drizzle the zucchini with 1 tablespoon of the reserved oil-lemon juice mixture.

3. **Into the remaining** 2 tablespoons oil mixture, whisk the lemon zest, yogurt, tahini and ¼ teaspoon each salt and pepper. Spread the yogurt mixture on a serving platter, place the zucchini on top and sprinkle with the walnuts and mint.

Sicilian Caponata

Caponata, a sweet and sour eggplant dish from Sicily, gets its distinctive flavor from a blending of the island's Mediterranean and North African influences. We batch-cook the eggplant, zucchini and onion plus bell pepper to better preserve each vegetable's character. This keeps the caponata bright and full of texture rather than stewy and one-dimensional. A tangy-sweet vinegar-sugar glaze, added at the end of cooking, brings the elements together. If you prefer a sweeter caponata, stir in additional sugar when seasoning with salt and pepper. Serve warm or at room temperature with crusty bread as an appetizer or as a side to grilled or roasted meats and seafood.

START TO FINISH: 45 MINUTES
SERVINGS: 4

___

6 tablespoons extra-virgin olive oil, divided

1 medium eggplant (about 1 pound), trimmed and cut into 1-inch chunks

Kosher salt and ground black pepper

1 medium zucchini, trimmed, halved lengthwise and cut into 1-inch pieces

1 large yellow onion, cut into 1-inch pieces

1 red bell pepper, stemmed, seeded and cut into 1-inch pieces

½ cup red wine vinegar

2 tablespoons white sugar, plus more to serve

1 tablespoon tomato paste

¼ cup lightly packed fresh basil, torn

Don't forget to stir the vegetables while they cook. Occasionally moving them around the pan ensures they cook and brown evenly. To preserve the basil's bright color, don't tear and add the leaves until you are ready to serve.

1. **In a 12-inch nonstick skillet** over medium, heat 4 tablespoons of oil until shimmering. Add the eggplant and ½ teaspoon salt, stir, then distribute in an even layer. Cover and cook, stirring occasionally, until the eggplant is browned and a fork inserted in the largest piece meets no resistance, 10 to 15 minutes. Using a slotted spoon, transfer to a large bowl.

2. **In the same skillet** over medium-low, heat 1 tablespoon of the remaining oil until shimmering. Add the zucchini and a pinch of salt, stir, then distribute in an even layer. Cover and cook, stirring occasionally, until the zucchini is browned and a fork inserted in the largest piece meets no resistance, 5 to 8 minutes. Transfer to the bowl with the eggplant.

3. **In the same skillet over medium,** heat the remaining 1 tablespoon oil until shimmering. Add the onion, bell pepper and a pinch of salt, stir, then spread evenly. Cover and cook, stirring occasionally, until the vegetables are lightly browned and softened, 7 to 10 minutes. Add the vinegar, sugar and tomato paste, then stir until the sugar has dissolved. Cook, stirring, until the liquid turns syrupy, 1 to 2 minutes. Add to the bowl with the eggplant and zucchini and stir. Taste and season with salt, pepper and sugar. Serve warm or at room temperature, stirring in the basil just before serving.

Baked Zucchini Fritters with Feta-Yogurt Sauce

Zucchini fritters are commonly pan-fried on the stovetop, but we discovered that cooking them on a well-oiled baking sheet in a hot oven delivers equally tasty results with a fraction of the hassle. We shred the zucchini and onion on the large holes of a box grater, but if you prefer, the medium shredding disk of a food processor works, too. We use panko bread-crumbs as a binder because their fluffy, airy texture yielded lighter fritters than fine dry breadcrumbs. And we season the batter with za'atar, a Levantine blend of herbs, spices and seeds. A tangy, creamy sauce of yogurt, feta and fresh mint is the perfect accompaniment to these crisp, lacy fritters.

START TO FINISH: 50 MINUTES
SERVINGS: 4 TO 6

3 medium zucchini (about 1½ pounds total), shredded on the large holes of a box grater

1 medium yellow onion, shredded on the large holes of a box grater

Kosher salt and ground black pepper

3 large eggs

1 cup panko breadcrumbs

2 teaspoons za'atar

¼ cup plus 3 tablespoons chopped fresh mint **OR** fresh dill **OR** a combination, divided

¼ cup extra-virgin olive oil

1 cup plain whole-milk yogurt

2 ounces feta cheese, crumbled (½ cup)

Don't be shy about wringing out the liquid *from the zucchini-onion mixture. The drier, the better, for light, flavorful fritters. Don't use a flimsy baking sheet. Use one that's sturdy and heavyweight so that it conducts heat well and won't warp in the oven. Finally, don't skimp on the oil for coating the baking sheet. A quarter cup may seem excessive but that amount is needed for crisping and browning.*

1. **Heat the oven to 450°F** with a rack in the middle position. In a large bowl, toss the zucchini and onion with 1 teaspoon salt, then let stand for about 10 minutes. Place the mixture in a clean kitchen towel and wring out the moisture. Wipe out the bowl, add the eggs and whisk to combine. Add the zucchini-onion mixture, the panko, za'atar, ¼ cup mint and ¼ teaspoon pepper, then mix until well combined.

2. **Coat a heavyweight rimmed baking sheet** with the oil. Form the zucchini mixture into 20 evenly sized balls, each about 1½ inches in diameter, then space them evenly on the prepared baking sheet. Press each ball into a ½-inch-thick round. Bake until crisp and deeply browned, 25 to 30 minutes, using a wide metal spatula to flip the fritters once about halfway through. Meanwhile, in a small bowl, stir together the yogurt, feta, the remaining 3 tablespoons mint and salt and pepper to taste; set aside until ready to serve. When the fritters are done, sprinkle them lightly with salt. Serve hot or warm with the yogurt sauce.

Bell Peppers

Mild, fruity and sweet; green, red, yellow or orange; bell peppers are part of a culinary kaleidoscope that includes everything from crisp salads to sturdy stews.

In Italy, stewed or roasted sweet peppers may be served as appetizers, stirred into pastas or be used as a topping for flatbreads.

Caponata is popular in Sicily and uses bell peppers along with other vegetables. We cook the vegetables separately for better texture, p. 10. A similar dish, peperonata, is a mix of sweet peppers and alliums. Our version, p. 289, is agrodolce-style, a Sicilian sweet and sour combination. We pair the peperonata with polenta to make a light main. Bell peppers and raisins bring the sweet, capers and balsamic vinegar balance with salt and tang.

In Syria, roasted red peppers combine with walnuts for the spicy-tart dip known as muhammara, served with flatbread. Our version, p. 6, also is great as a dip for fresh vegetables or as a sandwich spread.

Turkish cooks make a fast and fresh spread, ezme, with red bell peppers, tomatoes and a touch of spice. We liked serrano chilies for heat in our version, p. 7, and also endorse the optional step some cooks follow of adding pomegranate molasses for sweet-tart flavor and deep color.

Fried noodles are common in Asia. In Indonesia, bell peppers are part of a mix that goes into the dish called mee goreng (the name translates as fried noodles). Sweet sautéed peppers, along with cabbage and shallots, are balanced by savory soy sauce and oyster sauce, then tossed with fried noodles. We found that yellow wheat noodles, sometimes known as lo mein, worked best for our take, p. 296.

In Spain, peppers are grilled for the Catalonian dish known as escalivada. Escalivar means to char or roast in embers, and the dish usually is a mix of eggplant, sweet peppers, onions and tomatoes. To make this year-round, our version, p. 208, cooks the vegetables whole in a hot oven (no need to peel); they're cut into pieces when done and dressed with sherry vinegar.

Patatas Bravas

Patatas bravas is a popular Spanish tapa, and for good reason. Potatoes fried until perfectly crisp and served piping hot with alioli (the Spanish version of aioli) and a smoked paprika sauce (called bravas sauce) have universal appeal. To avoid having to fry the potatoes—the classic preparation—we first parcook chunked russets in the microwave, then coat them with cornstarch and finish them on a well-oiled baking sheet in a hot oven. This technique delivers fluffy-creamy interiors and ultra crisp exteriors without the hassle and mess of deep-frying.

START TO FINISH: 1¾ HOURS (40 MINUTES ACTIVE)
SERVINGS: 6

_____

For the potatoes:

⅓ cup plus 1 tablespoon extra-virgin oil

3 pounds russet potatoes, peeled and cut into 1½- to 2-inch chunks

2 tablespoons cornstarch

Kosher salt

For the alioli:

2 medium garlic cloves, finely grated

2 tablespoons lemon juice or sherry vinegar

½ cup mayonnaise

2 tablespoons extra-virgin olive oil

Kosher salt

For the bravas sauce:

3 tablespoons extra-virgin olive oil, divided

1 medium shallot, minced

1 tablespoon all-purpose flour

½ to 1 teaspoon cayenne pepper

Kosher salt and ground black pepper

¼ cup sweet vermouth

2 teaspoons sherry vinegar

1 tablespoon smoked sweet paprika

For serving:

Kosher salt and ground black pepper

1 tablespoon smoked sweet paprika

Don't use lower-starch potatoes. To get the correct browning and crispness, it's important to use high-starch russet potatoes. Also, don't cut the potatoes into small pieces. Largish two-bite chunks can roast long enough to achieve deep browning without overcooking on the inside.

1. **To make the potatoes,** heat the oven to 450°F with a rack in the middle position. Pour ⅓ cup oil onto a rimmed baking sheet and tilt to coat; set aside. In a large microwave-safe bowl, combine the potatoes and ¼ cup water. Cover loosely and microwave on high until just shy of tender, about 8 minutes, stirring once about halfway through.

2. **Drain the potatoes,** spread them on a kitchen towel and pat dry. Dry the bowl and return the potatoes to the bowl. Sprinkle with the cornstarch and ¾ teaspoon salt, then toss until evenly coated. Drizzle with the remaining 1 tablespoon oil and toss again. Distribute in an even layer on the prepared baking sheet and roast until deeply browned and well crisped, about 40 minutes, flipping with a metal spatula once halfway through.

3. **While the potatoes roast,** make the alioli and bravas sauce. To make the alioli, in a small bowl, mix the garlic and lemon juice, then let stand for 5 minutes. Whisk in the mayonnaise, oil and ¼ teaspoon salt, then set aside until ready to serve.

4. **To make the bravas sauce,** in an 8-inch skillet over medium, heat 2 tablespoons of oil until shimmering. Add the shallot and cook, stirring, until just beginning to soften, about 2 minutes. Whisk in the flour, cayenne and ¼ teaspoon salt, then cook, whisking constantly, until the flour is very lightly browned, 1 to 2 minutes. Gradually whisk in the vermouth and ¼ cup water followed by the vinegar. Whisking constantly, bring to a full simmer, then remove from the heat. Whisk in the paprika and the remaining 1 tablespoon oil. Taste and season with salt and pepper, then transfer to a serving bowl; cover and set aside at room temperature until ready to serve.

5. **When the potatoes are done,** use a slotted spoon to transfer them to a serving dish. Sprinkle with paprika and salt and black pepper to taste, then toss. Serve with the alioli and bravas sauce.

Quick Cucumber-Scallion Kimchi

While many types of Korean kimchi require slow fermentation, this cucumber and scallion version can be eaten the same day it's made. A splash of fish sauce adds depth and umami and is balanced by an equal amount of rice vinegar, which keeps the flavor fresh and bright and adds a hint of sweetness. Korean red pepper flakes, called gochugaru, are seedless, deep-red and fragrant. Look for them in Asian markets or in well-stocked supermarkets; if not available, red pepper flakes are a decent stand-in, but since they're more aggressive in spiciness, use less. The kimchi will keep in an airtight container in the refrigerator for up to two days; serve chilled or at room temperature.

START TO FINISH: 1 HOUR 20 MINUTES
(15 MINUTES ACTIVE)
SERVINGS: 4 TO 6

---

2 pounds Persian cucumbers **OR** pickling (Kirby) cucumbers, thinly sliced

Kosher salt

1 tablespoon plus 1 teaspoon unseasoned rice vinegar

1 tablespoon plus 1 teaspoon fish sauce

1 to 2 tablespoons Korean red pepper flakes (gochugaru; see headnote) **OR** ½ to 1 teaspoon red pepper flakes

1 medium garlic clove, finely grated

1 bunch scallions, whites thinly sliced, green parts cut into 1-inch lengths

Don't use regular or English cucumbers for this. Small Persian or pickling (also called Kirby) cucumbers contain fewer seeds, are less watery and have better texture for quick-pickling. Also, be sure to rinse, drain and pat the cucumbers dry after salting.

1. **In a large bowl,** toss the cucumbers with 1 tablespoon salt until well combined, then let stand for 10 minutes. Meanwhile, in a medium bowl, stir together the vinegar, fish sauce, gochugaru and garlic; set aside.

2. **Transfer the cucumbers** to a colander, rinse under running cool water and drain well. Pat the cucumbers dry, then add to the vinegar mixture along with the scallion whites and greens; toss until well combined. Cover and let stand at room temperature for about 1 hour before serving.

Crisp Oven-Charred Okra

START TO FINISH: 40 MINUTES
SERVINGS: 4

This okra is fragrantly spiced and oven fried until the pods are deeply browned and irresistibly crisp. We prefer to keep the okra whole, but this means it's best to choose evenly sized pods so they cook at the same rate. We like this as a side with lemon wedges for squeezing, but it's also a great appetizer or snack with sour cream-dill sauce (see following recipe) for dipping.

2 teaspoons curry powder	Kosher salt and ground black pepper
2 teaspoons ground coriander	1 pound okra, trimmed
2 teaspoons ground cumin	¼ cup extra-virgin olive oil
½ teaspoon cayenne pepper	Lemon wedges, to serve

Don't skip the foil lining on the baking sheet. The foil prevents the okra from sticking and also makes cleanup a breeze. Don't stir the okra during roasting. Letting the pods cook undisturbed allows them to crisp and brown deeply, but do rotate the baking sheet about halfway through to help ensure even cooking.

1. **Heat the oven to 450°F** with a rack in the middle position. Line a rimmed baking sheet with foil. In a small bowl, stir together the curry powder, coriander, cumin, cayenne, ½ teaspoon salt and 1 teaspoon black pepper. In a large bowl, toss the okra with the oil until evenly coated. Sprinkle with the spice mix and toss again.

2. **Distribute in an even layer** on the prepared baking sheet. Roast without stirring until the okra is tender and deeply browned, 30 to 35 minutes, rotating the baking sheet about halfway through. Transfer to a platter and serve warm or at room temperature with lemon wedges.

Sour Cream and Dill Dipping Sauce

START TO FINISH: 10 MINUTES
MAKES ABOUT 1 CUP

1 cup sour cream	¼ teaspoon granulated garlic
2 tablespoons finely chopped fresh dill	Kosher salt and ground black pepper
1½ tablespoons lemon juice	

In a small bowl, whisk together the sour cream, dill, lemon juice and garlic. Taste and season with salt and pepper.

Mushroom and Cheese Quesadillas

You'll find quesadillas of all types in Mexico. In Mexico City, they're often made from fresh masa and without cheese; in other parts of the country, they're made with flour tortillas and lots of melty Oaxaca cheese. Fillings vary from stewed or griddled meat to squash blossoms to nopales (cactus paddles). In this recipe, we stuff tortillas with a mixture of sautéed mushrooms and cheese, with a little smoky and spicy heat from a chipotle chili. Made with 4- to 5-inch flour tortillas, the quesadillas are perfect for a lunch or snack. If you can't find queso Oaxaca, any mild melting cheese, such as mozzarella or muenster, will work. Lard is traditional for cooking these quesadillas, but for a vegetarian version, use grapeseed or another neutral oil. For best browning, cook these in a nonstick skillet.

START TO FINISH: 30 MINUTES
SERVINGS: 4 TO 6

4 tablespoons lard **OR** neutral oil, divided

1 medium white onion, chopped

1 pound mixed mushrooms, such as cremini, oyster, portobello or shiitakes (stemmed), roughly chopped

Kosher salt and ground black pepper

2 medium garlic cloves, minced

1 chipotle chili in adobo sauce, finely chopped

3 ounces queso Oaxaca **OR** mozzarella cheese **OR** muenster cheese, shredded (¾ cup)

⅓ cup lightly packed fresh cilantro, chopped

Eight 4- to 5-inch flour tortillas

Don't use a conventional (i.e., not nonstick) skillet. The quesadillas brown best in a nonstick pan.

1. **In a 12-inch nonstick skillet** over medium-high, heat 2 tablespoons of lard until shimmering. Add the onion and cook, stirring occasionally, until softened and beginning to brown, 4 to 5 minutes. Add the mushrooms and ½ teaspoon each salt and pepper, then cook, stirring occasionally, until tender and well browned, 7 to 8 minutes. Add the garlic and chipotle; cook, stirring, until fragrant, 30 to 60 seconds. Transfer to a medium bowl, then stir in the cheese and cilantro. Taste and season with salt and pepper. Wipe out the skillet with paper towels; set aside.

2. **Divide the mushroom mixture** evenly among the tortillas, spreading it over half of each. Fold the unfilled sides over and press to seal.

3. **In the same skillet** over medium-high, heat 1 tablespoon of the remaining lard until shimmering. Add 4 of the quesadillas and cook until the tortillas are golden brown on the bottom, about 2 minutes. Flip and cook, adjusting the heat as needed, until the second sides are browned, another 2 to 3 minutes. Transfer to a platter and repeat with the remaining quesadillas using the remaining 1 tablespoon lard.

Charred Zucchini and Tahini Dip

This creamy dip, a variation on baba ghanoush, uses zucchini as its base instead of eggplant. The mild, subtle flavor of the summer squash benefits greatly from deep charring (we use the broiler), a dose of garlic and a hit of lemon juice. Once tender and browned, the zucchini is processed with rich, nutty tahini until smooth. If your food processor is small, process in two batches and transfer to a large bowl to combine. The dip can be refrigerated in an air-tight container for two to three days and can be eaten warm, chilled or room temperature. We recommend serving with pita chips or warm flatbread.

START TO FINISH: 35 MINUTES
SERVINGS: 4 TO 6

8 medium zucchini (4 pounds total), halved lengthwise and seeded

¼ cup extra-virgin olive oil, plus more to serve

Kosher salt and ground black pepper

3 tablespoons lemon juice

2 medium garlic cloves, finely grated

⅓ cup tahini

¼ teaspoon cayenne pepper, plus more to serve

2 tablespoons pine nuts, toasted

Sweet paprika, to serve

Don't forget to seed the zucchini. The core, where the seeds are located, is watery and turns mushy and limp with cooking. Use a spoon to scoop and scrape out the core from each zucchini half, creating hollowed-out boats.

1. **Heat the broiler** with a rack about 4 inches from the element. Set a wire rack in a broiler-safe rimmed baking sheet. In a large bowl, toss the zucchini with the oil and 1 teaspoon each salt and pepper. Arrange the zucchini halves cut sides up on the prepared rack. Broil until charred, 5 to 6 minutes, rotating the baking sheet about halfway through.

2. **Flip the zucchini halves** cut sides down and broil until tender and the skin sides are charred, 5 to 6 minutes, rotating the baking sheet about halfway through. Meanwhile, in a small bowl, stir together the lemon juice and garlic; set aside.

3. **When the zucchini is done,** cool for 5 to 10 minutes. Transfer to the bowl of a food processor. Add the lemon juice-garlic mixture, the tahini, cayenne, ½ teaspoon salt and ¼ teaspoon black pepper, then process until smooth, 15 to 20 seconds, scraping the bowl as needed. Taste and season with salt and pepper.

4. **Transfer to a shallow** serving bowl. Sprinkle with the pine nuts, dust with paprika and cayenne and drizzle with additional oil.

Summer Tomato Tian

In Provence, France, a tian is a casserole of sliced vegetables as well as the round, shallow earthenware vessel in which the dish is baked. A classic tian showcases an assortment of summer produce, but here the focus is on tomatoes seasoned with garlic and herbs. We opt for plum tomatoes, which are firmer and drier than regular round tomatoes, and because they withstand long baking and yield deep, rich, concentrated flavor. Ripe, in-season tomatoes are best, of course, but even less-than-stellar fruits are good. We love this served warm with crusty bread and cheese, but it can be refrigerated for up to a week and tucked into sandwiches or offered alongside grilled or roasted meats and seafood.

START TO FINISH: 1¾ HOURS
(15 MINUTES ACTIVE), PLUS COOLING
SERVINGS: 4

_____

6 tablespoons extra-virgin olive oil, divided

4 medium garlic cloves, minced

2 pounds ripe plum tomatoes, cored and cut crosswise into ¼- to ½-inch slices

Kosher salt and ground black pepper

6 sprigs fresh basil OR 4 sprigs fresh rosemary

Crusty bread, to serve

Don't worry if the tomatoes are tightly packed in the baking dish. *They will reduce in volume as they bake.*

1. **Heat the oven to 425°F** with a rack in the middle position. Coat the bottom and sides of a 9-inch pie plate with 2 tablespoons of oil. Sprinkle half of the garlic over the bottom. Arrange the tomatoes in concentric rings in the pie plate, shingling and tightly packing the slices.

2. **Sprinkle with salt and pepper,** then tuck the herb sprigs into the tomatoes and scatter on the remaining garlic. Drizzle evenly with the remaining 4 tablespoons oil. Bake until the tomatoes are browned, bubbling and meltingly tender, about 1½ hours. Cool for about 15 minutes. Serve with crusty bread.

Optional garnish: Burrata cheese **OR** fresh mozzarella cheese **OR** flaky sea salt

Artichoke Tart with Gouda and Herbs

Pastel de alcachofas, or artichoke cake or tart, is popular in Peru, one of the world's largest producers of the prickly edible flower buds. This tart is similar to quiche, with artichokes enveloped in rich custard, flavored with garlic, herbs and Gouda and Parmesan cheeses. For ease, we use frozen puff pastry as the crust instead of homemade pie dough. Leftovers can be covered and refrigerated for up to three days; bring to room temperature before serving.

START TO FINISH: 1¼ HOURS,
PLUS CHILLING AND COOLING
SERVINGS: 6 TO 8

1 sheet frozen puff pastry, thawed

14-ounce can artichoke hearts, drained, quartered if whole and patted dry

1 tablespoon extra-virgin olive oil

1 medium garlic clove, minced

¾ cup lightly packed fresh flat-leaf parsley, finely chopped

¾ cup lightly packed fresh basil, finely chopped

8 large eggs

½ cup half-and-half

Kosher salt and ground black pepper

2 ounces Gouda cheese, shredded (½ cup)

1 ounce Parmesan cheese, finely grated (½ cup)

Don't use marinated artichokes, which are too highly seasoned. Canned artichoke hearts packed in water are the right type for this recipe. Be sure to pat the artichokes dry so their moisture doesn't water down the filling. When placing the artichokes in the filling, don't fully submerge them in the custard. The finished tart looks best when pieces are visible on the surface.

1. **Heat the oven to 400°F** with a rack in the middle position. With a rolling pin, roll the pastry into a 12-inch square. Invert a 9-inch glass pie plate onto the square and, using a paring knife or pizza cutter and the rim of the pie plate as a guide, cut the pastry into a circle about 1 inch larger than the pie plate all the way around.

2. **Lift off the pie plate** and set it right side up on the counter. Remove and discard the pastry scraps. To transfer the dough, roll the pastry circle around the rolling pin, then unroll it onto the pie plate. Ease the pastry into the corners and up the sides of the plate. Fold the edges under, then crimp. Refrigerate, uncovered, until slightly firmed and chilled, about 15 minutes.

3. **Meanwhile, in a medium bowl,** toss the artichokes with the oil, garlic and half each of the parsley and basil; set aside. In a large bowl, whisk together the eggs, half-and-half, the remaining herbs and ½ teaspoon each salt and pepper.

4. **Remove the pastry-lined pie plate** from the refrigerator. Using a fork, poke holes all over the bottom and sides of the pastry to prevent it from puffing up. Evenly sprinkle both cheeses over the bottom of the pastry, then pour in the egg mixture. Place the artichokes in the filling, laying them so the interior layers are visible, and sprinkle on any herb-garlic mixture remaining in the bowl.

5. **Bake until the center** of the filling does not jiggle when the pie plate is gently shaken, 30 to 35 minutes. Cool on a wire rack for at least 15 minutes before slicing and serving.

Upside-Down Tomato Tart

This savory tart is impressive yet simple to make, thanks to store-bought pie dough sold in a 9-inch round (skip the type already fitted into a pie plate, but if you like, feel free to use homemade). To prevent sogginess, we minimize the tomatoes' juiciness. First, we use plum tomatoes, a variety that's relatively dry. Second, we salt the tomatoes in a colander for about 10 minutes to pull out moisture and drain it away. Third, we roast the tomatoes for about 15 minutes before laying on the pie dough; this not only cooks off additional moisture, it also concentrates flavor. Crumbled blue cheese or fresh goat cheese is a salty, creamy counterpoint to the crisp crust and sweet tomatoes. Serve the tart warm or at room temperature.

1 pound ripe plum tomatoes, cored and sliced into ¼-inch-thick rounds

Kosher salt and ground black pepper

2 tablespoons extra-virgin olive oil, plus more for the pie plate and to serve

1 large shallot, halved and thinly sliced

2 teaspoons minced fresh thyme **OR** finely chopped fresh tarragon, divided

3 tablespoons sherry vinegar

9-inch unbaked pie crust (see headnote)

2 ounces blue cheese **OR** fresh goat cheese (chèvre), crumbled (½ cup)

Honey, to serve (optional)

Don't worry if the tomatoes shift around when you flip the tart. They can be easily rearranged.

1. **Heat the oven to 450°F** with a rack in the middle position. In a colander set over a bowl, toss the tomato slices with ½ teaspoon salt; let stand for 10 minutes. Meanwhile, generously grease a 9-inch deep-dish pie plate with oil. Add to it the shallot, 1 teaspoon of thyme, the oil and ¼ teaspoon pepper; toss, then distribute in an even layer.

2. **Pat the tomatoes dry** with paper towels; discard the liquid in the bowl. Arrange the tomatoes over the shallots, overlapping them slightly, then drizzle with the vinegar. Bake until the tomatoes have softened and most of the liquid has cooked off, 15 to 20 minutes. Remove from the oven and cool on a wire rack for 5 minutes.

3. **Lay the pie dough** over the tomatoes, carefully folding and tucking the edges under around the edge of the pie plate. Using the tip of a paring knife, poke holes spaced about 1 inch apart into the dough. Bake until the crust is well browned and juices are bubbling around the edges, 15 to 18 minutes.

4. **Cool on a wire rack** for about 5 minutes. Run a knife around the edge of the pie plate to loosen the tart, then invert onto a serving platter. Lift off the pie plate. Sprinkle the tart with the remaining 1 teaspoon thyme and the cheese. Lightly drizzle with additional oil and honey (if using).

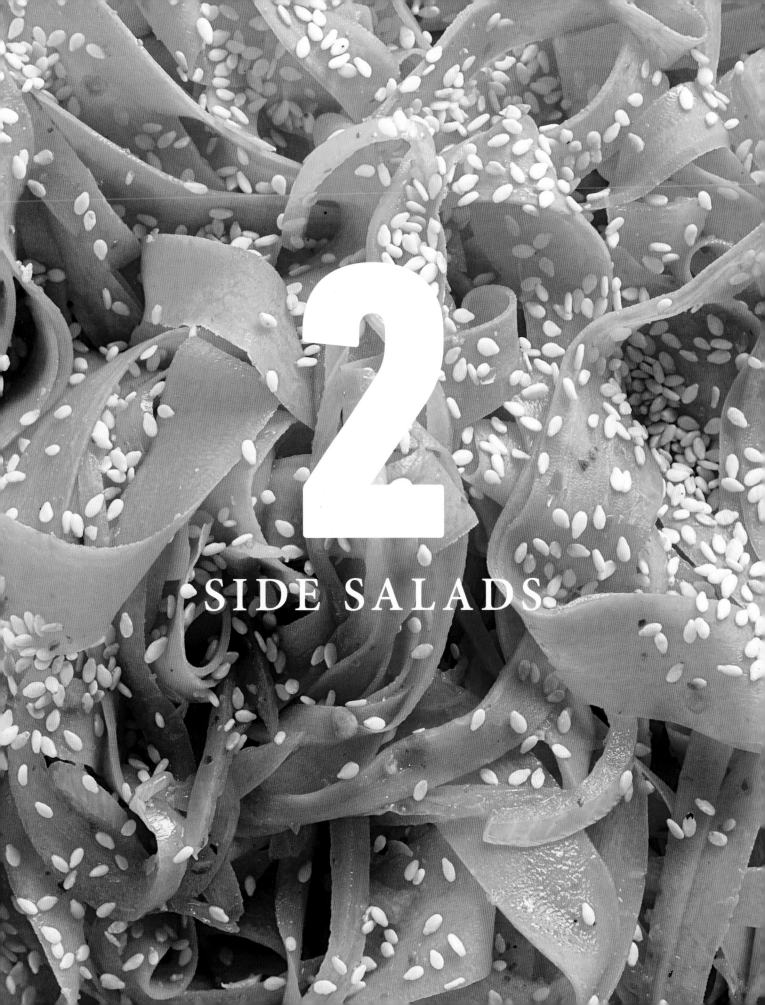

2

SIDE SALADS

Bok Choy Salad with Cucumber and Peanuts

Full of texture and savory with umami, this slaw-like salad gets loads of salty, nutty flavor from a generous amount of roasted peanuts that are finely chopped, toasted, then mixed with a little of the dressing. Be sure to use baby bok choy rather than the mature variety, as the young leaves and stalks are sweeter and more tender. To prep the bok choy, trim off and discard the thick, tough base before cutting the head in half lengthwise and slicing crosswise into ½-inch pieces.

START TO FINISH: 30 MINUTES
SERVINGS: 4 TO 6

_____

3 tablespoons lime juice

2 tablespoons soy sauce

2 tablespoons grapeseed or other neutral oil

¼ cup finely chopped fresh cilantro

2 teaspoons white miso

1 teaspoon finely grated fresh ginger

Ground black pepper

1 Fresno **OR** jalapeño chili, stemmed and seeded, half minced, half thinly sliced, reserved separately

3 scallions, whites minced, greens thinly sliced on the diagonal, reserved separately

¾ cup salted dry-roasted peanuts, finely chopped

1 pound baby bok choy, trimmed, halved lengthwise and sliced crosswise into ½-inch pieces

½ English cucumber, halved lengthwise, seeded and sliced ¼ inch thick, thinly sliced **OR** 6 radishes, thinly sliced

Don't skip the step of toasting the peanuts even though they're dry-roasted. Heating them and tossing them while warm with a little dressing makes them extra-flavorful, as the nuts absorb seasonings as they cool.

1. **In a large bowl,** whisk together the lime juice, soy sauce, oil, cilantro, miso, ginger, ½ teaspoon pepper, the minced chili and the scallion whites; set aside.

2. **In a 10-inch skillet** over medium, toast the peanuts, stirring occasionally, until fragrant and beginning to brown, about 1 minute. Transfer to a small bowl, add 2 tablespoons of the dressing and stir to combine; let cool.

3. **To the remaining dressing,** add the bok choy, cucumber, the sliced chili, the scallion greens and about a third of the peanut mixture. Toss, then taste and season with salt and pepper. Transfer to a serving dish and top with the remaining peanut mixture.

Daikon-Carrot Salad with Sesame and Lemon

As Sonoko Sakai, author of "Japanese Home Cooking" explains, many vinegared Japanese salads fall somewhere between a pickle and a conventional salad, and this namasu is a good example. Meant to be served in small portions, as most Japanese pickles are, this daikon and carrot salad is traditional at New Year's, but there's no reason the refreshingly crunchy, tangy-sweet tangle of textures can't be served year-round. For our adaptation of Sakai's recipe, we skipped the harder-to-source ingredients (such as dried persimmon and yuzu) for the more widely available substitutes that she suggests (dried apricots and lemon). We also use water instead of dashi (Japanese stock) for the marinade, but if you have dashi, use an equal amount; it will add umami to make the vegetables taste fuller and richer. Though the salad is simple to make, it requires a two-step process: first, the vegetables are rubbed with salt and squeezed of moisture. Then they are dressed and marinated for at least four hours (or up to one week). A mortar and pestle works well for grinding the sesame seeds, or give them two or three pulses in an electric spice grinder.

START TO FINISH: 30 MINUTES, PLUS MARINATING
MAKES ABOUT 3 CUPS

___

1 pound daikon radish, peeled and cut into 2-inch matchsticks

1 medium carrot, peeled and cut into 2-inch matchsticks

Table salt

¾ cup unseasoned rice vinegar

¼ cup white sugar

¼ cup dried apricots, cut into thin strips

1 tablespoon sesame seeds, toasted and coarsely ground (see headnote)

1 teaspoon grated lemon zest

¼ teaspoon red pepper flakes

Don't be shy about massaging the daikon and carrots with the salt. Use your hands to work the salt into the vegetables until they begin to wilt. A technique used in many types of Japanese pickles, this step forces the vegetables to release some of their water and renders their texture crunchy-crisp. Table salt has a fine texture that works best for this, so don't use kosher salt.

1. **In a large bowl,** toss together the daikon, carrots and 1 teaspoon salt. Using your hands, massage the salt into the vegetables until they begin to wilt, about 2 minutes. Set aside for about 5 minutes.

2. **Meanwhile, in a small bowl,** combine the vinegar, sugar and ¾ teaspoon salt and ¾ cup water. Whisk until the sugar and salt dissolve.

3. **A handful at a time,** squeeze the water from the vegetables. Discard any liquid accumulated in the bowl, then return the vegetables to it. Pour the vinegar mixture over the daikon and carrots, then toss to combine. Cover and refrigerate for at least 4 hours or up to 1 week.

4. **When ready to serve,** add the apricots, sesame seeds, lemon zest and pepper flakes, then toss to combine. Serve chilled or at room temperature.

Spicy "Korean-Style" Shaved Carrot Salad

START TO FINISH: 30 MINUTES, PLUS MARINATING
SERVINGS: 4

The provenance of the carrot salad called koreyskaya morkovka (which translates from the Russian as "Korean carrots") is murky, but it is said to have originated with ethnic Koreans in Russia. It's a spicy, garlicky, tangy-sweet, slaw-like affair. To give the dish more substance, we turned it into a shaved carrot salad, as we learned in Argentina. A sharp Y-style vegetable peeler makes it easy to shave the carrots into long, thin ribbons. We pour the hot dressing mixture over the ribbons and let the salad marinate for at least 1 hour (or up to three days). This slightly softens the carrots and allows them to absorb the seasonings. Use Korean red pepper flakes (gochugaru) if you can find them; if not, cayenne pepper works, but use half the amount.

4 or 5 large carrots (about 1½ pounds), peeled

Kosher salt

¼ cup grapeseed or other neutral oil

2 medium garlic cloves, minced

1 tablespoon Korean chili flakes (gochugaru) **OR** 1½ teaspoons cayenne pepper

½ teaspoon ground coriander

1 small yellow **OR** red onion, halved and thinly sliced

¼ cup white vinegar

1 tablespoon white sugar

1 tablespoon sesame seeds, toasted

Don't purchase small carrots for this recipe. Look for large ones, as they're easier to shave. Stop shaving the carrot when you reach the core, which tends to be tough and fibrous.

1. Use a Y-style peeler to shave the carrots from top to bottom into long, wide ribbons, rotating as you go. Stop shaving when you reach the core; discard the cores. In a large bowl, toss the carrots with ¾ teaspoon salt; set aside.

2. In a small saucepan over medium, cook the oil, garlic, chili flakes and coriander, stirring, until the garlic begins to brown, 1 to 2 minutes. Reduce to low and stir in the onion. Add the vinegar and sugar; cook, stirring, until the onion is slightly softened, about 2 minutes. Pour the hot mixture over the carrots and toss. Let stand for about 15 minutes, then cover and refrigerate for at least 1 hour or up to 3 days.

3. Taste and season with salt and pepper. Add the sesame seeds and toss. Serve chilled or at room temperature.

Shredded Kale Salad with Lemon, Olives and Pecorino

The green, minerally flavor of kale pairs well with sharp lemon, briny olives and funky Pecorino cheese. We rub the grated lemon zest with a little salt to fully extract the fragrant essential oils. This gives the salad extra brightness and a flavor reminiscent of preserved lemons. We like pecorino Romano, but Parmesan works nicely, too. Serve this salad as a side, or pile it on cooked rice or quinoa for a satisfying light main.

START TO FINISH: 20 MINUTES
SERVINGS: 4 TO 6

1 tablespoon grated lemon zest, plus ¼ cup lemon juice

Kosher salt and ground black pepper

1 medium shallot, minced

1 teaspoon honey

⅓ cup extra-virgin olive oil

2 medium bunches lacinato kale (1 pound), stemmed and thinly sliced

1 cup lightly packed fresh basil, roughly chopped

3 scallions, cut into ½-inch pieces on the diagonal

½ cup pitted green olives, chopped

2 ounces pecorino Romano OR Parmesan cheese, finely grated (1 cup), plus more to serve

Don't serve the salad immediately after tossing. Let it stand for about 15 minutes so the kale softens a bit and the flavors meld.

1. **In a large bowl,** combine the lemon zest and ½ teaspoon salt. Rub the mixture with your fingers until fragrant and some of the lemon oil has been extracted. Add the lemon juice and the shallot to the zest-salt mixture; whisk to combine, then let stand for about 10 minutes.

2. **Add the honey,** 1 teaspoon pepper and the oil; whisk to combine. Add the kale, basil, scallions, olives and the grated cheese to the bowl, then toss until well combined. Let stand for about 15 minutes to allow the kale to soften slightly.

3. **Taste and season** with salt and pepper. Transfer the salad to a serving bowl and sprinkle with additional cheese.

German Cucumber-Dill Salad (Gurkensalat)

Cucumber salad is the traditional accompaniment to German Schnitzel. This recipe is based on the salad we tasted at Restaurant Lohninger in Frankfurt. Instead of tart and vinegary, like Gurkensalat from other areas of Germany, ours is creamy but not overly rich. We salt the cucumbers after slicing. This step not only seasons the slices, it draws out moisture to prevent the salad from becoming too watery and leaves the cucumbers with a pleasant crispness. Champagne vinegar lends the dressing subtle acidity and brightness; if you can't find Champagne vinegar, unseasoned rice vinegar is an acceptable substitute.

START TO FINISH: 35 MINUTES
SERVINGS: 4

———

2 English cucumbers, peeled and sliced into ⅛-inch-thick rounds

Kosher salt and ground black pepper

½ cup sour cream

1 tablespoon Champagne vinegar (see headnote)

½ teaspoon white sugar, plus more if needed

1 medium carrot, peeled and shredded on the large holes of a box grater

2 tablespoons finely chopped fresh chives

1 cup lightly packed fresh dill, chopped

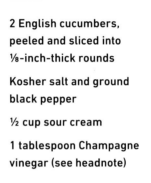

Don't forget to toss the cucumbers once or twice while they are salting. This helps the moisture drain out of the colander. Don't rinse the cucumbers after salting. A good amount of salt drains off with the water that the cucumbers release, so the salad won't taste overseasoned.

1. **In a large colander** set over a bowl, toss the cucumbers with 1½ teaspoons salt. Let stand for 30 minutes, tossing once or twice to encourage liquid to drain. Meanwhile, in a large bowl, stir together the sour cream, vinegar, sugar and ½ teaspoon pepper; set aside. In a small bowl, toss the carrot with the chives and ¼ teaspoon each salt and pepper; set aside.

2. **Using your hands,** firmly squeeze the cucumbers to remove as much water as possible; discard the liquid. Add the cucumbers to the sour cream mixture, then gently toss to combine. Stir in the dill. Taste and season with salt, pepper and sugar. Transfer to a serving dish, then top with the carrot mixture.

Turkish Tomato and Onion Salad with Olive Oil and Pomegranate Molasses

This is our version of the bright, bracing salad that we had at Manzara Restaurant in Söğüt, Turkey. The dish often is part of a Turkish meze spread, but we think it also is an ideal accompaniment to just about any type of grilled meat or kebabs. The salad comes together easily, but it's important to use ripe, flavorful tomatoes. We find cocktail tomatoes (sometimes sold as Campari tomatoes) to be dependably sweet and tasty no matter the season. Also, look for pomegranate molasses made without sugar (check the label), as its flavor is fruitier and more nuanced than brands containing added sweetener.

START TO FINISH: 45 MINUTES
(20 MINUTES ACTIVE)
SERVINGS: 4

½ medium white onion, thinly sliced

3 tablespoons pomegranate molasses

2 tablespoons lemon juice

Kosher salt and ground black pepper

⅓ cup extra-virgin olive oil

1½ pounds cocktail tomatoes, cored, each cut into 6 wedges

2 teaspoons dried mint (optional)

1 cup lightly packed fresh flat-leaf parsley, torn

½ cup lightly packed fresh dill, minced

Don't bypass the step of allowing the onion to marinate in the pomegranate molasses-lemon mixture. The acidity mellows the allium's pungency. It's also important to let the salad stand at room temperature for about 15 minutes before serving to allow the tomatoes to soften slightly and to give the flavors a chance to meld.

1. **In a large bowl,** combine the onion, pomegranate molasses, lemon juice and 1 teaspoon each salt and pepper; let stand for 10 minutes.

2. **To the onion mixture,** add the oil and whisk to combine. Add the tomatoes, mint (if using), parsley and dill, then toss. Let stand at room temperature for about 15 minutes. Taste and season with salt and pepper, then transfer to a serving bowl.

Arugula Salad with Roasted Grapes

This simple salad recreates a dish we had in Shaffa Bar, Shira Petel's restaurant in Tel Aviv. It's a perfect fusion of sweet, sharp and peppery flavors. We prefer black grapes because they take on a lovely hue when roasted (broiled, really) and lend that color to the thinly sliced onion during their brief marination in vinegar. Look for mature arugula sold in bunches instead of packaged baby arugula; bunched arugula requires a little more prep but its more assertive flavor is a better match for the sweetness of the grapes.

START TO FINISH: 45 MINUTES (15 MINUTES ACTIVE)
SERVINGS: 4

─────

2 cups seedless black
or red grapes (see headnote)

1 teaspoon plus
1 tablespoon extra-virgin
olive oil, divided

½ small red onion,
thinly sliced

Kosher salt and ground
black pepper

¼ cup red wine vinegar

1 ounce pecorino Romano
cheese, finely grated
(½ cup; optional)

1 bunch arugula, trimmed
of tough stems (about
8 lightly packed cups;
see headnote)

Don't overcrush the roasted grapes. Crush them only enough to break the skins and release the juices; the grapes should still retain their shape. When transferring the crushed grapes from the baking sheet to the bowl, don't add their juices, which would dilute the dressing

1. Heat the broiler with a rack about 4 inches from the element. On a broiler-safe rimmed baking sheet, toss the grapes with 1 teaspoon oil. Broil until the grape skins begin to split, about 5 minutes, shaking the pan once about halfway through.

2. Using the bottom of a cup or ramekin, lightly crush the warm grapes to burst them. Transfer the grapes to a large bowl, leaving behind the juices. To the grapes, add the onion, ¼ teaspoon salt and ½ teaspoon pepper, and the vinegar; toss to combine. Let stand for about 30 minutes, stirring occasionally.

3. To the bowl, add the remaining 1 tablespoon oil and the cheese (if using), then gently toss. Add the arugula and toss to coat. Taste and season with salt and pepper, then transfer to a platter.

Austrian Potato Salad
(Erdäpfelsalat)

Austrian cooks add flavor and creaminess to their potato salad without mayonnaise by cooking the potatoes in chicken stock, then using the starchy cooking liquid as the base for the dressing. That means you can skip the mayonnaise. Cornichon brine, red wine vinegar and Dijon mustard provide sharp notes; celery and fresh dill add crunch and bright flavor. Many recipes call for waxy potatoes, but we chose Yukon Golds for their rich flavor and creamy texture. If your potatoes are quite large, quarter them instead of halving before slicing.

START TO FINISH: 30 MINUTES
SERVINGS: 4

2 pounds Yukon Gold potatoes, peeled, halved and sliced ¼-inch thick

2 cups low-sodium chicken broth

Kosher salt and ground black pepper

¼ cup finely chopped cornichons, plus 1 tablespoon brine

2 tablespoons red wine vinegar, divided

½ medium red onion, finely chopped (about ½ cup)

½ teaspoon caraway seeds

¼ cup grapeseed or other neutral oil

1 tablespoon Dijon mustard

2 medium celery stalks, finely chopped (about ½ cup)

2 hard-cooked eggs, peeled and chopped (optional)

¼ cup chopped fresh dill

Don't overcook—or undercook—the potatoes. The cooked potatoes should be firm but not grainy, creamy at the center and just starting to fall apart at the edges. This is important, as some of the potatoes will break down into the salad.

1. **In a large saucepan,** combine the potatoes, broth and 1 teaspoon salt. Add enough water to just cover the potatoes. Bring to a boil over medium-high, then reduce to medium-low and cook until a skewer inserted into the potatoes meets no resistance, 8 to 10 minutes. Reserve ½ cup of the cooking liquid, then drain the potatoes and transfer them to a large bowl. Sprinkle with the cornichon brine, 1 tablespoon of the vinegar and ½ teaspoon pepper.

2. **In the same saucepan,** combine the reserved cooking liquid with the onion and caraway seed, then bring to a simmer over medium-high. Pour the mixture over the potatoes and stir well. Let stand, stirring occasionally, until the liquid has been absorbed, about 10 minutes

3. **In a liquid measuring cup** or small bowl, whisk together the oil, mustard, the remaining 1 tablespoon vinegar, ¼ teaspoon salt and ½ teaspoon pepper until emulsified. Pour the mixture over the potatoes and add the celery, cornichons, dill and eggs (if using), then fold until well combined. Taste and season with salt and pepper. Serve at room temperature.

Carrots

Carrots' good-for-you reputation often translates as dull. But in France, no one puts carrots in the corner. The classic salade de carottes râpées consists of grated carrots dressed with a bit of oil, some sugar and a touch of acid. Refreshing and full of earthy-sweet flavor, the dish works because grating ruptures cells, releasing sugars for fresher, sweeter flavor. It also creates a porous surface to better absorb the dressing. Ours, p. 41, uses mild white balsamic vinegar in the dressing for tangy, but not too tangy, flavor.

An entirely different, but equally carrot-forward, salad is koreyskaya morkovka, believed to have originated with ethnic Koreans in Russia. The carrots are doused in a warm, spicy, oil-based dressing. For our take, p. 28, we shave the carrots, producing thin curls with a pleasant texture and ample surface area to absorb the dressing.

Stir-fry may not be a technique we typically associate with Indian cooking (or with carrots, for that matter), but it's used by cooks in the southeastern state of Andhra Pradesh. Our version, p. 243, uses garlic, cumin and cilantro to bring sharp-savory balance to the sweetness of the carrots. We also use curry leaves, which are no relation to the spice—they're sold fresh or frozen in Indian groceries. But don't worry, the dish still is delicious without them.

In Turkey, olive oil is the key to zeytinaygli pirasa, a dish of braised carrots and leeks. Orange zest in the braise and lemon wedges served at the table add a refreshing burst of citrus to ours, p. 155.

As to carrots' victual virtue, there's a bit of a backstory. World War II British food authorities assured blackout-weary Britons that eating carrots would improve their night vision. That's not quite true, but carrots do contain beta-carotene, which the body uses to make vitamin A, important for eyesight. Good for you, yes, but far from boring.

Guatemalan-Style Radish and Mint Salad

Guatemalan picado de rábano is a chopped radish salad. The combination of the radish's pepperiness, tangy-sweet citrus and fresh mint makes a vibrantly hued, deliciously refreshing side. For our version, instead of chopping, we halve and slice the radishes so they have greater presence in the dish. You can use any variety of small radish, including French breakfast radishes or Easter egg radishes. Serve with just about any grilled meat, or offer alongside rice and beans. The optional garnish of chopped fried pork rinds (also known as cracklings) turns the salad into the Guatemalan dish called chojín.

START TO FINISH: 55 MINUTES
SERVINGS: 4 TO 6

3 scallions, whites thinly sliced and greens cut into 1-inch pieces, reserved separately

1 serrano **OR** jalapeño chili, stemmed, seeded and thinly sliced

1 teaspoon grated lime zest, plus 1 tablespoon lime juice

1 teaspoon grated orange zest, plus 1 tablespoon orange juice

Kosher salt

2 tablespoons grapeseed or other neutral oil

1 pound red radishes (without greens), halved and thinly sliced

1 cup lightly packed fresh mint, sliced into thin ribbons

Don't add the mint until just before serving so it retains its bright, fresh flavor and color. In fact, a good time to prep the herb is while the salad is chilling. But don't refrigerate it for longer than an hour or the radishes will lose some of their crispness.

1. **In a large bowl,** stir together the scallion whites, chili, lime zest and juice, orange zest and juice and ¼ teaspoon salt. Let stand for at least 10 minutes.

2. **Stir the oil into the dressing.** Add the radishes and the scallion greens, then toss. Cover and refrigerate until chilled, 30 to 60 minutes. Mix in the mint, then taste and season with salt.

Optional garnish: Fried pork rinds, chopped

Zucchini Salad with Lemon, Ricotta and Herbs

At Masseria Potenti in Puglia, Italy, Maria Grazia Di Lauro served an elegant first course of raw zucchini ribbons wrapped around a lemony ricotta filling, the open ends dipped in nutty toasted sesame seeds. This salad is a much-simplified version of that starter. We macerate the zucchini slices in the dressing for about 15 minutes before assembling the dish. This softens the raw edge, making the texture more silky and less crunchy, and also allows the zucchini to absorb flavor.

START TO FINISH: 30 MINUTES
SERVINGS: 4

_____

3 tablespoons extra-virgin olive oil, divided, plus more to serve

2 teaspoons grated lemon zest, plus 2 tablespoons lemon juice

1 teaspoon honey

4 tablespoons finely chopped chives **OR** basil **OR** mint **OR** a combination, divided

Kosher salt and ground black pepper

3 medium zucchini (about 1½ pounds total) halved lengthwise, seeded and sliced about ¼ inch thick

½ cup whole-milk ricotta cheese

½ cup sliced almonds, toasted **OR** chopped roasted pistachios

Don't skip the step of seeding the zucchini. If left in place, the seeds and the spongy area around them will turn the salad watery and dilute. Seed each zucchini half as you would a cucumber half—using a spoon, scrape down the length of the center of the vegetable.

1. **In a large bowl,** whisk together 2 tablespoons of oil, the lemon juice, honey, 2 tablespoons of chives and ½ teaspoon each salt and pepper. Add the zucchini and toss. Let stand for about 15 minutes, tossing once or twice. In a small bowl, stir together the ricotta, the remaining 1 tablespoon oil, the lemon zest, ⅛ teaspoon salt and ¼ teaspoon pepper.

2. **Taste the zucchini** and season with salt and pepper. Transfer to a serving dish and top with the ricotta mixture. Sprinkle with the almonds and the remaining 2 tablespoons chives, then drizzle with additional oil.

Spinach Salad with Tomatoes and Melon

This summery, savory-sweet salad balances the succulence of peak-season tomatoes and melon with the mineral notes of baby spinach (or kale) and the subtle heat of a seeded and sliced jalapeño. If you'd like a little more chili burn, leave in some or all of the jalapeño seeds. And if you'd like to add a creamy, tangy element to the salad, top it with some crumbled fresh goat cheese (chèvre) or feta cheese just before serving.

START TO FINISH: 30 MINUTES
SERVINGS: 4

2 pounds ripe tomatoes, cored and cut into 1-inch chunks

Kosher salt and ground black pepper

¼ cup cider vinegar

1 large shallot, sliced into thin rings

1 jalapeño chili, stemmed, seeded and thinly sliced crosswise

3 tablespoons extra-virgin olive oil

2 cups cubed (1-inch pieces) honeydew **OR** cantaloupe melon

5-ounce container baby spinach **OR** baby kale

¼ cup pumpkin seeds, toasted

Don't skip the step of salting the tomatoes, even if yours are perfectly ripe. This draws off some of their moisture which otherwise would water down the dish and also adds seasoning to enhance their flavor

1. In a colander set over a medium bowl, toss the tomatoes with ½ teaspoon salt; set aside to drain. In a large bowl, stir together the vinegar, shallot, chili and ¼ teaspoon salt; let stand for about 10 minutes.

2. Into the vinegar-shallot mixture, stir the oil. Add the tomatoes (discard the juices) and the melon, then toss. Add the spinach and toss again. Taste and season with salt and pepper. Transfer to a serving bowl and sprinkle with the pumpkin seeds.

Apple, Celery Root and Fennel Salad with Hazelnuts

A winter salad needs to stand up to hearty stews and roasts, and that calls for bold, bright flavors. We started with tart apples and thin slices of fennel bulb, the latter adding a pleasant anise flavor. Celery root added a fresh crispness while grated fresh horseradish gave the dish kick. If you own a mandoline, it makes quick work of slicing the apple, celery root and fennel. Grating the horseradish triggers a chemical reaction that enhances the root's bite. Tossing it with vinegar and salt helps preserve that heat, which otherwise dissipates quickly. Make sure you grate horseradish in an open and well-ventilated space.

START TO FINISH: 20 MINUTES
SERVINGS: 6

1 small shallot, grated

1½ tablespoons cider vinegar

3 tablespoons lightly packed grated fresh horseradish

3 tablespoons extra-virgin olive oil

1 teaspoon honey

Kosher salt and ground black pepper

1 Granny Smith apple, cored and cut into matchsticks

½ small celery root (about 8 ounces), peeled and cut into matchsticks

1 medium fennel bulb, trimmed and thinly sliced

½ cup chopped fresh flat-leaf parsley

¼ cup chopped fresh mint

½ cup hazelnuts, toasted and roughly chopped

Don't use prepared horseradish in this recipe. It's bottled with vinegar and salt which would alter the balance of flavors.

1. **In a large bowl,** combine the shallot and vinegar. Let stand for 10 minutes.

2. **Stir in the horseradish,** oil, honey, and ½ teaspoon each salt and pepper. Add the apple, celery root and fennel, then toss to combine. Stir in the parsley and mint, then taste and season with salt and pepper. Transfer to a serving dish and sprinkle with hazelnuts.

French Carrot Salad

Carrots tend to be a woody afterthought on U.S. salad bars. Here, we transform them into a lively side dish by taking a tip from France, where grated carrots stand alone as an iconic side dish—salade de carottes râpées. Shredding fresh carrots releases their sugars and aromas, creating an earthy sweetness that just needs a bit of acid for balance. Using relatively mild white balsamic vinegar allowed us to up the vinegar-to-oil ratio (1:2) for a punchy but not overwhelming flavor. White balsamic also paired well with a touch of honey, which heightened the carrots' natural sweetness. No tarragon? Use 1½ teaspoons chopped fresh thyme instead.

START TO FINISH: 20 MINUTES
SERVINGS: 6

2 tablespoons white balsamic vinegar

2 tablespoons chopped fresh tarragon

1 tablespoon minced shallot

1 teaspoon honey

⅛ teaspoon cayenne pepper, plus more as needed

Kosher salt

¼ cup extra-virgin olive oil

1¼ pounds carrots, peeled and shredded on the large holes of a box grater

1 cup chopped fresh flat-leaf parsley

Don't use old bagged carrots. This salad is all about the earthy, sweet carrot flavor. Large carrots can be woody, dry and bitter; small baby carrots are too juicy. Look for bunches of medium carrots with the greens still attached.

1. **In a large bowl,** whisk together the vinegar, tarragon, shallot, honey, cayenne and ½ teaspoon salt. Let stand for 10 minutes.

2. **Add the oil** and whisk to combine. Add the carrots and parsley, then stir until well combined. Taste and season with salt and cayenne pepper. Serve right away or cover and refrigerate for up to 24 hours.

Celery and Cucumbers

A high water content makes the cucumber the epitome of cool. That's also the biggest barrier to enjoying this fresh, crisp vegetable; too much water can create a watery mush that dilutes flavor and texture.

In Asia, cooks smash, salt and/or sugar their way out of that problem. The smashing doesn't require a lot of drama. A firm thump with your hand against something like the flat of a knife will do it. Cracking the cucumber open ruptures cells, which allows water to escape. Adding salt and sugar, then letting the cucumber pieces sit for a bit in a colander, further reduces the water content by osmotic pressure. The result: firmer, drier cucumbers that better absorb dressing. Either Persian or English cucumbers work, although the former, which are smaller, are preferable. Our version of China's smashed cucumber salad, see recipe p. 45, features a dressing made tangy with fresh ginger and rice vinegar.

Germans typically pair cucumber salad with Schnitzel; it's a cool, light contrast to the tender, crisp-crusted meat. Ours, p. 30, is based on a salad we had at Restaurant Lohninger in Frankfurt. We salt the slices to draw out excess water, and make our dressing with Champagne vinegar. (Unseasoned rice vinegar also works.) A dollop of sour cream makes the salad pleasantly creamy but not too rich.

As with cucumber, celery is a good way to add crunch to salad, though it sometimes gets overlooked as just a garnish. Our take on celery salad, see recipe p. 54, is based on Chilean apio con palta, or celery with avocado. Sliced radishes add color and peppery punch.

Throughout Asia, celery is a go-to for stir-fries; it stays crisp and is difficult to overcook and has a naturally high sodium content that plays well with savory flavors. For our take, see recipe p. 244, we pair celery with umami-rich shiitake mushrooms and a good amount of sliced fresh ginger.

Kale Salad with Smoked Almonds and Picada Crumbs

Flavorful and seasonal, kale is a prime candidate for a winter salad. But when eaten raw, the hardy leaves can be unpleasantly tough. We start with lacinato kale, also known as dinosaur or Tuscan kale. Its long blue-green leaves are sweeter and more tender than curly kale. Thinly slicing the greens makes them more salad-friendly. Then we massage the leaves with chopped smoked almonds that act as an abrasive to further soften them. An acidic shallot-sherry vinaigrette also helps to tenderize and brighten the kale (look for a sherry vinegar aged at least three years). Intensely flavorful paprika breadcrumbs, inspired by the Catalan sauce picada, tie everything together.

2 medium shallots, halved and thinly sliced

5 tablespoons sherry vinegar

Kosher salt and ground black pepper

2 tablespoons honey

8 tablespoons extra-virgin olive oil

1 cup smoked almonds

4 ounces chewy white bread, cut into 1-inch cubes

2 teaspoons fresh thyme

1 tablespoon sweet paprika

2 bunches lacinato kale, stemmed, washed, spun dry and thinly sliced crosswise (10 cups)

1 cup lightly packed fresh mint, chopped

Don't slice the kale until you're ready to make the salad; it will wilt. You can, however, stem, wash and dry it ahead of time.

1. **In a small bowl,** whisk together the shallots, vinegar and ¼ teaspoon salt. Let stand for 10 minutes. Whisk in the honey, 5 tablespoons of the oil and ½ teaspoon pepper; set aside.

2. **In a food processor,** process the almonds until roughly chopped, about 8 pulses; transfer to a large bowl. Add the bread to the processor and process to rough crumbs, about 20 seconds. Add the thyme, the remaining 3 tablespoons oil, paprika, ¼ teaspoon salt and ½ teaspoon pepper. Process until incorporated, about 10 seconds.

3. **Transfer the crumb mixture** to a 12-inch skillet. Cook over medium, stirring often, until the mixture is crisp and browned, 8 to 10 minutes. Transfer to a plate and let cool.

4. **Add the kale and mint** to the bowl with the almonds. Massage the greens until the kale softens and darkens, 10 to 20 seconds. Add the dressing and crumbs, then toss to combine. Taste and season with salt and pepper.

Smashed Cucumber Salad

Seasoning watery vegetables such as sliced cucumbers can be a challenge; dressings won't adhere to the slick surfaces. Our answer came from China's pai huang gua, or smashed cucumber salad. Smashing the cucumbers ruptures more cell walls than slicing and dicing, making it easier to remove the seeds, the main culprit in watery cucumbers. And, it creates craggy, porous surfaces that absorb more dressing. The easiest way to smash cucumbers is to place a rolling pin or the flat side of a chef's knife over them and smack it sharply with your hand. For a simple variation on this recipe, add ¼ cup creamy peanut butter and 2 tablespoons water with the soy sauce and sesame oil to smooth the dressing.

START TO FINISH: 40 MINUTES (15 MINUTES ACTIVE)
SERVINGS: 6

---

2 pounds English cucumbers (about 2 large)

4 teaspoons white sugar

Kosher salt

4 teaspoons unseasoned rice vinegar

1 medium garlic clove, peeled and smashed

2 tablespoons grapeseed or other neutral oil

½ teaspoon red pepper flakes

1½ tablespoons soy sauce

1 tablespoon toasted sesame oil

1 tablespoon finely grated fresh ginger

Don't substitute conventional, thick-skinned cucumbers for English. The ratio of seeds to flesh is higher and the skins are too tough.

1. Trim the ends off the cucumbers, then halve lengthwise. Place each half cut side down, then press a rolling pin or the flat side of a broad knife against the cucumber and hit firmly with the heel of your hand. Repeat along the length of the cucumbers until they crack. Pull the sections apart, scraping and discarding the seeds. Cut into rough ¾-inch pieces and transfer to a large bowl.

2. In a small bowl, combine the sugar and 1½ teaspoons salt; toss the cucumbers with 5 teaspoons of the mixture. Transfer to a colander set over a bowl. Refrigerate for 30 to 60 minutes, tossing occasionally. Meanwhile, stir the vinegar and garlic into the remaining sugar-salt mixture. Set aside.

3. In a small skillet over medium-low, combine the grapeseed oil and pepper flakes. Cook, stirring, until sizzling and the pepper flakes begin to darken, 2 to 4 minutes. Strain the oil, discarding the solids.

4. Remove and discard the garlic from the vinegar mixture. Stir in the soy sauce, sesame oil and ginger. Transfer the drained cucumbers to a kitchen towel and pat dry. In a bowl, combine the cucumbers and dressing. Stir for 1 minute, then stir in half of the chili oil. Serve drizzled with more chili oil and sprinkled with cilantro, scallions and sesame seeds, if desired.

Optional garnish: Fresh cilantro leaves **OR** sliced scallions **OR** toasted sesame seeds **OR** a combination

Thai-Style Coleslaw with Mint and Cilantro

Looking for a brighter, fresher, more dynamic cabbage slaw than the mayonnaise-rich American version, we were inspired by a recipe from San Antonio chef Quealy Watson that featured Southeast Asian flavors. Coconut milk in the dressing—instead of mayonnaise—has just the right amount of richness and body. Fish sauce adds savory pungency, while sugar balances with sweetness. For heat, we like fresh chili "cooked" in lime juice, which mellows the bite and helps disperse the heat more evenly. For vegetables, we use tender yet crunchy napa cabbage along with sliced red radishes and snap peas for vivid color and even more texture.

START TO FINISH: 25 MINUTES
SERVINGS: 6

3 tablespoons lime juice

4 teaspoons white sugar

1 tablespoon fish sauce, plus more as needed

1 medium serrano chili, stemmed, seeded and minced

⅓ cup coconut milk

1 pound napa cabbage (1 small head), thinly sliced crosswise (about 8 cups)

6 radishes, trimmed, halved and thinly sliced

4 ounces sugar snap peas, strings removed, thinly sliced on the diagonal

½ cup roughly chopped fresh cilantro

½ cup roughly chopped fresh mint

½ cup roasted, salted cashews, roughly chopped

Don't use "light" coconut milk or sweetened "cream of coconut" for this recipe. The former is too thin, and the latter is too sweet (think piña coladas). And don't forget to vigorously shake the can before opening to ensure that the fat and liquid are fully emulsified.

1. **In a liquid measuring cup** or small bowl, mix together the lime juice, sugar, fish sauce and chili. Let stand for 10 minutes. Whisk in the coconut milk, then taste and adjust seasoning with additional fish sauce if desired.

2. **In a large bowl,** combine the cabbage, radishes, peas, cilantro and mint. Add the dressing and toss until evenly coated. Stir in the cashews and transfer to a serving bowl.

Jicama and Orange Salad with Queso Fresco

Jicama, a root vegetable native to Mexico, has a ruddy, tough brown skin which must be removed before eating. Once peeled, it resembles a raw potato. Often eaten raw, jicama's texture is crisp, snappy and a little starchy and its flavor is mild with a hint of sweetness. This cool, refreshing salad combines slices of jicama with sweet-tangy oranges, along with herbal cilantro and salty queso fresco. Serve it alongside grilled meat or chicken, or as a side dish for a Mexican-inspired meal.

START TO FINISH 30 MINUTES (15 MINUTES ACTIVE)
SERVINGS: 6 TO 8

2 navel oranges

2 tablespoons lime juice

2 tablespoons light agave syrup **OR** honey

2 tablespoons grapeseed or other neutral oil

⅛ teaspoon ancho chili powder

Kosher salt and ground black pepper

1-pound jicama, peeled, cut into 8 wedges and very thinly sliced crosswise

¼ cup lightly packed fresh cilantro, roughly chopped

2 ounces queso fresco **OR** feta cheese, crumbled (½ cup)

Don't use regular chili powder. It typically is a blend that includes dried chilies, cumin, oregano and garlic; it'll muddy the flavors in this salad. Instead, look for pure ancho chili powder, which is made by pulverizing nothing more than ancho chilies.

1. **Using a sharp knife,** slice off the top and bottom ½ inch from each orange. One at a time, stand the oranges on a cut end and cut from top to bottom following the contours of the fruit to remove the peel and white pith. Hold each orange over a small bowl and cut between the membranes to release the segments, letting them drop into the bowl. Once all of the segments have been cut free, squeeze the membranes over a large bowl to extract all the juice; discard the membranes.

2. **To the bowl with the orange juice,** add the lime juice, agave, oil, chili powder and ¼ teaspoon each salt and pepper; whisk to combine. Add the jicama and orange segments with accumulated juices, then toss. Cover and refrigerate for about 30 minutes.

3. **Add the cilantro and cheese** to the jicama mixture, then toss. Taste and season with salt and pepper.

Cucumber and Shrimp Salad with Chili, Garlic and Lime

This fragrant, flavor-packed salad was loosely inspired by Malaysian kerabu, raw vegetable or fruit salads boldly seasoned with ingredients such as dried shrimp or shrimp paste, chilies and lime. We make a flavor paste by pureeing fresh chilies, garlic, shallots, lime zest and juice, and sugar, add some to the shrimp as they cook and mix the rest into sliced cucumbers that have been salted and squeezed of excess water. Serve as a part of a multi-dish Southeast Asian meal or as a light main course with jasmine rice.

START TO FINISH: 35 MINUTES
SERVINGS: 4

———

2 pounds cucumbers, peeled, halved lengthwise, seeded and sliced about ½ inch thick on the diagonal

Kosher salt

3 or 4 Fresno **OR** serrano chilies, stemmed and seeded

3 medium garlic cloves, smashed and peeled

2 large shallots, chopped

2 teaspoons white sugar

2 teaspoons grated lime zest, plus 3 tablespoons lime juice, divided

2 tablespoons grapeseed or other neutral oil, divided

½ cup wide-flake coconut, toasted

1 pound extra-large shrimp (21/25 per pound) peeled, deveined and patted dry

½ cup lightly packed fresh cilantro, chopped

Don't forget to salt and then squeeze the cucumbers. This removes excess moisture and yields cucumber slices with a satisfying crunch. Either regular cucumbers or English cucumbers work well, so use whichever you prefer.

1. In a colander set in a large bowl, toss the cucumbers with ¾ teaspoon salt. Using your hands, lightly rub the salt into the slices just until they begin to wilt, then let stand for about 20 minutes.

2. Meanwhile, in a food processor, combine the chilies, garlic, shallots, sugar, lime zest, 2 tablespoons of lime juice, 1 tablespoon of oil and ¼ teaspoon salt. Process until smooth, 1 to 2 minutes, scraping the bowl as needed. Transfer to a small bowl.

3. In a 12-inch nonstick skillet over medium, toast the coconut, stirring often, until light golden brown, 2 to 3 minutes. Transfer to a small bowl and set aside.

4. In the same skillet over medium-high, heat the remaining 1 tablespoon oil until shimmering. Add the shrimp in a single layer and cook without stirring until golden brown on the bottom, about 2 minutes. Add ¼ cup of the chili-shallot puree, then cook, stirring often, until the shrimp are just opaque, 1 to 2 minutes. Remove the pan from the heat, add the remaining 1 tablespoon lime juice and toss; set aside.

5. Using your hands, gently squeeze the cucumbers to remove excess liquid and transfer to a serving bowl. Add the remaining chili-shallot puree, the toasted coconut and the cilantro; toss to combine. Taste and season with salt, then top with the shrimp.

Fennel-Orange Salad with Harissa and Yogurt

This recipe, our adaptation of a salad from Coal Office restaurant in London, is a crisp, creamy update of the classic North African pairing of fennel, orange and olives. Harissa adds spice; Greek yogurt is a cooling counterpoint. Use your olive of choice—we tried several varieties and liked them all. Sweet mini peppers are sold in bags in grocery stores everywhere; if you prefer a spicier salad, use a jalapeño chili instead.

START TO FINISH: 45 MINUTES (25 MINUTES ACTIVE)
SERVINGS: 4

2 medium fennel bulbs, trimmed, halved lengthwise, cored and thinly sliced crosswise

2 tablespoons lemon juice

Kosher salt

1 navel orange

¼ cup extra-virgin olive oil

2 tablespoons harissa paste, plus more as needed

½ teaspoon white sugar

1 sweet mini pepper (see headnote), stemmed, sliced into thin rings

½ cup pitted olives, roughly chopped

⅓ cup roasted slivered almonds, roughly chopped

⅓ cup plain whole-milk Greek yogurt

¼ cup lightly packed fresh mint, torn if large

Don't slice the fennel paper-thin. Aim for slices between ⅛ to ¼ inch thick. This salad is all about contrasting textures. By rubbing the fennel with salt and lemon, the thicker slices will become pleasingly crisp-tender. Fennel sliced too thin will wilt and become soggy.

1. **In a large bowl,** toss the fennel, lemon juice and ¾ teaspoon salt, gently rubbing the salt into the fennel. Set aside for 30 minutes.

2. **Meanwhile, grate the zest** from the orange (about 1 tablespoon); set aside. Slice ½ inch off the top and bottom of the orange. Stand the orange on a cut end and cut from top to bottom following the contours of the fruit to remove the peel and white pith. Halve the orange from top to bottom, then slice each half into ¼-inch-thick half-rounds.

3. **After the fennel has rested** for 30 minutes, add the orange zest, oil, harissa and sugar; toss to combine. Add the orange slices, pepper rings, olives and almonds, then toss again. Taste and season with salt and harissa.

4. **Dollop the yogurt** onto the center of a platter, spreading it in an even layer. Using a slotted spoon, mound the salad on top of the yogurt. Sprinkle with mint, then serve.

Fennel

Fennel, both cultivated and wild, thrives in the warm, dry Mediterranean climate. So it's no surprise its light, mildly anise flavor is put to delicious use in the cooking of countries throughout the region—fronds, bulbs, seeds and all.

Sicilian cooks add fennel to their orange and olive salads; for ours, p. 50, we let the fennel sit in lemon juice and salt for 30 minutes to wilt the slices and soften their texture.

Roasted vegetables are popular in Italy and elsewhere, and roasting is a good way to bring out the tender, sweet side of fennel. Our version, p. 233, a loose adaptation of a French gratin, pairs fennel with onions and requires just 15 minutes hands-on time; the oven takes care of the rest. Cumin, coriander, cinnamon and the spicy hit of hot paprika (or sweet paprika plus cayenne) add layers of flavor while red onions nestled next to the fennel cook down to jammy sweetness.

We also roast fennel, along with pears, for our warm salad, p. 68, topped with radicchio, toasted walnuts and cheese.

Fennel and fire have a classical affinity. Legend has it that Prometheus used a fennel stalk to carry an ember of the gods' sacred fire to mortals. We give fennel (and zucchini) a good charring under the broiler for a simple side or first course, see p. 215. The fennel is sliced thin, broiled and then tossed with basil, lemon juice, and a little extra-virgin olive oil.

For a cooler take on fennel, we were inspired by antipasto salads, which are based on the Italian first course "antipasto" of cured meats, cheeses and marinated peppers or other vegetables. For our take, p. 86, we use sliced peperoncini mixed with fresh, shaved fennel and sliced mushrooms; the fennel combines beautifully with the earthy mushrooms. Sliced salami and Parmesan add both elegance and substance, and a lemony vinaigrette ties the flavors together.

Chilean Celery and Avocado Salad

Apio con palta, or celery with avocado, is a common Chilean salad. Our version includes sliced radishes for beautiful contrasting color and a pepperiness that plays off the smooth, creamy avocado. Look for bunched celery with leaves attached and include the leaves, which are tender and flavorful.

START TO FINISH: 25 MINUTES
SERVINGS: 6

1 small shallot, halved and thinly sliced

2 tablespoons white wine vinegar

Kosher salt and ground black pepper

2 tablespoons extra-virgin olive oil, plus more to serve (optional)

6 medium celery stalks with leaves, thinly sliced on the diagonal

4 red radishes, thinly sliced

1 ripe avocado, halved, pitted, peeled and cut into ½-inch cubes

¼ cup pitted Kalamata olives, halved

¼ cup walnuts, toasted and roughly chopped

Don't prep the avocado until right before use so it doesn't have a chance to discolor. The 10 minutes that the shallot mellows in the vinegar is a good time to do it.

1. **In a large bowl,** stir together the shallot, vinegar and ¼ teaspoon salt; let stand for about 10 minutes.

2. **Whisk the oil** into the shallot-vinegar mixture. Add the celery, radishes, avocado, olives and walnuts; gently toss to combine. Taste and season with salt and pepper. Transfer to a serving bowl and drizzle with additional oil, if desired.

Cucumber, Celery and Apple Salad with Yogurt and Walnuts

This crisp-creamy salad is reminiscent of a classic Waldorf salad, but tangy yogurt replaces the mayonnaise, for a lighter, fresher flavor. Thin half-rounds of cool cucumber and chopped dill fit seamlessly into the mix of apples and celery. For a light main dish or an elegant first course, lay slices of smoked salmon on each serving before sprinkling with the dill and walnuts.

START TO FINISH: 30 MINUTES
SERVINGS: 6

¾ cup plain
whole-milk yogurt

2 tablespoons
extra-virgin olive oil

1 tablespoon Dijon mustard

1 tablespoon lemon juice,
plus more as needed

3 tablespoons finely chopped
fresh dill, divided

Kosher salt and ground
black pepper

½ English cucumber,
halved lengthwise and
very thinly sliced crosswise

1 Honeycrisp **OR** Gala apple,
quartered, cored and very
thinly sliced crosswise

1 cup red **OR** green seedless
grapes, halved

2 medium celery stalks,
thinly sliced on the diagonal

¾ cup walnuts, toasted and
roughly chopped, divided

Don't make this salad too far ahead of serving it. It's best as soon as the ingredients are mixed.

1. **In a large bowl,** stir together the yogurt, oil, mustard, lemon juice, 2 tablespoons of dill and ½ teaspoon each salt and pepper. Add the cucumber, apple, grapes, celery and ½ cup walnuts, then fold to combine. Taste and season with salt, pepper and additional lemon juice.

2. **Transfer to a serving bowl** and sprinkle with the remaining walnuts.

Sweet and Sour Roasted Peppers with Feta and Mint

Persian sekanjabin, a sweet and sour syrup made with vinegar, mint, sugar or honey and sometimes infused with cucumber, inspired the dressing that we use here on silky roasted peppers. To add to the contrasting flavors, we finished the dish with crumbled feta cheese, which provides a deliciously savory, salty counterpoint and also adds creamy texture. Serve the salad at room temperature or even lightly chilled as a side to kebabs or roasted lamb or chicken, or offer it as a part of a meze spread, with flatbread alongside.

START TO FINISH: 1 HOUR (30 MINUTES ACTIVE)
SERVINGS: 4

———

4 large red **OR** yellow **OR** orange bell peppers **OR** a combination

⅓ cup raw pistachios **OR** whole almonds, roughly chopped

2 tablespoons extra-virgin olive oil, plus more to serve

⅓ cup cider vinegar

2 tablespoons honey

1 teaspoon dried mint

¼ teaspoon cayenne pepper

Kosher salt and ground black pepper

3 ounces feta cheese, crumbled (¾ cup)

½ cup lightly packed fresh mint **OR** dill **OR** basil **OR** a combination, roughly chopped

Don't forget to check on the peppers as they roast and turn them as needed so they char on all sides. Once charred let them stand, covered, for 15 to 30 minutes, which will further soften the skin, making them easy to peel.

1. Heat the broiler with a rack about 6 inches from the element. Place the peppers on a broiler-safe rimmed baking sheet and broil, turning them as needed, until charred on all sides, 14 to 16 minutes. As they are done, transfer to a large bowl. Cover and let the peppers steam to loosen the skins, about 20 minutes.

2. Meanwhile, in a small saucepan over medium-high, combine the pistachios and oil. Cook, stirring often, until the nuts are toasted and fragrant, 2 to 3 minutes. Off heat, whisk in the vinegar, honey, dried mint, cayenne and ¼ teaspoon salt; set aside.

3. Peel the peppers and remove and discard the stems and seeds; reserve the bowl. Tear or cut the peppers into strips, then return to the bowl. Add the dressing and toss to coat, then taste and season with salt and pepper. Let stand for about 10 minutes.

4. Add the feta and mint to the pepper mixture. Toss to combine, then transfer to a serving bowl.

Optional garnish: Flaky salt

Greek Cabbage Salad with Carrots and Olives (Politiki Salata)

Cabbage-based politiki salata may be a dish for fall and winter in Greece, but the bright flavors and crisp textures are great any time of the year. We were introduced to it at the Avissinia Café in Athens and find it is an excellent accompaniment to grilled meats and fish. The salad is best eaten the day it is made, but it can be refrigerated for up to four hours in advance; hold off on adding the feta and olives until just before serving.

START TO FINISH: 45 MINUTES
(15 MINUTES ACTIVE)
SERVINGS: 4

½ medium head green cabbage, cored and thinly sliced (about 4 cups)

3 medium carrots, peeled and coarsely shredded (about 1¼ cups)

5 tablespoons lemon juice, divided

Kosher salt

3 tablespoons extra-virgin olive oil

½ teaspoon white sugar

1 medium garlic clove, finely grated

3 medium celery stalks, thinly sliced on the diagonal (about 1 cup)

1 small or ½ large red bell pepper, stemmed, seeded and cut into rough matchsticks

4 ounces feta cheese, crumbled (1 cup)

½ cup chopped pitted green olives

Don't massage the lemon and salt into the cabbage and carrots. Gentle tossing will wilt the vegetables, but allow them to retain much of their crispness.

1. In a large bowl, combine the cabbage, carrots, 3 tablespoons of lemon juice and ¼ teaspoon salt. Toss gently, just until the vegetables begin to wilt, about 1 minute. Let stand at room temperature 30 minutes, or until the cabbage softens slightly. Alternatively, cover and refrigerate for up to 4 hours.

2. In a small bowl, whisk together the olive oil, sugar, garlic, remaining 2 tablespoons lemon juice and ¾ teaspoons salt.

3. Add the celery and bell pepper to the cabbage mixture. Drizzle with the dressing and toss. Using tongs, transfer the salad to a serving bowl, leaving behind any accumulated liquid. Top with feta and olives.

Kale Salad with Dates, Pistachios and Green Tahini

START TO FINISH: 45 MINUTES (25 MINUTES ACTIVE)
SERVINGS: 6

Green tahini is a popular variation on a basic tahini sauce. It's made by blending parsley (and sometimes other leafy herbs) into tahini with water, lemon juice, garlic and salt. The herbs tint the sauce green while also balancing the sesame's nutty, slightly bitter flavor with fresh, grassy notes. For this hearty salad, we make a green tahini enriched with olive oil and honey to create a dressing that nicely coats sliced kale and complements its assertive, minerally taste. For pops of contrasting flavor and texture, we toss chopped dates and roasted pistachios into the mix. Unlike salads made with delicate greens, many kale salads, including this one, benefit from standing for a few minutes after dressing; this allows the leaves to wilt slightly and soften for better texture.

½ small red onion, thinly sliced

2 tablespoons plus ¼ cup lime juice

Kosher salt and ground black pepper

1¼ cups lightly packed fresh flat-leaf parsley

⅓ cup lightly packed fresh cilantro

½ cup tahini

¼ cup extra-virgin olive oil

2 teaspoons honey

1 medium garlic clove, smashed and peeled

2 bunches lacinato kale (about 1½ pounds total), stemmed, leaves thinly sliced (about 12 cups lightly packed)

1 cup pitted dates, roughly chopped

1 cup roasted pistachios, roughly chopped

2 tablespoons sesame seeds, toasted

Don't use bagged pre-cleaned kale, as it tends to lack freshness. It also contains a lot of tough, fibrous stems. Lacinato kale, also known as Tuscan or dinosaur kale, is best.

1. **In a large bowl,** stir together the onion, 2 tablespoons lime juice and ½ teaspoon salt; set aside for about 10 minutes to allow the onion to mellow.

2. **Meanwhile, in a blender** combine the parsley, cilantro, tahini, oil, honey, garlic, ⅓ cup water, the remaining ¼ cup lime juice ¼ teaspoon salt and ½ teaspoon pepper. Blend until smooth, about 1 minute, scraping the blender jar as needed.

3. **To the bowl** with the onion mixture, add the kale, dates, pistachios and dressing. Toss well, then taste and season with salt and pepper. Let stand for about 15 minutes to allow the kale to soften slightly.

4. **Transfer to a serving bowl** and sprinkle with the sesame seeds.

Watercress Salad
with Olives and Feta

Peppery watercress is a perfect foil for salty feta and olives. We like pimento-stuffed olives for both their flavor and the burst of color provided by the pimento. We add some olive brine to the dressing, along with white wine vinegar and a touch of pomegranate molasses, for sweetness.

START TO FINISH: 25 MINUTES
SERVINGS: 4 TO 6

———

¼ cup extra-virgin olive oil

3 tablespoons
white wine vinegar

2 tablespoons
pomegranate molasses

½ cup pimento-stuffed green olives, roughly chopped, plus 1 tablespoon olive brine

Kosher salt and ground black pepper

2 bunches watercress (about 13 ounces total), trimmed of tough stems, cut into 2- to 3-inch lengths

½ cup lightly packed fresh mint, roughly chopped

2 ounces feta cheese, crumbled (½ cup)

Don't forget to wash and dry the watercress, especially if using regular bunched watercress, which tends to be sandy and gritty ("live" watercress, sold with roots still attached, requires less attention when cleaning). Also, don't dress the salad until just before you plan to serve it, as the watercress quickly turns limp.

In a large bowl, whisk together the oil, vinegar, pomegranate molasses, olive brine and ¼ teaspoon each salt and pepper. Add the watercress, mint, olives and feta; toss well. Taste and season with salt and pepper, then transfer to a platter.

Cabbage and Roasted Pepper Slaw with Pickled Raisins

Crisp, mild cabbage pairs well with bolder, more attention-grabbing ingredients. Here, thinly sliced cabbage is tossed with sweet, silky roasted red peppers, toasted nuts and raisins quick-pickled in vinegar that dot the slaw with sweet-sour flavor. This is a great accompaniment to roasted or grilled lamb or pork, or meaty fish such as salmon and swordfish; it's also great in sandwiches. Stored in an airtight container in the refrigerator, the slaw keeps well for up to three days.

START TO FINISH: 30 MINUTES
SERVINGS: 4 TO 6

_____

1 pound red cabbage **OR** green cabbage **OR** a combination, cored and thinly sliced (about 4 cups)

Kosher salt and ground black pepper

½ cup raisins **OR** golden raisins **OR** a combination

3 tablespoons sherry vinegar **OR** red wine vinegar, divided

3 tablespoons extra-virgin olive oil

1 tablespoon Dijon mustard

½ cup walnuts **OR** pecans, toasted and chopped

½ cup roasted red peppers, patted dry and chopped

½ cup lightly packed fresh tarragon **OR** basil, finely chopped

Don't skip the step of salting the cabbage and letting it stand for about 15 minutes. Salting helps draw out excess moisture from the vegetable while also seasoning it throughout.

1. **In a large bowl,** toss the cabbage with ½ teaspoon salt; let stand for about 15 minutes. Meanwhile, in a small microwave-safe bowl, stir together the raisins and 2 tablespoons vinegar. Microwave on high until the raisins are plumped and heated through, about 1 minute; set aside. In another small bowl, whisk together the remaining 1 tablespoon vinegar, oil, mustard, ¼ teaspoon salt and ½ teaspoon pepper.

2. **Pour off and discard any liquid** released by the cabbage. Add the raisins and any vinegar remaining in the bowl, the walnuts, roasted peppers and dressing to the cabbage. Toss, then taste and season with salt and pepper. Add the tarragon and toss again.

3

SUPPER SALADS

Romaine and Radicchio Salad with Olives, Eggs and Pomegranate Vinaigrette

This crisp, colorful salad gets meaty, briny flavor from oil-cured olives and fruity tang from pomegranate molasses. We supplement sweet romaine lettuce with pleasantly bitter radicchio and also toss in some parsley (or mint, or a combination of the two) for added aroma and herbal notes. Hard-cooked eggs cut into wedges lend substance to the salad, making it hearty enough to serve as a light main. Either whole-grain or Dijon mustard works nicely in the dressing, balancing the sweetness of the pomegranate molasses, so use whichever you prefer or what you have on hand.

START TO FINISH: 20 MINUTES
SERVINGS: 4 TO 6

3 tablespoons orange juice **OR** white wine vinegar

2 tablespoons pomegranate molasses

2 tablespoons extra-virgin olive oil

4 teaspoons whole-grain mustard **OR** 1 tablespoon Dijon mustard

Kosher salt and ground black pepper

1 small head romaine lettuce (about 12 ounces), cut crosswise into 2- to 3-inch pieces

1 small head radicchio (about 8 ounces), quartered lengthwise, then cut crosswise into 1-inch pieces

½ cup lightly packed fresh parsley **OR** mint **OR** a combination, torn if large

⅓ cup pitted oil-cured black olives, chopped

2 hard-cooked eggs, peeled, each cut into 6 wedges

Don't forget to pull off and discard *the bruised outer leaves from the head of romaine. Closer to the core, the leaves are sweeter.*

1. In a large bowl, whisk together the orange juice, molasses, oil, mustard, ½ teaspoon salt and ¼ teaspoon pepper.

2. To the bowl, add the romaine, radicchio, parsley and olives; toss until well combined. Taste and season with salt and pepper. Transfer to a serving platter and top with the eggs.

Optional garnish: Pomegranate seeds

Tomatoey Tabbouleh

Tabbouleh is a Levantine salad that's parsley-centric, with bulgur, tomatoes, allium, lemon juice, olive oil and sometimes cucumbers in important but supporting roles. For this version, we shifted the flavor and color balance by upping the amount of tomatoes. Our secret for toothsome tabbouleh is to slightly under-hydrate the bulgur with boiling water before combining it with the other ingredients. The bulgur soaks up the tomatoes' juices, resulting in both better flavor and a drier, fluffier texture. We season our tabbouleh generously with sumac, the ground dried berries of the sumac plant. The deep-red powder has a tart, subtly fruity, wholly unique flavor. Look for it in well-stocked grocery stores, spice shops or Middle Eastern markets. You will need about two bunches of flat-leaf parsley for this recipe, and be sure to dry it thoroughly after washing to prevent the parsley from becoming soggy when chopped.

START TO FINISH: 30 MINUTES
SERVINGS: 4

———

½ cup boiling water

½ cup fine bulgur

1½ teaspoons ground sumac, plus more as needed

Kosher salt and ground black pepper

1 pound ripe tomatoes, cored and diced

1 tablespoon lemon juice

1 large or 2 small shallots, minced

½ teaspoon ground allspice

4 cups lightly packed fresh flat-leaf parsley, finely chopped

¼ cup extra-virgin olive oil

Don't use medium or coarse bulgur, as it won't hydrate and soften properly. Fine bulgur is key. Don't use plum tomatoes. They tend to be dry and won't release juices for the bulgur to absorb, so the grain will remain al dente instead of fully plumping and softening.

1. In a medium bowl, stir together the boiling water, bulgur, sumac and ¼ teaspoon salt. Cover and let stand for 10 minutes, then fluff with a fork.

2. In a large bowl, stir together the tomatoes, lemon juice, shallot, allspice and ½ teaspoon salt. Add the bulgur and stir to combine. Let stand another 5 minutes. Stir in the parsley and oil. Taste and season with salt, pepper and additional sumac.

Optional garnish: Chopped fresh mint **OR** dill **OR** both

Radicchio Salad with Roasted Fennel and Pears

START TO FINISH: 35 MINUTES
SERVINGS: 6

A salad of fresh pears, fennel and walnuts was the starting point for this autumnal mix of sweet, salty and bitter notes. We roast fresh fennel and Bosc pears under the broiler to soften them and concentrate their flavors before combining them with ribbons of radicchio, toasted walnuts and cheese. Shaved Parmesan or crumbled Gorgonzola both work beautifully in the salad, so use whichever you prefer.

¼ cup extra-virgin olive oil

¼ cup cider vinegar, plus more if needed

2 teaspoons minced fresh thyme

Kosher salt and ground black pepper

1 medium fennel bulb, trimmed, halved lengthwise, cored and sliced ½ inch thick against the grain

2 ripe but firm Bosc pears, stemmed, halved, cored and cut into 1-inch chunks

1 tablespoon honey

1 medium head radicchio (about 8 ounces), quartered, cored and cut crosswise about ½ inch thick

½ cup walnuts, toasted and roughly chopped

1 ounce Parmesan cheese, shaved with a vegetable peeler (about ⅓ cup) OR Gorgonzola cheese, crumbled (½ cup)

Don't use pears that are ripened to the point of custardy softness. *They still should have some crunch or roasting may make them mushy. Don't peel the pears. Their skins add a burnished russet hue to the salad and also help keep the pieces intact. Finally, don't forget to drizzle the flavorful juices accumulated on the baking sheet over the just-assembled salad.*

1. **Heat the oven to broil** with a rack about 6 inches from the element. Mist a broiler-safe rimmed baking sheet with cooking spray. In a small bowl, whisk together the oil, vinegar, thyme and ¼ teaspoon each salt and pepper. In a large bowl, toss the fennel with 2 tablespoons of the dressing, then distribute in an even layer on one side of the prepared baking sheet.

2. **In the same bowl,** toss the pears with the honey. Distribute in an even layer on the other side of the baking sheet; reserve the bowl. Broil without stirring until the fennel is tender-crisp and the pears are browned at the edges, 10 to 12 minutes. Remove from the oven and cool for about 5 minutes.

3. **Transfer just the fennel** to the same bowl (leave the pears on the baking sheet) and add the radicchio, walnuts, cheese and the remaining dressing. Toss, then taste and season with salt and pepper and, if desired, additional vinegar. Transfer to a serving platter, scatter the pears on top and drizzle on any accumulated juices from the baking sheet.

Ensalada Rusa

Ensalada rusa translates from the Spanish as "Russian salad." Said to be created in the 19th century by chef Lucien Olivier at the Hermitage, a French restaurant in Moscow, the dish, which in its original form contained lavish ingredients such as caviar, was wildly popular and eventually made its way into the cuisines of other countries. Spain, in particular, took a liking to it, and the salad now is a fixture in tapas bars throughout the country. It also is much loved in many Latin American countries. A mayonnaise-based dressing is standard in ensalada rusa, potatoes are a must and beets are common. Some versions even include hearty ingredients, such as tuna or hard-cooked eggs. We like carrots in ours and, for easy prep, we opt for store-bought cooked beets. The salad is delicious at room temperature or even chilled.

START TO FINISH: 45 MINUTES
SERVINGS: 4 TO 6

1 pound small (1- to 1½-inch diameter) Yukon Gold potatoes, unpeeled, halved

Kosher salt and ground black pepper

2 medium carrots, peeled and sliced ¼ inch thick on the diagonal

¼ cup extra-virgin olive oil, plus more to serve

3 tablespoons mayonnaise

1 tablespoon plus 1 teaspoon sherry vinegar, divided

2 scallions, thinly sliced on the diagonal OR ½ small red onion, chopped

8 ounces cooked, peeled red OR yellow beets, cut into 1-inch chunks

⅓ cup lightly packed fresh flat-leaf parsley OR dill OR a combination

Don't let the potato-carrot mixture cool too much before tossing it with the mayonnaise mixture. It still should be quite warm when dressed so the vegetables better absorb the seasonings. When mixing in the beets, do so with a light hand to prevent them from turning the entire salad pink.

1. **Add the potatoes** to a large saucepan, cover with about 2 inches water and add 2 teaspoons salt. Bring to a simmer over medium-high and simmer until a skewer inserted into the potatoes meets just a little resistance, 3 to 5 minutes. Add the carrots and cook until the potatoes are tender and the carrots are tender-crisp, about 3 minutes. Drain in a colander.

2. **In a large bowl,** whisk together the oil, mayonnaise, 1 tablespoon vinegar, ½ teaspoon salt and ¼ teaspoon pepper. Add the warm potato-carrot mixture and the scallions. Stir, then let stand until cooled to room temperature.

3. **In a small bowl,** toss the beets with the remaining 1 teaspoon vinegar and ¼ teaspoon each salt and pepper. Gently stir the beets into the potato-carrot mixture. Taste and season with salt and pepper. Transfer to a serving dish, top with the parsley and drizzle with additional oil.

Zucchini and Chickpea Salad with Tahini Yogurt

This is our re-creation of a salad we loved at Coal Office, a restaurant in London that serves up modern Middle Eastern food. With raw zucchini, earthy chickpeas, nutty tahini and creamy yogurt, the dish is both fresh and hearty, light and rich. Za'atar, which seasons the chickpeas, is a dried herb and seed blend; look for it in the spice section of the supermarket, in specialty spice shops or in Middle Eastern grocery stores. If you're shopping for za'atar, also look for sumac, the dried ground berries of the sumac bush. Its tart flavor and deep-red hue are a nice, though optional, accent for the salad. For eye-catching presentation, we spoon the yogurt mixture in the center of a serving platter, then surround it with the zucchini-chickpea mixture. To serve, spoon some of the salad along with a bit of the yogurt onto each plate.

START TO FINISH: 35 MINUTES
SERVINGS: 4 TO 6

———

¾ cup plain whole-milk Greek yogurt

2 tablespoons tahini

1 teaspoon grated lemon zest, plus 1 tablespoon lemon juice

1½ teaspoons plus 2 tablespoons extra-virgin olive oil, plus more to serve

Kosher salt and ground black pepper

15½-ounce can chickpeas, rinsed and drained

1 small shallot, halved and thinly sliced

2 tablespoons red wine vinegar

2 teaspoons za'atar

2 small zucchini (12 ounces total), quartered lengthwise and thinly sliced on a steep diagonal

¼ cup lightly packed fresh mint, finely chopped

¼ cup lightly packed fresh dill, finely chopped

¼ cup lightly packed fresh cilantro

Ground sumac, to serve (optional)

Don't forget to cover the bowl containing the chickpeas and shallots when microwaving. Covering traps steam that helps wilt the shallots and soften the chickpeas. And remember to occasionally stir the chickpea-shallot mixture as it cools. This helps ensure the chickpeas evenly absorb the seasonings pooled at the bottom of the bowl while also hastening the cooling.

1. **In a medium bowl,** whisk together the yogurt, tahini, lemon zest and juice, 1½ teaspoons oil, ½ teaspoon salt and ¼ teaspoon pepper; set aside.

2. **In a large microwave-safe bowl,** stir together the chickpeas, shallot, vinegar and za'atar. Cover and microwave until the shallot is wilted, 1½ to 2 minutes. Uncover and cool to room temperature, stirring occasionally.

3. **When the chickpeas have cooled,** stir in the remaining 2 tablespoons oil, the zucchini, mint, dill and cilantro. Taste and season with salt and pepper.

4. **Scoop the yogurt mixture** into a mound in the center of a large platter. Transfer the chickpea-zucchini mixture to the platter, spooning it around the yogurt mixture. Drizzle with additional oil and sprinkle sumac (if using).

Shaved Brussels Sprouts with Browned Butter Vinaigrette

Most slaws are an uninspiring mashup of raw cabbage and sweet mayonnaise. We wanted tender texture and more nuanced taste, and got that by using browned butter in the vinaigrette instead of the traditional oil. We also opt for flavorful Brussels sprouts over cabbage. For speed, shred the sprouts with a food processor fitted with a thin slicing disk (4 millimeters or thinner). Otherwise, halve, then thinly slice them by hand using a chef's knife. We further tenderize the sprouts by salting them before adding the dressing. Whole-grain mustard adds flavor as well as a bit of texture to the vinaigrette.

START TO FINISH: 30 MINUTES
SERVINGS: 8

1 pound Brussels sprouts, trimmed and finely shredded (see headnote)

Kosher salt and ground black pepper

⅔ cup sherry vinegar

4 teaspoons whole-grain mustard

8 tablespoons (1 stick) salted butter

⅓ cup finely chopped fresh dill

1 cup smoked almonds, chopped

½ cup dried cranberries

Don't dress the shredded sprouts without first salting and letting them sit for 15 minutes. This slightly tenderizes the shreds.

1. **In a large bowl,** toss the shredded sprouts with ¾ teaspoon salt. Let stand for 15 minutes.

2. **Meanwhile, in a medium bowl,** whisk together the vinegar, mustard and ½ teaspoon salt. In a small saucepan over medium-low, melt the butter, then cook, swirling the pan, until the milk solids at the bottom are golden brown and the butter has a nutty aroma, 5 to 6 minutes.

3. **While whisking,** gradually add the browned butter to the vinegar mixture, then continue to whisk to cool the mixture slightly, about 20 seconds. Stir in the dill and ½ teaspoon pepper.

4. **Add the smoked almonds** and cranberries to the sprouts, then pour the dressing over the mixture and toss well. Let stand at room temperature for at least 15 minutes to thoroughly season the sprouts, or cover and let stand for up to 1 hour. Taste and season with salt and pepper, then transfer to a serving bowl.

Snow Pea and Summer Squash Salad with Goat Cheese

This bright salad pairs crisp snow peas with silky summer squash, the two briefly cooked together in the microwave. We meld the vegetables and balance their sweetness with a simple vinaigrette and creamy, tangy fresh goat cheese (or feta, if you prefer). Steeping the sliced onion in the vinegar for a few minutes mellows its raw allium bite, so don't skip this step.

START TO FINISH: 30 MINUTES
SERVINGS: 4

½ small red onion, thinly sliced **OR** 1 medium shallot, halved and thinly sliced

3 tablespoons sherry vinegar **OR** unseasoned rice vinegar

Kosher salt and ground black pepper

1 medium yellow summer squash (about 8 ounces), halved lengthwise, then sliced crosswise about ¼ inch thick

8 ounces snow peas, trimmed and halved

¼ cup extra-virgin olive oil

2 tablespoons chopped fresh dill **OR** oregano, divided

2 ounces fresh goat cheese (chèvre) **OR** feta cheese, crumbled (½ cup)

Don't forget to stir the squash-snow pea mixture about halfway through microwaving to ensure the vegetables cook evenly. And after microwaving, don't forget to pour off the liquid the mixture releases during cooking or it will water down the salad.

1. **In a small bowl,** stir together the onion, vinegar and a pinch of salt; set aside. In a large microwave-safe bowl, toss the summer squash and snow peas with ½ teaspoon salt. Cover and microwave on high until the squash is tender and the peas are tender-crisp, 2 to 3 minutes, stirring once about halfway through. Immediately pour off and discard the liquid in the bowl.

2. **To the warm** squash-snow pea mixture, add the onion-vinegar mixture, the oil and ½ teaspoon pepper, then toss to combine. Let cool to room temperature, about 15 minutes. To the vegetables, add 1 tablespoon of dill and half of the cheese, then toss. Taste and season with salt and pepper. Transfer to a serving dish and sprinkle with the remaining 1 tablespoon dill and the remaining cheese.

Snap Pea and Radish Salad with Olive Oil Tuna

Italian tonnato is a silky sauce made with olive oil–packed tuna. It traditionally is served with chilled slices of veal, but we use it as a sauce for a crisp, colorful salad of blanched sugar snap peas and peppery red radishes. It's important to use tuna packed in olive oil for this recipe. Its texture and taste are richer than tuna in water or vegetable oil, and you will use some of the oil as a flavor-boosting ingredient. Some varieties of snap peas are stringless; if yours are, you need only to trim the stem ends.

START TO FINISH: 30 MINUTES
SERVINGS: 6

———

Kosher salt and ground black pepper

1 pound sugar snap peas, trimmed, strings removed if present

1-pound bunch red radishes, trimmed and thinly sliced

2 tablespoons poppy seeds OR toasted sliced almonds

5 tablespoons extra-virgin olive oil, divided

Two 5-ounce cans olive oil–packed tuna, drained, oil reserved, flaked into bite-size pieces

2 tablespoons grated lemon zest, plus 2 tablespoons lemon juice

¼ cup mayonnaise

Don't let the snap peas stand for more than a couple of minutes in the ice water or they will become waterlogged. After draining the peas, be sure to dry them well so residual water won't dilute the salad. We suggest laying them out on a clean kitchen towel, patting them dry and leaving them uncovered to air-dry while you continue with the recipe.

1. **Fill a large bowl with ice water.** In a large saucepan, bring 2 quarts water to a boil. Stir in 1 tablespoon salt and the snap peas, then cook until the peas are bright green and tender-crisp, about 2 minutes. Drain in a colander, transfer to the ice water. Let stand until completely cooled, about 2 minutes. Drain again, reserving the bowl, then pat the peas dry.

2. **In the same bowl,** toss together the peas, radishes, poppy seeds, 2 tablespoons of olive oil and ¼ teaspoon each salt and pepper. In a medium bowl, toss the tuna with 3 tablespoons of the reserved tuna oil, the lemon zest and juice and ¼ teaspoon each salt and pepper.

3. **In a blender,** combine half of the tuna mixture, the mayonnaise and 1 tablespoon water. Puree, drizzling in the remaining 3 tablespoons olive oil, until the mixture is smooth. Taste and season with salt and pepper. Spread the puree on a serving platter. Spoon the vegetables on top, then scatter on the remaining tuna mixture.

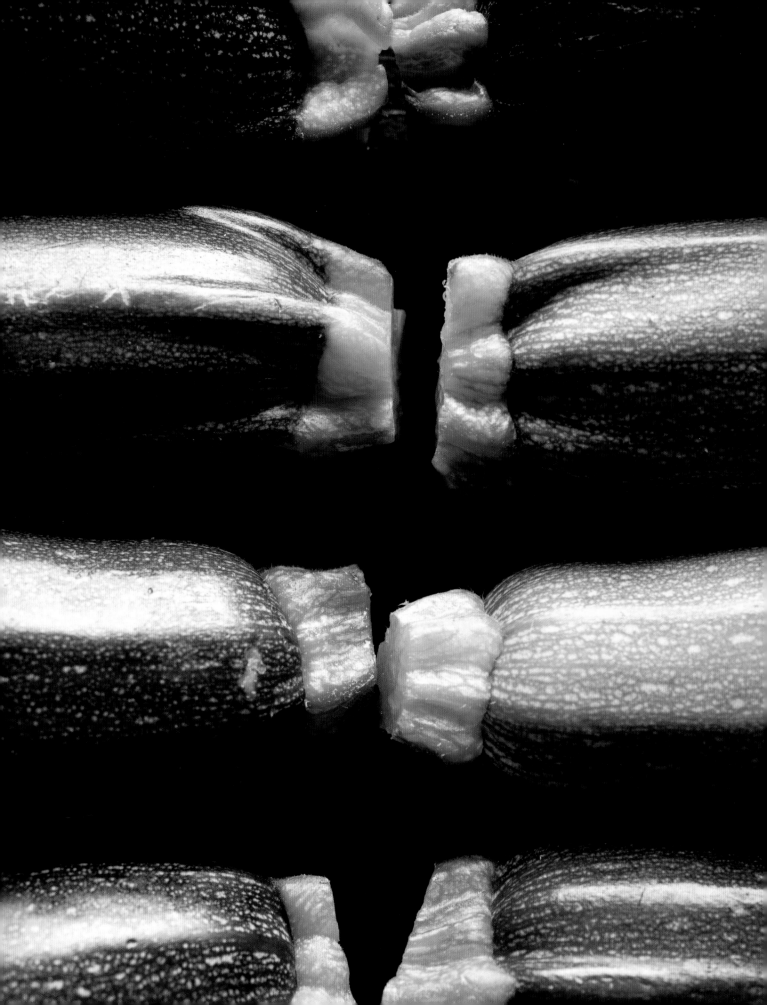

Summer Squash

Thin-skinned, juicy, and horticulturally prolific, summer squash are the user-friendly version of the gourd family—no need to get out the big knife to cut up a crookneck. The name is derived from "askutasquash," a Narragansett Indian word that means "eaten raw or uncooked." And for summer squash, this is literally true. The delicate vegetable can be shaved thin and eaten raw.

In Puglia, Italy, we were served an elegant first course of zucchini ribbons wrapped around lemony ricotta. We simplify, slicing the zucchini and topping it with ricotta spiked with lemon zest, p. 37. We macerate the zucchini slices in an herb-flecked dressing to take the raw edge off.

In Korea, seasoned sliced zucchini is served as a side dish called hobak muchim. The zucchini is often sautéed for this, but our version, p. 192, starts with broiled zucchini that get a brief rest, the better to release excess liquid, before being coated by a salty-sweet dressing spiked with gochujang, a spicy red chili paste.

Jamaican jerk seasoning contrasted by the mellow richness of coconut milk adds complexity to our squash soup, p. 115. When using crookneck squash, we halve and seed the squash before cooking; it turns spongy and soft and is just right for pureeing into a thick soup. Yellow squash work, too, although there's no need to seed them. Make this soup as fiery as you like, or not. We recommend checking your jerk seasoning for heat and adjusting the amount accordingly. And while we seed our habanero chili to tame the heat, feel free to leave in some or all of the seeds.

With its mild flavor and gentle crunch, zucchini make a good filling for omelettes (French) or frittatas (Italian). We look Down Under for a variation that Australians refer to as a "slice." The egg mixture gets some flour and leavener, which results in a firmer, more sliceable texture. In our take, p. 318, we shred, then salt and squeeze the zucchini to make sure the slice stays firm. Plenty of nutty Gruyère and some deli ham (optional) rounds out the dish, then everything goes into the oven to bake until golden. The recipe comes together quickly and simply, as befits fuss-free squash.

Sweet Potato and Arugula Salad with Chimichurri Vinaigrette

Argentinian chimichurri, the much-loved herbal, garlicky, vinegary sauce often paired with grilled meats, gave us the idea for the vinaigrette that dresses this hearty but easy-to-make salad. We cook the diced sweet potatoes in the microwave—no need to dirty pots or pans—and they're done in about five minutes. It's important to dress the potatoes while they're still warm so they absorb the flavorings. We especially like the pepperiness and tender texture of arugula in this salad, but baby spinach works nicely, too.

START TO FINISH: 35 MINUTES
SERVINGS: 4 TO 6

———

1 medium shallot,
halved and thinly sliced

3 tablespoons
red wine vinegar

Kosher salt and
ground black pepper

¼ cup extra-virgin olive oil

1 tablespoon fresh
oregano, chopped

½ to 1 teaspoon
red pepper flakes

1 medium
garlic clove, minced

½ cup flat-leaf parsley,
chopped

1 pound orange-fleshed
sweet potatoes, peeled and
cut into ½- to ¾-inch chunks

5-ounce container baby
arugula OR baby spinach

½ cup pecans, toasted
and roughly chopped

Don't forget to drain the sweet potatoes after microwaving, *otherwise the water that collects in the bottom of the bowl will dilute the dressing.*

1. In a medium bowl, stir together the shallot, vinegar and ¼ teaspoon salt; set aside for about 10 minutes to allow the shallot to mellow. Whisk in the oil, oregano, pepper flakes, garlic, parsley, ½ teaspoon salt and ¼ teaspoon pepper.

2. In a medium microwave-safe bowl, combine the sweet potatoes and 3 tablespoons water. Cover and cook until a skewer inserted into the largest piece meets no resistance, 4 to 5 minutes, stirring once about halfway through. Immediately drain the sweet potatoes in a colander, wipe out the bowl and return the potatoes to the bowl.

3. To the hot potatoes, add all but 1 tablespoon of the shallot mixture, then toss. Taste and season with salt and pepper. To the remaining shallot mixture, add the arugula and toss, then taste and season with salt and pepper. Transfer the arugula to a serving platter, arranging it in a bed. Top with the sweet potatoes and sprinkle with the pecans.

Tomato, Arugula and Bread Salad with Fresh Corn and Mozzarella

This vibrant, summery salad includes elements of Italian panzanella (bread salad). For best flavor and texture, we mix the tomato wedges and onion slices with the vinaigrette and allow them to marinate briefly before tossing in the leafy greens, basil, cheese, and toasted bread and corn. Crisp, juicy kernels cut from cobs of peak-season corn are, of course, ideal, but in a pinch or during winter months, frozen corn that has been thawed and patted dry is fine. Fresh mozzarella is sold in orbs of different sizes; smallish bocconcini and even smaller ciliegine are great for this salad because they're easily torn into bite-size pieces.

START TO FINISH: 20 MINUTES
SERVINGS: 4 TO 6

---

6 ounces crusty white bread, sliced ½-inch thick and torn into bite-size pieces (about 6 cups)

6 tablespoons extra-virgin olive oil, divided

Kosher salt and ground black pepper

2 tablespoons white balsamic vinegar OR sherry vinegar

1 pound ripe tomatoes, cored and cut into ½-inch-thick wedges

1 small red onion, halved and thinly sliced

1½ cups corn kernels (from 2 ears corn)

2 cups lightly packed baby arugula OR watercress OR mixed greens

4 ounces fresh mozzarella cheese (see headnote), torn into bite-size pieces

½ cup lightly packed fresh basil OR mint, torn

Don't use a soft, fine-crumbed bread for this salad. Choose a crusty, rustic bread that will toast up with a crisp-chewy texture and won't turn soggy when soaked with the salad's dressing and juices.

1. **Heat the oven to 450°F** with a rack in the middle position. In a large bowl, toss the bread with 3 tablespoons of oil, ½ teaspoon salt and 1 teaspoon pepper. Distribute in a single layer on a rimmed baking sheet; reserve the bowl. Bake for 5 minutes. Meanwhile, in the same bowl, whisk together the remaining 3 tablespoons oil, the vinegar and ½ teaspoon each salt and pepper. Add the tomatoes and onion, then toss; set aside.

2. **After the bread has toasted** for 5 minutes, add the corn to the baking sheet and stir to combine. Bake until the croutons are golden brown, 5 to 7 minutes, stirring once about halfway through. Cool to room temperature. To the tomato-onion mixture, add the bread-corn mixture, the arugula, mozzarella and basil, then toss to combine. Taste and season with salt and pepper. Transfer to a serving bowl.

Spicy Potato Salad with Tomatoes and Pigeon Peas

Solterito, often described as Peruvian chopped salad, was our inspiration for this colorful dish. Classic solterito (which translates from the Spanish as "little bachelor") is made with choclo, a starchy Peruvian corn, and labor-intensive fresh fava beans. To simplify, we took a few liberties with the ingredients. We use Yukon Gold potatoes as a buttery, starchy salad base and add canned pigeon peas (or butter beans). And in place of Peruvian rocoto chili, we spice things up with a combination of habanero (for heat) and a mini red sweet pepper (for color). Tomatoes and cilantro bring bright notes, and olive and queso fresco counter with savoriness.

START TO FINISH: 40 MINUTES, PLUS COOLING
SERVINGS: 4 TO 6

1 mini red sweet pepper **OR** ¼ red bell pepper, stemmed, seeded and roughly chopped

1 habanero chili, stemmed, seeded and roughly chopped

¼ cup extra-virgin olive oil

3 tablespoons white wine vinegar

Kosher salt and ground black pepper

1 pint grape **OR** cherry tomatoes, halved

15½-ounce can pigeon peas **OR** butter beans, rinsed and drained

1 medium shallot, finely chopped

1½ pounds small Yukon Gold potatoes (1 to 1½ inches in diameter), unpeeled, halved

½ cup lightly packed fresh cilantro, chopped

½ cup pitted Kalamata olives, halved

3 ounces queso fresco, crumbled (¾ cup)

Don't allow the potatoes to cool before adding them to the dressed tomato mixture. The hot potatoes soak up flavor as they cool, which means every bite is well seasoned.

1. In a blender, combine the sweet pepper, habanero, oil, vinegar and ½ teaspoon each salt and pepper. Puree until mostly smooth, about 1 minute, stopping the blender once and scraping down the sides, then transfer to a large bowl. Add the tomatoes, pigeon peas and shallot. Stir to combine, then set aside while the potatoes cook.

2. In a large saucepan, combine the potatoes, ½ teaspoon salt and 2 quarts water. Bring to a simmer over medium-high, then cover, reduce to medium and cook, stirring occasionally, until a skewer inserted into the largest pieces meet no resistance, about 12 minutes.

3. Drain the potatoes, then immediately add them to the tomato mixture. Stir to combine and let cool for about 10 minutes, stirring occasionally. Stir in the cilantro, olives and cheese, then taste and season with salt and pepper.

Roasted Sunchokes with Capers and Creamy Tarragon Sauce

We roast sunchokes (which sometimes are referred to as Jerusalem artichokes) with slices of red onion, then toss them with capers and dress them with a sour cream sauce containing tarragon and garlic.

START TO FINISH: 50 MINUTES (15 MINUTES ACTIVE)
SERVINGS: 4

———

2 pounds sunchokes, scrubbed but not peeled, cut into 1-inch chunks

1 medium red onion, halved and thinly sliced

3 tablespoons extra-virgin olive oil

Kosher salt and ground black pepper

⅓ cup sour cream **OR** plain whole-milk yogurt

1 medium garlic clove, finely grated

¼ cup lightly packed fresh tarragon, finely chopped

4 teaspoons lemon juice, divided

2 tablespoons drained capers

2 ounces (about 4 cups lightly packed) watercress **OR** baby arugula **OR** pea shoots

Don't forget to toss the just-roasted sunchokes and onions with the capers and lemon juice and let them stand for 10 minutes. The vegetables will absorb the lemon juice and cool just enough that the greens won't wilt when they're added.

1. **Heat the oven to 450°F** with a rack in the lowest position. In a large bowl, toss together the sunchokes, onion, oil and ½ teaspoon each salt and pepper. Distribute in an even layer on a rimmed baking sheet; reserve the bowl. Roast, stirring once halfway through, until the vegetables are browned and a skewer inserted into the sunchokes meets no resistance, 25 to 35 minutes.

2. **Meanwhile, in a small bowl,** whisk together the sour cream, garlic, tarragon, 2 teaspoons lemon juice and ½ teaspoon pepper. Taste and season with salt.

3. **When the vegetables are done,** return them to the bowl. Add the capers and the remaining 2 teaspoons lemon juice; toss to combine, then let stand for about 10 minutes. Toss in the greens. Transfer to a serving platter and drizzle with the sour cream mixture.

Shaved Fennel, Mushroom and Parmesan Salad

This is an elegant take on an American favorite: the Italian deli salad. We dress thinly sliced vegetables, cheese and salami with a lemony vinaigrette that keeps the flavors bright and fresh. The salad tastes best the day it's made, but still is delicious if refrigerated overnight; bring to room temperature before serving.

START TO FINISH: 15 MINUTES
SERVINGS: 4

⅓ cup lemon juice

⅓ cup extra-virgin olive oil

3 medium garlic cloves, minced

6 peperoncini, stemmed, seeded and sliced into thin rings, plus 1 tablespoon brine

Kosher salt

1 large fennel bulb, trimmed and halved

8 ounces white button mushrooms, stemmed

3-ounce chunk Parmesan cheese (without rind)

2 ounces thinly sliced salami, chopped

¾ cup lightly packed flat-leaf parsley leaves, finely chopped

Don't attempt to slice your own salami on the mandoline. It's best to purchase it already sliced. Don't worry if the Parmesan ends up in irregular shapes and sizes after slicing. This adds to the visual appeal of the salad.

1. **In a small bowl,** whisk together the lemon juice, oil, garlic, peperoncini brine and 1 teaspoon salt. Set aside.

2. **Adjust the blade** of your mandoline to slice ¹⁄₁₆ inch thick. One at a time, hold each fennel half by the base and slice against the grain as far as is safe; discard the base. Transfer to a large bowl. Next, slice each mushroom cap on the mandoline and add to the bowl. Finally, slice the Parmesan on the mandoline, roughly crumbling any large slices, and add to the fennel-mushroom mixture.

3. **Add the peperoncini,** salami and parsley to the bowl, then toss. Drizzle with the dressing and toss again.

Fresh Fennel and Brussels Sprouts Tabbouleh

START TO FINISH: 40 MINUTES (25 MINUTES ACTIVE)
SERVINGS: 4 TO 6

Classic tabbouleh tosses summery tomatoes, cucumbers and herbs with nutty, nubby bulgur. For this riff on the perennial favorite, we switched to cool-weather Brussels sprouts and fennel and make a sweet-tart dressing by combining dark, syrupy pomegranate molasses with olive oil and a touch of cinnamon. We also use coarse bulgur—and a good amount of it—to make the salad more grain-centric. A food processor fitted with the thin (2-millimeter) slicing disk makes quick work of the vegetable prep, but, if you prefer, the vegetables also can be sliced by hand. This tabbouleh is delicious either at room temperature or slightly chilled.

6 tablespoons extra-virgin olive oil

¼ cup pomegranate molasses

¼ teaspoon ground cinnamon

Kosher salt and ground black pepper

6 ounces Brussels sprouts, trimmed

1 medium fennel bulb, trimmed, halved lengthwise and cored

½ medium red onion, trimmed and peeled

1½ cups coarse bulgur

4 cups boiling water

½ cup chopped fresh flat-leaf parsley

¼ cup chopped fresh mint

½ cup sliced, toasted almonds **OR** chopped roasted pistachios

Don't forget to rinse the hydrated bulgur before adding it to the vegetables. Rinsing stops the cooking process and cools down the bulgur so its heat doesn't cause the vegetables to wilt and lose their texture. If your fennel bulb has feathery fronds attached, don't discard them. Chop the fronds and sprinkle them on as a garnish along with the almonds.

1. **In a large bowl,** whisk together the oil, pomegranate molasses, cinnamon, ½ teaspoon each salt and pepper and 1 tablespoon water; set aside. Using a food processor fitted with the thin (2-millimeter) slicing disk, slice the Brussels sprouts, fennel and onion, cutting the vegetables if needed to fit into the feed tube. Add the sliced vegetables to the dressing and toss, then let stand at room temperature while you soak the bulgur.

2. **Add the bulgur** to a medium bowl, then stir in the boiling water. Let stand for 15 minutes to allow the bulgur to hydrate. Drain in a fine-mesh strainer, rinse under cool water and drain again.

3. **Add the bulgur** to the bowl with the vegetables, along with the parsley and mint. Toss well, then taste and season with salt and pepper. Transfer to a serving dish and sprinkle with the almonds.

Escarole Salad with Charred Grapes, Apples and Blue Cheese

A warm, charred grape vinaigrette dresses this winter salad. Apple slices add crunch and sweetness and are a welcome contrast to the bitter escarole and creamy blue cheese. Purchase a chunk of blue cheese, not crumbles, that can be cut into wedges for placing atop the greens. The dish is hearty enough to be a light main course, especially with chunks of crusty bread alongside.

START TO FINISH: 25 MINUTES
SERVINGS: 4

1 teaspoon
extra-virgin olive oil

½ cup seedless black
OR red grapes

1 medium shallot,
finely chopped

2 tablespoons Champagne
vinegar OR white balsamic
vinegar

2 tablespoons chopped fresh
tarragon OR fresh chives

Kosher salt and ground
black pepper

1 medium head escarole,
tough outer leaves
removed and discarded OR
2 small heads frisée OR a
combination, torn into
bite-size pieces

1 large crisp apple such as
Honeycrisp OR Asian pear,
cored and thinly sliced

4 ounces creamy blue
cheese, such as Gorgonzola
OR cambozola, cut into
4 wedges

Don't forget to pull away the darkest, toughest layers of the escarole. This salad is meant to showcase the tender, innermost leaves.

1. **In a small saucepan** over medium-high, heat the oil until shimmering. Add the grapes and cook, occasionally shaking the pan, until the grapes char in spots and burst, about 4 minutes. If the grapes have charred but haven't burst, gently press on them with a potato masher until they break open. Off heat, stir in the shallot, vinegar, tarragon, ½ teaspoon salt, ¼ teaspoon pepper and 2 tablespoons water.

2. **Put the escarole in a large bowl,** pour the warm grape vinaigrette over and toss. Let stand for 5 minutes to cool slightly. Add the apple and toss, then taste and season with salt and pepper. Divide the salad among 4 plates and top each with a wedge of blue cheese.

Potato Salad with Capers, Olives and Olive Oil Tuna

This mayo-free potato salad was inspired by classic salade Niçoise. It combines big, bold Mediterranean ingredients and uses a generous amount of capers to add pops of savory, briny flavor in every forkful (you'll need two 4-ounce jars to obtain the ½ cup capers called for in the recipe). The optional tuna makes the salad hearty enough to serve as a light main, especially if it's served on top of a bed of greens, but if you like, you can omit the tuna.

START TO FINISH: 25 MINUTES
SERVINGS: 4 TO 6

_____

½ small red onion, thinly sliced

¾ teaspoon dried oregano

3 tablespoons red wine vinegar

1½ pounds Yukon Gold potatoes **OR** red potatoes **OR** a combination, unpeeled, cut into 1-inch chunks

Kosher salt and ground black pepper

½ cup drained capers, plus 1 tablespoon caper brine

⅓ cup pitted black olives, chopped

¼ cup extra-virgin olive oil

5-ounce can olive oil–packed tuna, drained and broken into large flakes (optional)

½ cup lightly packed fresh flat-leaf parsley **OR** basil **OR** a combination, roughly chopped

Don't allow the potatoes to cool before tossing them with the dressing. They more readily absorb seasonings when they're hot. Don't skip the tablespoon of caper brine. The unique flavor is a welcome addition to this salad.

1. **In a large bowl,** stir together the onion, oregano and vinegar; set aside. Add the potatoes and 2 teaspoons salt to a large saucepan and add water to cover by about 1 inch. Bring to a boil over medium-high, then reduce to medium-low and cook, stirring occasionally, until a skewer inserted into the potatoes meets no resistance, 8 to 10 minutes.

2. **Drain the potatoes in a colander.** To the bowl with the onion-vinegar mixture, stir in the capers and brine, the olives, oil, ¼ teaspoon salt and ½ teaspoon pepper. Add the hot potatoes and toss to coat. Add the tuna (if using). Taste and season with salt and pepper, then add the parsley and toss again.

Rice Noodle, Cucumber and Herb Salad

This refreshing noodle salad is our take on a dish that we tasted in Cambodia combined with a recipe from "The Elephant Walk Cookbook" by Longteine de Monteiro and Katherine Neustadt. Thin rice noodles are tossed with cucumber, peanuts and tons of fresh herbs, then dressed in a punchy salty-sweet fish sauce-based dressing. Dried shrimp, soaked in hot water to soften, then chopped, adds unique, umami-rich flavor and texture to the salad, but it's an optional ingredient (the dish is delicious even without it). Rice vermicelli are thin, wiry noodles; they're sometimes labeled as maifun or thin rice sticks; don't confuse them with wide, flat rice sticks used in pad thai or pho. We think the salad is a perfect companion to rich, fatty roasted pork or nicely charred grilled pork skewers.

START TO FINISH: 30 MINUTES
SERVINGS: 4

___

4 ounces rice vermicelli (see headnote)

⅓ cup fish sauce

¼ cup white sugar

3 tablespoons lime juice, plus lime wedges to serve

1 medium shallot, halved and thinly sliced

2 medium garlic cloves, finely grated

Kosher salt and ground black pepper

1 medium English cucumber, halved lengthwise, seeded and cut into 2-inch matchsticks

2 tablespoons dried shrimp, soaked in hot water for 10 minutes, drained and finely chopped (optional)

2 Fresno **OR** jalapeño chilies, stemmed, seeded and thinly sliced

¼ cup salted, roasted peanuts, chopped

1 cup lightly packed fresh basil **OR** mint **OR** a combination, torn if large

Don't serve the salad immediately after tossing the noodles and cucumbers with the dressing. A 15-minute rest allows the noodles to absorb the flavors and the cucumbers to soften slightly.

1. **Bring a large pot** of water to a boil. Add the vermicelli, stir to combine and turn off the heat. Let stand until the noodles are fully tender, about 3 minutes. Drain in a colander, rinse under running cold running water until completely cooled, then drain again. Transfer to a medium bowl. If the noodles are very long, use kitchen shears to snip them into more manageable lengths.

2. **In a small saucepan,** combine the fish sauce and sugar. Bring to a boil over medium, stirring to dissolve the sugar. Remove from the heat and stir in the lime juice, shallot, garlic and ½ teaspoon pepper. Pour the mixture over the noodles, then add the cucumbers. Toss to combine, then let stand, tossing occasionally, for about 15 minutes.

3. **Add the dried shrimp** (if using), chilies and peanuts; toss to combine. Taste and season with salt and pepper. Toss in the herbs then transfer to a serving dish. Serve with lime wedges.

4
SOUPS

Andalusian Chilled Tomato and Bread Soup (Salmorejo)

If perfectly ripe summer tomatoes are available, use them in this simple but richly flavored, no-cook chilled soup, called salmorejo, from Andalusia in southern Spain. Campari or cocktail tomatoes also are a good choice, as they tend to be sweet year-round. Excellent results also require high-quality extra-virgin olive oil, so make sure the oil you use does not have bitter or harsh notes. Bread thickens the soup and gives it its creamy consistency; choose a crusty, country-style loaf with a relatively soft interior so the bread blends easily into the soup, but remember to remove the crust.

START TO FINISH: 15 MINUTES, PLUS CHILLING
SERVINGS: 4

———

2 pounds ripe tomatoes (see headnote), cored

2½ ounces country-style white bread (see headnote), crust removed, torn into small pieces (about 1½ cups)

½ medium red bell pepper, stemmed, seeded and chopped

1 medium garlic clove, smashed and peeled

1 teaspoon white sugar

3 tablespoons sherry vinegar, plus more to serve

Kosher salt and ground black pepper

¾ cup plus 1 tablespoon extra-virgin olive oil, plus more to serve

4 hard-cooked eggs, peeled and quartered

Don't forget to taste the soup for seasoning after refrigerating, just before serving. Chilling blunts flavor, so though the soup may have tasted perfectly seasoned immediately after blending, once cold, it likely will need additional salt and pepper.

1. **In a blender,** combine the tomatoes, bread, bell pepper, garlic, sugar, vinegar and 1 teaspoon each salt and pepper. Blend until completely smooth and no bits of tomato skins remain, about 1 minute. With the blender running, stream in the ¾ cup oil. Transfer to a large bowl, then taste and season with salt and pepper. Cover and refrigerate until well chilled, 2 to 4 hours.

2. **Re-season the soup** with salt and pepper. Serve drizzled with additional vinegar and oil and topped with the eggs.

Optional garnish: Chopped fresh flat-leaf parsley

¼ teaspoon saffron threads, crumbled

1 tablespoon boiling water

2 tablespoons extra-virgin olive oil

1 medium yellow onion, chopped

¼ cup smooth almond butter

1 teaspoon ground coriander

Kosher salt and ground black pepper

1 pound carrots, peeled and chopped into 1½-inch pieces

1 quart low-sodium chicken broth **OR** vegetable broth

1 cup plain whole-milk yogurt

2 tablespoons lemon juice

¼ cup finely chopped fresh mint

Don't use almond butter that contains added sugar (check the ingredients listed on the label). *The carrots themselves already are rich in natural sugars.*

1. In a small bowl, stir together the saffron and boiling water, then set aside to cool and allow the water to infuse.

2. Meanwhile, in a large saucepan over medium, heat the oil until shimmering. Add the onion and cook, stirring occasionally, until softened but not browned, about 5 minutes. Add the almond butter, coriander and 1 teaspoon each salt and pepper; cook, stirring, until fragrant, about 30 seconds. Add the carrots, broth and ½ cup water. Bring to a simmer, then reduce to medium-low and cook, uncovered and stirring occasionally, adjusting the heat as needed to maintain a gentle simmer, until a skewer inserted into the carrots meets no resistance, 20 to 25 minutes.

3. While the carrot mixture is simmering, in a small bowl, stir together the yogurt, lemon juice, mint and ¼ teaspoon each salt and pepper. Set a fine-mesh strainer over the bowl and pour the saffron water into the strainer; discard the solids in the strainer. Stir the yogurt mixture until well combined.

4. When the carrots are tender, remove the pan from the heat and cool for about 5 minutes. Using a blender and working in 2 or 3 batches to avoid overfilling the jar, puree the mixture until smooth. Return the soup to the pan and reheat over medium, stirring occasionally. Taste and season with salt and pepper. Serve topped with some of the yogurt mixture.

Carrot and Almond Soup with Mint-Saffron Yogurt

This rich, creamy, elegant soup is completely creamless. It gets its velvety texture from pureeing carrots that are simmered until tender along with a small measure of smooth almond butter. Tangy yogurt mixed with lemon, mint and saffron is a colorful finishing touch that brightens the carrots' flavor and balances their natural sweetness. If you own an immersion blender, you can use it to puree the soup directly in the pot.

Pozole with Collard Greens

Traditional Mexican pozole is a stew of hominy and pork flavored with fresh or dried chilies. In this simpler, lighter version, hearty collard greens stand in for the meat. Cooking the puree of ancho chilies, tomatoes and onion eliminates excess moisture and concentrates the ingredients for a robustly flavored soup. Serve with warmed tortillas and garnishes such as shredded cabbage, radishes, crumbled queso fresco and avocado.

START TO FINISH: 1¼ HOURS
(20 MINUTES ACTIVE)
SERVINGS: 4

___

2 ancho chilies (about 1 ounce), stemmed, seeded, soaked in boiling water for 10 minutes and drained

1 white onion, roughly chopped

1 pound plum tomatoes, cored and halved

2 teaspoons dried oregano

2 teaspoons cumin seeds

2 tablespoons grapeseed or other neutral oil

28-ounce can hominy, drained

1 bunch collard greens, stemmed and chopped

1 quart low-sodium chicken broth or water

Kosher salt and ground black pepper

2 tablespoons lime juice, plus lime wedges, to serve

1. In a blender, combine the chilies, onion, tomatoes, oregano and cumin. Puree until smooth, scraping down the blender as needed, about 1 minute.

2. In a large pot over medium-high, heat the oil until shimmering. Add the puree and cook, stirring, until slightly thickened and darker, about 10 minutes. Add the hominy and collards, then cook, stirring, until the collards begin to wilt and turn bright green, about 2 minutes. Add the broth, 2 cups water and 1 teaspoon each salt and black pepper. Bring to a boil over high, then cover and reduce to medium and cook, stirring occasionally, until the collards are tender, about 45 minutes.

3. Stir in the lime juice, then taste and season with salt and pepper. Serve with lime wedges on the side.

Cauliflower Soup
with Harissa Butter

This soup gets a burst of bold, rich flavor as well as stunning color from a drizzle of harissa bloomed in browned butter. Look for harissa, a North African spice paste, in well-stocked supermarkets and Middle Eastern markets. Spiciness varies by brand so we suggest a range. We prefer to puree this soup in a conventional jar blender for a perfectly smooth, silky texture. If you own an immersion blender, though, you can puree it directly in the pot after the mixture has cooled for a few minutes; the texture will be a little chunkier. Pita chips served on the side offer contrasting crunchiness.

START TO FINISH: 45 MINUTES (20 MINUTES ACTIVE)
SERVINGS: 4 TO 6

———

6 tablespoons salted butter, cut into 1-tablespoon pieces, divided

1 to 2 tablespoons harissa paste (see headnote)

1 large yellow onion, halved and thinly sliced

Kosher salt and ground black pepper

3-pound head cauliflower, trimmed and cut into 1-inch florets

1 quart low-sodium chicken OR vegetable broth

Chopped fresh dill, to serve

Pita chips, to serve

Don't hesitate to rewarm the harissa butter if it cools and solidifies while you prepare the soup. This can be done in the microwave or on the stovetop. To prevent hot soup from spouting out the top of the blender, make sure to puree it in batches and fill the blender jar only about halfway.

1. In a large pot over medium-high, melt 4 tablespoons of butter and cook, stirring often, until browned, 2 to 3 minutes. Add the harissa and cook, stirring, until fragrant, about 30 seconds, then transfer to a small bowl; set aside. In the same pot over medium, melt the remaining 2 tablespoons butter. Add the onion and ½ teaspoon salt, then cover and cook, stirring occasionally, until softened but not browned, 6 to 8 minutes. Add the cauliflower, broth and 3½ cups water. Bring to a simmer, cover and cook until the cauliflower is fully tender, 15 to 20 minutes. Cool uncovered for about 5 minutes.

2. Using a blender and working in 2 or 3 batches to avoid overfilling the jar, puree the mixture until smooth. Return the soup to the pot and reheat over medium, stirring, adding water as needed to thin. Taste and season with salt and pepper. Serve drizzled with the harissa butter, sprinkled with dill and with pita chips on the side.

Zucchini and Green Chili Soup

START TO FINISH: 40 MINUTES
SERVINGS: 4

This simple pureed soup is rich and creamy but contains no dairy. Rather, the velvety consistency comes from zucchini cooked until fully tender and toasted pumpkin seeds simmered then pureed with the soup ingredients. To toast the pumpkin seeds, put them in a small skillet over medium heat and cook, stirring often, until lightly browned and fragrant. Though the soup is blended, be sure to finely chop the poblano chili so the pieces are fully softened by the time the zucchini is tender.

2 tablespoons grapeseed or other neutral oil

3 medium zucchini (about 1½ pounds), halved and thinly sliced

1 large poblano chili, stemmed, seeded and finely chopped

2 tablespoons fresh oregano

¼ cup plus 2 tablespoons pumpkin seeds, toasted

1 bunch scallions, thinly sliced

Kosher salt and ground black pepper

Diced ripe avocado, to serve

Crumbled tortilla chips, to serve

Lime wedges, to serve

Don't be shy about the heat when cooking the zucchini. Putting the slices into smoking-hot oil helps them brown quickly. The goal is to thoroughly tenderize the vegetables so they process into a smooth puree, and to do so as quickly as possible so they retain their fresh flavors. Don't use an immersion blender to puree this soup; a conventional blender is best.

1. **In a large Dutch oven** over high, heat the oil until barely smoking. Add the zucchini and cook, stirring once or twice, until beginning to brown. Add the poblano, oregano, the ¼ cup pumpkin seeds, all but 2 tablespoons of the scallions and 1 teaspoon salt. Cook, stirring often, until the poblano is tender, 2 to 3 minutes. Add 3 cups water and 1 teaspoon pepper, bring to a simmer and cook, uncovered and stirring occasionally, until the zucchini is just tender, about 4 minutes. Cool uncovered for about 5 minutes.

2. **Using a blender** and working in batches to avoid overfilling the jar, puree in batches until smooth. Return the soup to the pot and reheat over medium, stirring occasionally. Taste and season with salt and pepper. Serve sprinkled with the remaining scallions, the remaining pumpkin seeds, avocado and tortilla chips. Offer lime wedges on the side.

Optional garnish: Crumbled queso fresco **OR** hot sauce **OR** both

3 tablespoons extra-virgin olive oil, plus more to serve

1 head garlic, top third cut off and discarded

4 medium leeks, white and light green parts, halved lengthwise, thinly sliced, rinsed and drained (4 cups)

4 bay leaves

Kosher salt and ground black pepper

1½ pounds Yukon Gold potatoes, unpeeled, cut into 1- to 1½-inch chunks

3 medium carrots **OR** parsnips, **OR** a combination, peeled and sliced into ¼-inch rounds

2 teaspoons lemon juice

Crusty bread, to serve

Don't skip the flavor-building step of browning the garlic.
We sear the cut side of the garlic head until nicely caramelized to create compounds that add complexity to the soup. This is especially important because water, not broth, is the liquid here.

1. In a large pot over medium-high, heat the oil until shimmering. Add the garlic head cut side down and cook undisturbed until well browned, 2 to 4 minutes. Transfer the garlic to a small plate, then add the leeks, bay and ½ teaspoon salt to the pot. Cook, stirring occasionally, until the leeks are lightly browned, about 6 minutes.

2. Add the potatoes, ½ teaspoon each salt and pepper, then continue to cook, stirring occasionally, until the potatoes begin to brown and stick to the pot, about 4 minutes. Add 6 cups water and bring to a boil. Stir in the carrots and garlic head, reduce to medium-low and cook, at a gentle simmer, uncovered and stirring occasionally, until a skewer inserted into the head of garlic and potatoes meets no resistance, 35 to 45 minutes.

3. Remove and discard the bay. Using tongs, remove the garlic head and squeeze the cloves into a small bowl. Mash the garlic to a smooth paste, then stir into the soup and cook, stirring occasionally, for about 5 minutes. Off heat, add the lemon juice, then taste and season with salt and pepper. Serve the soup drizzled with additional oil and with bread alongside.

Optional garnish: Flaked smoked trout

Basque-Style Leek and Potato Soup

Porrusalda, a rustic leek and potato soup from Spain's Basque Country, takes a few humble ingredients and transforms them into a light but satisfying meal in a bowl. Some versions are made with salt cod or meat, but ours is vegetarian. Carrots are classic in porrusalda; parsnips are not, but we like their nutty notes and earthiness. Use whichever you prefer, or even a mix. Leeks' many layers trap dirt and sand, so be sure to thoroughly wash the sliced leeks, then drain them well in a colander so excess water doesn't cause steaming, which will delay browning. Serve the soup drizzled with olive oil, with warm, crusty bread alongside.

Alliums

In Valencia, Spain, home to juicy, sweet-tart oranges, paella and a vibrant tapas scene, we visited Casa Montaña, a 19th-century bodega where wine barrels blackened with age line the walls. There we had a simple side of leek hearts poached in olive oil, sprinkled with sea salt and drizzled with a balsamic glaze. The leeks were silky; offset by the sweet-tangy glaze.

Quite a change from the U.S., where onions, scallions, garlic, shallots and leeks are generally relegated to the background. They may provide sharp bite as a raw or pickled relish or melt to a sweet, jammy base for a sauce or broth, but they're rarely the star of the plate.

That's a shame, as we learned in Valencia. Our version of that dish, p. 142, takes the same uncomplicated approach. You do have to get rid of the grit, always the admission price for leeks (we recommend soaking, washing, then drying the leeks for best results), but after that the leeks cook mostly hands-off in a skillet. Once done, they rest on a platter while vinegar and honey are stirred into the pan drippings to make a sweet, tangy and syrupy dressing.

North of Valencia, in Basque Country, cooks take garlic, leeks and potatoes and turn them into porrusalda, a meal in a bowl. Our version, p. 101, starts by searing the cut side of a head of garlic—the caramelization really boosts the flavor—then dropping the garlic into the soup where it gently simmers to mashable tenderness.

In Senegal, well-caramelized onions are a big part of a popular dish known as yassa chicken. Raw scallions, garlic, parsley and chilies are used for the garnish/stuffing known as rof. We skip the chicken and make an onion soup, p. 113, that starts by caramelizing yellow onions and finishes with a bracing topping of scallions, parsley and lime zest. The alliums have a starring role, and they shine.

2 tablespoons extra-virgin olive oil

Eight ¼-inch-thick baguette slices

Kosher salt and freshly ground black pepper

5 tablespoons salted butter, cut into pieces

2½ pounds ripe tomatoes, cored and cut into large chunks

1 quart low-sodium chicken OR vegetable broth

1 large white onion, chopped

Pesto (homemade or store-bought), to serve

Shaved Parmesan cheese, to serve

Don't use underripe tomatoes. The best soup is made with ripe, in-season tomatoes. However, in non-summer months, Campari tomatoes (also known as cocktail tomatoes) work almost as well. We don't recommend cherry or grape tomatoes, as their tough skins don't puree well.

1. In a large Dutch oven over medium-high, heat the oil until shimmering. Add the bread and cook until golden brown on both sides, about 2 minutes per side; transfer to a large plate and sprinkle with salt and pepper.

2. To the same pot over medium-high, add the butter and tomatoes, then cook, stirring occasionally, until the tomatoes begin to break apart and the skins start to peel away, about 5 minutes. Add the broth, onion and a large pinch each of salt and pepper. Bring to a boil, reduce to medium-low and cook, uncovered and stirring occasionally, until the onion has softened and the tomatoes have broken down, about 20 minutes; adjust the heat as needed to maintain a steady simmer. Cool uncovered for about 5 minutes.

3. Using a blender and working in 2 or 3 batches to avoid overfilling the jar, puree in batches until smooth. Return the soup to the pot and reheat over medium, stirring occasionally. Taste and season with salt and pepper. Ladle the soup into bowls and top with pesto, toasted bread and shaved Parmesan.

Butter-Braised Tomato Soup

In "The Essentials of Classic Italian Cooking," Marcella Hazan shared her now-famous recipe for a sublimely delicious, remarkably simple sauce made with nothing more than tomatoes, onion and butter. This soup turns that sauce into a light meal. If you own an immersion blender, the soup can be pureed directly in the pot, but the texture won't be as velvety as if processed in a conventional blender. We top individual bowlfuls with olive oil-toasted baguette slices, a dollop of pesto and shaved Parmesan. Homemade pesto is best, of course, but store-bought is fine; we've found that refrigerated pesto tastes fresher than the shelf-stable type sold in jars. A Y-style vegetable peeler is the best tool for planing off wide, thin shavings from a chunk of Parmesan cheese.

Miso Soup with Mixed Vegetables and Tofu

START TO FINISH: 35 MINUTES
SERVINGS: 4

Kenchinjiru is a Japanese vegetable and tofu soup that, if made the traditional way, is vegan. For ease, we use instant dashi (Japanese stock), which typically counts katsuobushi (bonito flakes) as a primary ingredient, so vegans and vegetarians take note. Look for instant dashi sold boxed or in packets in the international aisle of the supermarket or in Asian grocery stores. Follow the package instructions for preparing the 6 cups dashi needed for this recipe. Just a couple tablespoons of soy sauce add color, seasoning and umami to the soup, and to further enrich it with salty-sweet notes, we also include some white miso.

6 cups dashi (see headnote)

4 medium dried shiitake mushrooms

3 scallions, thinly sliced on the diagonal, white and green parts reserved separately

14-ounce container firm **OR** extra-firm tofu, drained and cut or torn into ½-inch pieces

3 small carrots, peeled and cut crosswise into ½-inch pieces

5 ounces daikon radish, peeled and cut into ½-inch cubes (about 1 cup)

3 tablespoons sake

2 tablespoons soy sauce

¼ cup white miso

Kosher salt and ground black pepper

Don't forget to trim off the shiitake stems after the mushrooms are rehydrated. The stems are fibrous and tough and, unlike the caps, will not tenderize with additional cooking.

1. **In a large saucepan** over medium-high, bring the dashi and mushrooms to a simmer. Reduce to medium and simmer, uncovered, for 10 minutes. Using a slotted spoon, transfer the mushrooms to a cutting board. To the broth, add the scallion whites, tofu, carrots, daikon, sake and soy sauce.

2. **Remove and discard the stems** from the mushrooms, thinly slice the caps and return them to the pan. Bring to a gentle simmer over medium and cook, uncovered and stirring occasionally, until the vegetables are tender, 5 to 9 minutes.

3. **In a small bowl,** whisk together the miso and ¼ cup of the hot broth until the miso is dissolved, then stir the mixture into the soup. Taste and season with salt and pepper. Ladle into bowls and sprinkle with the scallion greens.

Optional garnish: Toasted sesame oil **OR** shichimi togarashi **OR** both

Thai Red Curry Squash Soup

We take a shortcut and reach for store-bought Thai red curry paste to make this silky, rich soup. Together with coconut milk, ginger and lemon grass, the paste gives the soup incredible body and fragrance, as well as a little heat. To add another level of flavor, we fry shallots in oil until crisp, then reserve them for a garnish. Firm, dense kabocha squash is our first choice, but you can substitute delicata or butternut; note that if you're using delicata squash, it does not need to be peeled.

START TO FINISH: 1 HOUR (40 MINUTES ACTIVE)
SERVINGS: 4

_____

¼ cup grapeseed or other neutral oil

3 medium shallots, halved and thinly sliced

Kosher salt and ground black pepper

2-inch piece fresh ginger, peeled and minced

1 to 2 tablespoons Thai red curry paste (see headnote)

14-ounce can coconut milk

1 stalk lemon grass, trimmed to the lower 6-inches, dry outer layers discarded, halved and bruised

1 tablespoon white **OR** packed light brown sugar

2 teaspoons grated lime zest, plus 2 tablespoons lime juice, plus more grated zest, to serve

2 pounds kabocha **OR** butternut squash, peeled, seeded and cut into 2-inch chunks **OR** delicata squash, seeded and cut into 2-inch chunks

½ cup chopped fresh cilantro **OR** basil **OR** mint **OR** a combination

__Don't overcook the shallots.__ Remove them from the oil when they're lightly golden. As they cool, they continue to darken, by a shade or two, and also become crisp.

1. **In a large pot** over medium-high, heat the oil until shimmering. Add the shallots, reduce to medium and cook, stirring occasionally at first but more often as they begin to color, until light golden brown, 7 to 11 minutes; if browning too quickly, reduce the heat slightly. Remove the pot from the heat and, using a slotted spoon, transfer the shallots to a paper towel-lined plate, leaving the oil in the pot. Sprinkle the shallots with salt and set aside.

2. **To the oil** remaining in the pot, add the ginger and curry paste. Cook over medium, stirring often, until browned and fragrant, about 2 minutes. Add the coconut milk, lemon grass, sugar and lime zest, scraping up any browned bits. Stir in the squash and bring to a simmer over medium-high, then add 2½ cups water and ½ teaspoon salt. Return to a simmer, then cover, reduce to low and cook, stirring occasionally, until a skewer inserted into the squash meets no resistance, 20 to 25 minutes. Cool uncovered for about 5 minutes, then remove and discard the lemon grass.

3. **Using a blender** and working in 2 or 3 batches to avoid overfilling the jar, puree the squash mixture until smooth. Return the soup to the pot, add the lime juice and heat over medium, stirring, until heated through. Taste and season with salt and pepper. Serve topped with the fried shallots, cilantro and additional lime zest.

Optional garnish: Chopped roasted peanuts

Spinach and Green Lentil Soup with Roasted Peppers

This hearty soup, which happens to be vegan, gets loads of flavor from a base of sautéed shallots, tomato paste, cumin and smoked paprika. The earthiness of green lentils is offset by the sweetness and bright color of roasted red peppers. Spinach, added at the end of cooking, wilts into the broth, yielding a complete meal in a bowl. We use water as the cooking liquid, but you could use vegetable broth if you're so inclined. And if the finished soup is too thick for your taste, thin it with some hot water. Serve with warm crusty bread.

START TO FINISH: 50 MINUTES
SERVINGS: 4 TO 6

———

¼ cup extra-virgin olive oil, plus more to serve

4 medium shallots, halved and thinly sliced

2 tablespoons tomato paste

1 tablespoon ground cumin

1 teaspoon smoked paprika

2 bay leaves

Kosher salt and ground black pepper

1 cup green lentils

1 cup chopped drained roasted red peppers

5-ounce container baby spinach

Don't use lentils du Puy for this soup; they hold their shape and remain too firm. Regular green lentils, on the other hand, will soften to a silky texture that lends body to the broth.

1. **In a large saucepan** over medium, heat the oil until shimmering. Add the shallots and cook, stirring occasionally, until softened, about 5 minutes. Add the tomato paste, cumin, paprika, bay and 1 teaspoon pepper; cook, stirring, until fragrant, 1 to 2 minutes.

2. **Stir in the lentils,** roasted peppers, 1 teaspoon salt and 6 cups water. Bring to a simmer over medium-high, then cover, reduce to low and cook, stirring occasionally, until the lentils have softened and begin to fall apart, about 40 minutes.

3. **Remove and discard the bay.** Add the spinach and cook, stirring, until wilted, about 2 minutes. Taste and season with salt and pepper. Serve drizzled with additional oil.

Corn Bisque with Yogurt and Saffron

For this simple yet luxurious soup we combine saffron and corn. With so few ingredients, it's important to use fresh summer corn; frozen is not up to the task. To extract every drop of flavor, after slicing off the kernels, we simmer the cobs in the soup base until they relinquish all of their sweet, grassy flavor. At the very end, we stir in Greek yogurt, which adds creaminess along with a pleasing tanginess that balances the sweetness of the corn.

START TO FINISH: 45 MINUTES (25 MINUTES ACTIVE)
SERVINGS: 4 TO 6

————

4 tablespoons salted butter

4 cups corn kernels (from about 5 ears corn), cobs reserved

Kosher salt and ground black pepper

1 quart low-sodium chicken OR vegetable broth

¼ teaspoon saffron threads

1 cup plain whole-milk Greek yogurt

Fresh basil, chopped or torn, to serve

Don't use an immersion blender. A conventional jar blender is necessary for achieving a velvety smooth puree. Don't use low-fat or nonfat Greek yogurt. Whole-milk Greek yogurt is the only type that will not separate when stirred into the hot soup. But even so, be sure the pot is off the burner and, after the yogurt is added, don't allow the soup to return to a simmer, as additional heat may cause curdling.

1. **In a large pot** over medium-high, melt the butter. Add the corn kernels and ½ teaspoon each salt and pepper. Cook, stirring occasionally, until the corn begins to brown, about 5 minutes. Add the reserved cobs, the broth and saffron. Bring to a boil, then reduce to medium-low and cook, uncovered and stirring occasionally, for 30 minutes; adjust the heat as needed to maintain a simmer. Cool for about 5 minutes, then remove and discard the cobs.

2. **Using a blender** and working in 2 or 3 batches to avoid overfilling the jar, puree until smooth. Return the soup to the pot and reheat over medium, stirring occasionally. Remove the pot from the heat and whisk in the yogurt; if the soup is too thick, stir in water to thin. Taste and season with salt and pepper. Serve sprinkled with basil.

Optional garnish: Lime wedges **OR** halved cherry tomatoes **OR** both

2 tablespoons plus
1 teaspoon extra-virgin
olive oil, divided

2-pound butternut squash,
peeled, seeded and cut into
½-inch chunks (4 cups)

2 medium carrots, peeled
and cut into ½-inch chunks

Kosher salt

1 medium yellow onion,
chopped

1 tablespoon finely
grated fresh ginger

1½ teaspoons ground cumin

1 teaspoon ground coriander

½ to ¾ teaspoon cayenne
pepper, divided

½ cup pumpkin seeds

½ cup plain whole-milk
yogurt, plus more to serve

Don't bring the soup to a full simmer after adding the yogurt. Simmering will cause the yogurt to curdle.

1. In a large pot over medium-high, heat 2 tablespoons oil until barely smoking. Add the squash, carrots and 1 teaspoon salt, then cook, stirring occasionally, until the squash begins to brown, about 4 minutes. Add the onion and continue to cook, stirring occasionally, until the onion has softened, 3 to 4 minutes.

2. Stir in the ginger, cumin, coriander, ¼ teaspoon of cayenne and ½ teaspoon salt, then cook until fragrant, about 30 seconds. Pour in 5 cups water and bring to a simmer. Cover, reduce to medium-low and cook, stirring occasionally, until a skewer inserted into the squash meets no resistance, 10 to 15 minutes. Remove from the heat and let cool, uncovered, for about 15 minutes.

3. Meanwhile, in a 10-inch skillet over medium, stir together the remaining 1 teaspoon oil, the remaining ¼ to ½ teaspoon cayenne, the pumpkin seeds and ¼ teaspoon salt. Cook, stirring frequently, until toasted and fragrant, 3 to 5 minutes. Transfer to a small bowl and set aside.

4. Using a blender and working in 2 or 3 batches to avoid overfilling the jar, puree the squash mixture and its cooking liquid, processing until mostly smooth, 15 to 30 seconds. Return the pureed soup to the pot. Whisk in the yogurt and heat over low, stirring occasionally, just until warmed; do not allow the soup to simmer. (Alternatively, puree the soup directly in the pot with an immersion blender, then stir in the yogurt; the soup won't need reheating.) Taste and season with salt. Ladle the soup into serving bowls and top with additional yogurt and spiced pumpkin seeds just before serving.

Indian-Spiced Butternut Squash Soup with Yogurt

Fresh ginger and warm spices complement the natural sweetness of squash for a vibrant yet comforting soup. Because butternut often has a one-note flavor, we include carrots for earthiness and depth. A spoonful of yogurt and some spiced pumpkin seeds add color and texture.

Habanero-Onion Soup with Lime

This soup requires only a handful of ingredients but hits a wide range of flavor notes: savory, sweet, spicy, tangy and herbal. Habanero chilies are intensely spicy but also fruity. To achieve a soup with the right flavor but without scorching heat, we mince one chili and leave the other whole, cutting slits into its sides so it releases its flavor, then fish it out before serving. While the soup is simmering, we throw together a fragrant mix of lime and herbs for garnishing individual servings.

START TO FINISH: 45 MINUTES
SERVINGS: 4 TO 6

3 tablespoons extra-virgin olive oil

2 large yellow onions, halved and thinly sliced

2 habanero chilies, 1 slit a couple times with a paring knife, 1 stemmed, seeded and minced

2 bay leaves

1 teaspoon white sugar

Kosher salt and ground black pepper

1½ quarts low-sodium chicken broth

1 cup lightly packed fresh flat-leaf parsley, finely chopped

3 scallions, finely chopped

2 teaspoons grated lime zest, plus 2 tablespoons lime juice, plus lime wedges to serve

Don't touch your face with your hands after handling the chilies, as residual capsaicin will cause a burning sensation. If you have disposable food safe gloves, it's a good idea to use them to prep the chilies.

1. **In a large Dutch oven** over medium-high, heat the oil until shimmering. Add the onions, the whole and minced chilies, bay, sugar and ½ teaspoon salt. Cook, stirring occasionally, until the onions are deep golden brown, 15 to 18 minutes. Add the broth and bring to a simmer, scraping up any browned bits. Reduce to medium-low, cover and cook, stirring occasionally, until the onions are meltingly tender, 10 to 15 minutes.

2. **Meanwhile, in a small bowl,** stir together the parsley, scallions, lime zest, ¼ teaspoon salt and 1 teaspoon pepper; set aside.

3. **When the soup is done,** remove the pot from the heat. Remove and discard the bay and whole habanero, then stir in the lime juice. Taste and season with salt and pepper. Serve topped with the parsley mixture and with lime wedges.

Jerk-Seasoned Yellow Squash Soup with Coconut

This soup pairs the lively flavor of Jamaican jerk spices with rich coconut milk and buttery, subtly sweet yellow crookneck squash. Crookneck squash is in the same family as zucchini, but its skin is thicker and its seeds are heartier. When cooked, it becomes soft and spongy, perfect for pureeing into a velvety soup. If crookneck isn't available, yellow summer squash works instead, though its flavor is milder, and there's no need to remove the seeds because they're more tender. The spiciness of jerk seasoning—an herb, spice and chili blend—varies brand to brand, so you may want to taste yours and adjust the amount you add. The habanero also lends spiciness, but we seed it to remove some of its capsaicin. Fans of heat, however, may wish to leave in the seeds. If you own an immersion blender, you can use it to puree the soup directly in the pot.

START TO FINISH: 45 MINUTES
SERVINGS: 4

3 tablespoons coconut oil **OR** neutral oil

1 medium yellow onion, chopped

Kosher salt and ground black pepper

2 tablespoons minced fresh ginger

3 medium garlic cloves, minced

1½ teaspoons jerk seasoning, plus more to serve

1 habanero chili, stemmed, halved and seeded

6 thyme sprigs

3 pounds yellow crookneck squash, halved lengthwise, seeded and chopped **OR** yellow summer squash, chopped

14-ounce can coconut milk

Pecans, toasted and chopped, to serve

Don't forget to remove the thyme sprigs before blending. Also, don't fill the blender jar more than halfway. If overfilled, hot soup may spout out the top when the blender is turned on.

1. **In a large Dutch oven** over medium-high, heat the oil until shimmering. Add the onion and ½ teaspoon salt, then cook, stirring occasionally, until golden brown, 7 to 10 minutes. Add the ginger, garlic, jerk seasoning, habanero and thyme. Cook, stirring often, until the ginger is lightly browned, about 2 minutes. Add the squash, coconut milk, 2 cups water and a generous pinch each of salt and pepper. Bring to a boil, scraping up any browned bits. Cover, reduce to medium and cook, stirring occasionally, until the squash is tender, 6 to 10 minutes. Cool uncovered for about 5 minutes, then remove and discard the thyme.

2. **Using a blender** and working in 2 or 3 batches to avoid overfilling the jar, puree the mixture until smooth. Return the soup to the pot and reheat over medium, stirring occasionally. Taste and season with salt and pepper. Served sprinkled with pecans and additional jerk seasoning.

Optional garnish: Chopped fresh cilantro

Asparagus

In a world of year-round produce, asparagus remains a messenger of spring, showing up in markets as winter begins to relax its grip. Elegant and luxurious, the plants take up to three years to become established, and, once harvested, the stalks won't tolerate more than a brief stay in the crisper drawer. It's worth the effort because asparagus is ideal for celebratory, colorful recipes.

Asparagus isn't a common vegetable in Asian kitchens, but we think its natural sweetness is delicious paired with mỡ hành, or Vietnamese scallion oil. The condiment is spooned onto everything from grilled seafood to steamed rice. The fat carries flavor and is delicious spooned over asparagus that's been briefly seared, then steamed until tender in a scant amount of water, p. 143.

Delicate asparagus contrasts nicely with a bittersweet char, but we find broiling can be disappointing; if the oven's not hot enough, the insides turn mushy. In Spain, vegetables often are cooked a la plancha, on a hot griddle, and we take that approach with our charred asparagus, p. 168, cooking it in a hot cast-iron skillet.

From Israel, we borrow the concept of pashtida, a crustless, quiche-like dish that often features a mix of vegetables and cheese. Our recipe, p. 313, is brightened by the fresh grassiness of chopped dill and sharp white cheddar or nutty, salty Gruyère.

Lemon grass, prized for its herbal, citrus notes, is common in Southeast Asian cooking, often paired with fish sauce. We keep things vegetarian, pairing lemon grass with Chinese five-spice powder and soy sauce for our stir-fry of asparagus and mushrooms, p. 264. The asparagus sets off the meatiness of the mushrooms and a citrusy sauce ties everything together.

For an elegantly simple dish, we combine campanelle and slender asparagus spears, p. 271. Noodles and asparagus finish in a gentle simmer of half-and-half for a creamy, one-pot pasta—a great way to welcome spring.

Chilled Beet Soup
with Fresh Dill

START TO FINISH: 20 MINUTES
SERVINGS: 6

Chlodnik, a simple chilled beet soup, is a summertime staple in Poland. It was our inspiration for this recipe, but instead of mixing sour cream or another creamy, tangy dairy product directly into the soup, we dollop it on as a garnish. Refrigerated cooked beets, found in the produce section of most grocery stores, and jarred pickled beets make the soup a breeze to prepare. We blend the beets with ice so it can be served right away (no chilling required), but it also can be made ahead and refrigerated for up to a day before serving, and its flavor actually improves as it sits. If you don't have ice on hand, add an additional ½ cup cold water to each batch of puree and chill the soup until cold. To keep the soup cold at the table, chill your bowls in the freezer briefly before ladling in the soup.

4 red radishes,
cut into ¼-inch cubes

½ English cucumber,
cut into ¼-inch cubes

¾ cup drained sliced
pickled beets, finely
chopped, plus ¼ cup pickled
beet juice

2 tablespoons lemon juice

3 tablespoons chopped
fresh dill, divided

Kosher salt and
ground black pepper

Three 8.8 ounce-packages
refrigerated cooked
red beets, drained (liquid
reserved) and roughly
chopped

2 cups ice, divided

Sour cream **OR** plain
whole-milk yogurt,
to serve

Don't discard the beet juice from the packages of refrigerated cooked beets. The liquid is colorful and flavorful, so we puree it with the beets.

1. **In a medium bowl,** stir together the radishes, cucumber, pickled beets, lemon juice, 1 tablespoon dill, ¾ teaspoon salt and ¼ teaspoon pepper; set aside.

2. **In a blender,** combine half of the cooked beets, the reserved cooked beet juice, ¾ cup water and 1 cup ice. Puree until smooth, then transfer to a large bowl. Puree the remaining cooked beets, the remaining 1 cup ice and 1 cup water until smooth and add to the bowl. To the puree, add the pickled beet juice and ¼ teaspoon pepper. Stir, then taste and season with salt.

3. **Ladle the soup** into serving bowls. Top each with a spoonful of sour cream, some of the radish-cucumber mixture, the remaining dill and a few grinds of pepper.

Asparagus and Barley Soup with Lemon and Dill

Barley soups tend to be heavy and stodgy, but this one is light and bright with asparagus, lemon and dill. We use a few tablespoons of butter to sauté a shallot and create a flavor base with just enough richness to yield a satisfying soup in which each ingredient holds its own. The barley requires about 35 minutes of simmering to become tender; this is a good time to prep both the asparagus and the dill. Leftover soup will thicken because of the barley; add water or broth during heating to thin it.

START TO FINISH: 50 MINUTES
SERVINGS: 4 TO 6

———

3 tablespoons salted butter

1 medium shallot, minced

Kosher salt and ground black pepper

1 cup pearled barley

2 quarts low-sodium chicken broth

1 pound asparagus

½ cup chopped fresh dill

1 teaspoon grated lemon zest, plus 3 tablespoons lemon juice

Don't cover the pot during simmering. Allowing some evaporation helps concentrate the flavors for a richer-tasting soup. Also, be sure to taste the barley to gauge its doneness before adding the asparagus. The grain should be tender before the asparagus goes in because once it does, the soup needs only a few more minutes to cook.

1. **In a large pot over medium,** melt the butter. Add the shallot and ¼ teaspoon salt; cook, stirring occasionally, until the shallot is softened, 2 to 3 minutes. Stir in the barley. Add the broth and ½ teaspoon pepper. Bring to a simmer over medium-high, then reduce to medium-low and cook, uncovered and stirring occasionally, until the barley is tender, 35 to 40 minutes; adjust the heat as needed to maintain a gentle simmer.

2. **Meanwhile, trim off and discard** the tough, woody base of the asparagus spears. Slice the stalks into ¼-inch pieces on the diagonal, leaving the tips about 1 inch in length. Set aside until ready to use.

3. **When the barley is tender,** add the asparagus and cook, stirring occasionally, until tender-crisp, 2 to 3 minutes. Off heat, stir in the dill and lemon zest and juice. Taste and season with salt and pepper.

Mushroom and Sauerkraut Soup with Paprika and Caraway

Sauerkraut soup is a German and Eastern European classic. It often is made with meat, but for our vegetarian version, we lean on mushrooms—both fresh cremini and dried porcini—to provide savory depth. Crushing the caraway seeds helps them fully release their flavor into the broth. Either pulse them in an electric spice grinder or bash them with a mortar and pestle. Serve with hearty brown bread smeared with butter.

START TO FINISH: 50 MINUTES
SERVINGS: 4

¼ cup grapeseed or other neutral oil

8 ounces cremini mushrooms, trimmed and thinly sliced

6 medium garlic cloves, minced

2 tablespoons hot paprika OR 2 tablespoons sweet paprika plus ⅛ teaspoon cayenne pepper

2 teaspoons caraway seeds, lightly crushed

12 ounces Yukon Gold potatoes, unpeeled, cut into ½-inch chunks

Kosher salt and ground black pepper

1 medium carrot, peeled, halved lengthwise and thinly sliced

¼ cup dried porcini mushrooms, broken into small pieces, rinsed and drained

2 cups drained refrigerated sauerkraut

½ cup lightly packed fresh dill, chopped

Don't use canned sauerkraut for this soup. Fresh kraut, sold in jars or bags, tastes fresher, has better texture and lends the right amount of tang.

1. In a large pot over medium-high, heat the oil until shimmering. Add the cremini mushrooms and cook, stirring occasionally, until the liquid they release has evaporated and the mushrooms are well browned, 8 to 12 minutes. Add the garlic, paprika and caraway; cook, stirring, until fragrant, about 1 minute.

2. Stir in the potatoes and ½ teaspoon salt, then add 6 cups water, the carrots, porcini and ½ teaspoon pepper, scraping up any browned bits. Bring to a boil, then reduce to medium and simmer, uncovered, until the potatoes are just tender, 12 to 17 minutes.

3. Add the sauerkraut and cook, stirring occasionally, until the potatoes and carrots are tender, about another 10 minutes. Off heat, stir in ¼ cup of dill. Taste and season with salt and pepper. Serve sprinkled with the remaining dill.

Optional garnish: Sour cream

Paprika-Cumin Potato and Bell Pepper Soup

With a smooth, creamy consistency and sunny color, the potato soup known as locro de papas—variations of which are found in both Ecuador and Peru—is both humble and elegant. It often is made with milk and cheese, but we skip most of the dairy to keep the flavors lighter and fresher, instead adding queso fresco at the end only as a garnish. Ecuadorian locro do papas gets its yellow-orange hue from annatto seeds (also called achiote), but we achieve a similar color by using red or orange bell peppers and sweet paprika.

START TO FINISH: 1 HOUR 10 MINUTES
SERVINGS: 6

————

2 tablespoons
extra-virgin olive oil

1 large white onion, halved
and thinly sliced

3 red **OR** orange bell
peppers, stemmed, seeded
and sliced

1 bunch cilantro, chopped,
stems and leaves reserved
separately

1 bunch scallions, thinly
sliced, white and green
parts reserved separately

6 medium garlic cloves,
smashed and peeled

2 tablespoons
sweet paprika

1 tablespoon ground cumin

2 pounds russet potatoes,
unpeeled, cut into 1-inch
cubes

2 quarts low-sodium
chicken broth or water

Kosher salt and
ground black pepper

2 tablespoons lime juice

Crumbled or grated
queso fresco, to serve

Diced avocado, to serve

Don't peel the potatoes. The skins add an earthiness that complements the other flavors. If using a conventional blender, make sure to allow the potato mixture to cool for about 10 minutes before pureeing and don't try to puree all the soup mixture in a single batch.

1. In a large Dutch oven over medium, heat the oil until shimmering. Add the onion, bell peppers, cilantro stems and scallion whites. Cook, stirring occasionally, until the vegetables are softened and beginning to brown, 6 to 9 minutes. Add the garlic, paprika and cumin, then cook, stirring, until fragrant, about 30 seconds. Stir in the potatoes, broth and 1½ teaspoons salt.

2. Bring to a boil over medium-high, then cover, reduce to low and cook, stirring occasionally and adjusting the heat as needed to maintain a simmer, until a skewer inserted into the potatoes meets no resistance, about 40 minutes. Remove from the heat and cool for about 10 minutes.

3. Using a blender and working in batches, puree the mixture until completely smooth. (Alternatively, use an immersion blender and puree directly in the pot.) Return the soup to the pot and cook over medium, stirring occasionally, until heated through.

4. Off heat, stir in the lime juice, then taste and season with salt and pepper. Serve the soup topped with the cilantro leaves, scallion greens, queso fresco and avocado.

Collard Greens and Potato Soup with Chili Oil

This vegetarian soup is hearty and satisfying, but not at all heavy. When creating it we had in mind caldo verde, the classic Portuguese soup of greens and chouriço. We skipped the sausage to keep the focus on the flavors and textures of the vegetables, and we tossed in some carrots for a jolt of color and sweetness. As a flourish to transform the humble soup into something special, we make a spicy, vibrant infused oil with dried chilies, garlic, rosemary and oregano for drizzling at the table. Serve with warm, crusty bread.

START TO FINISH: 1 HOUR
SERVINGS: 4

_____

½ cup plus 2 tablespoons grapeseed or other neutral oil, divided

¼ cup árbol chilies, coarsely crumbled **OR** 2½ teaspoons red pepper flakes

2½ teaspoons sweet paprika, divided

2 medium garlic cloves, chopped

1 teaspoon dried oregano

2 small sprigs rosemary, divided

Kosher salt and ground black pepper

12 ounces red **OR** Yukon Gold potatoes, unpeeled, cut into ½-inch chunks

1 medium carrot, peeled and cut into ½-inch pieces

1 bunch (1 pound) collard greens, stemmed and torn into rough 1-inch pieces

1½ quarts low-sodium vegetable broth

1 tablespoon red wine vinegar **OR** sherry vinegar

Don't strain the infused oil right away. _Allow it to steep while you make the soup so the ingredients bloom and the oil intensifies in flavor._

1. In a small saucepan over medium-low, combine the ½ cup oil, the chilies, 1½ teaspoons paprika, the garlic, oregano, 1 rosemary sprig and ¼ teaspoon black pepper. Cook, stirring occasionally, until the garlic is lightly toasted and the oil is aromatic and bright red, 5 to 7 minutes. Remove from the heat and set aside.

2. In a large pot over medium-high, heat the remaining 2 tablespoons oil until shimmering. Add the potatoes, carrots, the remaining rosemary sprig, the remaining 1 teaspoon paprika, 1 teaspoon salt and ½ teaspoon black pepper. Cook, stirring occasionally, until the potatoes are lightly browned,

about 5 minutes. Add the collards and cook, stirring occasionally, until slightly wilted, about 3 minutes. Pour in the broth and bring to a boil over medium-high. Cover, reduce to low and cook, stirring occasionally, until the collards are completely tender and the potatoes break apart when pressed, about 30 minutes.

3. While the soup is simmering, pour the infused oil through a fine-mesh strainer set over a small bowl; press on the solids to extract as much oil as possible.

4. When the soup is done, remove the pot from the heat. Remove and discard the rosemary. Stir in the vinegar, then taste and season with salt and black pepper. Ladle into bowls and serve, offering the oil alongside for drizzling.

Double Carrot Soup with Fennel and Lime

START TO FINISH: 35 MINUTES
SERVINGS: 4

To make this silky soup, we simmer carrots in carrot juice, resulting in a vibrant and full-flavored puree. The addition of baking soda may seem unusual, but it helps break down and tenderize the carrots so they blend into a smooth, velvety texture. Fennel seeds and cumin add earthiness and spice to balance the carrots' natural sweetness, while a little lime juice added at the end brightens the flavors. Butter-toasted sliced almonds sprinkled onto individual bowlfuls add crunchy contrast.

4 tablespoons salted butter, cut into 1-tablespoon pieces, divided

½ cup sliced almonds

1½ pounds carrots, peeled and cut into 1-inch pieces

4 cups carrot juice

½ cup chopped fresh cilantro, plus cilantro leaves to serve

1 tablespoon fennel seeds

1 tablespoon ground cumin

½ teaspoon baking soda

Kosher salt and ground black pepper

2 tablespoons lime juice, plus lime wedges to serve

Don't substitute water or broth for the carrot juice. The juice bolsters the carrots' flavor as well as their color. Don't use an immersion blender for this soup; a conventional blender is best for achieving a flawless puree.

1. **In a large saucepan** over medium-high, melt 1 tablespoon of butter. Add the almonds and cook, stirring, until golden brown, 3 to 5 minutes. Remove the pan from the heat and, with a slotted spoon, transfer the almonds to a small bowl; set aside.

2. **To the same pan,** add the carrots, carrot juice, cilantro, fennel seeds, cumin, baking soda and ¾ teaspoon salt; stir to combine. Bring to a boil over medium-high then reduce to low and cook, uncovered and stirring occasionally, until the carrots are tender enough to be smashed with a fork, about 20 minutes. Cool uncovered for about 5 minutes.

3. **Using a blender** and working in 2 batches, puree the carrot mixture until smooth. Return the soup to the pot and heat over medium, stirring, until heated through. Off heat, add the remaining 3 tablespoons butter and the lime juice; stir until the butter melts. Taste and season with salt and pepper. Serve topped with the toasted almonds and cilantro leaves and with lime wedges on the side.

Optional garnish: Plain whole-milk yogurt

Kale, Fennel and White Bean Soup with Parmesan Croutons

We love ribollita, the rustic, hearty Tuscan meal in a bowl. But for this recipe we wanted a lighter vegetable and bean soup, one that kept the focus on the freshness of the ingredients. So we took out the stale bread that's simmered into ribollita to thicken it and instead made some crisp, craggy croutons that we tossed with grated Parmesan and scattered on top of individual bowlfuls. This soup uses water instead of broth; the flavor backbone comes from the aromatics as well as from the umami-rich tomato paste and the chunk of Parmesan rind that's simmered in the mix.

START TO FINISH: 1¼ HOURS
SERVINGS: 4 TO 6

_____

8 ounces rustic bread, torn into bite-size pieces (4 cups)

4 tablespoons extra-virgin olive oil, divided, plus more to serve

Kosher salt and ground black pepper

2 ounces Parmesan cheese, finely grated (1 cup), plus a 2-inch piece of Parmesan rind

1 medium red OR yellow onion, chopped

1 medium fennel bulb, trimmed, halved lengthwise, cored and sliced ½ inch thick against the grain

1 bunch lacinato kale, stems removed and chopped, leaves roughly chopped, reserved separately

2 tablespoons tomato paste

2 medium garlic cloves, minced

½ cup dry white wine

2 sprigs thyme

½ teaspoon red pepper flakes

15½-ounce can cannellini beans, drained but not rinsed

Don't discard the stems from the kale. Chop them and reserve separately from the leaves. We sauté the stems with the onion and fennel to bolster the soup's green, minerally flavor. Lacinato kale is sometimes sold as Tuscan kale, dinosaur kale or cavolo nero. Also, drain but don't rinse the beans. The starchy liquid that clings to them lends body to the broth.

1. **Heat the oven to 375°F** with a rack in the middle position. Distribute the bread on a rimmed baking sheet. Drizzle with 2 tablespoons oil and sprinkle with ½ teaspoon each salt and black pepper. Toss, then bake until browned and crisp, about 10 minutes, stirring once about halfway through. Remove from the oven, sprinkle with about half of the Parmesan and toss; set aside.

2. **In a large pot** over medium, heat the remaining 2 tablespoons oil until shimmering. Add the onion, fennel, kale stems and ½ teaspoon salt. Cook, stirring occasionally, until the vegetables begin to soften, about 5 minutes. Add the tomato paste and garlic; cook, stirring, until the tomato paste begins to brown and stick to the bottom of the pot, about 1 minute. Add the wine, thyme and pepper flakes, then cook, scraping up any browned bits, until the liquid has almost evaporated, about 2 minutes.

3. **Stir in the beans,** the kale leaves, Parmesan rind (if using), 5 cups water, 1½ teaspoons salt and ½ teaspoon black pepper. Bring to a simmer over medium-high, then reduce to medium and cook, uncovered and stirring occasionally, until the kale is very tender, 20 to 25 minutes.

4. **Remove and discard the thyme** and Parmesan rind (if used). Taste and season with salt and black pepper. Ladle the soup into bowls, top with the croutons and the remaining Parmesan and drizzle with additional oil.

5

STOVETOP STANDOUTS

Radishes and Snap Peas with Orange and Mint

Snap peas (or snow peas, if you prefer) and red and white radishes make this a colorful dish that's also full of crisp-tender texture. With mustard seeds for savoriness and orange for brightness and acidity, plus the sweetness of the peas and the pepperiness of the radishes, this easy-to-make side features layers of complexity. Radishes vary greatly in size, so cutting them into evenly sized wedges helps them cook evenly. Smaller radishes may only require quartering, while larger ones may need to be cut into eighths.

START TO FINISH: 25 MINUTES
SERVINGS: 4

———

3 tablespoons salted butter **OR** extra-virgin olive oil

1 tablespoon yellow mustard seeds

1 sprig fresh mint, plus ½ cup chopped fresh mint

Kosher salt and ground black pepper

1 pound radishes, cut into ½-inch wedges

1 pound sugar snap peas **OR** snow peas, trimmed, strings removed, if present

1 teaspoon grated orange zest, plus 2 tablespoons orange juice

Don't stir the vegetables too often during the first 3 minutes of cooking. Each time the lid is removed, heat escapes, which slows down the cooking.

1. In a large Dutch oven over medium-high, melt the butter with the mustard seeds and mint sprig. Cook, stirring, until fragrant, 1 to 2 minutes. Add 1¼ cups water, ¾ teaspoon salt and ¼ teaspoon pepper, then bring to a simmer.

2. Stir in the radishes and snap peas, cover and cook, stirring just once or twice, until the peas are tender-crisp, 3 to 5 minutes. Uncover and cook until the moisture evaporates and the vegetables begin to sizzle, about 5 minutes.

3. Off heat, discard the mint sprig, then stir in the chopped mint and orange juice. Taste and season with salt and pepper and sprinkle with the orange zest.

Optional garnish: Crumbled blue cheese

"Creamed" Corn with Scallions

All-American creamed corn typically is made with heavy cream, and sometimes even is thickened with starch. But we think these ingredients blunt the sweet, grassy flavor of fresh corn, so instead we scrape the "milk" from the cobs after cutting away the kernels and blend it with a little water plus half of the kernels. Cooked with the whole kernels, the puree becomes creamy and velvety thanks to the corn's natural starches. We don't shy away from the butter, though, as it adds a luxurious richness, and we use savory scallions to balance the sugariness of the corn. Peak-season fresh yellow corn is best, of course, but thawed frozen corn works, too. Since you won't have any cobs to "milk," add an additional ¾ cup kernels to the blender for pureeing.

START TO FINISH: 25 MINUTES
SERVINGS: 4

_____

4 cups corn kernels (from about 5 ears corn), divided, cobs reserved

6 tablespoons salted butter

1 bunch scallions, thinly sliced, white and green parts reserved separately

Kosher salt and ground black pepper

Lime wedges, to serve

Don't forget to stir often and scrape the bottom of the pan while cooking the corn. The natural sugars in the corn tend to stick and will easily scorch. Using a nonstick skillet helps prevent sticking, but it still is important to stir frequently.

1. **One at a time,** stand the cobs on their base and, using the back of a chef's knife, scrape down the length of the cob to remove the "milk." In a blender, combine the corn milk, 2 cups of the kernels and ½ cup water. Puree until smooth, about 1 minute.

2. **In a 12-inch nonstick skillet** over medium-high, melt the butter. Add the puree, the remaining 2 cups corn kernels, the scallion whites and a large pinch each salt and pepper. Bring to a simmer, stirring, then reduce to medium and cook, stirring often and scraping along the bottom to prevent scorching, until the mixture begins to thicken, about 10 minutes. Off heat, taste and season with salt and pepper. Transfer to a serving dish, sprinkle with the scallion greens and serve with lime wedges.

Green Beans with Mushrooms and Sherry Vinaigrette

We borrowed some of the flavors from classic green bean casserole to create this simple, bright green bean side. The soy sauce in the vinaigrette boosts the natural umami of the mushrooms, and a mixture of chopped and sliced mushrooms makes the dish more visually and texturally interesting. The vinaigrette can be refrigerated up to a day in advance; bring to room temperature before using. The mushroom and shallot mixture can also be cooked ahead. To do so, after they're well browned, pour ¼ cup water into the pan and scrape up any browned bits; let cool, then refrigerate in an airtight container for up to a day. When ready to serve, in a 12-inch skillet over medium, heat the mushroom mixture, stirring occasionally, until hot, then stir in the blanched green beans (no additional water needed) and cook until warmed through. Dress the beans off heat as instructed in the recipe.

START TO FINISH: 20 MINUTES
SERVINGS: 8

6 tablespoons extra-virgin olive oil, divided

⅓ cup sherry vinegar

2 tablespoons Dijon mustard

1 tablespoon soy sauce

2 teaspoons grated lemon zest

Kosher salt and ground black pepper

1 pound cremini mushrooms (8 ounces chopped, 8 ounces thinly sliced)

5 medium shallots, halved and thinly sliced

1½ pounds green beans, trimmed, halved and blanched

Don't dress the green beans until ready to serve.

1. **In a small bowl,** whisk together 4 tablespoons of oil, the vinegar, mustard, soy sauce, lemon zest and 1 teaspoon pepper; set aside.

2. **In a 12-inch skillet** over medium, heat the remaining 2 tablespoons oil until shimmering. Add all of the mushrooms, the shallots and ½ teaspoon salt, then stir to combine. Cover and cook, stirring occasionally, until the mushrooms release their moisture, about 5 minutes. Uncover and continue to cook, stirring occasionally, until the mushrooms and shallots are well browned, 5 to 7 minutes.

3. **Pour in ¼ cup water** and scrape up any browned bits. Add the green beans and cook, stirring occasionally, until the beans are heated through, about 5 minutes. Off heat, stir in the dressing and toss until the beans are well coated. Taste and season with salt and pepper. Transfer to a dish and serve warm or at room temperature.

Broccoli with Scallions, Miso and Orange

The broccoli in this recipe starts with a simmer and finishes with a sizzle. First, we cook the brassica, covered, until tender-crisp in a mixture of water, miso and sesame oil, then remove the lid and keep cooking until the moisture evaporates and the flavors concentrate. Orange zest and juice added at the very end wake up the dish with citrusy brightness. Either white or red miso works, so use whichever you prefer or have on hand.

START TO FINISH: 25 MINUTES
SERVINGS: 4

3 tablespoons extra-virgin olive oil **OR** salted butter

1 bunch scallions, thinly sliced, whites and greens reserved separately

1½ tablespoons white miso **OR** red miso

1 tablespoon toasted sesame oil, plus more to serve

Kosher salt and ground black pepper

2 pounds broccoli, stems sliced ½ inch thick and florets cut into 1-inch pieces

1 tablespoon grated orange zest, plus 2 tablespoons orange juice

Don't forget to reserve the scallion whites and greens separately, as they're added at different times. The whites are sautéed before the broccoli is added to the pot; the greens go in at the end.

1. **In a large Dutch oven,** combine the olive oil and scallion whites. Cook over medium-high, stirring, until lightly browned, about 5 minutes. Add 1¼ cups water, the miso, sesame oil, ¼ teaspoon salt and ½ teaspoon pepper. Bring to a boil, stirring to dissolve the miso, then stir in the broccoli. Cover and cook, stirring occasionally, until tender-crisp, about 7 minutes.

2. **Uncover and cook,** stirring occasionally, until the moisture evaporates and the broccoli begins to sizzle, about 4 minutes. Off heat, stir in the orange zest and juice along with the scallion greens, then taste and season with salt and pepper. Transfer to a serving dish and drizzle with additional sesame oil.

Optional garnish: Toasted sesame seeds **OR** Sriracha **OR** both

Charred Kale with Garlic, Chilies and Lime

Charring kale gives it a bittersweet flavor and a nutty edge, reminiscent of oven-roasted kale chips. The volume of raw kale here may seem overwhelming, but it will cook down. Use the largest bowl you have to toss the leaves with oil, and the largest Dutch oven you own to cook the greens. Beware the vapors when you add the chili and garlic to the hot pot.

START TO FINISH: 35 MINUTES
SERVINGS: 4

————

2 large bunches lacinato kale (about 1½ pounds total), stemmed, leaves torn into 2- to 3-inch pieces

1 tablespoon plus 1 teaspoon grapeseed or other neutral oil

Kosher salt and ground black pepper

5 medium garlic cloves, thinly sliced

1 Fresno **OR** jalapeño chili, stemmed, seeded and thinly sliced

4 scallions, thinly sliced on the diagonal, white and green parts reserved separately

1 teaspoon grated lime zest, plus 1 tablespoon lime juice

1 tablespoon extra-virgin olive oil

Don't use olive oil to char the kale, as it has a lower smoke point than neutral oil. And don't be afraid to get the oil super hot before piling the kale into the pot; light wisps of smoke are an indication that the oil and pot are ready.

1. **In a large bowl,** toss the kale with 1 tablespoon of neutral oil and ½ teaspoon salt, rubbing with your hands to coat each leaf. In a large Dutch oven over high, heat the remaining 1 teaspoon neutral oil until barely smoking. Add the kale, cover and cook, occasionally turning the kale with tongs, until wilted and charred, about 10 minutes.

2. **Push the kale to the sides of the pot** and add the garlic, chili and scallion whites. Cook, stirring, until fragrant, about 30 seconds, then stir the mixture into the kale. Quickly add ½ cup water to the pot and immediately cover. Cook, without stirring, until the kale is tender and the water has evaporated, about 2 minutes.

3. **Off heat,** stir in the scallion greens and lime zest and juice. Taste and season with salt and pepper. Transfer to a serving dish and drizzle with the olive oil.

Butter-and-Soy-Glazed Vegetables

The richness of butter plus umami-rich soy sauce makes vegetables taste full and satisfying without eclipsing their flavors or weighing them down. And the combination, along with a little sliced fresh ginger, is a fantastic pairing for just about any type of vegetable, so this is a great way to use up small amounts of produce hanging out in the crisper drawer. Serve with steamed rice.

START TO FINISH: 20 MINUTES
SERVINGS: 4

5 tablespoons salted butter, cut into several pieces

3 medium shallots, halved and thinly sliced

1-inch piece fresh ginger, peeled and thinly sliced

1 pound mixed vegetables (such as thinly sliced broccoli and/or cauliflower florets, trimmed and halved snow or snap peas, trimmed green beans, sliced bell peppers, sliced mushrooms, sliced cabbage, thinly sliced carrots, and asparagus cut into 1-inch sections)

¼ cup soy sauce

Sesame seeds, toasted (optional)

Sliced scallions (optional)

Don't cut broccoli or cauliflower, if using, into large florets. Rather, thinly slice the florets so they cook in the same time as the other vegetables.

1.   **In a 12-inch skillet** over medium-high, melt the butter. Add the shallots and ginger, then cook, stirring, until the shallots have softened, about 1 minute. Add the vegetables and cook, stirring occasionally, until just beginning to soften, 3 to 5 minutes.

2.   **Add ¼ cup water** and the soy sauce. Increase to high and cook, stirring, until the liquid has reduced and the vegetables are tender-crisp and lightly glazed, 2 to 3 minutes. Transfer to a serving dish and sprinkle with sesame seeds and/or sliced scallions (if using).

Braised Swiss Chard with Raisins and Pine Nuts

Savory-sweet chard with plump raisins and rich, resinous pine nuts is a common vegetable offering in Catalonia, Spain. In our version, we've accentuated the contrast of tangy and sweet by adding a touch of floral honey and woodsy sherry vinegar, and we toss in a small measure of red pepper flakes to add a hint of heat. Any variety of Swiss chard works here, but if you can find rainbow chard, the colorful stems make for an especially vibrant dish. To be efficient, toast the pine nuts while the chard cooks. In a small skillet over medium, they'll take only 3 to 4 minutes to turn fragrant and golden brown.

START TO FINISH: 40 MINUTES
SERVINGS: 4 TO 6

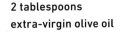

2 tablespoons extra-virgin olive oil

1 medium red onion, halved and thinly sliced

2 medium garlic cloves, thinly sliced

1 bunch Swiss chard (about 1 pound), stems chopped, leaves cut crosswise into rough 2-inch pieces, reserved separately

⅓ cup golden raisins

Kosher salt and ground black pepper

1 tablespoon honey

¼ teaspoon red pepper flakes

¼ cup pine nuts, toasted

1 tablespoon sherry vinegar

Don't forget to reserve the chard stems separately from the leaves. *We chop the stems and sauté them with the aromatics so they spend more time in the pot than the quicker-cooking leaves.*

1. **In a large pot over medium,** heat the oil until shimmering. Add the onion, garlic, chard stems, raisins and ½ teaspoon salt. Cook, stirring occasionally, until the onion and stems are softened, 6 to 8 minutes.

2. **Add the chard leaves,** honey, pepper flakes and ¼ cup water. Cook, stirring, until the leaves are wilted, about 1 minute. Cover and cook, stirring occasionally, until the leaves are tender and only a little liquid remains in the pot, 8 to 10 minutes.

3. **Off heat,** stir in the pine nuts and vinegar. Taste and season with salt and pepper.

Corn

To wander the streets of Ho Chi Minh City is to be immersed in a swirl of street vendors, markets and ripe produce spilling into pathways, all of it set to a soundtrack that thrums with the buzz of 2 million scooters. Food, and its seductive aromas, is everywhere. Women stir-fry corn with butter, scallions, fish sauce and dried shrimp for the snack known as bắp xào tôm khô. It's served hot from the skillet, sweet, savory, crisp—and a world away from the one-note, overpowering sweetness that can so easily beset this vegetable.

What makes the dish work is the balance between savory ingredients and corn's natural sweetness. Our take, p. 241, uses easier-to-find cooked, shelled shrimp in place of dried shrimp. And, bonus, it works fine with frozen kernels (be sure to pat them dry).

Savory is one way to complement the sweetness of corn. Spices also work, as does the simple appeal of bittersweet char.

In Mexico, corn, zucchini and other summer vegetables are paired with the kick of chilies in the dish known as calabacitas, which translates from the Spanish as "little squash." It typically is cooked on the stovetop, which can lead to sogginess. So, in our version, p. 195, we instead broil the vegetables, which preserves the character of the individual components and adds a bit of extra flavor through caramelization of the sugars. Jalapeños add heat and toasted pumpkin seeds bring crunch.

American cooks have plenty to say about corn, not surprising since, according to the USDA, there are around 91 million acres of corn—food, feed and fuel—planted in the U.S. (What is that in terms of football fields you ask? Sixty-nine million, the government helpfully points out.) Creamed corn is a classic, and our version, p. 132, is dairy-free. We scrape "milk" from the stripped cobs and blend it with half of the kernels in the dish; the natural starches create a creamy texture.

Corn is ideal for tossing on a backyard grill. We leave ours, p. 179, in their husks to start so the kernels get a chance to steam to plumpness. Then we strip off the husks, give the cobs a slather of butter and let them char. For balance, we came up with sweet, savory and spicy butters that take this side from good to great.

Braised Leeks
with Balsamic Glaze

At Casa Montaña in Valencia, Spain, we tasted leeks poached in olive oil until meltingly soft and finished with a sweet-tart balsamic glaze. This is our re-creation of that delicious side. When shopping for this recipe, look for leeks that are slender, with long white and light green sections, as these are the desirable parts (the dark green tops are too tough for braising). Leeks' many layers trap sand and dirt, so it's important to wash them thoroughly before cooking, then dry them well so they brown, rather than steam, in the oil.

1 pound leeks (see headnote), white and light green parts only, outer layers removed, ends trimmed

¼ cup extra-virgin olive oil

Kosher salt and ground black pepper

6 thyme sprigs, plus 1 teaspoon chopped fresh thyme

¼ cup balsamic vinegar

1 teaspoon honey

3 tablespoons sliced almonds, toasted

Don't stir the leeks too vigorously or too often when browning them in the oil. Stir gently just once or twice so they color evenly. And once the water goes into the pan and the cover goes on, it's best to gently shake the skillet, not stir its contents, so the leeks hold together.

1. **Cut the leeks** in half lengthwise. Fill a large bowl with water, submerge the leek halves and swish them around to remove the grit between the layers. Pour off the water and repeat until the leeks are clean, then pat dry. Cut the leeks on the diagonal into 2-inch sections, keeping the layers intact as much as possible.

2. **In a 12-inch skillet,** combine the oil and the leeks. Set the pan over medium-high and cook, gently stirring only once or twice so the layers do not separate, until the leeks are lightly browned, 4 to 6 minutes. Add ¼ teaspoon salt and ½ teaspoon pepper, then slowly add ⅔ cup water. Add the thyme sprigs, cover and reduce to medium-low. Cook, occasionally shaking the skillet, until a knife inserted into the leeks meets no resistance and most of the water has evaporated, about 20 minutes.

3. **Using a slotted spoon,** transfer the leeks to a platter, leaving the oil in the skillet. Remove and discard the thyme sprigs. Add the vinegar and honey to the pan, then cook over medium, stirring often, until the mixture is syrupy, 2 to 4 minutes. Taste and season with salt and pepper, then pour over the leeks. Sprinkle with the chopped thyme and the almonds.

Asparagus with Vietnamese Scallion Oil

START TO FINISH: 20 MINUTES
SERVINGS: 4

Vietnamese scallion oil, called mỡ hành, is used as a garnish or condiment on a number of different foods, from grilled clams on the half shell to steamed rice. It adds allium notes as well as bright color to any dish it's drizzled onto. And since fat carries flavor, it also acts as a flavor booster. Our version includes savory fish sauce (or soy sauce), pungent ginger and a little sugar to build complexity. We spoon it onto sautéed asparagus, but it's also delicious on corn, steamed dumplings and grilled meats and seafood. You likely will have leftover scallion oil; refrigerate it in an airtight container for up to three days; bring to room temperature before serving.

½ cup chopped scallions

Kosher salt and ground black pepper

¼ cup plus 1 tablespoon peanut or neutral oil, divided

1½ tablespoons fish sauce OR soy sauce

1½ tablespoons finely grated fresh ginger

1 teaspoon white sugar

1½ pounds asparagus, trimmed and halved on the diagonal

Don't just slice the scallions. For proper texture and flavor, the scallions should be chopped. Slice them first, then run the knife over them a few times to further break them down.

1. **In a medium heatproof bowl,** combine the scallions, a pinch of salt and 1 teaspoon pepper. Using your fingers, gently rub the salt and pepper into the scallions until the scallions begin to wilt.

2. **In a small saucepan** over medium-high, heat the ¼ cup oil until shimmering, then pour the hot oil over the scallions; the scallions will sizzle. Stir, then stir in the fish sauce, ginger and sugar. Cool to room temperature.

3. **In a 12-inch skillet** over medium-high, heat the remaining 1 tablespoon oil until barely smoking. Add the asparagus and ¼ teaspoon salt, then cook, stirring only a few times, until lightly charred, about 3 minutes. Add 3 tablespoons water, then immediately cover. Reduce to low and cook, stirring just once or twice, until the asparagus is tender-crisp and the pan is dry, 2 to 3 minutes. Transfer to a serving dish and spoon on scallion oil to taste.

Mashed Vegetable Curry with Toasted Buns (Pav Bhaji)

Pav bhaji, a much-loved fast food in India, is like a vegetarian sloppy Joe. Fragrantly spiced cooked vegetables are mashed to a chunky pulp and served with buttered pav, or soft rolls, for making open-faced sandwiches and mopping up the curry. The dish is such a mainstay that spice blends, called pav bhaji masala, exist to make the seasoning simpler. For our version, in addition to ground turmeric, we use whole coriander, cumin and fennel, and we crush them only lightly so they lend some texture to the curry. You can pulse the seeds all together (rather than one spice at a time) in an electric spice grinder or bash them in a mortar with a pestle. If you're sensitive to chili heat, you may wish to seed the serranos before chopping them.

START TO FINISH: 50 MINUTES
SERVINGS: 4

1 pound russet potatoes, peeled and cut into ½-inch cubes

1 pound cauliflower, cored and cut into ½-inch pieces

1 cup frozen peas

Kosher salt and ground black pepper

5 tablespoons ghee **OR** coconut oil, divided

1 medium red onion, finely chopped

1 or 2 serrano chiles, stemmed and finely chopped

1 tablespoon coriander seeds, lightly crushed

1½ teaspoons cumin seeds, lightly crushed

1 teaspoon fennel seeds, lightly crushed

1 teaspoon ground turmeric

12 ounces ripe tomatoes, cored and chopped

⅓ cup lightly packed fresh cilantro, chopped

4 soft buns or rolls, split

Don't forget to reserve about 2 tablespoons of the chopped onion to use as garnish. Also, don't use a nonstick skillet because the vegetables are mashed directly in the pan with a potato masher, which may scratch the surface. If you have no choice but to use nonstick, transfer the vegetable mixture to a bowl before mashing.

1. In a 12-inch skillet, combine the potatoes, cauliflower, peas, 1½ cups water and ½ teaspoon salt. Bring to a simmer over medium-high. Cover and cook until the cauliflower and potatoes are fully tender, 8 to 10 minutes. Remove from the heat and mash the mixture with a potato masher until almost smooth. Transfer to a medium bowl and cover to keep warm; wipe out the skillet.

2. In the same skillet over medium-high, heat 3 tablespoons of ghee until shimmering. Add all but 2 tablespoons of the onion and cook, stirring often, until softened and beginning to brown, 3 to 4 minutes. Stir in the chili(es), coriander, cumin, fennel and turmeric; cook, stirring, until fragrant, 30 to 60 seconds. Add the tomatoes and cook, stirring occasionally, until they soften and release their liquid, 3 to 4 minutes. Transfer the mixture to the bowl with the mashed vegetables and stir. Taste and season with salt and pepper, then re-cover to keep warm; set aside.

3. Wipe out the skillet, set it over medium and melt the remaining 2 tablespoons ghee. Add the buns cut sides down and toast until lightly browned, 2 to 3 minutes; transfer to a platter. Transfer the vegetable mixture to a serving dish and sprinkle with the reserved chopped onion and the cilantro. Serve with the toasted buns.

Collard Greens Stewed with Tomato, Shallots and Ginger

These silky, long-cooked collard greens are fortified by a base of shallots and tomato paste and brightened by the addition of fresh ginger. The result is rich yet light, bringing the collards' vegetal flavor to the forefront. Serve as a side dish or as the main attraction, with cornbread alongside to soak up the braising liquid.

START TO FINISH: 1¼ HOURS (20 MINUTES ACTIVE)
SERVINGS: 4

———

2 tablespoons extra-virgin olive oil

4 medium shallots **OR** 1 small red onion, halved and thinly sliced

Kosher salt and ground black pepper

¼ cup tomato paste

1 tablespoon soy sauce

1 tablespoon packed light brown sugar

2 teaspoons minced fresh ginger

1 bunch (1 pound) collard greens, stemmed, leaves chopped into rough 1-inch pieces

Don't rush the cooking time. Cooked slowly over low heat, the collards become meltingly tender.

1. **In a large Dutch oven** over medium, heat the oil until shimmering. Add the shallots and ¼ teaspoon salt, then cook, stirring occasionally, until softened and translucent, about 4 minutes.

2. **Add the tomato paste,** soy sauce, sugar and ginger; cook, stirring often, until the liquid has evaporated and the ginger and tomato paste begin to stick to the bottom of the pot, 1½ to 2 minutes. Stir in the collards a handful at a time, then add 4 cups water, scraping up any browned bits, and bring to a simmer over medium-high. Cover, reduce to low and cook, stirring occasionally, until the collards are completely tender, 50 to 60 minutes. Taste and season with salt and pepper.

Optional garnish: Fried shallots **OR** toasted sesame seeds **OR** both

Asparagus Gomae

In the Japanese kitchen, gomae refers to a dish, commonly a vegetable, dressed with a savory-sweet toasted sesame sauce. Here we give tender-crisp, skillet-cooked asparagus the gomae treatment. Look for medium-size asparagus, ones that are about the size of a pencil, and make sure to trim off the tough, woody parts at the base of the spears. This can be served warm, at room temperature or even lightly chilled.

START TO FINISH: 35 MINUTES
SERVINGS: 4

¼ cup sesame seeds

1 tablespoon mirin

1 tablespoon soy sauce

1 tablespoon sake

2 teaspoons white sugar

⅛ to ¼ teaspoon cayenne pepper (optional)

1 tablespoon grapeseed or other neutral oil

1½ pounds medium asparagus, trimmed and cut on the diagonal into 2-inch lengths

Kosher salt and ground black pepper

Don't forget to dry the asparagus before adding it to the skillet. Any remaining water droplets will create steam and prevent browning.

1. **In a 12-inch skillet** over medium, toast the sesame seeds, stirring often, until lightly browned, 2 to 3 minutes. Cool completely, then pulse in an electric spice grinder or grind with a mortar and pestle until fragrant and coarse

2. **In a large bowl,** stir together the sesame seeds, mirin, soy sauce, sake, sugar and cayenne (if using). In a 12-inch skillet over medium-high, heat the oil until barely smoking. Add the asparagus and ¼ teaspoon salt, then cook, stirring only a few times, until lightly charred, about 3 minutes.

3. **Add 3 tablespoons water,** then immediately cover. Reduce to low and cook, stirring just once or twice, until the asparagus is tender-crisp and the pan is dry, 2 to 3 minutes. Add the asparagus to the bowl with the sesame mixture and toss to coat. Taste and season with salt and black pepper, then transfer to a serving dish.

Gochujang-Glazed Potatoes (Gamja Jorim)

Gamja jorim, or salty-sweet soy-simmered potatoes, is a common banchan (small plate) on the Korean table. For our version, we added gochujang (Korean fermented chili paste) for a little heat and extra umami. Yukon Gold potatoes 1½ to 2 inches in diameter worked best, but creamier potatoes were good, too. If your potatoes are very small (about 1 inch in diameter), cut them in half; if larger than 2 inches, cut them into eighths. Depending on the sugar content of your potatoes, they may or may not brown lightly as they cook before the soy mixture is added. This is a great side dish to grilled meats and seafood.

START TO FINISH: 30 MINUTES
SERVINGS: 4

3 tablespoons plus
2 teaspoons soy sauce

¼ cup mirin

1 tablespoon gochujang

1 tablespoon white sugar

2 large garlic cloves,
finely grated

Kosher salt and ground
black pepper

1 tablespoon grapeseed
or other neutral oil

2 pounds small Yukon Gold
potatoes (1½ to 2 inches
in diameter), quartered

2 teaspoons toasted
sesame oil

2 teaspoons unseasoned
rice vinegar

2 teaspoons sesame
seeds, toasted

2 scallions, thinly sliced

Don't stir vigorously once the potatoes are nearly glazed. *Doing so may cause the pieces to break apart.*

1. **In a small bowl,** whisk together ½ cup water, 3 tablespoons of the soy sauce, the mirin, gochujang, sugar, garlic and ½ teaspoon each salt and pepper.

2. **In a 12-inch nonstick skillet** over medium, heat the oil until shimmering. Add the potatoes and stir to coat. Cover and cook, stirring occasionally, until the edges of the potatoes are translucent, 10 to 12 minutes.

3. **Stir in the soy sauce mixture.** Bring to a simmer over medium-high, then reduce to medium, cover and cook, stirring occasionally, until the tip of a knife inserted into the largest piece meets no resistance, about 10 minutes.

4. **Uncover and cook** over medium-high, stirring gently but frequently, until the liquid completely evaporates and the potatoes are glazed, about 5 minutes.

5. **Off heat,** stir in the remaining 2 teaspoons soy sauce, the sesame oil, vinegar and sesame seeds. Taste and season with salt and pepper. Transfer to a platter and sprinkle with scallions.

3 tablespoons coconut oil, preferably unrefined

1 tablespoon honey

1 tablespoon brown mustard seeds

2 teaspoons ground turmeric

2 teaspoons curry powder

Kosher salt and ground black pepper

2 pounds parsnips, peeled and sliced ½ inch thick on a sharp diagonal

½ cup lightly packed fresh basil, torn

3 tablespoons unsweetened wide-flake coconut, toasted

Lime wedges, to serve

Don't use super-sized parsnips, as we've found they can taste bitter. Look for ones that are medium to large and weigh about 6 ounces each. Also, don't stir more than once or twice while the parsnips are simmering in the covered pot. Lifting the lid allows heat and steam to escape, which slows the cooking and may cause the pot to run dry.

1. **In a large Dutch oven** over medium, combine the oil, honey, mustard seeds, turmeric and curry powder. Cook, stirring, until the mixture is fragrant, about 1 minute. Add 1¼ cups water and ½ teaspoon each salt and pepper, then bring to a simmer. Stir in the parsnips and return to a simmer. Cover and cook, stirring once or twice, until the parsnips are almost tender, 5 to 7 minutes.

2. **Uncover and cook,** stirring occasionally, until most of the water has evaporated, the parsnips begin to sizzle and a skewer inserted into the largest piece meets no resistance, another 3 to 5 minutes. Taste and season with salt and pepper.

3. **Transfer to a serving dish** and spoon on any liquid remaining in the pot. Sprinkle with the basil and coconut; serve with lime wedges.

Curried Parsnips with Basil and Coconut

This recipe uses a one-pot, two-step cooking technique, first simmering parsnips in a small amount of water in a covered pot, then removing the lid and letting the liquid cook off. This ensures perfectly cooked vegetables that are nicely glazed. The flavors of curry, turmeric and mustard seeds are a good counterpoint to the naturally sweet parsnips; crisp coconut flakes add another layer of flavor and some crunch. To toast the coconut, spread in an even layer on a rimmed baking sheet and bake at 350°F until light golden brown, 3 to 5 minutes.

Lebanese Braised Green Beans

The Lebanese dish called loubieh bi zeit, or green beans in olive oil, typically is prepared with flat, sturdy runner beans. The beans are braised until tender in a tomato sauce that's sometimes seasoned with a mix of spices but always enriched with a glug of olive oil. We opted for easier-to-find standard green beans, and made a seasoning blend with a few common spices. We got the most flavor out of canned whole tomatoes by crushing and cooking them until thick and jammy, and using some of their juices as the cooking liquid for the beans.

START TO FINISH: 40 MINUTES
SERVINGS: 4

1 teaspoon ground cumin

1 teaspoon ground coriander

½ teaspoon grated nutmeg

¼ teaspoon ground cardamom

¼ teaspoon ground cinnamon

Kosher salt and ground black pepper

¼ cup extra-virgin olive oil

2 medium shallots, halved and thinly sliced

1½ pounds green beans, trimmed

28-ounce can whole peeled tomatoes, drained, 1 cup juices reserved, tomatoes crushed by hand and reserved separately

Don't forget to reserve the tomatoes and 1 cup of their juices separately because they are added at different times during cooking.

1. **In a small bowl,** stir together the cumin, coriander, nutmeg, cardamom, cinnamon and 1 teaspoon pepper.

2. **In a large Dutch oven** over medium-high, heat the oil until shimmering. Add the shallots and cook, stirring occasionally, until golden brown, 2 to 3 minutes. Add the beans and spice mixture, then stir to coat. Stir in the tomatoes (not the reserved juices) and ¾ teaspoon salt. Cook, stirring occasionally, until the tomatoes begin to brown, 5 to 8 minutes.

3. **Add the reserved juices,** cover and reduce to medium-low. Cook until the beans are tender, 15 to 18 minutes, stirring only once or twice. Taste and season with salt and pepper, then transfer to a serving bowl.

Soy-Braised Baby Bok Choy with Scallions

In traditional recipes for Chinese soy-braised greens, the greens are likely to be blanched before they're quickly cooked with ingredients that supply high-impact flavor. In this recipe, however, we stir-fry baby bok choy with aromatics, then braise them in a mixture of Shaoxing rice wine and soy sauce, with sugar for sweetness and sesame oil for nuttiness. A few minutes of uncovered cooking drives off excess moisture, leaving the greens meltingly tender and coated in a light savory-sweet sauce. Serve with steamed fish or spooned atop a bowl of rice.

START TO FINISH: 25 MINUTES
SERVINGS: 4

——

2 tablespoons grapeseed or other neutral oil

2 pounds baby bok choy, trimmed and cut crosswise into 1-inch pieces

1 bunch scallions, whites thinly sliced, greens thinly sliced on the diagonal, reserved separately

1 tablespoon minced fresh ginger

2 medium garlic cloves, minced

3 tablespoons Shaoxing wine **OR** dry sherry **OR** sake

3 tablespoons soy sauce

1 tablespoon packed light brown sugar **OR** white sugar

2 teaspoons toasted sesame oil

Don't forget to wash the bok choy, as the inner leaves often trap dirt or sand. But make sure to drain and dry it so it browns rather than steams when it hits the hot skillet.

1. **In a 12-inch skillet** over medium-high, heat the neutral oil until shimmering. Add the bok choy and cook, stirring occasionally, until wilted and lightly browned, 3 to 4 minutes. Add the scallion whites, ginger and garlic, then cook, stirring, until fragrant, 30 to 60 seconds. Reduce to medium and stir in the Shaoxing wine, soy sauce, sugar and sesame oil, then immediately cover. Cook until the bok choy is tender-crisp, 2 to 3 minutes.

2. **Uncover and cook,** stirring occasionally, until the liquid is lightly thickened and the bok choy is fully tender, 2 to 3 minutes. Transfer to a serving dish and sprinkle with the scallion greens.

Braised Carrots and Leeks with Olives and Herbs

This recipe was inspired by zeytinaygli pirasa, a classic Turkish dish of leeks and carrots cooked with a generous amount of olive oil. We add chopped olives for briny, salty contrast against the natural sweetness of the vegetables and a shower of tender herbs at the end for freshness and color. Serve warm or at room temperature. They make a great accompaniment to seared fish and simple roasts of almost any sort or can be a part of a vegetarian meal.

START TO FINISH: 35 MINUTES
SERVINGS: 4 TO 6

———

¼ cup extra-virgin olive oil, plus more to serve

1 pound carrots, peeled and sliced ½ inch thick on the diagonal

2 medium leeks, white and light green parts sliced ½ inch thick, rinsed, drained and patted dry (see headnote)

½ cup pitted green **OR** black olives, roughly chopped

Two 3-inch strips orange zest

Kosher salt and ground black pepper

¼ cup lightly packed fresh dill, chopped

¼ cup lightly packed fresh tarragon, chopped

Lemon wedges, to serve

Don't forget to rinse, drain and dry the sliced leeks, but use a gentle touch so the layers remain intact, which allows the leeks to have more presence in the finished dish and makes for a more attractive presentation. Swirling the pan during cooking instead of stirring also helps keep the leek slices intact.

1. **In a 12-inch skillet** over medium-high, heat the oil until shimmering. Add the carrots and cook, stirring occasionally, until lightly browned, 4 to 5 minutes. Using a slotted spoon, transfer to a large plate. Add the leeks to the pan in an even layer and cook without stirring until well browned on the bottom, 2 to 3 minutes. Using a spatula, flip the leeks and cook until well browned on the second sides, another 2 to 3 minutes.

2. **Return the carrots** to the pan and add the olives, zest strips, 1 cup water and ¼ teaspoon each salt and pepper; swirl the pan to combine. Bring to a simmer, then cover and cook without stirring, until a skewer inserted into the carrots meets no resistance, 10 to 12 minutes.

3. **Uncover and cook,** occasionally swirling the pan, until the liquid has almost fully evaporated, 2 to 4 minutes. Remove the pan from the heat, then remove and discard the zest strips. Taste and season with salt and pepper. Transfer to a serving dish, sprinkle with the dill and tarragon and drizzle with additional oil. Serve with lemon wedges.

Hot Oil–Flashed Chard with Ginger, Scallions and Chili

We tenderize Swiss chard with sizzling oil, a technique we learned from cookbook author Fuchsia Dunlop. Her recipe is modeled on a classic Cantonese method in which hot oil is poured over lightly blanched greens. We scatter fresh ginger, scallions and serrano chilies over the greens; the hot oil blooms the flavors. The clean flavor and light texture of grapeseed oil was ideal, but vegetable oil works, too.

START TO FINISH: 20 MINUTES
SERVINGS: 4

Kosher salt

2 bunches Swiss chard (about 2 pounds total), stemmed, leaves cut crosswise into rough 3-inch pieces

2 scallions, thinly sliced on the diagonal

1 tablespoon finely grated fresh ginger

1 serrano chili, stemmed and thinly sliced

2 tablespoons grapeseed or other neutral oil

1 tablespoon toasted sesame oil

1 tablespoon unseasoned rice vinegar

1 tablespoon soy sauce

2 teaspoons toasted sesame seeds (optional)

Don't use the chard stems, but also don't throw them away. The stems are tougher than the leaves and won't cook through in the short time it takes to wilt the leaves. Chard stems do have good flavor, however, and can be sautéed, pickled or added to soups and stews.

1. **In a 12-inch skillet** over medium-high, bring ¼ cup water and ¼ teaspoon salt to a boil. Pile the chard into the pan and cover (the lid may not close completely). Cook until the chard is wilted, about 5 minutes, stirring halfway through. Remove the lid and continue to cook, stirring occasionally, until most of the liquid has evaporated, 1 to 3 minutes. Transfer the chard to a serving platter and wipe out the skillet.

2. **Distribute the scallions,** ginger and chili evenly over the chard. Add both oils to the skillet and return to medium-high until very hot, 1 to 2 minutes. Pour the oils directly over the greens and aromatics (you should hear them sizzle) and toss to distribute. Drizzle the vinegar and soy sauce over the chard and toss again. Sprinkle with the sesame seeds (if using).

2 tablespoons grapeseed or other neutral oil

¼ cup white sugar

1 tablespoon soy sauce

2 teaspoons unseasoned rice vinegar

1 teaspoon toasted sesame oil

Kosher salt and ground black pepper

Two 12-ounce orange-fleshed sweet potatoes **OR** Japanese sweet potatoes, scrubbed but not peeled, quartered lengthwise and cut crosswise into 1½-inch pieces

2 teaspoons white **OR** black sesame seeds **OR** a combination, toasted

Don't raise the heat above medium while the potatoes cook covered. A moderately low temperature helps ensure even cooking without scorching. Also, sweet potatoes vary in water content depending on the variety. If you find that the moisture in the pan is gone before the potatoes are tender, just add a tablespoon or two of water as needed and continue cooking.

1. **In a 12-inch skillet,** combine ½ cup water, the neutral oil, sugar, soy sauce, vinegar, sesame oil and ½ teaspoon each salt and pepper, then stir until the sugar dissolves. Add the sweet potatoes and stir to coat. Cover the pan and cook over medium, stirring and turning the potatoes about every 4 minutes, until a skewer inserted into the largest piece meets no resistance, 16 to 20 minutes. If the skillet looks dry before the potatoes are tender, add 1 or 2 tablespoons water as needed and continue cooking.

2. **Uncover, increase to medium-high** and cook, stirring constantly, until the potatoes are glazed and sizzling, about 2 minutes. Off heat, toss in the sesame seeds, then taste and season with salt and pepper.

Optional garnish: Chopped fresh chilies **OR** shichimi togarashi **OR** sliced scallions

Japanese-Style Glazed Sweet Potatoes with Sesame

Candied sweet potatoes, or daigaku imo, a favorite Japanese snack, inspired this recipe. To make daigaku imo, chunks of Japanese sweet potatoes, or satsuma imo, are deep-fried then coated in a syrup and sprinkled with sesame seeds. In this recipe, we cook the potatoes in a skillet with water and seasonings, then cook off the moisture at the end, leaving the potatoes coated with a savory-sweet glaze. Common orange-fleshed sweet potatoes work in this recipe, but use Japanese sweet potatoes if you can find them. They have dry, starchy flesh and a sweet, chestnut-like flavor.

Garlicky Quick-Cooked Collard Ribbons

This speedy side is a vegetarian (vegan, even) version of the Brazilian dish known as couve à mineira, which often is flavored with smoky bits of meat. The collards are cut so thinly that their cooking time is a mere two minutes and their finished texture is tender-crisp, giving the dish a slaw-like quality. Couve à mineira is the traditional accompaniment to the Brazilian bean-and-meat stew called feijoada; we think the greens are a great side to barbecued or grilled meats or beans of any kind.

START TO FINISH: 25 MINUTES
SERVINGS: 4

1 bunch (1 pound) collard greens, stemmed, leaves halved lengthwise

2 mini sweet red peppers OR ½ medium red bell pepper, stemmed and thinly sliced

¼ teaspoon red pepper flakes

Kosher salt and ground black pepper

3 tablespoons extra-virgin olive oil

6 medium garlic cloves, minced

1 tablespoon plus 1 teaspoon white balsamic vinegar

Don't walk away from the garlic as it is cooking. Be sure to stir often and don't turn the heat up higher than medium. It can go from sweet and golden brown to acrid and burnt in a flash.

1. **Stack 4 or 5 collard leaf halves,** roll them up into a cigar shape and slice crosswise into thin ribbons. Transfer to a large bowl and repeat with the remaining leaves. Add the sweet peppers, pepper flakes and ½ teaspoon salt, then toss.

2. **In a large Dutch oven** over medium, combine the oil and garlic. Cook, stirring often, until the garlic is golden brown, 4 to 5 minutes. Stir in the collards mixture, increase to medium-high and cook, stirring constantly, until the greens are bright green and just wilted, about 1½ minutes. Add the vinegar and cook, stirring, until just incorporated, about 1 minute. Remove from the heat, then taste and season with salt and pepper.

Sake and Soy-Braised Kabocha Squash

Kabocha, which translates from the Japanese as "pumpkin," is a variety of winter squash originating in Japan. Short, squat and green with light mottling and stripes that run from top to bottom, kabocha is orange on the interior, with sweet flesh that is slightly starchy and quite dense. In the Japanese kitchen, it often is cut into chunks and simply braised with soy sauce and a little sweetener (we use mirin). We add a small measure of toban djan (a spicy Asian chili-bean sauce) as a flavor accent. Look for toban djan sold in jars in the international aisle of the grocery store or in Asian markets. If it's not available, chili-garlic sauce is a fine substitute.

START TO FINISH: 30 MINUTES
SERVINGS: 4 TO 6

___

2 tablespoons sake

2 tablespoons mirin

1 tablespoon soy sauce

2-pound kabocha squash, rougher parts of the skin peeled, squash seeded and cut into rough 2-inch pieces

1 tablespoon toasted sesame oil

2 teaspoons chili-bean sauce (toban djan) **OR** chili-garlic sauce

Kosher salt

Don't bother peeling the entire squash. Just shave off the areas of skin that are very bumpy and scarred using a sturdy vegetable peeler. With cooking, the skin becomes tender and soft enough to eat.

1. **In a 12-inch skillet** over medium-high, combine the sake, mirin, soy sauce and ⅔ cup water. Add the squash pieces, peel side down, and bring to a simmer. Cover and simmer until a skewer inserted into the squash meets just a little resistance, 15 to 17 minutes. Meanwhile, in a small bowl, stir together the sesame oil, chili-bean sauce and 1 tablespoon water; set aside.

2. **Uncover the skillet** and cook over medium-high until the liquid has almost completely evaporated and a skewer inserted into the squash meets no resistance, 4 to 5 minutes. Transfer to a serving dish, scraping any cooking liquid onto the squash, then drizzle with the sesame oil mixture.

Optional garnish: Toasted sesame seeds

Green Beans with Browned Butter and Almonds

This easy one-pot side was inspired by classic green bean almondine. First, the beans simmer in a small amount of water until tender-crisp. Then, the liquid is cooked off, leaving them lightly glazed with butter. We especially like the texture of slivered almonds in this dish, but just about any type of nut pairs well with the beans. Red pepper flakes add a touch of piquancy and lemon zest and juice brightens up the flavors.

START TO FINISH: 25 MINUTES
SERVINGS: 4

⅓ cup slivered almonds
OR chopped walnuts **OR** chopped hazelnuts

3 tablespoons salted butter

3 medium shallots, sliced into thin rings

¼ to ½ teaspoon red pepper flakes

Kosher salt and ground black pepper

2 pounds green beans, trimmed

1 teaspoon grated lemon zest, plus 2 tablespoons lemon juice

Don't remove all of the almonds from the pot after toasting. Leave about half of them to cook with the beans; they soften slightly with cooking and add richness and textural interest to the dish.

1. **In a large Dutch oven** over medium, toast the almonds, stirring occasionally, until lightly browned and fragrant, about 5 minutes. Transfer about half of the almonds to a small bowl and set aside for garnish. Add the butter to the pot. When melted, add the shallots and pepper flakes, then increase to medium-high and cook, stirring occasionally, until the shallots are lightly browned, about 2 minutes.

2. **Add 1 cup water,** ½ teaspoon salt and ¼ teaspoon black pepper, then bring to a boil. Stir in the beans, cover and cook, stirring occasionally, until tender-crisp, 5 to 7 minutes. Uncover and cook, stirring occasionally, until the moisture evaporates and the beans begin to sizzle, 5 to 7 minutes. Off heat, stir in the lemon zest and juice, then taste and season with salt and pepper. Transfer to a serving dish and sprinkle with the reserved almonds.

Optional garnish: Chopped fresh chives **OR** toasted walnut oil **OR** both

Broccolini with Sesame-Miso Sauce

Even with just a handful of ingredients—many of them likely already in your pantry—the flavor payout here is huge. A thick, nubby mixture of toasted and coarsely ground sesame seeds and umami-rich miso is the perfect flavor accent to skillet-cooked Broccolini; the sauce, tossed with the just-cooked vegetable, clings beautifully to the florets and bias-cut stalks. A shower of scallions finishes the dish and adds fresh, oniony bite.

START TO FINISH: 30 MINUTES
SERVINGS: 4 TO 6

¼ cup sesame seeds

3 tablespoons white miso

2 tablespoons seasoned rice vinegar, plus more if needed

1 tablespoon soy sauce, plus more if needed

2 tablespoons grapeseed or other neutral oil

1½ pounds Broccolini, trimmed and cut into 1-inch pieces on the diagonal

4 scallions, thinly sliced on the diagonal

Don't use red miso or any type of miso that's very dark and strong. Mellow, slightly sweet white miso is the best choice here. Also, be sure to use seasoned rice vinegar. It contains both salt and sugar, which balances the flavors in the dressing.

1. In a 12-inch skillet over medium, toast the sesame seeds, stirring often, until lightly browned, 2 to 3 minutes. Cool completely, then grind in an electric spice grinder or with a mortar and pestle until fragrant and coarsely ground. Reserve the skillet.

2. In a medium bowl, whisk together the ground sesame seeds, miso, vinegar and soy sauce; set aside. In the 12-inch skillet over medium-high, heat the oil until shimmering. Add the Broccolini and cook, stirring occasionally, until beginning to char, 3 to 4 minutes. Stir in ¼ cup water, then immediately cover and reduce to low. Cook, stirring once or twice, until the Broccolini is tender-crisp, about 4 minutes.

3. Transfer the Broccolini to the bowl with the sesame mixture and toss. Taste and season with additional soy sauce and vinegar, if needed. Transfer to a serving dish and sprinkle with the scallions.

4 tablespoons salted butter

1 medium red onion, halved and thinly sliced **OR** 1 bunch scallions, thinly sliced

3 medium garlic cloves, thinly sliced

1 tablespoon minced fresh ginger

1 teaspoon ground coriander

½ teaspoon curry powder

1½ pounds lacinato kale (2 large bunches), stemmed, leaves torn into 2-inch pieces

1 pint cherry **OR** grape tomatoes, halved

Kosher salt and ground black pepper

½ cup plain whole-milk yogurt

2 teaspoons lemon juice

Don't bother drying the kale after washing. A little water clinging to the leaves helps create the steam needed to wilt the kale.

1. In a large pot over medium, melt the butter. Add the onion and cook, stirring occasionally, until softened, 5 to 6 minutes. Add the garlic, ginger, coriander and curry, then cook, stirring, until the onion and garlic begin to brown, 2 to 3 minutes.

2. Increase to medium-high, then add the kale a large handful at a time. Cook, stirring, until the leaves are just wilted, about 1 minute, before adding more. Stir in the tomatoes, ½ teaspoon salt, ¼ teaspoon pepper and ¼ cup water. Cover, reduce to medium-low and cook, stirring occasionally, until tender, 35 to 40 minutes.

3. Uncover, increase to medium and cook, stirring occasionally, until little moisture remains in the pot, 3 to 5 minutes. Off heat, stir in the yogurt and lemon juice. Taste and season with salt and pepper.

Curried Braised Kale and Tomatoes with Yogurt

Lighter than creamed spinach, more interesting than simple sautéed greens, this kale gets its flavor from a combination of ginger, coriander and curry powder. We prefer lacinato, or dinosaur, kale, with its long, deep green leaves and silky texture, but curly kale works, too. If you use curly kale, shorten the cooking time to 20 to 30 minutes, as it becomes tender more quickly than lacinato. Plain yogurt stirred in at the end adds a refreshing tang that balances the buttery richness of the braised kale. Warm naan or steamed rice is the perfect accompaniment.

Greens

Greens call out for robust flavorings and an unctuous touch of fat, and cooks around the world have come up with myriad ways to do that.

In the Caribbean, chilies bring the heat for callaloo, a dish of spicy stewed greens. Recipes vary by region, our version, p. 353, uses Swiss chard, peppy habanero or Scotch bonnet chilies, and coconut milk for richness.

In the Mediterranean, especially the Catalonia region of Spain, greens often are paired with plump raisins and rich pine nuts. Our take, p. 139, adds a bit of honey and sherry vinegar for sweet-savory contrast and red pepper flakes for kick.

Brazilian cooks keep it simple for the side known as couve à mineira, which at its most basic is collard greens, garlic and olive oil, with the greens cooked quickly for crisp-chewy texture. Some versions call for bacon,

some for sweet peppers. For our riff, p. 159, we keep the greens vegetarian, include peppers to balance the savoriness of the greens, and add a splash of white balsamic vinegar.

A classic Cantonese technique infuses greens with flavor by scattering chilies and aromatics over lightly blanched greens and then pouring sizzling oil over the whole thing. Our version, p. 157, uses ginger, scallions and a serrano chili.

Kale is a hearty and versatile green that brings vibrant color and texture to the table, but when eaten raw it does require a little extra handling to keep it from crossing the line between chewy and tough. Asian cooks sometimes massage raw greens with salt to tenderize them. We adopt that technique, but use chopped smoked almonds instead of salt for our salad, p. 44. Breadcrumbs flavored with paprika (inspired by

picada sauce from Catalonia) add flavorful crunch. For another kale salad, this one with briny olives and pecorino Romano cheese, p. 29, we thinly slice the kale and let it sit in a lemony dressing to tame its texture.

Kale is equally at home in soup as it is in salad. In Portugual, there's caldo verde, a hearty soup of greens and spicy sausage. We skip the sausage and add carrots for color and sweetness for our take, p. 124. Even though there's no sausage, we keep things spicy with oil that's infused with dried chilies, garlic and herbs.

Beans and greens are a hit in many different culinary styles. Armenian cooks pair spinach or chard softened in olive oil with chickpeas for the dish known as nivik. We liked Swiss chard for our version, p. 323, and boost the flavor with onion, garlic, tomatoes and a finishing shot of lemon.

Skillet-Charred Asparagus with Lemon and Tarragon

START TO FINISH: 30 MINUTES
SERVINGS: 4 TO 6

For charring vegetables on the stovetop, nothing works quite as well as cast iron, which retains and distributes heat better than other cookware. We use a 12-inch cast-iron skillet to char asparagus that has been cut into 2-inch pieces. Even so, we cook in two batches to avoid overcrowding in the pan, which would result in steaming. We found that in a conventional skillet, the asparagus doesn't char as deeply. And afterward, the pan requires serious effort to scrub clean. We keep the flavors simple and finish the asparagus with butter, lemon juice and tarragon, ingredients that complement the vegetables' green, grassy notes.

2 pounds asparagus, trimmed and cut into 2-inch pieces on a sharp diagonal

3 teaspoons grapeseed or other neutral oil, divided

Kosher salt and ground black pepper

2 tablespoons salted butter, cut into 2 pieces, room temperature

2 tablespoons lemon juice

1 tablespoon finely chopped fresh tarragon

Don't use asparagus that's very fat or especially thin or it will wind up over- or undercooked. Look for spears that are slightly thicker than pencil-sized. After transferring the first batch of cooked asparagus to the bowl, don't cover tightly. Partially or loosely covering the bowl will allow some heat to escape so the asparagus doesn't overcook while it waits for the second batch.

1. **In a large bowl,** toss the asparagus with 2 teaspoons of oil and ¼ teaspoon each salt and pepper. In a 12-inch cast-iron skillet over medium-high, heat the remaining 1 teaspoon oil, spreading it with a silicone spatula or heatproof brush to cover the surface, until barely smoking. Add half the asparagus, distributing it in an even layer, and cook without stirring until well charred on the bottom, 5 to 6 minutes. Stir, redistribute in an even layer, then continue to cook until tender-crisp, about 2 minutes. Transfer to a medium bowl and partially cover.

2. **Return the skillet to medium-high** and heat until barely smoking. Cook the remaining asparagus in the same way, then transfer to the bowl with the first batch. To the asparagus, add the butter and toss until melted. Add the lemon juice and tarragon, then toss again. Taste and season with salt and pepper, then transfer to a serving platter.

Soy-Glazed Braised Brussels Sprouts

Tare (pronounced tah-reh) is a Japanese seasoning liquid typically made with a soy sauce base, often enhanced by mirin, sake, ginger and garlic. Here, we use those ingredients with Brussels sprouts. We first brown the halved sprouts in butter to develop rich, nutty flavor notes, braise them until tender, then allow the moisture to cook off, leaving the sprouts coated with a salty-sweet glaze.

START TO FINISH: 35 MINUTES
SERVINGS: 4

_____

2 tablespoons salted butter

1½ pounds Brussels sprouts, trimmed and halved

Kosher salt and ground black pepper

¼ cup mirin

¼ cup sake

1 tablespoon packed light brown sugar

1 tablespoon finely grated fresh ginger

2 medium garlic cloves, finely grated

2 tablespoons soy sauce

2 scallions, thinly sliced **OR** 1 tablespoon chopped fresh cilantro **OR** both

**Don't stir the sprouts too often** in the first step. The key is to let them brown and char slightly in order to produce a rich, complex sauce.

1. **In a large Dutch** oven over medium-high, melt the butter. Add the sprouts and ¼ teaspoon each salt and pepper, then cook, stirring only once or twice, until browned in spots, 3 to 5 minutes.

2. **Add the mirin,** sake, sugar, ginger, garlic and ¼ cup water. Cover, reduce to medium-low and cook, stirring occasionally, until the sprouts are tender but still hold their shape, 8 to 13 minutes. Uncover and stir in the soy sauce. Increase to medium and cook, uncovered and stirring occasionally, until the sprouts are lightly glazed, 5 to 8 minutes.

3. **Off heat,** stir in the scallions, then taste and season with salt and pepper.

Optional garnish: Shichimi togarashi **OR** toasted sesame seeds **OR** chili oil

Lebanese-Style Spicy Potatoes with Lemon and Cilantro

This is our simplified version of Lebanese batata harra—or "spicy potatoes" as translated from the Arabic—which typically is made by deep-frying potatoes until crisp, then tossing them in a fragrant mixture of garlic and spices. We get everything done in a nonstick skillet. First, the potatoes are simmered in a modest amount of water until tender, then drained and dried, and finally returned to the pan with olive oil for crisping before the seasonings are introduced. Aleppo pepper is a key ingredient here. The seedless, bright-red pepper flakes have a slightly smoky, subtly fruity flavor with hints of cumin and moderate spiciness. Look for it in Middle Eastern markets, spice shops and well-stocked supermarkets.

START TO FINISH: 35 MINUTES
SERVINGS: 4 TO 6

2½ pounds Yukon Gold potatoes, unpeeled, cut into 1-inch chunks

Kosher salt

¼ cup extra-virgin olive oil

3 medium cloves garlic, minced

1 tablespoon Aleppo pepper, plus more to serve

½ teaspoon hot paprika OR ½ teaspoon sweet paprika plus ⅛ teaspoon cayenne pepper

½ cup lightly packed fresh cilantro, chopped

2 tablespoons lemon juice

Don't drain the potatoes of their simmering liquid until they're fully tender. When they're added back to the pan, they'll brown on the exteriors but the interiors will not cook through any more. Also, be sure to dry the potatoes well after draining so they brown and crisp with a minimal amount of splatter.

1. **In a 12-inch nonstick skillet,** combine the potatoes, 3 cups water and 2 teaspoons salt. Bring to a simmer over medium-high, then cover and cook until a skewer inserted into the potatoes meets no resistance, 10 to 12 minutes. Drain the potatoes in a colander; wipe out the skillet. Distribute the potatoes on a clean kitchen towel or a doubled layer of paper towels and thoroughly pat dry.

2. **In the same skillet** over medium-high, heat the oil until shimmering. Add the potatoes and cook, stirring occasionally, until well browned all over, 8 to 10 minutes. Add the garlic and cook, stirring, until the garlic is lightly browned, 1 to 2 minutes. Add the Aleppo pepper and paprika; cook, stirring, until fragrant, 30 to 60 seconds. Remove the pan from the heat and stir in half the cilantro and the lemon juice. Taste and season with salt, then transfer to a serving dish. Top with the remaining cilantro and an additional sprinkle of Aleppo pepper.

¼ cup grapeseed or other neutral oil

5 dried Thai bird **OR** árbol chilies, stemmed, broken in half, seeds shaken out and discarded

1 teaspoon Sichuan peppercorns, lightly crushed

1 teaspoon sweet paprika

1 pound shiitake mushrooms, stemmed and halved (if small) or quartered (if medium or large) **OR** cremini mushrooms, halved (if small)

or quartered (if medium or large) **OR** beech mushrooms, pulled apart into small clusters **OR** a combination

3 medium garlic cloves, minced

Kosher salt

2 tablespoons Shaoxing wine **OR** dry sherry **OR** sake

½ cup low-sodium chicken broth **OR** vegetable broth

1 tablespoon salted butter

½ cup lightly packed fresh cilantro

Don't use pre-sliced mushrooms, as they tend to be dry. Flavorful results rely on the moisture released by the mushrooms as they cook to build the foundation for the sauce. You could use just one variety of mushroom, but two or more types add visual, textural and flavor appeal.

1. In a 12-inch skillet over medium, combine the oil, chilies, Sichuan peppercorns and paprika. Cook, stirring often, until the oil is fragrant and takes on a reddish hue, 1 to 3 minutes. Pour the mixture through a fine-mesh strainer set over a small bowl, pressing on the solids to extract as much oil as possible; discard the solids. Wipe out the skillet.

2. Return the strained oil to the skillet; heat over medium-high until shimmering. Add the mushrooms, garlic and ½ teaspoon salt; cook, stirring often, until the mushrooms are lightly browned, 2 to 4 minutes. Reduce to medium, add the Shaoxing wine and cover. Cook, occasionally shaking the skillet, until the mushrooms release their liquid, about 4 minutes. Stir in the broth and bring to a simmer. Re-cover, reduce to medium and cook, stirring occasionally, until the mushrooms are tender, about 10 minutes. If a lot of liquid remains in the skillet, cook, uncovered and stirring occasionally, until only a small pool remains.

3. Remove the pan from the heat. Stir in the butter and half the cilantro, then taste and season with salt and pepper. Transfer to a serving dish and sprinkle with the remaining cilantro.

Braised Mushrooms with Sichuan Chili Oil

This savory, spicy mushroom braise starts with an oil infused with dried chilies and Sichuan peppercorns and finishes with a tablespoon of butter, which gives the dish silky richness, balancing the spices and rounding out the meaty mushroom flavors. To crush the Sichuan peppercorns, which brings out more of their tongue-tingling spiciness, pulse them a few times in an electric spice grinder or bash them in a mortar with a pestle.

Cider and Honey–Glazed Turnips

Turnips are members of the Brassica family, which also includes broccoli, cauliflower and cabbage. The white turnips commonly found in grocery stores often have purple-hued tops. Their crunchy texture and slightly bitter, spicy flavor mellows with cooking. We cut our turnips into wedges and simmer them in apple cider. When they're tender, we turn up the heat to allow the liquid to reduce to a glossy glaze. This is a perfect side to a pork roast or chops.

START TO FINISH: 45 MINUTES
SERVINGS: 6 TO 8

2 tablespoons salted butter

1 large shallot, finely chopped

2 medium garlic cloves, minced

Kosher salt and ground black pepper

2 pounds white turnips, peeled and cut into ¾-inch wedges

1 cup apple cider

1 teaspoon minced fresh thyme

1 tablespoon honey

Don't forget to add 1 cup water with the apple cider. The liquid is necessary to cook the turnips evenly and thoroughly. But don't use additional cider in place of the water or the liquid will be too sugary and apt to scorch when reduced.

1. **In a 12-inch nonstick skillet** over medium-high, melt the butter. Add the shallot, garlic and ¼ teaspoon salt, then cook, stirring occasionally, until the shallot is softened, about 2 minutes. Add the turnips, cider, thyme and 1 cup water, then bring to a boil. Reduce to medium and cook, uncovered and stirring occasionally, until a skewer inserted into the turnips meets no resistance, 20 to 25 minutes.

2. **Increase to high and cook** without stirring until only a little liquid remains and the turnips are lightly browned on the bottom, 2 to 3 minutes. Using a silicone spatula, scrape up and flip the turnips, then cook, stirring, until glazed on all sides, about another 1 minute. Off heat, stir in the honey, then taste and season with salt and pepper.

Skillet-Charred Brussels Sprouts with Garlic, Anchovy and Chili

We loved the Brussels sprouts at Gjelina in Los Angeles. Chef Travis Lett served them with chili-lime vinaigrette and they were both wonderfully charred and tender. We assumed they'd been roasted in a very hot oven. In fact, Lett had used a cast-iron skillet, a quicker and more efficient way to transfer heat. We tried it and loved the way the searing-hot skillet gave the sprouts a delicious char we'd never achieved in the oven. For the sauce, we were inspired by bagna cauda, the warm garlic- and anchovy-infused dip from Northern Italy with red pepper flakes and a splash of lemon juice. A drizzle of honey in the dressing added a note of sweetness.

START TO FINISH: 25 MINUTES
SERVINGS: 4

___

1 pound small to medium Brussels sprouts, trimmed and halved

4 tablespoons extra-virgin olive oil, divided

4 teaspoons honey, divided

Kosher salt

4 medium garlic cloves, minced

4 oil-packed anchovy fillets, minced

Red pepper flakes

2 teaspoons lemon juice

Don't use a stainless steel skillet. A well-seasoned cast-iron pan was key to this recipe. Stainless steel didn't hold the heat well enough to properly char. To comfortably accommodate the recipe, the pan needed to be at least 12 inches. And stick to small or medium sprouts; large ones didn't taste as good, containing a higher concentration of the compounds that lead to bitterness. Even smaller sprouts were best when cut in half, creating more surface area and contact with the skillet and therefore more charring.

1. **In a large bowl,** toss the sprouts with 1 tablespoon of oil, 2 teaspoons of honey and ¼ teaspoon salt; set aside.

2. **In a 12- to 14-inch cast-iron skillet** over high, combine the remaining 3 tablespoons of oil, the garlic, anchovies and ¼ teaspoon pepper flakes. Cook, stirring, until the garlic begins to color, 3 to 4 minutes. Scrape the mixture, including the oil, into a small bowl and set aside.

3. **Return the skillet to high.** Add the sprouts (reserve the bowl) and use tongs to arrange them cut-side down in a single layer. Cook, without moving, until deeply browned and blackened in spots, 3 to 7 minutes, depending on your skillet. Use the tongs to flip the sprouts cut-side up and continue to cook until charred and just tender, another 3 to 5 minutes.

4. **As they finish,** return the sprouts to the reserved bowl. Add the garlic mixture, the remaining 2 teaspoons of honey and the lemon juice, then toss to combine. Taste and season with salt and pepper flakes.

Broccoli with Lemon, Toasted Garlic and Smoked Almonds

In this recipe, simple steamed broccoli gets big, bold flavor when it's tossed after cooking with a lemony, toasted-garlic dressing. We double up on the smokiness by using both smoked almonds and Spanish smoked paprika; the nuts also add a welcome texture that plays off the tender-crisp broccoli. Mint, with its menthol freshness, lightens up all the deep, earthy notes in the dish.

START TO FINISH: 30 MINUTES
SERVINGS: 4 TO 6

¼ cup extra-virgin olive oil

4 medium garlic cloves, thinly sliced

2 tablespoons grated lemon zest, plus 3 tablespoons lemon juice

¼ teaspoon smoked paprika

½ cup smoked almonds, chopped

Kosher salt and ground black pepper

1½ pounds broccoli, stems peeled and cut into 1½-inch pieces, florets cut into 1-inch pieces

⅓ cup lightly packed fresh mint

Don't wait to serve the broccoli; it is best immediately after dressing. If left to stand, the acidity of the lemon juice will turn the broccoli yellow-green.

1. **In a 10-inch skillet** over medium, heat the oil and garlic, stirring, until the garlic is golden brown, 1 to 2 minutes. Scrape the mixture into a large bowl. Whisk in the lemon zest and juice, smoked paprika, almonds and ½ teaspoon each salt and pepper; set aside.

2. **Fill a large Dutch oven** with about 1 inch of water, cover and bring to a simmer over medium-high. Distribute the broccoli in an even layer in a steamer basket, then carefully place the basket in the pot. Cover, reduce to medium and cook until the broccoli is tender-crisp, 8 to 10 minutes.

3. **Transfer the broccoli** to the bowl with the dressing, add the mint and toss. Taste and season with salt and pepper.

Sesame-Soy Spinach

The Korean name for this dish is sigeumchi namul. It's a classic banchan (side dish); sigeumchi means spinach and namul is a category of cooked and seasoned vegetable dishes. The spinach is blanched, drained and rinsed under cold water to stop the cooking before it is tossed with a flavorful dressing made with toasted and ground sesame seeds. Like most other namul, the spinach is best served at room temperature or slightly chilled.

START TO FINISH: 25 MINUTES
SERVINGS: 4

2½ tablespoons
sesame seeds

2 tablespoons soy sauce,
plus more if needed

1 tablespoon toasted
sesame oil

1 medium garlic clove,
minced

Kosher salt

2 bunches spinach
(about 2 pounds), trimmed
of bottom 1½ inches,
washed and drained

3 scallions, thinly sliced
on the diagonal

Don't use baby spinach, which is too delicate in flavor and texture. Mature spinach sold in bunches is better. Be sure to wash and drain the spinach to remove any sand or grit, but there's no need to dry it since it will be blanched.

1. In a large pot over medium-high, bring 4 quarts water to a boil. Meanwhile, in an 8-inch skillet over medium, toast the sesame seeds, stirring often, until lightly browned, 2 to 3 minutes. Cool completely. In an electric spice grinder or in a mortar with a pestle, coarsely grind 2 tablespoons of the seeds; reserve the remainder for garnish. Transfer the ground seeds to a medium bowl, then stir in the soy sauce, sesame oil and garlic; set aside.

2. To the boiling water, add 1 tablespoon salt and the spinach. Cook, stirring, until the leaves are wilted and the stems are tender-crisp, 1 to 2 minutes. Immediately drain in a colander, rinse under running cold water, tossing the spinach, until cool to the touch, then drain well. Using your hands, firmly squeeze the spinach to remove the water (no need to wring it completely dry).

3. Add the spinach to the sesame mixture along with the scallions and toss until well combined. Taste and season with soy sauce, if needed. Transfer to a serving dish, then sprinkle with the reserved sesame seeds.

Grilled Corn

Few vegetables do as well on the grill as fresh, sweet corn. Tossing ears still in their husks onto the hot grate allows the kernels to steam so they're plump and tender, not tough and dry. We then strip off the husks and return the corn to the grill for a few minutes for a light charring, which adds smoky, toasty flavors. If you're looking for ways to kick up the flavor of grilled corn, see the recipes that follow. All employ the same grilling technique; the seasonings are added after husking, when the ears are tossed with a compound butter (see recipes p. 180) and briefly returned to the heat.

START TO FINISH: 35 MINUTES, PLUS GRILL PREP
SERVINGS: 6

6 ears corn, husks on

6 tablespoons salted butter, room temperature

Kosher salt and ground black pepper

Compound butters to serve (see recipes p. 180)

Don't bother removing the silk before grilling. It's easy to pull off when stripping the husks off the grilled corn, and any residual silk will be burned off when the ears are returned to the grill to char.

1. Remove only the outermost layer of husk from each ear of corn, leaving the inner layers intact. If needed, trim off the silk that extends past the tip.

2. Prepare a charcoal or gas grill. For a charcoal grill, ignite a large chimney of coals, let burn until lightly ashed over, then distribute the coals evenly over one side of the grill bed; open the bottom grill vents. Heat the grill, covered, for 5 minutes, then clean and oil the grate. For a gas grill, turn all burners to high and heat, covered, for 15 minutes, then clean and oil the grate. Turn off 1 burner, leaving the remaining burner(s) on high.

3. Place the corn (still in the husks) on the hot side of the grill. Cover and cook until charred on all sides, about 15 minutes, turning every 5 minutes or so. Transfer to a rimmed baking sheet. When the corn is just cool enough to handle, remove and discard the husks and silk. Slather the butter onto the ears, then return the corn to the hot side of the grill. Cook, uncovered and turning occasionally, until lightly charred on all sides, 5 to 7 minutes; move the ears to the cool side if flare-ups become too intense. Transfer to a platter and sprinkle with salt and pepper.

Compound Butters for Grilled Corn

Grilled Corn with Tamarind-Chutney Butter

In a large bowl, mix together **6 tablespoons salted butter** (room temperature), **3 tablespoons tamarind chutney, 2 tablespoons garam masala** and **¼ teaspoon each kosher salt** and **ground black pepper.** Prepare, grill and husk the corn as directed. Add the husked ears a few at a time to the bowl with the butter mixture and turn to coat. Return the corn to the hot side of the grill and cook, uncovered and turning occasionally, until lightly charred on all sides, 5 to 7 minutes; move the ears to the cool side if flare-ups become too intense. Transfer the ears to a platter, then sprinkle with **⅓ cup unsweetened shredded coconut** (toasted) and **⅓ cup lightly packed fresh cilantro** (chopped).

Grilled Corn with Hoisin Butter

In a large bowl, mix together **6 tablespoons salted butter** (room temperature), **3 tablespoons hoisin sauce, 1 tablespoon plus 1 teaspoon Chinese five-spice powder** and **¼ teaspoon each kosher salt** and **ground black pepper.** Prepare, grill and husk the corn as directed. Add the husked ears a few at a time to the bowl with the butter mixture and turn to coat. Return the corn to the hot side of the grill and cook, uncovered and turning occasionally, until lightly charred on all sides, 5 to 7 minutes; move the ears to the cool side if flare-ups become too intense. Transfer to a platter, then sprinkle with **4 scallions** (thinly sliced) and **⅓ cup roasted salted peanuts** (finely chopped).

Grilled Corn with Harissa Butter

In a large bowl, stir together **6 tablespoons salted butter** (room temperature), **3 tablespoons harissa paste, 2 tablespoons cider vinegar, 1 teaspoon grated orange zest** and **¼ teaspoon each kosher salt** and **ground black pepper.** Prepare, grill and husk the corn as directed. Add the husked ears a few at a time to the bowl with the butter mixture and turn to coat. Return the corn to the hot side of the grill and cook, uncovered and turning occasionally, until lightly charred on all sides, 5 to 7 minutes; move the ears to the cool side if flare-ups become too intense. Transfer to a platter, then sprinkle with **⅓ cup lightly packed fresh mint** (chopped).

Grilled Corn with Za'atar Butter

In a large bowl, stir together **6 tablespoons salted butter** (room temperature), **2 tablespoons za'atar, 1 tablespoon ground sumac, 1 teaspoon grated lemon zest** and **¼ teaspoon each kosher salt** and **ground black pepper.** Prepare, grill and husk the corn as directed. Add the husked ears a few at a time to the bowl with the butter mixture and turn to coat. Return the corn to the hot side of the grill and cook, uncovered and turning occasionally, until lightly charred on all sides, 5 to 7 minutes; move the ears to the cool side if flare-ups become too intense. Transfer to a platter, then sprinkle with **½ cup crumbled feta cheese, ⅓ cup lightly packed fresh flat-leaf parsley** (chopped) and **Aleppo pepper.**

Green Beans with Garlic-Herb Yogurt

For this simple, fresh take on green beans, we steam them in water with a few tablespoons of butter, then the lid comes off the pot so the water can evaporate, leaving the beans tender and lightly slicked with flavorful fat. The garlic-herb yogurt, spooned on before serving, is a creamy yet light flourish. This side is as good served at room temperature as it is warm.

START TO FINISH: 25 MINUTES
SERVINGS: 4

½ cup whole-milk plain Greek yogurt

¼ cup finely chopped fresh chives

2 tablespoons finely chopped fresh mint, plus 2 tablespoons torn fresh mint

2 tablespoons finely chopped fresh dill

2 tablespoons lemon juice

1 tablespoon extra-virgin olive oil

2 teaspoons honey

1 medium garlic clove, finely grated

3 tablespoons salted butter, cut into 2 or 3 pieces

Kosher salt and ground black pepper

1½ pounds green beans, trimmed

Don't forget to cover the beans for the first half of cooking; stir only once to ensure even doneness and prevent too much steam-heat escaping the pot.

1. **In a medium bowl,** stir together the yogurt, chives, the chopped mint, dill, lemon juice, oil, honey and garlic. Season with salt and pepper; set aside.

2. **In a Dutch oven** over medium-high, bring the butter, ½ cup water and ½ teaspoon salt to a boil. Stir in the green beans, then cover and cook until just tender when pierced with the tip of a knife, about 5 minutes; stir once about halfway through. Uncover, increase to high and cook, stirring occasionally, until the water evaporates and the beans begin to sizzle, about 5 minutes.

3. **Transfer the beans** to a platter. Drizzle with the yogurt mixture and sprinkle with the torn mint.

Lebanese-Style Greens
with Caramelized Onions

Hindbeh is the name of both a common Lebanese side dish and its star ingredient, wild dandelion. The bitter greens are blanched in salted water, then sautéed with olive oil and served topped with deeply caramelized onions. Dandelion greens aren't always available, but collard greens, which are milder and sweeter, are delicious prepared in the same way; use whichever you prefer. A scallion-yogurt accompaniment, though not traditional, is a creamy contrast to the greens and onions and pulls together all the flavors and textures. To make a complete vegetarian meal, serve the greens with a nutty bulgur pilaf.

START TO FINISH: 40 MINUTES
SERVINGS: 4

_____

Kosher salt and
ground black pepper

2 bunches (about 2 pounds)
collard greens, stemmed
and chopped into 2- to
3-inch pieces OR 2 pounds
dandelion greens, bottom
2 inches trimmed, chopped
into 2- to 3-inch pieces

⅓ cup extra-virgin olive oil

2 medium yellow onions,
halved and thinly sliced

¾ cup plain whole-milk
yogurt

4 scallions, chopped

½ teaspoon ground allspice

½ teaspoon ground cumin

2 tablespoons lemon juice

Don't squeeze the blanched greens totally dry. Some of the residual water helps ensure the greens stay silky; just give them a light squeeze to remove excess moisture.

1. In a large pot, bring 4 quarts water to a boil. Add 1 tablespoon salt and the collards, then cook, stirring occasionally, until tender, 3 to 5 minutes. Drain in a colander and rinse under cold running water until cool enough to handle. Using your hands, lightly squeeze out some of the excess moisture; do not wring them completely dry.

2. In a 12-inch skillet over medium-high, heat the oil until shimmering. Add the onions and cook, stirring only occasionally at first then more often once browning begins at the edges of the pan, until the onions are deeply caramelized and crisped, 15 to 20 minutes; reduce the heat if the onions brown before they become tender.

3. Meanwhile, in a small bowl, stir together the yogurt, scallions and ¼ teaspoon pepper. Taste and season with salt; set aside.

4. When the onions are done, using a slotted spoon, transfer about ½ cup to a paper towel-lined plate and spread in an even layer. Sprinkle with salt and set aside; the onions will crisp as they cool. To the remaining onions in the skillet, add the greens, allspice, cumin, ½ teaspoon pepper and ¼ cup water. Cook over medium-high, stirring often, until the greens are warmed through and most of the water has evaporated, about 3 minutes.

5. Off heat, stir in the lemon juice, then taste and season with salt. Transfer to a serving bowl and top with the yogurt mixture, followed by the reserved onions.

6

OVEN-BAKED

Roasted Sweet Potatoes with Toasted Spices and Cilantro (Sabzi)

START TO FINISH: 45 MINUTES
SERVINGS: 4

2 pounds orange-flesh sweet potatoes, peeled and cut into 1-inch chunks

5 tablespoons grapeseed or other neutral oil, divided

Kosher salt and ground black pepper

½ cup unsweetened shredded coconut

2 tablespoons sesame seeds

1 tablespoon yellow mustard seeds

1 tablespoon cumin seeds

4 medium garlic cloves, finely chopped

1 jalapeño chili, stemmed, seeded and finely chopped

1 cup lightly packed fresh cilantro, chopped

Don't add the mustard seeds and cumin seeds to the skillet at the same time as the coconut and sesame or the spices will end up overdone and taste acrid.

1. **Heat the oven to 475°F** with a rack in the middle position. Line a rimmed baking sheet with kitchen parchment. In a large bowl, combine the sweet potatoes, 2 tablespoons of oil and ½ teaspoon salt. Toss to coat, then transfer to the prepared baking sheet, distributing in an even layer; reserve the bowl. Roast until golden brown and a skewer inserted into a piece meets no resistance, 30 to 35 minutes, stirring once about halfway through.

2. **Meanwhile, in a 12-inch skillet** over medium, heat the remaining 3 tablespoons oil until shimmering. Add the coconut and sesame seeds, then cook, stirring often, until light golden brown, 2 to 3 minutes. Add the mustard seeds, cumin seeds, garlic and jalapeño. Cook, stirring often, until golden brown and the mixture has a toasty aroma, 1 to 2 minutes. Pour the mixture into the reserved large bowl.

3. **When the potatoes are done,** transfer while still hot to the bowl. Toss to coat with the spice mixture, then add the cilantro and toss again. Taste and season with salt and pepper.

In the Indian kitchen, sabzi refer to a wide range of cooked vegetable dishes. In our recipe, a nutty, fragrant mix of toasted coconut, sesame seeds and sizzled aromatics coats oven-caramelized roasted sweet potatoes. The contrast of crunchy seeds and creamy potato is deliciously compelling, as is the balance of sweet, savory and spicy flavors. To up the chili heat, leave the seeds in the jalapeño before chopping. If you like, for a touch of acidity, serve with lemon wedges.

Braised and Glazed Carrots and Parsnips with Orange and Cardamom

START TO FINISH: 1 HOUR 50 MINUTES
(20 MINUTES ACTIVE)
SERVINGS: 4 TO 6

For these simple but luxurious root vegetables we use a high oven temperature to reduce the braising liquid, and we finish the roots with a little butter to give them a rich, glossy glaze. The sweet, fruity orange is nicely rounded out by the floral, piney notes of ground cardamom and a sprinkle of fresh herbs. The start-to-finish time for this side dish is long but the cooking is largely hands-off. This is delicious alongside a simple roast, but also is elegant enough for the holiday table.

3 tablespoons extra-virgin olive oil

4 scallions, whites minced, greens thinly sliced on the diagonal, reserved separately

1 tablespoon grated orange zest, plus 1 cup orange juice, divided

1 teaspoon ground cardamom

¼ teaspoon red pepper flakes

Kosher salt and ground black pepper

1 pound medium carrots (about 5), peeled and sliced ½ inch thick on a sharp diagonal

1 pound medium parsnips (about 4), peeled and sliced ½ inch thick on a sharp diagonal

2 tablespoons salted butter, cut into 2 pieces

¼ cup lightly packed fresh dill **OR** fresh mint **OR** a combination, chopped

Don't use carrots and parsnips that are very slender, as they will overcook. Look for ones that are medium in size, and don't slice them thinner than ½ inch. Also, don't bother stirring the vegetables as they braise. There's simply no need to.

1. **Heat the oven to 350°F** with a rack in the middle position. In a large Dutch oven over medium, cook the oil and scallion whites, stirring occasionally, until beginning to soften, about 2 minutes. Add ¾ cup of orange juice, the cardamom, pepper flakes and 1 teaspoon salt, then bring to a simmer. Stir in the carrots and parsnips. Cover, transfer to the oven and cook until almost no liquid remains and browning has formed on the bottom of the pot, about 1½ hours.

2. **Remove the pot from the oven.** Uncover and stir in the remaining ¼ cup orange juice, the orange zest, butter and herbs, scraping up the browned bits. Taste and season with salt and black pepper. Transfer to a serving dish and sprinkle with the scallion greens.

Roasted Romanesco with Smoked Paprika Yogurt

Romanesco, sometimes referred to as Roman cauliflower, is pale green and the florets that comprise the head display a unique, intricate design. Its flavor is similar to broccoli and cauliflower, its brassica brethren, and we think less is more when it comes to cooking it. Simply cutting the heads into wedges and roasting them in a super-hot oven capitalizes on romanesco's unique shape while also developing sweet, nutty flavors and crisping the filigreed surfaces. If romanesco is not available, this technique also works with cauliflower, but use a single larger head and cut it into six wedges (romanesco tends to be smaller than cauliflower). This can be served as a side but is hearty enough to be a vegetarian main.

START TO FINISH: 35 MINUTES
SERVINGS: 4 TO 6

Two 1½-pound heads romanesco, trimmed, each cut into 4 wedges **OR** one 2- to 2½-pound head cauliflower, trimmed and cut into 6 wedges

5 tablespoons extra-virgin olive oil, divided

Kosher salt and ground black pepper

1 medium garlic clove, minced

2 teaspoons smoked paprika, divided

½ cup plain whole-milk Greek yogurt

2 teaspoons grated lemon zest, plus 1 tablespoon lemon juice

¼ cup chopped fresh dill **OR** mint **OR** a combination

Don't remove the core of the romanesco. *Simply trim off the leaves and the base of the stem, then cut the heads in half, then each half in half again.*

1. **Heat the oven to 500°F.** Brush the romanesco wedges all over with 3 tablespoons of oil and sprinkle with salt. Place with a cut side down on a rimmed baking sheet and roast for 15 minutes. Meanwhile, in a small bowl, whisk together the remaining 2 tablespoons oil, the garlic, 1 teaspoon of paprika and ¼ teaspoon pepper; set aside. In another small bowl, stir together the yogurt, the remaining 1 teaspoon paprika and the lemon zest and juice, then taste and season with salt and pepper; set aside.

2. **Using a wide metal spatula,** flip the wedges onto the second cut sides and drizzle evenly with the oil mixture. Continue to roast until the romanesco is well browned and a skewer inserted into the cores meets no resistance, about another 10 minutes. Spread the yogurt mixture on a serving platter, place the romanesco wedges on top and sprinkle with dill.

Charred Zucchini with Gochujang and Scallions

Hobak muchim is a Korean side dish of seasoned sliced zucchini. In this boldly flavorful—yet ultra-simple—version, the charred bitter notes and subtle sweetness of the zucchini (or yellow summer squash) are a perfect match for the spicy, pungent, sesame-fragrant, salty-sweet dressing that coats the zucchini after broiling. When shopping, look for medium-size zucchini (ones that weigh about 8 ounces each) so the slices aren't too small and numerous nor too large and few. Gochujang is an umami-packed Korean hot pepper paste; look for it in the international aisle of most supermarkets or in Asian grocery stores. Note that we use seasoned rice vinegar here, as it's an easy one-ingredient way to incorporate acidity, sweetness and salt.

START TO FINISH: 35 MINUTES
SERVINGS: 4

———

3 medium (1½ pounds total) zucchini **OR** yellow summer squash **OR** a combination, sliced into ¼- to ½-inch-thick rounds

1 tablespoon grapeseed or other neutral oil

Kosher salt and ground black pepper

2 to 3 tablespoons gochujang

3 tablespoons seasoned rice vinegar

2 tablespoons toasted sesame oil

2 teaspoons finely grated fresh ginger

1 medium garlic clove, finely grated

4 scallions, thinly sliced on the diagonal

Don't forget to rotate the baking sheet about halfway through broiling. This helps ensure that the zucchini browns evenly, especially if your oven has hot spots, as many do. Be sure to allow the zucchini to cool for 5 to 10 minutes after broiling. During this time, the slices release some liquid that would otherwise dilute the dressing.

1. Heat the broiler with a rack about 4 inches from the element. Set a wire rack in a broiler-safe rimmed baking sheet. In a large bowl, toss the zucchini with the neutral oil, ¼ teaspoon salt and ½ teaspoon pepper. Arrange the slices on the prepared rack in a single layer; reserve the bowl. Broil until the tops are well charred, 7 to 9 minutes, rotating the baking sheet about halfway through. Meanwhile, in the reserved bowl, whisk together the gochujang, vinegar, sesame oil, ginger, garlic and scallions.

2. When the zucchini is done, let it cool on the rack for 5 to 10 minutes. Transfer the slices to the bowl and toss gently until evenly coated. Taste and season with salt and pepper, then transfer to a serving dish. Serve warm or at room temperature.

Optional garnish: Toasted sesame seeds

Cauliflower Shawarma

Traditional Levantine shawarma is meat, commonly lamb, that's seasoned and spit-roasted. Modern meatless riffs opt for cauliflower because it pairs well with nearly any type of spicing and cooks up with a satisfying texture. Shawarma Bar in London boosts richness in their cauliflower shawarma with butter, and we agree it's a flavorful addition, but we also include a little olive oil for better browning. Tangy, deep-red sumac is made by grinding the dried berries of the sumac bush; look for it in the spice section of the supermarket or Middle Eastern grocery stores. If it's not available, use lemon zest; zest alters the flavor profile but the cauliflower still will taste great.

START TO FINISH: 35 MINUTES (15 MINUTES ACTIVE)
SERVINGS: 4

4 tablespoons salted butter, melted

2 tablespoons extra-virgin olive oil

3 medium garlic cloves, finely grated

1 tablespoon ground coriander

1 tablespoon plus ½ teaspoon ground sumac OR grated lemon zest

2- to 2½-pound head cauliflower, trimmed and cut into 1-inch florets

Kosher salt and ground black pepper

⅓ cup plain whole-milk yogurt, room temperature

Pita bread rounds, halved, to serve

Sliced onion OR sliced tomato OR sliced cucumber OR a combination, to serve

Don't stir the cauliflower more than once during roasting so the florets brown deeply. The best tool to use is a wide metal spatula to scrape up and flip the pieces.

1. **Heat the oven to 500°F** with a rack in the middle position. In a small bowl, stir together the butter, oil, garlic, coriander and 1 tablespoon of sumac. On a rimmed baking sheet, drizzle the cauliflower with ¼ cup of the butter mixture and sprinkle with salt and pepper; toss to combine. Roast until well browned and tender, 18 to 24 minutes, stirring once about halfway through.

2. **Into the remaining butter mixture,** stir the yogurt, then taste and season with salt, pepper and the remaining ½ teaspoon sumac. Tuck the cauliflower and sliced vegetable(s) into the pita and serve with the yogurt sauce.

Optional garnish: Fresh flat-leaf parsley **OR** fresh mint **OR** lemon wedges **OR** a combination

Mexican-Style Zucchini and Corn (Calabacitas)

Mexican calabacitas, which translates from the Spanish as "little squash," typically is cooked on the stovetop, yielding a stewy mix of summer vegetables. We prefer to char the veggies under the broiler to caramelize some of their natural sugars and allow each ingredient to keep its character. Zucchini lends the dish its name, but corn, green chilies and tomatoes also are part of the mix. Corn kernels freshly cut from the cob offer the best flavor and texture, but frozen corn that has been thawed and patted dry to wick away excess moisture will work, too. This is great as a vegetarian taco filling or as a side to grilled or roasted chicken.

2 medium zucchini (about 8 ounces each), halved lengthwise, then sliced crosswise ¼ to ½ inch thick

2 poblano chilies, stemmed, seeded and chopped

2 cups corn kernels (from about 3 ears corn) **OR** thawed frozen corn kernels, patted dry

1 pint grape **OR** cherry tomatoes, halved

2 tablespoons grapeseed or other neutral oil

4 teaspoons dried oregano

Kosher salt and ground black pepper

2 ounces queso fresco cheese, crumbled (½ cup)

⅓ cup drained pickled jalapeños, roughly chopped

¼ cup pumpkin seeds, toasted

Don't stir the vegetables as they cook under the broiler. This allows them to take on some char, which lends complex, subtle smoky notes to the dish.

1. Heat the broiler with a rack about 4 inches from the element. In a large bowl, toss together the zucchini, poblanos, corn, tomatoes, oil, oregano and ½ teaspoon each salt and pepper. Distribute in an even layer on a broiler-safe rimmed baking sheet and broil, without stirring, until the mixture is well-charred and the zucchini is tender, 8 to 10 minutes.

2. Remove the baking sheet from the oven. Let the vegetables cool for a few minutes, then taste and season with salt and pepper. Transfer to a serving dish and sprinkle with the queso fresco, pickled jalapeños and pumpkin seeds.

Optional garnish: Chopped fresh cilantro **OR** lime wedges **OR** both

Eggplant with Pomegranate Molasses, Fennel and Herbs

This dish of roasted eggplant garnished with a salad of fresh fennel and herbs is elegant yet easy. The contrast in texture between silky eggplant and crisp fennel, the tart-sweet flavor of pomegranate molasses and lemon juice and the freshness of parsley and mint creates layers of delicious complexity. Dark, viscous pomegranate molasses, often used in Middle Eastern cooking, is pomegranate juice that has been reduced to a syrupy consistency. Look for it sold in bottles in the international aisle of the grocery store or in Middle Eastern markets; if you can, choose, one without any added sugar or coloring.

START TO FINISH: 45 MINUTES
SERVINGS: 4

_____

Two 1-pound eggplants, trimmed, peeled lengthwise in sections (creating a striped effect), then cut crosswise into 1-inch-thick rounds

¼ cup extra-virgin olive oil, plus more to serve

Kosher salt and ground black pepper

1 medium fennel bulb, trimmed, halved lengthwise, cored and thinly sliced against the grain

1 medium garlic clove, peeled and finely grated

3 tablespoons lemon juice

2 tablespoons pomegranate molasses, plus more to serve

¾ cup lightly packed fresh flat-leaf parsley, torn if large

¼ cup lightly packed fresh mint, torn if large

3 tablespoons pomegranate seeds (optional)

Don't peel off all the skin from the eggplants. We like the contrast in texture of partially peeled eggplant. To partially peel, use a vegetable peeler to remove strips of skin along the length of the eggplant, creating a striped effect.

1. **Heat the oven to 475°F** with a rack in the lowest position. Brush the eggplant on both sides with the oil and season with salt and pepper. Arrange in a single layer on a rimmed baking sheet and roast until golden brown on the surface, 15 to 20 minutes. Meanwhile, in a medium bowl, toss together the fennel, garlic, lemon juice and ¼ teaspoon salt; set aside.

2. **When the eggplant is golden brown,** using a wide metal spatula, flip the pieces. Brush with the pomegranate molasses and continue to roast until deeply browned and a skewer inserted into the slices meets no resistance, about 5 minutes. Transfer the eggplant to a serving platter.

3. **To the fennel mixture,** add the parsley, mint and pomegranate seeds (if using), then toss. Taste and season with salt and pepper. Mound the mixture on the eggplant and drizzle with additional oil and pomegranate molasses.

Optional garnish: Chopped pistachios

Eggplant

The eggplant is treated as a vegetable (but is actually a berry) and gets its American name from history—early European versions were smaller and white or yellow, hence egg-like. It can be bitter or mushy, but conquer those challenges and you have a meaty and mellow vegetable that can really shine.

In Cairo, we encountered dish after dish of btingan mekhalel, deep-fried chunks of eggplant punched up with the snap of coarse-ground spices and plenty of vinegar. Our version, p. 223, swaps broiling for deep-frying (easier) and uses harissa paste for a quick yet complex hit of heat.

In Ho Chi Minh City, we encountered a different but equally delicious eggplant dish at an open-air lunch shop run by Vo Thi Dao. She charred slender eggplants over a large, stainless steel bowl filled with coals, cooking them until soft, heaping the smoky, tender flesh into a bowl and mashing it lightly before adding sliced scallions and a dressing of fish sauce, lime juice, sugar, garlic and chilies.

Our take on the dish, cà tím nướng, p. 200, again uses the broiler, moving the cooking indoors, and we add chopped peanuts and fresh herbs for crunch. (Like Vo Thi, we use the slender, thin-skinned Japanese or Chinese type of eggplant.)

Probably the best known iteration of eggplant is the large, glossy, deeply purple ovals known as globe eggplant which are popular in Mediterranean cooking. In Naples, we ate a pasta dish of lightly browned eggplant chunks simmered with tomatoes and some of the starchy pasta water, then tossed with creamy, pungent Gorgonzola cheese. Our version, p. 281, is straightforward and doesn't skimp on the cheese.

In India, eggplant, chickpeas and curry spices are paired in chole baigan. In our version, p. 357, we simplify by using only curry powder, but we boost flavor by browning the powder along with tomato paste. While that's happening, chunks of eggplant and onion brown under the broiler, getting soft and mellow. Canned chickpeas continue the convenience factor— the whole dish, hearty and flavorful, comes together in 40 minutes.

Vietnamese-Style Broiled Eggplant

Cà tím nướng is a popular Vietnamese dish of grilled eggplant with nước chấm, the ubiquitous savory-sweet dressing made with fish sauce, lime and garlic. For this recipe, we moved the cooking indoors and fired up the broiler for year-round convenience; its focused heat does a good job of charring the eggplant. With no sweetener other than the natural sugars in the shredded carrots, the dressing that sauces the eggplant after broiling has more savory-sour notes and a more restrained sweetness than is typical of nước chấm. Serve this with steamed jasmine rice as a light meal or offer it as a component of a Southeast Asian-inspired dinner.

1 medium carrot, peeled and shredded on the large holes of a box grater

2 Fresno **OR** jalapeño chilies, stemmed, halved lengthwise, seeded and sliced into thin half rings

2 tablespoons lime juice, plus lime wedges to serve

1 medium garlic clove, minced

Kosher salt and ground black pepper

1½ pounds Chinese **OR** Japanese eggplant, trimmed and halved lengthwise

2 tablespoons grapeseed or other neutral oil

2 tablespoons fish sauce

½ cup roasted, salted peanuts, chopped

½ cup lightly packed fresh cilantro, roughly chopped

Don't use globe eggplant for this recipe, as it is more bulbous and seedy than slender Chinese or Japanese eggplant. Broilers vary in heat output, so keep a close eye on the eggplant as it cooks and be sure to rotate the baking sheet halfway to help ensure even browning.

1. **In a small bowl,** stir together the carrot, chilies, lime juice, garlic and ¼ teaspoon each salt and pepper; set aside. Heat the broiler with a rack about 4 inches from the element. Brush the eggplant on all sides with the oil, then sprinkle with ½ teaspoon salt and 1 teaspoon pepper. Arrange cut side up on a broiler-safe rimmed baking sheet and broil until well charred and a skewer inserted through the thickest parts meets no resistance, 8 to 10 minutes, rotating the baking sheet halfway. Transfer the eggplant to a cutting board, cut into into 1½- to 2-inch pieces and place on a platter.

2. **Stir the fish sauce** into the carrot mixture. Using a fork, scatter the carrots over the eggplant, then spoon the liquid over the top. Top with the peanuts and cilantro.

Crisp Oven-Fried Cauliflower with Tahini-Yogurt Sauce

START TO FINISH: 45 MINUTES (15 MINUTES ACTIVE)
SERVINGS: 4 TO 6

½ cup cornstarch

1 tablespoon ground cumin

2 teaspoons ground fennel seed **OR** curry powder

1 teaspoon ground coriander

Kosher salt and ground black pepper

3-pound head cauliflower, trimmed and cut into 1-inch florets

½ cup grapeseed or other neutral oil

1 cup whole-milk plain yogurt

2 tablespoons tahini

2 tablespoons finely chopped fresh mint

1 tablespoon lemon juice

1 small garlic clove, finely grated

Don't skimp on the oil that's tossed with the cauliflower. One-half cup may seem excessive, but it's important to generously coat the florets. Use your hands to rub the oil into the pieces and ensure all surfaces are covered. This way, the cornstarch-spice mix will adhere well and form a crisp crust in the oven.

1. **Heat the oven to 475°F** with a rack in the middle position. In a small bowl, whisk together the cornstarch, cumin, fennel, coriander, 1 teaspoon salt and 2 teaspoons pepper. In a large bowl, toss the cauliflower with the oil, using your hands to rub the oil into the florets. Sprinkle with the cornstarch mixture and toss until evenly coated. Transfer the florets to a rimmed baking sheet, shaking off excess cornstarch mixture and turning the pieces cut side down as much as possible. Roast for 15 minutes.

2. **Using a metal spatula,** flip the florets, then continue to roast until deep golden brown, another 15 to 20 minutes. Meanwhile, in a small bowl, whisk together the yogurt, tahini, mint, lemon juice, garlic and ⅛ teaspoon salt. Serve the cauliflower with the yogurt-tahini sauce.

Optional garnish: Thinly sliced scallions **OR** lemon wedges **OR** both

We love the crisp exterior and creamy interior of arnabeet mekleh, or Lebanese fried cauliflower, but cooking the florets in a pot of oil on the stovetop is not our favorite kitchen activity. Luckily, roasting well-oiled, starch-coated cauliflower in a hot oven yields delicious results that come incredibly close to the real deal. We add a few spices here to layer in intriguing flavor and aroma. If the tahini-yogurt sauce isn't for you, try serving the cauliflower with mango chutney or aioli.

Oven-Charred Broccoli

Broccoli, like most cruciferous vegetables, is especially delicious when deeply charred, which develops nutty, bittersweet flavors while crisping the florets. Our method of choice is a preheated baking sheet in an intensely hot oven, as more broccoli can be cooked this way than in a skillet on the stovetop. Charred broccoli is great on its own—maybe with some freshly squeezed lemon for brightness—but tossing with a few high-impact ingredients immediately after coming out of the oven takes the flavors to another level (see the recipes below).

START TO FINISH: 35 MINUTES
SERVINGS: 4

2 pounds broccoli, florets cut into 2-inch pieces, stems peeled and sliced about ¼ inch thick

2 tablespoons grapeseed or other neutral oil

Kosher salt and ground black pepper

Don't forget to set a rimmed baking sheet on the oven rack placed in the lowest position when you turn on the oven. Make sure the baking sheet is heavyweight so it doesn't warp and can withstand a 500°F oven.

Heat the oven to 500°F with a rack in the lowest position. Set a heavyweight rimmed baking sheet on the rack. In a large bowl, toss the broccoli with the oil, ¼ teaspoon salt and ½ teaspoon pepper. Carefully remove the hot baking sheet from the oven and distribute the broccoli in an even layer. Roast without stirring until deeply charred and tender-crisp, 20 to 25 minutes. Transfer to a serving dish.

Oven-Charred Broccoli with Peanuts, Soy and Scallions

Follow the recipe for Oven-Charred Broccoli; while the broccoli is roasting, in the same bowl used to toss the broccoli with oil and seasonings, whisk together **3 tablespoons grapeseed or other neutral oil, 3 tablespoons seasoned rice vinegar, 3 tablespoons soy sauce, ½ cup roasted peanuts** (finely chopped), **1 teaspoon red pepper flakes and 2 scallions** (thinly sliced on the diagonal). As soon as the broccoli is done, scrape it into the bowl and toss to combine. Taste and season with **kosher salt** and **black pepper**. Transfer to a serving dish and sprinkle with another **2 scallions** (thinly sliced on the diagonal) and **toasted sesame seeds** (optional).

Oven-Charred Broccoli with Pistachios and Parmesan

Follow the recipe for Oven-Charred Broccoli; while the broccoli is roasting, in the same bowl used to toss the broccoli with oil and seasonings, stir together **3 tablespoons extra-virgin olive oil, 3 tablespoons lemon juice, 2 ounces Parmesan cheese** (shaved), **½ cup roasted pistachios** (roughly chopped) and **½ cup lightly packed fresh flat-leaf parsley** (chopped). As soon as the broccoli is done, scrape it into the bowl and toss to combine. Taste and season with **kosher salt** and **black pepper**, then transfer to a serving dish.

Oven-Charred Broccoli with Dates and Toasted Almonds

Follow the recipe for Oven-Charred Broccoli; while the broccoli is roasting, in the same bowl used to toss the broccoli with oil and seasonings, stir together **3 tablespoons extra-virgin olive oil, 3 tablespoons lemon juice, 1 cup pitted dates** (roughly chopped), **½ cup whole or slivered almonds** (toasted and finely chopped), **½ cup lightly packed fresh flat-leaf parsley** (chopped) and **1 tablespoon Aleppo pepper** (or 2 teaspoons sweet paprika plus ¼ teaspoon cayenne pepper). As soon as the broccoli is done, scrape it into the bowl and toss to combine. Taste and season with **kosher salt** and **black pepper,** transfer to a serving dish.

Oven-Charred Broccoli with Lime, Shallots and Fish Sauce

Follow the recipe for Oven-Charred Broccoli; while the broccoli is roasting, in the same bowl used to toss the broccoli with oil and seasonings, whisk together **3 tablespoons neutral oil, 2 or 3 Fresno or serrano chilies** (stemmed, seeded and thinly sliced), **2 medium shallots** (halved and thinly sliced), **3 tablespoons lime juice, 3 tablespoons fish sauce and 2 teaspoons packed brown sugar.** As soon as the broccoli is done, scrape it into the bowl and toss to combine. Taste and season with **kosher salt** and **black pepper.** Transfer to a serving dish and sprinkle with **chopped fresh cilantro** (optional).

Roasted Mushrooms with Garlic, Lemon and Parsley

Italian funghi trifolati are sautéed mushrooms with olive oil, garlic and parsley. In this recipe, instead of firing up the stovetop, we roast the mushrooms in the oven. At the same time, on the oven rack just below, we toast a couple slices of crusty bread that later are torn into pieces and tossed with the roasted mushrooms. The croutons add a chewy-crisp texture that complements the mushrooms' silkiness. To keep their flavors bright and fresh, lemon zest and juice are mixed in only at the very end, along with chopped parsley. Use at least a couple different mushroom varieties, if you can. Grocery stores often sell packages containing a few different types—these work perfectly in this recipe, even if only as a supplement to commonplace cremini mushrooms.

START TO FINISH: 30 MINUTES
SERVINGS: 4 TO 6

Two 1-inch-thick slices crusty bread

5 tablespoons extra-virgin olive oil, divided

1½ pounds mixed mushrooms (such as cremini, oyster and shiitake; see headnote), trimmed and cut into ½- to ¾-inch pieces

3 medium garlic cloves, minced

¼ to ½ teaspoon red pepper flakes

Kosher salt and ground black pepper

1 tablespoon grated lemon zest, plus 2 tablespoons lemon juice

1 cup lightly packed fresh flat-leaf parsley, finely chopped

Don't purchase presliced mushrooms, as they tend to be dried out and often are haphazardly cut. If you're using shiitakes, be sure to remove and discard the stems, which are too tough and fibrous to eat. Pass on the portobellos for this recipe; they're too large and their gills darken and muddy the mix.

1. Heat the oven to 400°F with racks in the middle and lower-middle positions. Brush both sides of the bread with 1 tablespoon of oil and place on a rimmed baking sheet.

2. On a second rimmed baking sheet, toss the mushrooms, 3 tablespoons of the remaining oil, the garlic, pepper flakes, ½ teaspoon salt and 1 teaspoon black pepper until well combined. Place the mushrooms on the middle rack and the bread on the lower-middle rack. Roast until the liquid released by the mushrooms has evaporated and the mushrooms begin to brown and the bread is golden brown, about 20 minutes, stirring the mushrooms and flipping the bread about halfway through.

3. Remove both baking sheets from the oven. When the bread is cool enough to handle, tear the slices into rough ½-inch pieces and add to the mushrooms along with the remaining 1 tablespoon oil, the lemon zest and juice and parsley. Toss to combine, then taste and season with salt and black pepper.

Roasted Vegetables
with Cilantro Yogurt

The Turkish vegetable medley called turlu turlu, often described as spiced-up ratatouille, inspired this recipe. The vegetables are sometimes stewed, sometimes roasted; we chose the latter approach, as we're fond of the browning and flavor concentration that results from cooking in the dry heat of the oven. Vegetables of all sorts—from turnips to okra—may go into turlu turlu. For our version, we limited it to a few types of summery produce with similar cooking times and complementary flavors and textures. Earthy, mildly spicy Aleppo pepper (or paprika mixed with cayenne), coriander and cinnamon perfume the vegetables, their flavors blooming during roasting. A final flourish of yogurt mixed with cilantro is by no means traditional (cilantro isn't often used in Turkish cuisine), but we think it adds a bright, creamy counterpoint to the deeply flavorful veggies.

START TO FINISH: 45 MINUTES
SERVINGS: 4 TO 6

⅓ cup extra-virgin olive oil

1 tablespoon Aleppo pepper **OR** 1 tablespoon sweet paprika plus ½ teaspoon cayenne pepper

1 tablespoon ground coriander

1 teaspoon ground cinnamon

Kosher salt and ground black pepper

Two 1-pound eggplants, trimmed and cut into 1-inch chunks

2 medium red onions, each cut into 8 wedges

1 medium poblano chili **OR** red bell pepper, stemmed, seeded and cut into 1-inch wedges

8 ounces green beans, trimmed

1 pint cherry **OR** grape tomatoes

1 cup whole-milk or low-fat plain Greek yogurt

1½ cups lightly packed fresh cilantro, finely chopped

Don't use a baking sheet or a low-sided pan to roast the vegetables. The higher sides of a roasting pan slow the rate of moisture evaporation so the vegetables don't dry out before they're fully tender.

1. **Heat the oven to 500°F** with a rack in the middle position. In a small bowl, whisk together the oil, Aleppo pepper, coriander, cinnamon, and 1 teaspoon each salt and black pepper.

2. **In a roasting pan,** combine the eggplants, onions, chili and beans. Add the spiced oil, toss until the vegetables are coated, then distribute in an even layer. Scatter the tomatoes over them. Roast, stirring every 15 minutes, until browned and tender, 35 to 40 minutes.

3. **While the vegetables cook,** in a small bowl, stir together the yogurt, cilantro, ½ teaspoon salt and ¼ teaspoon black pepper; set aside until ready to serve. Transfer the roasted vegetables to a serving platter and dollop with the cilantro yogurt.

Spanish-Style Roasted Vegetables with Sherry Vinegar

START TO FINISH: 50 MINUTES
(10 MINUTES ACTIVE)
SERVINGS: 4

The Catalonian dish known as escalivada is a medley of grilled vegetables—typically eggplant, sweet peppers, onions and tomatoes—all of them finished with a glug of olive oil before serving. The name comes from the verb escalivar, meaning to char or roast in embers. For an easy all-season rendition, we roast the vegetables in a hot oven and cut them into pieces after they're tender and lightly caramelized. A final toss with sherry vinegar adds nutty, woodsy notes and bright acidity. Serve this warm or at room temperature as a side to roasted meats or seafood, or as part of a tapas spread. Or, pile the vegetables onto crusty bread along with a sharp, aged cheese or a creamy, mild one.

2 medium red OR yellow OR orange bell peppers OR a combination, stemmed, halved and seeded

2 plum tomatoes, cored

1 Japanese eggplant OR Chinese eggplant OR Italian eggplant (about 6 ounces), trimmed

1 small red onion, root end intact, cut into 8 wedges

⅓ cup extra-virgin olive oil

Kosher salt and ground black pepper

2 tablespoons sherry vinegar

Don't bother peeling the peppers, tomatoes and eggplant after roasting. The browning on the exteriors lends bittersweet notes and complexity while also making the dish look appealingly rustic.

1. **Heat the oven to 450°F** with a rack in the middle position. In a large bowl, toss together the peppers, tomatoes, eggplant, onion, oil, 1½ teaspoons salt and ½ teaspoon pepper, rubbing the oil and seasonings into the vegetables. Using your hands or a slotted spoon, transfer the vegetables to a 9-by-13-inch baking pan; reserve the bowl and the oil that remains in it. Roast the vegetables until browned and a skewer inserted into the onion meets no resistance, 35 to 40 minutes; if you prefer your tomatoes on the firm side, remove them from the oven when they're softened but not collapsed, about 25 minutes into roasting.

2. **Transfer the roasted vegetables** to a cutting board, then cut them into large bite-size pieces. Return the vegetables and accumulated juices to the bowl with the oil. Add the sherry vinegar and toss. Taste and season with salt and pepper, then transfer to a serving dish. Serve warm or at room temperature.

Optional garnish: Fresh flat-leaf parsley OR flaky salt OR both

Spicy Roasted Cauliflower with Sun-Dried Tomatoes and Almonds

The inspiration for this cauliflower side comes from "Maximo," by renowned Mexico City chef Eduardo García. To capture some of García's complexly layered flavors while using a much-simplified approach, we make a thick puree of cilantro, sun-dried tomatoes, almonds, pumpkin seeds, jalapeños and olive oil. Most of it is applied as a seasoning paste to cauliflower florets; the remainder is made into a simple sauce for serving alongside. In this recipe, Marcona almonds yield excellent flavor. However, if Marconas aren't available, use regular roasted almonds. If you wish to temper the chili heat, remove some or all of the seeds from the jalapeños before adding the chilies to the food processor.

START TO FINISH: 50 MINUTES (35 MINUTES ACTIVE)
SERVINGS: 4

1 cup lightly packed
fresh cilantro

¾ cup grapeseed
or other neutral oil

½ cup oil-packed sun-dried
tomatoes

½ cup roasted almonds,
preferably Marcona almonds
(see headnote)

½ cup pumpkin seeds

2 jalapeño chilies,
stemmed and halved

2 teaspoons ground cumin

Kosher salt and
ground black pepper

2- to 2½-pound head
cauliflower, trimmed, cored
and cut into 1½-inch florets

3 tablespoons lime juice,
plus lime wedges to serve

2 tablespoons sour cream

Don't use pre-cut cauliflower, as the florets tend to be too small and unevenly sized. When distributing the cauliflower on the prepared baking sheet, be sure to turn the florets cut side down as much as possible. The more contact the pieces have with the metal, the better they will brown. Letting the florets roast without stirring also allows for deeper caramelization.

1. Heat the oven to 475°F with a rack in the middle position. Line a rimmed baking sheet with foil and mist it with cooking spray. In a food processor, combine the cilantro, oil, sun-dried tomatoes, almonds, pumpkin seeds, chilies, cumin, 1 teaspoon salt and ½ teaspoon pepper. Process until smooth, about 1 minute, scraping the bowl as needed; the puree will be very thick. Transfer to a 2-cup liquid measuring cup; you should have about 1¾ cups.

2. In a large bowl, combine the cauliflower and 1¼ cups of the puree. Toss to thoroughly coat the florets, massaging it into the crevices. Transfer to the prepared baking sheet and distribute in a single layer, turning the florets cut side down as much as possible. Roast without stirring until deep golden brown, 20 to 25 minutes.

3. Meanwhile, in a small bowl, stir together the remaining puree, the lime juice and sour cream. Taste and season with salt and pepper; set aside for serving. When the cauliflower is done, taste and season with salt and pepper, then transfer to a platter. Serve with the sauce and lime wedges.

Roots

Gnarled, hairy, often thick-skinned— root vegetables are unabashedly homely. But don't judge a vegetable by its cover. A bit of knife work is all it takes to uncover sweet-fleshed, brightly colored interiors waiting to be slid into a hot oven and roasted to meaty, earthy tenderness, pureed into thick and creamy soups, or sliced and tossed into a crisp and tangy salad.

Polish cooks turn beets into a chilled soup called chlodnik that is popular in summer. We were inspired to come up with a version, p. 118, but instead of incorporating sour cream or other dairy product directly into the soup we add it at the end as a garnish.

While some root vegetables must be cooked, others are good raw. In Mexico, jicama is often eaten raw with lime juice and chili powder. We've got a version, p. 47, that balances bright, fresh cilantro with creamy queso fresco. Radishes also usually are eaten raw. In Guatemala's picado de rábano, they're paired with chilies, a bitter orange dressing and mint for a brightly flavored salad. (With the addition of chicharrones, fried pork skins, this is known as chojin.) Bitter orange juice isn't a common ingredient so for our take, p. 36, we substitute a combination of fresh lime and orange juice.

Turnips, on the other hand, typically require heat. Cooking food until tender in liquid, then reducing the liquid to a glaze is a classic technique, and one we use on our cider-braised turnips, p. 173, a very autumnal pairing of flavors.

Rutabagas are roots with identity issues. They're purplish on the outside, orange on the inside and also known as Swedish turnips, yellow turnips, or (in Britain) swedes. For our take, p. 237, we roast for walk-away ease, adding cubed pears about two-thirds of the way in so they're done at the same time as the rutabagas. Minced rosemary contributes piney notes (half used during roasting, half added fresh at the end for brighter flavor), and a tangy-sweet sauce of browned butter, honey and vinegar finishes the dish.

Celery root, aka celeriac, is good raw, as in our wintry salad, enlivened by apples and hazelnuts, p. 40. It's also terrific roasted. Our take, p. 234, starts by cutting the roots into wedges so they cook faster. Once they've softened, we glaze them with a mixture of sesame, soy and mirin to give them a teriyaki-like finish.

Harissa Roasted Potatoes

Tossing raw potatoes with harissa before roasting muted the chili paste's flavor. Instead, we roasted the potatoes until browned and crispy, tossed them with harissa, then returned them to the oven to re-crisp. This gave the potatoes the right texture and a spicy crust. A quick toss with chopped parsley and a squeeze of lemon juice to serve kept the flavors bold and bright.

START TO FINISH: 1 HOUR (10 MINUTES ACTIVE)
SERVINGS: 4

———

3 pounds Yukon Gold potatoes, peeled and cut into 1-inch chunks

5 tablespoons extra-virgin olive oil, divided

Kosher salt and ground black pepper

5 tablespoons harissa paste, plus more to serve

¼ cup finely chopped fresh flat-leaf parsley

Lemon wedges, to serve

Don't use harissa without first tasting it; *brands vary in intensity. If it packs considerable heat, you may want to use only 2 or 3 tablespoons.*

1. **Heat the oven to 450°F** with a rack in the middle position. In a large bowl, toss the potatoes with 4 tablespoons of the oil, 1 teaspoon salt and ½ teaspoon pepper.

2. **With a slotted spoon,** transfer the potatoes to a rimmed baking sheet in an even layer, leaving the excess oil in the bowl; set the bowl aside. Roast the potatoes until well browned and crisp, about 50 minutes, stirring and rotating the baking sheet halfway through.

3. **Transfer the potatoes back to the bowl,** scraping up any browned bits. Add the harissa and remaining 1 tablespoon olive oil; toss well. Return the potatoes to the baking sheet in an even layer; again reserve the bowl. Roast until the potatoes have re-crisped, another 10 minutes, stirring halfway through.

4. **Return the potatoes to the bowl,** again scraping up any browned bits. Add the parsley and toss. Taste and season with salt and pepper. Serve with lemon wedges and harissa on the side.

Roasted Eggplant and Peppers with Aleppo Browned Butter and Yogurt

For a rich and flavorful dish, we broil sweet peppers and eggplant until tender and silky, toss the vegetables with browned butter infused with Aleppo pepper (or sweet paprika plus red pepper flakes) and serve them atop a creamy bed of butter-enriched yogurt. A sprinkle of toasted walnuts adds crunch. The smoky, caramelized notes balance the vegetables' natural sweetness and the cool tartness of the yogurt. Serve with warmed pita bread.

START TO FINISH: 50 MINUTES
SERVINGS: 6

_____

3 medium red **OR** yellow **OR** orange bell peppers **OR** a combination

Two 1-pound eggplants, trimmed and cut crosswise into 1-inch-thick rounds

¼ cup extra-virgin olive oil

Kosher salt and ground black pepper

4 tablespoons salted butter

1 tablespoon Aleppo pepper **OR** 2 teaspoons sweet paprika plus ½ teaspoon red pepper flakes

1 cup plain whole-milk Greek yogurt

¼ cup walnuts, toasted and chopped

Don't forget to allow the roasted peppers to steam in a covered bowl. This loosens the skins from the flesh so they're easier to peel. When peeling the peppers, don't worry about removing every last bit of skin, and don't rinse them under water, as doing so washes away some of their flavor.

1. **Heat the broiler** with a rack about 6 inches from the element. Lay the peppers on their sides on a broiler-safe rimmed baking sheet, then broil until well charred on all sides, about 16 minutes, turning them as needed. Transfer to a large bowl, cover and let steam to loosen the skins; reserve the baking sheet.

2. **Arrange the eggplant** in a single layer on the same baking sheet. Brush both sides of the rounds with the oil, then season with salt and black pepper. Broil until the eggplant is softened and well browned on both sides, 16 to 18 minutes, flipping the slices halfway through. Remove from the oven. Stem, seed and peel the peppers, then cut them into 1-inch pieces and return to the bowl. Cut the eggplant into 1-inch pieces and add to the peppers.

3. **In an 8-inch skillet** over medium, melt the butter, then cook, stirring often, until the milk solids at the bottom are golden brown and the butter has a nutty aroma, about 3 minutes. Add the Aleppo pepper and cook, stirring, until the butter is bright red and fragrant, about 1 minute. Transfer to a small bowl and let cool for a few minutes.

4. **Fold 2 tablespoons** of the infused butter into the pepper-eggplant mixture, then taste and season with salt and black pepper. Stir the yogurt into the remaining infused butter; taste and season with salt and black pepper. Spread the yogurt mixture on a serving platter. Top with the pepper-eggplant mixture and sprinkle with the walnuts.

Charred Zucchini and Fennel with Shaved Parmesan

Zucchini and fennel are subtly sweet vegetables that benefit from a good charring over high heat, which introduces some welcome complexity and bitterness. We found the heat of the broiler worked well. Be sure to set a rack as close as possible to the broiler element and keep an eye on the vegetables as they cook, as heat output varies greatly broiler to broiler. If you have a mandoline, use it to make short work of slicing the fennel. Slicing it against the grain makes it more tender.

START TO FINISH: 25 MINUTES
SERVINGS: 4 TO 6

2 medium zucchini (about 8 ounces each), cut crosswise into ½-inch rounds

3 tablespoons extra-virgin olive oil, divided

Kosher salt and ground black pepper

2 medium fennel bulbs, halved, cored and thinly sliced against the grain

½ cup lightly packed fresh basil, thinly sliced

1 tablespoon lemon juice

¾ ounce Parmesan cheese, shaved with a vegetable peeler (about ⅓ cup)

Don't try to broil all the vegetables at once. There won't be enough room on the baking sheet to prevent steaming and they won't char evenly.

1. **Heat the broiler** with a rack about 4 inches from the element. In a large bowl, toss the zucchini with 1 tablespoon oil, ½ teaspoon salt and ¼ teaspoon pepper. Arrange in a single layer on a broiler-safe rimmed baking sheet, reserving the bowl. Broil until charred and tender, 6 to 7 minutes, rotating the baking sheet about halfway through. Meanwhile, in the same bowl, toss the fennel with 1 tablespoon of the remaining oil, ½ teaspoon salt and ¼ teaspoon pepper; set aside.

2. **When the zucchini is done,** use a wide metal spatula to transfer it to a serving platter; leave the broiler on. Distribute the fennel in an even layer on the baking sheet, again reserving the bowl; broil until charred and tender, 8 to 9 minutes, rotating the baking sheet about halfway through.

3. **Return the fennel to the bowl.** Add the remaining 1 table-spoon oil, the basil and lemon juice, then toss. Taste and season with salt and pepper, then distribute evenly over the zucchini. Scatter the shaved Parmesan on top.

Yogurt-Roasted Carrots with Warm Spices

Garam masala is an Indian blend of a number of different warm, sweet spices, including cinnamon, cardamom and cloves, plus savory ones such as cumin and black pepper. Here we supplement garam masala with crushed fennel seeds and ground turmeric to create a perfect flavor match for the earthy sweetness of carrots. Inspired by the method used to make tandoori chicken, we toss the carrots with yogurt and spices before roasting. After roasting, they're finished with a spiced butter flavored with alliums and chopped fresh herbs.

START TO FINISH: 45 MINUTES
SERVINGS: 4

2 teaspoons garam masala

1 teaspoon fennel seeds, lightly crushed

½ teaspoon ground turmeric

Kosher salt and ground black pepper

¼ cup whole-milk Greek yogurt

2 bunches carrots with tops (1 pound total), tops removed and discarded, halved crosswise on a sharp diagonal

4 tablespoons salted butter

1 small shallot, finely chopped

1 medium garlic clove, finely grated

⅓ cup lightly packed fresh cilantro, chopped

⅓ cup lightly packed fresh mint, chopped

Don't forget to coat the baking sheet with cooking spray. The yogurt-covered carrots otherwise will char and stick to the pan. Don't use large carrots for this recipe. Bunched carrots with tops are thinner and more tender than bagged carrots.

1. **Heat the oven to 500°F** with a rack in the middle position. Mist a rimmed baking sheet with cooking spray. In a small bowl, mix together the garam masala, fennel, turmeric and ½ teaspoon each salt and pepper. In a large bowl, mix the yogurt with 4 teaspoons of the spice mix. Add the carrots and toss to coat. Distribute the carrots in an even layer on the prepared baking sheet. Roast until well charred and a skewer inserted into the carrots meets no resistance, 25 to 30 minutes; stir the carrots once about halfway through.

2. **Meanwhile, in an 8-inch skillet** over medium, melt the butter. Add the shallot and garlic, then cook, stirring, until beginning to brown and crisp, 3 to 5 minutes. Add the remaining spice mix and cook, stirring, until fragrant, 30 to 60 seconds. Remove from the heat and set aside.

3. **When the carrots are done,** add the spiced shallot mixture, cilantro and mint directly to the baking sheet and toss with tongs. Taste and season with salt and pepper, then transfer to a serving dish.

½ cup unsalted dry-roasted peanuts

2 teaspoons sweet OR hot paprika

2 teaspoons ground ginger

2 teaspoons granulated garlic

1 teaspoon packed light brown sugar

Kosher salt and ground black pepper

3 tablespoons grapeseed or other neutral oil, divided

1½ pounds small (1½ to 2 inches) Yukon Gold OR red potatoes, halved

3 plum tomatoes, cored and finely chopped

1 medium shallot, finely chopped

1 serrano chili, stemmed, seeded and finely chopped

½ cup lightly packed fresh flat-leaf parsley, chopped

2 tablespoons lime juice

Don't be shy about using your hands to thoroughly coat the halved potatoes with the seasoning mixture. After emptying the potatoes onto the baking sheet, be sure to scrape any seasoning remaining in the bowl onto the potatoes.

1. **Heat the oven to 475°F** with a rack in the middle position. Mist a rimmed baking sheet with cooking spray. In a food processor, combine the peanuts, paprika, ginger, garlic, sugar, ½ teaspoon salt and 1 teaspoon pepper. Process until finely ground, about 20 seconds. Add 2 tablespoons oil and pulse until evenly combined, 3 to 5 times, scraping the bowl as needed.

2. **In a large bowl, toss the potatoes** with the remaining 1 tablespoon oil and ¼ teaspoon salt. Add the nut-spice mixture, and use your hands to toss and press the seasoning onto the potatoes so it sticks. Scrape the potatoes and any residual seasoning onto the prepared baking sheet, then distribute in an even layer. Roast until well browned all around and a skewer inserted into the potatoes meets no resistance, 20 to 25 minutes; use a metal spatula to turn the potatoes about halfway through.

3. **While the potatoes roast,** in a small bowl, stir together the tomatoes, shallot, chili, parsley, lime juice, and ½ teaspoon each salt and pepper. When the potatoes are done, transfer to a serving dish and sprinkle with salt. Serve with the tomato mixture on the side.

Suya-Spiced Roasted Potatoes with Tomato-Chili Relish

Suya is a Nigerian street food of spiced sliced meat threaded onto skewers and grilled. We make our suya spice mix by processing peanuts, paprika, ginger, garlic and a touch of brown sugar and use it to add flavor and crunch to potatoes. We add a bit of oil and toss the mixture onto halved potatoes before roasting. A simple fresh tomato relish with chili and lime served on the side brightens up the dish.

Roasted Butternut Squash with Ginger and Five-Spice

Instead of pureeing butternut squash and loading it up with butter, we cut it into chunks and roast it, seasoning it with fresh ginger and Chinese five-spice to complement its natural sweetness. You will need two large, heavy rimmed baking sheets. The squash can be peeled, seeded, cut into chunks and refrigerated in zip-close bags for up to two days before cooking. Many grocery stores sell butternut squash that has already been peeled, seeded and cut into chunks. We found that this variety does not brown as well as squash we prepped ourselves, though it tasted equally good. If you purchase precleaned squash, you will still need about 4 pounds.

START TO FINISH: 40 MINUTES
SERVINGS: 8

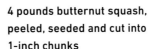

4 pounds butternut squash, peeled, seeded and cut into 1-inch chunks

3 tablespoons salted butter, melted

2 tablespoons finely grated fresh ginger

1½ teaspoons Chinese five-spice powder

Kosher salt and ground black pepper

¼ cup finely chopped fresh chives

2 tablespoons finely chopped crystallized ginger (optional)

Don't substitute oil for the butter. The milk solids in the butter brown during roasting, adding a nutty flavor and fragrance to the squash. Don't try to fit all of the squash onto a single baking sheet. Crowding impedes browning.

1. Heat the oven to 500°F with racks in the upper and lower-middle positions. Line 2 rimmed baking sheets with foil.

2. In a large bowl, toss the squash with the butter, ginger, five-spice powder, 1½ teaspoons salt and ½ teaspoon pepper. Divide evenly between the prepared baking sheets and distribute in even layers. Roast, switching and rotating the pans halfway through, until well browned, 25 to 35 minutes.

3. Taste and season with salt and pepper. Transfer to a platter and sprinkle with the chives and crystallized ginger (if using). Serve warm or at room temperature.

Stuffed Artichokes with Prosciutto and Garlic

Whether steamed, roasted, braised or fried, cooking fresh artichokes is a labor of love because the flower buds demand a lot of prep. For this recipe, we steam-roast halved artichokes until almost tender, stuff them with a savory mixture of crusty bread, prosciutto (or pancetta) and fontina cheese, then continue baking them until the craggy surface of the filling is crisp and golden brown. A simple roasted-garlic sauce completes the dish, and is perfect for dipping the base of the petals before scraping off the tender, sweet inner pulp. For this recipe, you will need a large roasting pan (one that measures about 13-by-16 inches), plus foil to cover the pan.

START TO FINISH: 2 HOURS (45 MINUTES ACTIVE)
SERVINGS: 4 TO 8

___

1 lemon, halved crosswise

4 medium artichokes
(7 to 8 ounces each)

1 head garlic, top third
cut off and discarded

Kosher salt and ground
black pepper

1 large egg

6 ounces crusty bread,
torn into ½-inch pieces
(about 4 cups)

2 ounces prosciutto
OR pancetta, chopped

2 ounces fontina cheese,
shredded (½ cup)

1 cup lightly packed fresh
mint **OR** basil, chopped

¼ cup extra-virgin olive oil,
plus more to serve

Don't prep the artichokes until you are ready to cook them. Once cut, artichokes oxidize quickly. Squeezing lemon juice onto the cut surfaces slows the discoloration, so be sure to have a lemon half close by. When prepping the artichokes, don't remove the stems, which turn succulent and sweet with cooking. Simply trim off the cut ends, peel off the outer layer and squeeze on some lemon juice to slow the browning.

1. **Heat the oven to 375°F** with a rack in the middle position. In a large roasting pan, combine 4 cups water and ¾ teaspoon salt, then squeeze in some of the juice from 1 of the lemon halves. Working with one artichoke at a time, use scissors to trim off the thorny tips from the petals, then pull off and discard any bruised outer petals. Trim and peel the stem. Using a chef's knife, halve the artichoke lengthwise, then squeeze some lemon juice from the same lemon half onto the cut surfaces. Using a spoon, dig out and discard the fuzzy choke at the center of each half; squeeze lemon juice onto the exposed heart. Place the artichoke halves cut side down in the prepared roasting pan. Repeat with the remaining artichokes.

2. **Add the garlic head,** cut side down, to the pan. Cover tightly with foil and bake until a skewer inserted into the wide base of the artichokes meets just a little resistance, 50 to 60 minutes. Meanwhile, in a large bowl, beat the egg. Add the bread, prosciutto, fontina, mint, oil, ½ teaspoon salt and 1 teaspoon pepper; mix until well combined, then set aside.

3. **When the artichokes are done,** remove the pan from the oven and uncover. Using a wide metal spatula, flip the artichokes cut sides up; leave the garlic cut side down. Divide the bread mixture evenly among the artichoke halves, packing it in. Return the pan to the oven, uncovered, and bake until the filling is golden brown, about 30 minutes; there should be about 1 cup water remaining in the pan.

4. **Transfer the artichokes** to a platter, squeeze on the juice from the remaining lemon half and drizzle with additional oil. Squeeze the garlic cloves from the head into the liquid remaining in the roasting pan and, using a fork, mash and mix with the liquid to make a sauce. Taste and season with salt and pepper, transfer to a small bowl and serve with the artichokes.

Roasted Cauliflower
with Miso Glaze

This recipe—inspired by a dish at Fujisaki, a Japanese restaurant along the Sydney waterfront—coats chunks of cauliflower with a thick, miso-based glaze that is sweet and savory. We roast the cauliflower before tossing the richly browned florets with miso blended with vinegar and ginger, then top it with toasted pistachios, scallions and cilantro. The result is fresh, warm and rich.

START TO FINISH: 30 MINUTES
SERVINGS: 4

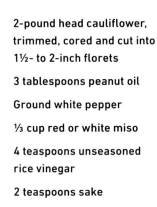

2-pound head cauliflower, trimmed, cored and cut into 1½- to 2-inch florets

3 tablespoons peanut oil

Ground white pepper

⅓ cup red or white miso

4 teaspoons unseasoned rice vinegar

2 teaspoons sake

1 teaspoon honey

1 teaspoon finely grated fresh ginger

¼ cup shelled roasted pistachios, chopped

1 bunch scallions, thinly sliced

¼ cup chopped fresh cilantro

Don't forget to heat the baking sheet while preparing the cauliflower. A heated baking sheet—along with allowing the cauliflower to roast without stirring—ensures flavor-building caramelization.

1. Heat the oven to 500°F with a rack in the lowest position. Line a rimmed baking sheet with foil and place the baking sheet in the oven.

2. Place the cauliflower in a large bowl. Add the oil and ¼ teaspoon pepper, then toss to coat. When the oven is at temperature, quickly remove the baking sheet and distribute the cauliflower in an even layer; reserve the bowl. Roast until the cauliflower is just tender and browned in spots, 15 to 18 minutes; do not stir.

3. Meanwhile, in the reserved bowl, whisk together the miso, vinegar, sake, honey, ginger and 2 tablespoons water. As soon as the cauliflower is done, transfer to the bowl with the miso mixture and gently toss. Carefully stir in the pistachios, scallions and cilantro. Transfer to a serving platter.

1 tablespoon
coriander seeds

1 tablespoon cumin seeds

Two 1-pound globe or
Italian eggplants, trimmed

6 tablespoons
extra-virgin olive oil

¼ cup harissa paste

¼ cup cider vinegar

3 tablespoons honey

1 medium garlic clove,
finely grated

¼ cup finely chopped
fresh mint

3 tablespoons finely
chopped fresh dill, divided

Kosher salt and ground
black pepper

Don't allow the eggplant to cool *before tossing it with the harissa mixture. As they cool, the chunks absorb the flavorings. Allow the mixture to stand for at least 10 minutes before serving.*

1. In a small skillet over medium, toast the coriander and cumin, shaking the pan, until fragrant, about 2 minutes. Transfer to a spice grinder and let cool slightly, then pulse until coarsely ground; set aside.

2. Heat the oven to broil with a rack about 6 inches from the element. Line a broiler-safe rimmed baking sheet with foil and mist with cooking spray. Cut each eggplant crosswise into 1½-inch-thick rounds, then cut each round into 1½-inch cubes. In a large bowl, toss the eggplant with the oil to coat. Distribute in an even layer on the prepared baking sheet; reserve the bowl. Broil without stirring until tender and lightly charred on top, 10 to 12 minutes.

3. Meanwhile, in the reserved bowl, whisk together the harissa, vinegar, honey, garlic, mint, 2 tablespoons of dill and the coriander and cumin. When the eggplant is done, immediately add it to the bowl, then gently toss to combine. Taste and season with salt and pepper. Let stand for 10 minutes. Transfer to a serving platter and sprinkle with the remaining 1 tablespoon dill.

Spicy Egyptian Eggplant with Fresh Herbs

The inspiration for this recipe was btingan mekhalel, a spicy, vinegary deep-fried eggplant dish sold by street vendors in Cairo. We made a lighter, easier oven-friendly version of the dish. But because broilers vary in heat output, check the eggplant for doneness after 10 minutes. For the same reason, it also may need longer than called for. The pieces should be tender and lightly charred, but not falling apart. Harissa is a North African red pepper paste seasoned with spices and other ingredients; our favorite brand is DEA, which usually is sold in a yellow tube. Serve warm or at room temperature.

Oven-Crisped Smashed Potatoes with Cilantro-Yogurt Hot Sauce

These potatoes are browned and crisp on the outside, and dense and creamy on the inside. To get that perfect contrast in texture, we first boil whole fingerlings or small Yukon Golds until tender, then flatten them until they split open, brush them with oil and roast them in a hot oven. It's a multistep process, but it requires only about 25 minutes of active time—and is well worth the effort. The spicy cilantro and yogurt accompaniment is a version of the Somali hot sauce called basbaas, and is made simply by pureeing the ingredients in a blender.

START TO FINISH: 1¼ HOURS (25 MINUTES ACTIVE)
SERVINGS: 4 TO 6

2½ pounds fingerling potatoes OR small (1- to 1½-inch) Yukon Gold potatoes, scrubbed

Kosher salt and ground black pepper

1 cup lightly packed fresh cilantro

½ cup plain whole-milk Greek yogurt

2 or 3 serrano OR jalapeño OR Fresno chilies, stemmed, seeded and roughly chopped

1 medium garlic clove, smashed and peeled

3 tablespoons lime juice OR lemon juice

1 tablespoon white vinegar

3 tablespoons grapeseed or other neutral oil

½ teaspoon ground ginger

Don't let the potatoes cool completely before smashing. They are easier to flatten and they hold their shape better when warm.

1. **Heat the oven to 500°F** with a rack in the middle position. In a large pot over high, bring 2 quarts water to boil. Add the potatoes and ½ cup salt, then cook, uncovered and stirring occasionally, until a skewer inserted into the largest potato meets no resistance, 18 to 22 minutes.

2. **Meanwhile, in a blender,** puree the cilantro, yogurt, chilies, garlic, lime juice and vinegar until smooth and bright green, about 1 minute. Season to taste with salt; set aside.

3. **Using a slotted spoon,** transfer the potatoes to a wire rack set in a rimmed baking sheet. Cool for about 10 minutes. In a small bowl, stir together the oil, ground ginger and ½ teaspoon pepper.

4. **Remove the rack** from the baking sheet. Wipe away any moisture on the baking sheet and place the potatoes in an even layer directly on the sheet. Using the bottom of a dry measuring cup or ramekin, press down on each potato so it is slightly flattened and splits open but remains intact. Brush the tops of the potatoes with the oil mixture, dividing it evenly.

5. **Roast the potatoes** without turning them until browned and crisp, 35 to 40 minutes. Using a wide metal spatula, transfer to a serving platter. Drizzle half of the cilantro-yogurt sauce over the potatoes. Pour the remaining sauce into a small bowl and serve on the side.

Optional garnish: Unsweetened shredded coconut, toasted

Roasted Acorn Squash with Orange-Herb Salad and Hazelnuts

With its green skin, golden-orange flesh and unique scalloped exterior, roasted acorn squash makes for an especially attractive autumnal dish. We like to use a very hot oven so the slices develop flavorful caramelization while becoming tender and creamy. A leafy bed of fresh herbs and greens tossed with orange segments and toasted hazelnuts is a perfect complement to the earthy, sweet squash. When prepping the oranges, be sure to reserve the juice, as you'll need 3 tablespoons to make the vinaigrette.

START TO FINISH: 45 MINUTES
SERVINGS: 4 TO 6

1½- to 2-pound acorn squash, halved lengthwise, seeded and sliced into 1-inch-thick half rings

2 tablespoons plus ⅓ cup extra-virgin olive oil, divided

Kosher salt and ground black pepper

2 navel oranges

2 tablespoons white wine vinegar

½ cup hazelnuts, toasted, skinned and chopped

1 cup lightly packed fresh flat-leaf parsley

1 cup lightly packed fresh mint

2 cups lightly packed baby arugula **OR** mesclun

Don't empty the salad onto the serving platter by tipping it out of the bowl. Use tongs to transfer it so that excess dressing remains in the bowl for tossing with the roasted squash before the slices are placed on top of the greens.

1. **Heat the oven to 475°F** with a rack in the middle position. Mist a rimmed baking sheet with cooking spray. Place the squash on the prepared baking sheet and toss with the 2 tablespoons oil and ½ teaspoon each salt and pepper. Distribute in an even layer and roast until a skewer inserted into a piece meets no resistance and the bottoms are nicely browned, 25 to 30 minutes.

2. **Meanwhile, grate 1 teaspoon zest** from 1 of the oranges; set aside. Using a sharp knife, slice off the top and bottom ½ inch from each orange. One at a time, stand the oranges on a cut end and cut from top to bottom following the contours of the fruit to remove the peel and white pith. Hold each orange over a large bowl and cut between the membranes to release the segments, allowing the juices to fall into the bowl; set the orange segments aside. Once all of the segments have been cut free, squeeze the juice from the membranes into the bowl; discard the membranes. You should have about 3 tablespoons orange juice.

3. **When the squash is done,** to the orange juice in the bowl, whisk in the orange zest, vinegar, remaining ⅓ cup oil, half of the hazelnuts, ½ teaspoon salt and ¼ teaspoon pepper. Add the parsley, mint, arugula and orange slices. Toss with tongs to combine, then taste and season with salt and pepper. Using the tongs, transfer the salad to a serving platter. To the dressing remaining in the bowl, add the squash and toss to coat. Place on top of the salad and sprinkle with the remaining hazelnuts.

Mashed Butternut Squash with Cumin and Chili

In this recipe, we balance the sweet, nutty flavor of butternut squash with earthy cumin and spicy, smoky chili. Rather than steam or boil the squash, we roast it in a moderately hot oven to caramelize some of the sugars and concentrate the flavors, and we toss raw pumpkin seeds onto the baking sheet midway through to add a little richness and texture. If you have only toasted pumpkin seeds on hand, instead of adding them to the squash in the oven, fold them in after the squash is mashed. Crema is a tangy Mexican cultured cream similar to sour cream but more pourable in consistency. If using sour cream, stir the lime juice into it before adding it to the squash prior to mashing.

2- to 2½-pound butternut squash, peeled, seeded and cut into 1½-inch chunks

2 tablespoons extra-virgin olive oil, plus more to serve

¾ teaspoon ancho powder **OR** chipotle chili powder, divided

½ teaspoon ground cumin

Kosher salt and ground black pepper

¼ cup raw pumpkin seeds (see headnote)

1 teaspoon grated lime zest, plus 2 teaspoons lime juice

2 tablespoons Mexican crema **OR** sour cream, plus more to serve

1 tablespoon chopped fresh cilantro

Don't skip the foil lining for the baking sheet. Without the foil, the squash has a tendency to stick and burn, and the burnt bits end up tough and stringy. Also, for the best texture, be sure to mash the squash straight out of the oven, while it's still hot.

1. **Heat the oven to 425°F** with a rack in the middle position. Line a rimmed baking sheet with foil. In a large bowl, toss the squash with the oil, ½ teaspoon chili powder, the cumin and ½ teaspoon salt. Distribute in an even layer on the prepared baking sheet; reserve the bowl. Roast for 25 minutes; the pieces will be lightly browned but not yet tender.

2. **Add the pumpkin seeds** to the baking sheet, stir to combine, then roast until the squash is well browned and a skewer inserted into the largest pieces meets no resistance, another 12 to 17 minutes.

3. **Return the squash mixture** to the bowl. Add the lime juice, crema, the remaining ¼ teaspoon chili powder and ¼ teaspoon pepper. Using a potato masher or large spoon, mix and mash to a coarse puree. Taste and season with salt. Transfer to a serving bowl, drizzle with additional crema and oil, then sprinkle with the cilantro and lime zest

Optional garnish: Crumbled queso fresco **OR** crumbled cotija cheese **OR** flaky salt

Spaghetti Squash with Lemon, Cream and Herbs

Spaghetti squash is a mildly flavored late summer to early fall variety with flesh that, as the name suggests, can be raked apart into long, spaghetti-like strands after cooking. In a recipe from "Root to Leaf," Atlanta chef Steven Satterfield tosses roasted spaghetti squash with a light, creamy herb sauce. Not only did we riff on his combination of ingredients, we learned that halving the squash crosswise instead of lengthwise will yield the longest, most spaghetti-like strands because the fibers grow in a spiral around the seedy core of the squash. We think pumpkin seeds and sage leaves toasted in butter are perfect flavor and textural accents for this autumnal dish.

START TO FINISH: 1¼ HOURS (25 MINUTES ACTIVE)
SERVINGS: 4

___

2½-pound spaghetti squash, halved crosswise and seeded

Kosher salt and ground black pepper

4 tablespoons salted butter, cut into 1-tablespoon pieces, 1 tablespoon softened

6 thyme sprigs OR 2 rosemary sprigs

¼ cup lightly packed fresh sage

2 tablespoons pumpkin seeds

1 medium garlic clove, minced

1 cup heavy cream

⅛ teaspoon freshly grated nutmeg

½ cup lightly packed fresh flat-leaf parsley, chopped

1 teaspoon grated lemon zest, plus 2 tablespoons lemon juice

Don't halve the squash lengthwise, as directed in most recipes. You'll get the longest spaghetti-like strands if the squash is cut crosswise. Also, be sure to remove the skillet from the heat while you remove some of the pumpkin seeds and sage so there's little risk of scorching.

1. **Heat the oven to 400°F** with a rack in the lower-middle position. Rub the cut sides and cavity of the squash halves with the 1 tablespoon softened butter, then season with salt and pepper. Place the squash halves cut sides down in a 9-by-13-inch baking dish. Add ¾ cup water and the thyme sprigs, then bake until the squash yields when pressed firmly and the flesh easily pulls away from the skin, 35 to 45 minutes. Remove from the oven and set aside until the squash is cool enough to handle.

2. **Using a fork,** scrape the flesh of each squash half, working around the circumference to loosen the flesh into spaghetti-like strands. Return the flesh to the baking dish and toss with any remaining liquid. Discard the skins and thyme sprigs.

3. **In a 12-inch skillet over medium,** melt the remaining 3 tablespoons butter. Add the sage and pumpkin seeds; cook, stirring occasionally, until the butter, seeds and sage are fragrant and lightly browned, 1 to 2 minutes. Remove the pan from the heat and, using a slotted spoon, transfer about half the sage and seeds to a paper towel–lined plate.

4. **To the remaining sage and seeds** in the skillet, add the garlic, cream, nutmeg and ¼ teaspoon each salt and pepper. Bring to a boil over medium-high, stirring, then add the squash. Cook, gently stirring and tossing, until the cream thickens and clings to the squash strands, 2 to 4 minutes.

5. **Off heat,** stir in half of the parsley, the lemon zest and juice, then taste and season with salt and pepper. Transfer to a serving dish and sprinkle with the remaining parsley and the reserved sage and pumpkin seeds.

Optional garnishes: Finely grated Parmesan cheese **OR** red pepper flakes **OR** both

2 tablespoons finely chopped toasted hazelnuts, divided

1 tablespoon coriander seeds, lightly crushed

1 medium garlic clove, finely grated

1 teaspoon grated grapefruit **OR** lemon zest, plus ¼ cup grapefruit **OR** lemon juice

Kosher salt and ground black pepper

4 tablespoons salted butter, cut into 1-tablespoon pieces and softened

2-pound head savoy **OR** napa cabbage, tough outer leaves removed, quartered

2 tablespoons whole-grain mustard **OR** Dijon mustard

2 teaspoons honey

2 tablespoons chopped fresh tarragon **OR** fresh chives **OR** fresh flat-leaf parsley **OR** a combination

Don't forget to allow the butter to soften. If cold and firm, the butter cannot be rubbed onto the surfaces and in between the layers of the cabbage wedges.

1. **Heat the oven to 475°F** with a rack in the middle position. Line a rimmed baking sheet with foil. In a small bowl, stir together half of the hazelnuts, the coriander, garlic, zest and ¾ teaspoon each salt and pepper.

2. **Using your hands** and 1 tablespoon of butter per cabbage wedge, rub the butter on all sides and into the layers of the cabbage. Sprinkle the wedges evenly with the spice mixture, rubbing it in to adhere; reserve the bowl. Place the cabbage wedges cut-side down on the prepared baking sheet. Cover tightly with foil and roast until a skewer inserted at the thickest part of the cabbage meets a little resistance, 20 to 30 minutes.

3. **Uncover the baking sheet and roast** until the cabbage is deeply browned on all sides, another 15 minutes, flipping the wedges with a wide metal spatula about halfway through. Meanwhile, in the reserved bowl, whisk together the grapefruit juice, mustard, honey, ½ teaspoon salt and ¼ teaspoon pepper; set aside.

4. **Transfer the cabbage** to a cutting board, then trim out and discard the core from each wedge. Place the wedges on a platter and drizzle each wedge with 1 tablespoon of the sauce. Sprinkle with the remaining hazelnuts and the tarragon. Serve with the remaining sauce on the side.

Butter-Roasted Cabbage with Citrus, Hazelnuts and Mustard

An amazingly delicious wood fire-roasted cabbage at Firedoor restaurant in Sydney, Australia, inspired us to do something similar, albeit in a conventional oven, and transform a humble vegetable into something special. We rub wedges of cabbage with butter and sprinkle them with a fragrant combination of hazelnuts, citrus zest, garlic and coriander. As they roast, the exterior leaves become deeply browned and crispy, while the interior remains silky, sweet and tender. A bright, citrusy dressing completes the dish. Be sure to use savoy cabbage rather than regular green cabbage; the frilly leaves cook up with better texture and flavor. Serve this as an accompaniment to roasted meats, or serve with creamy beans and sausage for a weeknight meal.

Sesame and Cumin Roasted Green Beans with Tahini Sauce

Roasting coaxes the sweetness out of green beans and develops caramelized flavors in a way that steaming and blanching cannot. Here, drawing inspiration from a recipe by Eddie Hernandez and Susan Puckett, we toss beans with sesame and cumin seeds before roasting, then pile the lightly charred beans on top of a tahini sauce that's bright with lemon and garlic. Keep an eye on the beans as they roast, as they can go from perfectly tender-crisp to mushy quickly.

START TO FINISH: 30 MINUTES
SERVINGS: 4

2 tablespoons lemon juice

1 medium garlic clove, finely grated

1 pound green beans, trimmed

1 tablespoon grapeseed or other neutral oil

1 tablespoon sesame seeds

2 teaspoons cumin seeds

Kosher salt and ground black pepper

¼ cup tahini

2 tablespoons extra-virgin olive oil

⅓ cup lightly packed fresh cilantro, chopped

Don't bother stirring the beans as they roast. They'll brown more deeply if they're left alone, and as long as they're spread in an even layer, they'll cook evenly.

1. **Heat the oven to 450°F** with a rack in the middle position. In a small bowl, stir together the lemon juice and garlic; let stand for about 10 minutes.

2. **In a large bowl,** toss the beans with the neutral oil, sesame seeds, cumin seeds and ½ teaspoon each salt and pepper. Distribute in an even layer on a rimmed baking sheet and roast until the beans are tender-crisp and well browned, 12 to 15 minutes.

3. **When the beans are almost done,** whisk the tahini and olive oil into the lemon-garlic mixture, then add 3 tablespoons water and whisk until smooth. Taste and season with salt and pepper. Spread the tahini sauce onto a serving platter.

4. **Remove the green beans** from the oven and transfer to the platter on top of the sauce. Sprinkle with the cilantro.

Slow-Roasted Fennel and Red Onions with Tahini and Spices

Slow-roasting fennel and onions is one of the best ways to coax out their inherent sweetness. We start them in a covered baking dish, mixed with olive oil, tahini and seasonings, as well as water that creates steam to help them tenderize. They finish roasting uncovered to cook off any remaining moisture and develop deep, rich, flavorful caramelization. The vegetables are delicious warm or even at room temperature (but hold off adding the mint until ready to serve).

START TO FINISH: 1¾ HOURS (15 MINUTES ACTIVE)
SERVINGS: 4 TO 6

⅓ cup extra-virgin olive oil

2 tablespoons tahini

1½ teaspoons ground cumin

1 teaspoon hot paprika
OR 1¾ teaspoons sweet paprika, plus ¼ teaspoon cayenne pepper

1 teaspoon ground coriander

½ teaspoon ground cinnamon

1 tablespoon grated lemon zest, plus 2 tablespoons lemon juice

Kosher salt and ground black pepper

2 large fennel bulbs, trimmed, halved lengthwise and cut into 1-inch wedges

2 medium red onions, sliced into ½-inch rounds

1 cup lightly packed fresh mint, chopped

Don't separate the layers after slicing the onion. It's fine if a few rings separate, but try to keep the rounds mostly intact. Also, be sure to cover the baking dish tightly with foil to prevent steam from escaping too quickly.

1. **Heat the oven to 450°F** with a rack in the middle position. In a 9-by-13-inch baking pan, stir together the oil, tahini, cumin, paprika, coriander, cinnamon, lemon juice, 1 teaspoon salt, 2 teaspoons pepper and ½ cup water. Add the fennel and onions; toss until well coated, then distribute in an even layer, making sure the onions are evenly dispersed amongst the fennel wedges. Cover tightly with foil and bake for 1 hour.

2. **Uncover and bake** until the liquid has cooked off and the vegetables are browned and very tender, about another 15 minutes. Cool on a wire rack for about 15 minutes. Sprinkle the lemon zest and mint over the top and serve.

Optional garnish: Chopped fennel fronds

Sesame and Soy-Glazed Roasted Celery Root

Celery root—also known as celeriac—has a parsnip-like texture and mild celery-like flavor. At the grocery story, look for firm 1-pound roots that are evenly round and not too knobby; the knobs make peeling off the tough skin more challenging. Though often served raw, celery root becomes soft and tender when roasted, and browning develops sweet, nutty notes. For this recipe, we cut the roots into wedges for relatively fast, even cooking and amp up the flavor with a glaze containing mirin, sugar, soy and sesame oil. But we hold off on brushing the wedges until midway through roasting to prevent scorching.

START TO FINISH: 1 HOUR 10 MINUTES
(35 MINUTES ACTIVE)
SERVINGS: 4

Two 1-pound celery roots, peeled, each cut into 4 wedges

2 tablespoons grapeseed or other neutral oil

Kosher salt and ground black pepper

2 tablespoons toasted sesame oil, plus more to serve

2 tablespoons soy sauce

1 tablespoon plus 1 teaspoon white sugar OR packed brown sugar

1 tablespoon mirin

2 teaspoons lemon juice

1 medium garlic clove, finely grated

2 teaspoons sesame seeds, toasted

Don't forget to flip the celery root often during the second half of the roasting time, reapplying glaze each time so the wedges are evenly coated all over. Some of the glaze may collect on the baking sheet and burn, but the celery root itself will be perfectly roasted.

1. **Heat the oven to 425°F** with a rack in the middle position. Line a rimmed baking sheet with foil and mist with cooking spray. On the prepared baking sheet, toss the celery root wedges with the grapeseed oil, ½ teaspoon salt and ¼ teaspoon pepper. Roast until the wedges are lightly browned and a skewer inserted into the center meets a little resistance, about 20 minutes.

2. **Meanwhile, in a small bowl,** combine the sesame oil, soy sauce, sugar, mirin, lemon juice, garlic and ¼ teaspoon pepper. Stir until the sugar dissolves; set aside.

3. **Brush the celery root all over** with about 2 tablespoons of the sesame-soy mixture and continue to roast, flipping the wedges and brushing them with the sesame-soy mixture every 10 minutes or so, until deeply browned and a skewer inserted into the centers meets no resistance, 25 to 35 minutes. Transfer the celery root to a platter. Drizzle any remaining sesame-soy mixture over the top and sprinkle with the sesame seeds.

Optional garnish: Shichimi togarashi **OR** scallions, thinly sliced on the diagonal **OR** both

Spiced Sweet Potato Tian

When you prepare sweet potatoes like this, you get the best of both worlds: tender, buttery rounds of flesh with crisped, browned edges. To balance the natural sweetness of the potatoes, we toss the slices with vinegar, spices and red pepper flakes, then tuck sliced shallot and sage or rosemary leaves in between the layers. Sweet potatoes can vary greatly in size. Try to choose medium-sized ones of about the same diameter so the slices fit neatly in the pie plate. The quickest way to slice the potatoes is with a mandoline—aim for slices about ⅛-inch thick. Serve this with a pork roast or pork chops, or alongside the roasted turkey on the Thanksgiving table.

START TO FINISH: 1 HOUR 20 MINUTES
(20 MINUTES ACTIVE), PLUS COOLING
SERVINGS: 4 TO 6

4 tablespoons salted butter, melted

2 tablespoons extra-virgin olive oil

1 tablespoon cider vinegar **OR** lime juice

½ teaspoon ground coriander **OR** ground cumin **OR** both

½ teaspoon red pepper flakes

2½ pounds medium orange-flesh sweet potatoes, peeled and sliced into ⅛-inch rounds

Kosher salt and ground black pepper

1 medium shallot, sliced into thin rings

⅓ cup lightly packed fresh sage **OR** rosemary

Maple syrup **OR** honey, to serve (optional)

Don't worry if you don't have a mandoline—you can slice the potatoes by hand. Just try to keep the slices thin and even, no thicker than ¼ inch, or they will take longer in the oven.

1. **Heat the oven to 450°F** with a rack in the middle position. In a small bowl, stir together the melted butter, oil, vinegar, coriander and red pepper flakes. Brush half of this mixture on the bottom and sides of a 9-inch deep-dish pie plate. Arrange the potatoes in 2 concentric rings in the pie plate, shingling and tightly packing the slices.

2. **Sprinkle with salt and black pepper,** then tuck the shallot slices and sage leaves between the potato slices. Drizzle with the remaining butter mixture. Cover tightly with foil and bake until a skewer inserted into the center of the potatoes meets just a little resistance, about 40 minutes.

3. **Uncover and bake** until the potatoes are lightly browned and the edges are beginning to crisp and char, another 15 to 20 minutes. Cool on a wire rack for 10 minutes. If desired, drizzle with maple syrup just before serving.

Roasted Rutabaga and Pears with Browned Butter, Honey and Rosemary

The sturdy, purple-shouldered root vegetable known as rutabaga also goes by the name swede or yellow turnip. Its interior is yellow-orange and its flavor earthy-sweet. Oven-roasting these roots is an easy way to render them tender on the inside and caramelized on the exterior. We pair rutabaga with piney rosemary and ripe but firm pears, adding the fruit about two-thirds into roasting so they become tender but not overdone. Nutty browned butter with honey and vinegar swirled in dresses the mixture for a sweet-tart finish.

START TO FINISH: 45 MINUTES
SERVINGS: 6

———

5 tablespoons salted butter

4 teaspoons minced fresh rosemary, divided

Kosher salt and ground black pepper

1½ pounds rutabaga, peeled and cut into 1-inch cubes

2 ripe but firm Bosc pears (about 1 pound), unpeeled, quartered, cored and cut into 1-inch pieces

1 tablespoon honey, plus more to serve (optional)

1 teaspoon sherry vinegar OR cider vinegar OR white wine vinegar

Don't confuse rutabagas with turnips. They're very different in both flavor and size. Whereas turnips are spicy and punchy like radishes and measure just a few inches in diameter, rutabagas are mild and sweet and often are larger than a softball.

1. **Heat the oven to 475°F** with a rack in the middle position. Mist a rimmed baking sheet with cooking spray. In a small saucepan over medium, melt the butter; remove from the heat and set aside.

2. **In a large bowl,** stir together 3 teaspoons of rosemary, ½ teaspoon each salt and pepper and 2 tablespoons of melted butter. Add the rutabaga and toss to coat, then distribute in an even layer on the prepared baking sheet; reserve the bowl. Roast the rutabaga for 20 minutes.

3. **Meanwhile, in the same bowl,** toss the pears with 1 tablespoon of the remaining melted butter; set aside. Set the pan with the remaining 2 tablespoons melted butter over medium and cook the butter, occasionally swirling the pan, until the milk solids at the bottom are golden brown and the butter has a nutty aroma, about 1 minute. Off heat, whisk in the remaining 1 teaspoon rosemary, the honey, vinegar and ¼ teaspoon each salt and pepper; cover and set aside.

4. **When the rutabaga has roasted for 20 minutes,** add the pears to the baking sheet and toss to combine with the rutabaga. Roast until a skewer inserted into the rutabaga and pears meets no resistance and the rutabaga is well browned, 10 to 12 minutes; stir once about halfway through.

5. **Remove the baking sheet** from the oven, immediately drizzle the rutabaga and pears with the browned butter mixture and toss to coat. Taste and season with salt and pepper, then transfer to a serving dish. If desired, drizzle with additional honey.

7

STIR-FRIES

⅓ cup low-sodium soy sauce

2 to 3 tablespoons chili-bean sauce (toban djan, see headnote)

2 tablespoons toasted sesame oil

14-ounce container firm OR extra-firm tofu, drained, halved lengthwise, cut crosswise into ½-inch-thick slices and pressed dry

3 tablespoons grapeseed or other neutral oil

1 pound Broccolini, trimmed and cut into 1- to 2-inch pieces

⅓ cup lightly packed fresh cilantro

Don't use medium firm tofu, as it's too delicate. Firm or extra-firm are the best options. After slicing the tofu, press the slices between paper towels to wick away excess moisture. Finally, when adding the tofu to the skillet, don't simply dump it in with the marinade. Rather, lift out the slices and place them in a single layer in the pan; reserve the marinade for cooking the Broccolini.

1. **In a large bowl,** stir together the soy sauce, chili-bean sauce and sesame oil. Add the tofu and toss to coat. In a 12-inch nonstick skillet over medium-high, heat 1 tablespoon of the neutral oil until barely smoking. Remove the tofu from the bowl and place the slices in the skillet in a single layer; reserve the marinade. Cook the tofu, turning the pieces once with tongs or a metal spatula, until well browned on both sides, about 3 minutes per side. Transfer to a serving platter and wipe out the skillet.

2. **In the same skillet** over medium-high, heat the remaining 2 tablespoons neutral oil until shimmering. Add the Broccolini and cook, stirring occasionally, until beginning to char, 3 to 4 minutes. Stir in ¼ cup water and the reserved marinade, then immediately cover and reduce to low. Cook, stirring once or twice, until the Broccolini is tender-crisp and the sauce is slightly thickened, about 4 minutes. Transfer the Broccolini with sauce onto the tofu and sprinkle with the cilantro.

Optional garnish: Toasted sesame seeds **OR** chili oil **OR** both

Spicy Broccolini with Seared Tofu and Sesame Oil

This hearty vegetarian main gets its spicy-salty earthiness from chili-bean sauce, or toban djan, a common ingredient in Sichuan cooking. The brownish red sauce is sold in jars; if it's not available, approximate the flavor by mixing 2 tablespoons red miso with 1 tablespoon Asian chili-garlic sauce. We use a sear-then-steam skillet technique to cook the Broccolini here; it builds flavor with browning but also allows the vegetable to cook up succulently crisp-tender. Serve with steamed rice.

Corn with Shrimp, Chilies and Scallions

This is our rendition of Vietnamese bắp xào tôm khô, or stir-fried corn with dried shrimp. Instead of dried shrimp, we add cooked fresh shrimp, which are easier to source and make the dish more substantial. Complementary flavors—salty, sweet, savory, spicy, rich and tangy—are what make this dish a standout. Make a light meal of it by serving with steamed jasmine rice.

START TO FINISH: 25 MINUTES
SERVINGS: 4

————

2 tablespoons grapeseed or other neutral oil

4 cups fresh corn kernels (from about 5 ears corn) **OR** thawed frozen corn kernels, patted dry

12 ounces cooked shelled shrimp, roughly chopped

2 Fresno **OR** jalapeño chilies, stemmed, seeded and chopped

2 tablespoons salted butter, cut into 2 pieces

2 tablespoons fish sauce **OR** soy sauce

1 bunch scallions, thinly sliced on the diagonal

1 tablespoon lime juice

Kosher salt and ground black pepper

Don't forget to thaw and pat dry the corn if using frozen. Removing excess moisture reduces splatter and also helps ensure the kernels char instead of steam when they hit the hot skillet.

1. In a 12-inch nonstick skillet over medium-high, heat the oil until barely smoking. Add the corn and cook, stirring occasionally, until it begins to char, 6 to 7 minutes.

2. Add the shrimp, chilies and butter, then cook, stirring, until the shrimp are heated through and the butter is melted, 1 to 2 minutes. Off heat, stir in the fish sauce, scallions and lime juice. Taste and season with salt and pepper.

Indian Carrot Stir-Fry

This spicy, fragrant and flavorful stir-fry is our adaptation of a recipe from "Five Morsels of Love" by Archana Pidathala. The natural sweetness of carrots is balanced by the savoriness of garlic, cumin, curry leaves and cilantro, while fresh chilies add clear, crisp heat. Curry leaves are completely unrelated to curry powder. Quite thick and leathery, they vaguely resemble fresh bay, but their pungent flavor and aroma are unique, with hints of citrus, spice and even browned garlic. The leaves are sold fresh or frozen in Indian grocery stores; if they're not available, not to worry—there is no substitute for them, but the stir-fry is delicious even made without. If you wish to temper the dish's spicy heat, remove the seeds from the chilies before chopping them.

START TO FINISH: 30 MINUTES
SERVINGS: 4

_____

¼ cup wide-flake unsweetened coconut

2 tablespoons ghee **OR** neutral oil

1½ pounds medium carrots (about 8 carrots), peeled and sliced ¼ inch thick on the diagonal

Kosher salt

20 curry leaves (optional, see headnote)

6 medium garlic cloves, finely grated

1½ teaspoons cumin seeds

1 or 2 Fresno **OR** serrano chilies, stemmed and finely chopped

1 tablespoon grated lime zest, plus 1 tablespoon lime juice

½ cup lightly packed fresh cilantro leaves

Don't use extra-large or super-slender carrots. Medium carrots cut on the diagonal yield pieces of just the right size. Also, as with all stir-fries, the cooking here goes quickly, so make sure all ingredients are prepped before you head to the stove.

1. **In a 12-inch skillet over medium,** toast the coconut, stirring often, until golden brown, about 4 minutes. Transfer to a small bowl and set aside.

2. **In the same skillet over high,** heat the ghee until barely smoking. Add the carrots and ½ teaspoon salt, then cook, stirring only once or twice, until beginning to char at the edges, 3 to 5 minutes. Reduce to medium-high and add the curry leaves (if using), garlic, cumin seeds and chilies. Cook, stirring, until fragrant, about 1 minute. Add 2 tablespoons water and cook, stirring constantly and scraping up any browned bits, until the liquid has evaporated and the carrots are tender-crisp, 1 to 3 minutes.

3. **Remove the pan from the heat.** Remove and discard the curry leaves. Taste and season with salt, then stir in the lime zest and juice, cilantro and toasted coconut.

Ginger-Shiitake Celery Stir-Fry

START TO FINISH: 30 MINUTES
SERVINGS: 4

Stir-frying slightly mellows the unique flavor and snappy texture of celery. Here, the oft-overlooked vegetable partners perfectly with nutty sesame oil, peppery ginger and the umami notes of soy sauce and shiitake mushrooms. Chinese chili-bean sauce, or toban djan, is a spicy, salty fermented mixture of soybeans, broad beans and chilies that gives this stir-fry lots of character; it's sold in jars in Asian grocery stores and in the international aisle of some supermarkets. If not available, use an equal amount of chili-garlic sauce; its sharper, more garlicky flavor gives the dish a slightly different, but still delicious, taste profile.

2 tablespoons unseasoned rice vinegar

1 tablespoon chili-bean sauce (toban djan) **OR** chili-garlic sauce (see headnote)

1 tablespoon low-sodium soy sauce

1 tablespoon toasted sesame oil, plus more to serve

½ teaspoon ground white pepper

3 tablespoons grapeseed or other neutral oil

8 ounces shiitake mushrooms, stemmed, caps thinly sliced

1½-inch piece fresh ginger, peeled, quartered lengthwise and thinly sliced

1 bunch scallions, thinly sliced, white and green parts reserved separately

2 pounds celery, stalks halved lengthwise and sliced ⅛ inch thick on the diagonal

Don't forget to reserve the scallion whites and greens separately, as they are added at different times in the recipe. Also, don't use regular soy sauce, especially if using chili-bean paste; both are high in sodium, and the combination may make the dish too salty (chili-garlic sauce is less salty than chili-bean paste, so if using it, regular soy sauce is fine).

1. **In a small bowl,** stir together the vinegar, chili-bean sauce, soy sauce, sesame oil, white pepper and ¼ cup water; set aside. In a 12-inch skillet over medium-high, heat the grapeseed oil until shimmering. Add the mushrooms and cook, stirring occasionally, until beginning to brown, 4 to 6 minutes.

2. **Add the ginger,** scallion whites and celery, then cook, stirring often, until the celery is crisp-tender and the ginger is golden brown, 5 to 7 minutes. Add the sauce mixture and cook, stirring, until the sauce thickens slightly and clings to the celery, 2 to 3 minutes. Transfer to a serving dish, then sprinkle with scallion greens and drizzle with additional sesame oil.

Hot and Sour Stir-Fried Cabbage

Hot and sour cabbage is a classic stir-fry that's ready in minutes. Napa cabbage is cooked hot and fast with aromatics until tender-crisp and lightly charred. Sauced with a mixture of soy sauce, vinegar and just a touch of sugar, the flavors are spicy, salty and tangy. Chinese black vinegar is made with rice and has a lightly smoky, subtly malty flavor. If not available, 1 tablespoon each of unseasoned rice vinegar and balsamic vinegar is a reasonably good substitute. For extra heat, drizzle with chili oil before serving.

2 tablespoons soy sauce

2 tablespoons Chinese black vinegar **OR** 1 tablespoon unseasoned rice vinegar plus 1 tablespoon balsamic vinegar

1 tablespoon white sugar

1 tablespoon cornstarch

Kosher salt and ground black pepper

2 tablespoons grapeseed or other neutral oil

3 árbol chilies, broken in half, seeds shaken out and discarded

1 or 2 jalapeño **OR** Fresno chilies, stemmed, seeded and thinly sliced

2 medium garlic cloves, peeled and thinly sliced

1 pound napa cabbage, sliced on the diagonal about ½ inch thick

½ medium red **OR** orange **OR** yellow bell pepper, stemmed, seeded and thinly sliced

Thinly sliced scallions, to serve

Don't forget to turn the heat to high before adding the cabbage. The vegetables should char hot and fast so they don't leach moisture that would dilute the flavors and make the stir-fry soggy. Also, be sure to stir the soy mixture before adding it to the skillet, as the cornstarch will settle to the bottom upon standing.

1. **In a small bowl,** whisk together the soy sauce, vinegar, sugar, cornstarch, ⅓ cup water and ¼ teaspoon pepper until the sugar dissolves; set aside.

2. **In a 12-inch nonstick skillet** over medium-high, combine the oil, árbol chilies, jalapeños and garlic; cook, stirring, until fragrant and lightly browned, 1 to 2 minutes. Increase to high, add the cabbage, bell pepper and a pinch of salt. Cook, stirring often and pressing the vegetables against the skillet to encourage browning, until charred at the edges and beginning to soften, about 3 minutes.

3. **Stir the soy mixture to recombine,** then stir it into the vegetables. Cook, stirring, until the cabbage is tender-crisp and the sauce has thickened, 2 to 4 minutes. Off heat, taste and season with salt and pepper. If desired, remove and discard the árbol chilies. Transfer to a serving dish and sprinkle with the scallions.

Stir-Fried Green Beans with Mustard Seeds and Chilies

For boldly aromatic green beans, we cook the vegetable in two stages, using the same pan. First they're steamed, then they're stir-fried. This technique delivers punchy, intense flavors because the parcooked beans can be stir-fried "dry" with the spices and aromatics—no additional liquid is needed to render them tender. Look for curry leaves in Indian grocery stores; if not available, not to worry—the stir-fry is delicious even made without. Serve this as part of an Indian meal, or as a light main with basmati rice alongside.

START TO FINISH: 35 MINUTES
SERVINGS: 4

_____

1 pound green beans, trimmed and cut into 2-inch pieces

Kosher salt and ground black pepper

2 tablespoons grapeseed or other neutral oil

1 teaspoon black **OR** brown mustard seeds

1 medium red onion, finely chopped

10 curry leaves (optional)

2 or 3 árbol chilies, broken in half and seeds discarded **OR** ¼ to ½ teaspoon red pepper flakes

3 medium garlic cloves, finely grated

1 teaspoon ground cumin

Don't skip the step of rinsing the green beans under cold water after cooking. This cools them down so they don't wind up soft and overcooked in the finished dish.

1. In a 12-inch skillet over medium-high, combine the green beans, 1 cup water and ¼ teaspoon salt. Bring to a simmer, cover and cook until the green beans are tender-crisp, 3 to 4 minutes. Drain the beans in a colander and rinse under running cold water until fully cooled. Drain well and dry them on a kitchen towel. Wipe out the skillet.

2. In the same skillet over medium-high, heat the oil until shimmering. Add the mustard seeds and cook, stirring, until fragrant and beginning to pop, 30 to 60 seconds. Add the onion, curry leaves (if using) and chilies, then cook, stirring often, until the onion begins to brown, 3 to 4 minutes.

3. Add the green beans, along with ½ teaspoon salt and ¼ teaspoon pepper. Cook, stirring occasionally, until the beans are tender, 2 to 3 minutes. Add the garlic and cumin, then cook, stirring, until fragrant, 30 to 60 seconds. Remove from the heat, then taste and season with salt and pepper.

Stir-Fried Chinese Broccoli with Oyster Sauce

Leafy and stemmy but with few florets, Chinese broccoli, also known as gai lan, typically is steamed or blanched before it is finished with salty-sweet oyster sauce that's been boosted with other seasonings. In this recipe we stir-fry the vegetable, separated into leaf and stem sections, so it takes on some flavorful browning. If you cannot find Chinese broccoli, broccoli rabe works well, though its flavor is more bitter. Serve as part of an Asian-inspired meal, with steamed rice alongside.

START TO FINISH: 30 MINUTES
SERVINGS: 4

————

1 pound Chinese broccoli (gai lan) **OR** broccoli rabe

¼ cup oyster sauce

2 tablespoons low-sodium soy sauce

1 teaspoon white sugar

2 tablespoons grapeseed or other neutral oil, divided

1-inch piece fresh ginger, peeled and cut into matchsticks

2 medium garlic cloves, minced

Don't forget to reserve the broccoli stems separately from the leaves. The stems need a head start on cooking, so they're added to the skillet several minutes before the leaves.

1. **If the broccoli stems** are very thick, peel them. Slice the stems ¼ inch thick on the diagonal until you reach the leafy sections. Cut the leafy sections into 1½- to 2-inch pieces; reserve separately from the sliced stems.

2. **In a small bowl,** stir together the oyster sauce, soy sauce, sugar and 1 tablespoon water; set aside. In a 12-inch nonstick skillet over medium-high, heat 1 tablespoon of oil until shimmering. Add the broccoli stems and cook, stirring occasionally, until browned and tender-crisp, 4 to 5 minutes. Add the leaves and cook, stirring, until wilted, 2 to 3 minutes. Transfer to a serving dish and wipe out the skillet.

3. **In the same skillet** over medium, heat the remaining 1 tablespoon oil until shimmering. Add the ginger and garlic and cook, stirring, until lightly browned, 1 to 2 minutes. Stir in the oyster sauce mixture; it will thicken slightly. Immediately pour the sauce over the broccoli and serve.

Optional garnish: Toasted sesame seeds

Thai Stir-Fried Spinach

This simple, bold stir-fry uses regular bunch spinach rather than the water spinach common in Thai cooking. The wilted leaves and crisp-tender stems combine for a pleasing contrast of textures. Be sure to dry the spinach well after washing (a salad spinner works well); excess water will cause splattering and popping when the spinach is added to the hot oil. We liked to serve this with steamed jasmine rice to soak up the sauce.

START TO FINISH: 20 MINUTES
SERVINGS: 4

1 tablespoon fish sauce

1 tablespoon oyster sauce

2 teaspoons white sugar

¾ teaspoon
red pepper flakes

4 tablespoons grapeseed
or other neutral oil, divided

3 tablespoons coarsely
chopped garlic

1½ pounds bunch spinach,
trimmed of bottom
1½ inches, washed and
dried well

Don't use baby spinach, which can't handle high-heat cooking and doesn't have stems to offer textural contrast. And don't allow the spinach leaves to fully wilt in the pan; some leaves should still look fairly fresh, but will continue to cook after being transferred to the bowl.

1. **In a small bowl,** whisk together the fish sauce, oyster sauce, sugar and pepper flakes until the sugar dissolves. Set aside.

2. **In a large skillet** over medium-high, heat 2 tablespoons of the oil until barely smoking. Remove the pan from the heat, add the garlic and cook, stirring, until just beginning to color, 20 to 30 seconds. Return the skillet to high and immediately add about ⅓ of the spinach. Using tongs, turn the spinach to coat with the oil and garlic. When the spinach is nearly wilted and the garlic has turned golden brown, 30 seconds or less, transfer to a large bowl. The leaves will continue to wilt but the stems should remain crisp-tender.

3. **Return the skillet** over high heat. Add 1 tablespoon of the remaining oil, swirl to coat the pan and heat until barely smoking. Add half of the remaining spinach and cook, as before, for 20 to 30 seconds. Transfer to the bowl and repeat with the remaining oil and spinach.

4. **Pour the fish sauce mixture** over the spinach and toss. Transfer to a platter and drizzle with any accumulated liquid.

Spicy Snow Peas
with Sichuan Pepper

In this simple stir-fry, Sichuan peppercorns provide their unique tongue-tingling heat while fresh chilies add a more direct spiciness. Either snow peas or snap peas work, so use whichever you prefer, and be sure to remove the strings from the pods, if present (some varieties of snap peas are stringless). The best way to grind the Sichuan peppercorns is in an electric spice grinder or with a mortar and pestle; process them as finely as possible to break down their woody, fibrous texture.

START TO FINISH: 25 MINUTES
SERVINGS: 4

2 tablespoons grapeseed or other neutral oil

1 pound snow peas **OR** sugar snap peas, trimmed, strings removed, if present

2 Fresno chilies **OR** 1 serrano chili, stemmed, seeded and sliced into thin half rings

2 medium shallots, halved and thinly sliced

1 tablespoon Sichuan peppercorns, finely ground

1 tablespoon soy sauce

Flaky sea salt **OR** kosher salt, to serve

Don't use a conventional (i.e., not nonstick) skillet for this recipe. In such a pan, browned bits tend to stick to the surface and scorch, then are loosened when the soy sauce is added, causing bitter notes in the dish. A nonstick pan prevents any sticking at all, resulting in better flavor. It also makes cleanup easier.

In a 12-inch nonstick skillet over medium-high, heat the oil until barely smoking. Add the snow peas, chilies and shallots, then cook, stirring occasionally, until the peas are tender-crisp and well-charred, 5 to 6 minutes. Add the Sichuan pepper and cook, stirring, until fragrant, about 1 minute. Off heat, stir in the soy sauce. Transfer to a serving dish and sprinkle with salt.

Spicy Stir-Fried Cabbage, Onion and Peas

Mild and subtly sweet cabbage is a blank canvas that's great at taking on other flavors and can be either crisp or velvety, depending on how it is treated. In this stir-fry, green cabbage is complemented by an array of spices and aromatics. If you're a fan of chili heat, leave the seeds in one or both of the serranos before chopping. Serve with chicken, fish or a curry and with basmati rice alongside.

START TO FINISH: 35 MINUTES
SERVINGS: 4 TO 6

_____

3 tablespoons ghee
OR neutral oil

1 small red onion, halved
and thinly sliced

2 serrano chilies, stemmed,
seeded and finely chopped

2 tablespoons finely
grated fresh ginger

½ teaspoon cumin seeds

1½ teaspoons
ground coriander

½ teaspoon ground turmeric

1 pound green cabbage,
cored and thinly sliced
(4 to 5 cups)

½ teaspoon white sugar

Kosher salt and
ground black pepper

1 cup frozen peas, thawed

2 tablespoons unsweetened
shredded coconut

½ cup lightly packed
fresh cilantro, chopped

Don't overcook the cabbage. _Its texture is best if it retains a little crispness._

1. In a 12-inch nonstick skillet over medium-high, heat the ghee until shimmering. Add the onion, chilies, ginger and cumin; cook, stirring occasionally, until the onion softens and begins to brown, 4 to 5 minutes. Add the coriander and turmeric, then cook, stirring, until fragrant, 30 to 60 seconds. Stir in the cabbage, sugar and ½ teaspoon each salt and pepper. Cover and cook, stirring occasionally and adjusting the heat if the onion browns too quickly, just until the cabbage is tender-crisp, 5 to 6 minutes.

2. Stir in the peas, coconut and half the cilantro. Cook, uncovered and stirring occasionally, until the peas are heated through, 1 to 2 minutes. Off heat, taste and season with salt and pepper. Transfer to a serving dish and sprinkle with the remaining cilantro.

Sichuan Dry-Fried Cauliflower

START TO FINISH: 25 MINUTES
SERVINGS: 4

The Mandarin term for dry-frying, sometimes called dry-searing, is gan bian. It's essentially a two-stage cooking technique. A protein or vegetable first is parcooked in oil until the surfaces are browned and any moisture on the exterior has evaporated. The food then is stir-fried with aromatics and seasonings that reduce and cling to the browned surfaces. The resulting dish is more or less sauce-free. Green beans are the vegetable most often cooked in this manner, but in our version we use cauliflower. Sichuan peppercorns provide their resinous heat, while optional árbol chilies add a more direct spiciness. Serve this with white or brown rice.

2-pound head cauliflower, trimmed

¼ cup grapeseed or other neutral oil

1 tablespoon Sichuan peppercorns

6 medium garlic cloves, smashed and peeled

3 árbol chilies, broken in half (optional)

2 tablespoons soy sauce

1 tablespoon dry sherry

1 teaspoon white sugar

4 scallions, cut into 1-inch lengths

1 tablespoon finely grated fresh ginger

Chili oil, to serve

Don't use a head of cauliflower larger than 2 pounds. The skillet will be too crowded to get the browning that's essential to the dish. Also, for proper browning, don't stir the cauliflower for the first several minutes after adding it to the pan, and once the Sichuan peppercorns are added, stir only every minute or so.

1. **Using a chef's knife,** cut the cauliflower in half top to bottom. Set each half flat side down and cut parallel with the stem into rough ¼-inch slices; the florets will break up a bit as you cut, especially at the ends.

2. **In a 12-inch skillet** over medium, heat the oil until shimmering. Add the cauliflower in an even layer and cook without stirring until browned, about 6 minutes. Sprinkle in the Sichuan peppercorns and cook, stirring about every minute or so, until the cauliflower is spotty brown all over, 5 to 7 minutes.

3. **Add the garlic** and árbol chilies (if using), then cook, stirring often, until fragrant, about 1 minute. Stir in the soy sauce, sherry and sugar. Cook until the skillet is mostly dry, about 1 minute. Stir in the scallions and ginger, then continue to cook until the scallions are slightly wilted, about another 1 minute. Transfer to a serving dish and serve with chili oil for drizzling.

Cabbage and Brussels Sprouts

Brussels sprouts and cabbage get a bad rap as bitter and boring. Turns out the problem isn't so much the vegetables as the way they are treated. Shredded fine and paired with a tangy dressing—think slaw but with an upgrade—or charred to play up earthy sweetness and tone down sulfurous tendencies, they can be delicious.

In the Japanese kitchen, a seasoning liquid called tare starts with soy sauce and often includes mirin, sake, ginger and garlic. We use this combination on Brussels sprouts that have first been browned in butter, p. 169. The browned sprouts braise until done, the moisture evaporates, creating nutty, tender sprouts coated with a sweet-salty glaze.

In India, fried cabbage often is combined with peas and plenty of spices. Our version, p. 252, is bright with ginger, chilies and cilantro.

We're not fans of typical slaws, too often limp and slathered in mayo. But a crisp tangle of shredded greens perked up with a flavorful dressing? We're in favor. For our cabbage slaw,

p. 46, we turned to Thai flavors for the dressing, which uses coconut milk, not mayonnaise, and is balanced by savory fish sauce.

In Athens, we learned that cabbage is the backbone of the winter salad known as politiki. Shredded cabbage and carrots are dressed with a blend of sugar, salt and acid and allowed to rest briefly for tender crunch. Our version, p. 58, adds crumbled feta, thinly sliced celery and some chopped bell pepper.

Charring works well with sprouts and cabbages because it softens texture, caramelizes sugars and neutralizes bitter-tasting compounds. At Firedoor restaurant in Sydney, Australia, we had cabbage that was wood fire-roasted for a showstopper side. We came up with a version, p. 230, that works in a regular oven. We rub butter into cabbage wedges and sprinkle them with nuts, citrus zest and other flavorings. The outer leaves crisp up during roasting; the interior cooks to silky, sweet tenderness.

Stir-Fried Ginger
Green Beans with Tofu

Seasoned with fish and soy sauces, sugar and ginger, this simple stir-fry features a Southeast Asian flavor profile. To contrast the beans' tender-crispness, we prefer the more yielding texture of firm tofu over the bounciness of extra-firm, but either works. Whichever you use, be sure to salt the tofu cubes and let them drain in a colander for five to 10 minutes as the recipe instructs. We found that salted tofu better absorbs the flavorings that are applied during cooking. Serve this as part of an Asian meal or offer it as a light main, with steamed rice on the side.

START TO FINISH: 40 MINUTES
SERVINGS: 4 TO 6

_____

14-ounce container firm tofu, drained, patted dry and cut into ½- to ¾-inch cubes

Kosher salt and ground black pepper

2 tablespoons fish sauce

2 tablespoons soy sauce

1 tablespoon packed brown sugar

3 tablespoons grapeseed or other neutral oil, divided

1 pound green beans, trimmed and halved on the diagonal

1 tablespoon finely grated fresh ginger

½ teaspoon red pepper flakes

2 tablespoons unseasoned rice vinegar

Don't forget to pat the tofu dry after draining so the cubes splatter less and brown well. Also, be sure to use a nonstick skillet to ensure the tofu won't stick, especially after the sauce mixture, which contains sugar, is added.

1. **In a colander** set over a medium bowl, toss the tofu with ¼ teaspoon salt and let stand for 5 to 10 minutes. In a small bowl, stir together the fish sauce, soy sauce and sugar until the sugar dissolves; set aside.

2. **Transfer the tofu** to paper towels and pat dry. In a 12-inch nonstick skillet over medium-high, heat 1 tablespoon of oil until shimmering. Add the tofu in an even layer and cook, stirring occasionally, until golden brown, 6 to 7 minutes. Add 2 tablespoons of the fish sauce-soy sauce mixture and cook, stirring occasionally, until the liquid thickens and coats the tofu, about 1 minute. Transfer to a plate and wipe out the skillet.

3. **In the same skillet** over medium-high, heat the remaining 2 tablespoons oil until shimmering. Add the green beans and cook, stirring occasionally, until charred and tender-crisp, 6 to 7 minutes. Add the ginger and pepper flakes, then cook, stirring, until fragrant, about 30 seconds. Add the remaining fish sauce-soy sauce mixture and cook, stirring occasionally, until the liquid thickens and coats the beans, about 1 minute. Off heat, stir in the tofu and vinegar. Taste and season with black pepper.

Stir-Fried Snap Peas with Scallions, Ginger and Mango Chutney

In this super-quick stir-fried side, we use spicy, fruity, savory-sweet mango chutney as an ingredient, not as a condiment. We combine it with other high-impact options, such as lime juice, fresh chilies, ginger and garlic, to kick up the flavor and complement the natural sweetness of fresh sugar snap peas.

START TO FINISH: 30 MINUTES
SERVINGS: 4

¼ cup mango chutney

2 tablespoons lime juice

2 tablespoons grapeseed or other neutral oil

1 bunch scallions, thinly sliced on the diagonal

1 large shallot, halved and thinly sliced

1 Fresno **OR** small jalapeño chili, stemmed, seeded and thinly sliced

Kosher salt and ground black pepper

3 medium garlic cloves, thinly sliced

2-inch piece fresh ginger, peeled and thinly sliced

1 pound sugar snap peas, trimmed, strings removed, if present

¼ cup lightly packed fresh mint, torn

Don't head to the stove *until all of your ingredients are prepped. Once you start cooking, it's a matter of minutes before the peas are ready to be served.*

1. In a medium bowl, whisk together the chutney and lime juice. In a 12-inch nonstick skillet over medium-high, heat the oil until shimmering. Add the scallions, shallot, chili and ½ teaspoon salt; cook, stirring often, until softened, about 3 minutes.

2. Add the garlic and ginger, then cook, stirring, until fragrant, about 30 seconds. Add the snap peas and cook, stirring occasionally, until the peas begin to soften, about 2 minutes. Add the chutney mixture and cook, stirring occasionally, until the peas are tender-crisp, 3 to 5 minutes. Off heat, taste and season with salt and pepper. Transfer to a serving dish and sprinkle with the mint.

2 tablespoons black peppercorns, coarsely cracked

¼ cup lime juice, plus lime wedges to serve

1 tablespoon oyster sauce

1 teaspoon packed brown sugar

Kosher salt

2 tablespoons grapeseed or other neutral oil

3 medium garlic cloves, minced

1 pound carrots, peeled and thinly sliced on the diagonal

8 ounces baby bok choy OR green cabbage, cut into rough 2-inch pieces

3 scallions, thinly sliced on the diagonal

Don't use pre-ground black pepper; it lacks the vibrancy this dish requires. Start with fresh, whole peppercorns, then use a mortar and pestle to coarsely crack them. If you don't have a mortar and pestle, you also can crush them beneath a heavy skillet, rocking the pan back and forth over the peppercorns so they crack rather than scatter.

1. In a 12-inch skillet over medium, toast the cracked peppercorns, stirring often, until fragrant and a wisp of smoke rises from the pan, 2 to 4 minutes. Transfer to a small bowl. Stir in 3 tablespoons water, the lime juice, oyster sauce, sugar and ¼ teaspoon salt; set aside.

2. In the same skillet over medium-high, combine the oil and garlic. Cook, stirring often, until the garlic is lightly browned, 1 to 2 minutes. Increase to high, then add the carrots and a pinch of salt. Cook, stirring constantly, until the garlic is browned and the carrots begin to brown around the edges, about 3 minutes.

3. Add the bok choy and cook, stirring, until beginning to wilt, 1 to 2 minutes. Add the black pepper mixture and cook, stirring constantly, until the carrots are just tender, 2 to 4 minutes. Off heat, stir in the scallions, then taste and season with salt. Serve with lime wedges.

Optional garnish: Fresh chilies, stemmed, seeded and minced **OR** chopped roasted cashews **OR** both

Stir-Fried Carrots and Bok Choy with Black Pepper and Lime

In the Khmer kitchen, black pepper and lime juice are combined to make a sharp, pungent dipping sauce called tuk meric. In this recipe, we apply those flavors to a vegetable stir-fry. The sweetness of the carrots is enhanced by the acid and spice of the lime and peppercorns, while a bit of oyster sauce adds umami. We like the addition of greens here, especially baby bok choy, which retains its crunch, but you can substitute green cabbage or mustard greens. Like all stir-fries, this comes together quickly, so have all your ingredients prepped and ready before you begin.

Thai-Style Vegetable Stir-Fry with Garlic and Black Pepper

In the Thai kitchen, kratiem prik Thai is an aromatic, flavor-packed paste of garlic, black pepper and cilantro root. It often is used to season meat and seafood, but in this recipe we combine the ingredients (we substitute cilantro stems for hard-to-find roots) to add punch to a simple vegetable stir-fry. Napa cabbage and mushrooms provide meaty flavor, while snow peas, or bell peppers, offer color, sweetness and crunch. If you don't have fish sauce or want to make the dish vegetarian, use an equal amount of low-sodium soy sauce.

START TO FINISH: 30 MINUTES
SERVINGS: 4

1½ tablespoons fish sauce

2 teaspoons packed light brown sugar

Kosher salt and ground black pepper

3 tablespoons grapeseed or other neutral oil

4 medium garlic cloves, minced

2 tablespoons minced cilantro stems, plus ¼ cup lightly packed leaves, roughly chopped

14-ounce head napa cabbage, halved lengthwise, bottom 1 inch trimmed, cut crosswise into ½-inch-wide pieces (about 7 cups)

4 ounces shiitake mushrooms, stemmed and thinly sliced OR cremini mushrooms, thinly sliced

4 ounces snow peas, trimmed OR 1 red bell pepper, stemmed, seeded and thinly sliced

Don't stir the vegetables too often during the first 4 to 6 minutes of cooking. Infrequent stirring allows the vegetables to get a nice amount of charring to mimic the browning of cooking in a hot wok.

1. **In a small bowl,** stir together the fish sauce, sugar and 1 teaspoon pepper. Whisk until the sugar dissolves, then set aside. In a 12-inch nonstick skillet over medium-high, cook the oil, garlic and cilantro stems, stirring occasionally, until golden brown, 2 to 4 minutes. Add the cabbage, mushrooms and peas, then cook, stirring occasionally, until the vegetables begin to char and soften, 4 to 6 minutes.

2. **Working quickly,** add the fish sauce mixture. Immediately cover the pan, reduce to medium and cook, occasionally shaking the pan without lifting the lid, for 2 minutes. Uncover and cook, stirring often, until the skillet is dry, about 2 minutes. Taste and season with salt and pepper. Transfer to a serving dish and sprinkle with the cilantro leaves.

Optional garnish: Scallions thinly sliced on the diagonal **OR** Sriracha sauce **OR** both

Hot and Sour Stir-Fried Potatoes

We don't often think to stir-fry potatoes, but that's how they're cooked in the classic Sichuan dish called tudou si. Cut into matchsticks, the potatoes are soaked to remove some of their starch, then are stir-fried until tender but with just a hint of crispness at the core, not until totally yielding in texture. We flavor the potatoes with finely ground Sichuan peppercorns (pulverize them in an electric spice grinder), dried chilies for supplemental heat and Chinese black vinegar (also known as Chinkiang vinegar; balsamic vinegar is a reasonably good substitute) to add tanginess. The potatoes should be cut into ⅛-inch matchsticks, though the length of the sticks isn't so important. We suggest using the julienne blade on a mandoline or, if you're up for some knife work, do the prep by hand with a chef's knife. Another option is to get a slicing assist from a mandoline or a food processor fitted with the ⅛-inch slicing disk, then cut the slices, stacked a few high, into matchsticks with a knife.

START TO FINISH: 30 MINUTES
SERVINGS: 4

—————

1 pound medium (2 to 2½ inches in diameter) red **OR** Yukon Gold potatoes, unpeeled, cut into matchsticks (see headnote)

2 tablespoons soy sauce

1 tablespoon toasted sesame oil

1 tablespoon Chinese black vinegar **OR** balsamic vinegar

½ teaspoon white sugar

2 tablespoons grapeseed or other neutral oil

2 medium garlic cloves, minced

1 to 2 teaspoons Sichuan peppercorns, finely ground

4 árbol chiles, broken in half **OR** ½ teaspoon red pepper flakes

2 scallions, thinly sliced on the diagonal

Don't use russet potatoes; they are high in starch and will cook up too soft and sticky. Lower-starch red potatoes or Yukon Golds are the best choice, but purchase ones that are medium (2 to 2½ inches) in size so that they're easier to prep, especially if you're using a mandoline.

1. **In a large bowl,** cover the potatoes with 6 cups water. Swish them around and let the potatoes soak for 10 to 15 minutes to remove excess starch. Meanwhile, in a small bowl, stir together the soy sauce, sesame oil, vinegar and sugar; set aside.

2. **Drain the potatoes in a colander** and rinse well under running cold water. Working in batches if needed, transfer to a clean kitchen towel and thoroughly wring dry.

3. **In a 12-inch nonstick skillet** over medium-high, heat the neutral oil until shimmering. Add the potatoes and cook, stirring occasionally, until lightly browned and tender-crisp, 5 to 6 minutes. Add the garlic, Sichuan pepper and chilies, then cook, stirring, until fragrant, 30 to 60 seconds. Add the soy-sauce mixture and cook, tossing, until the liquid reduces to a light glaze and the potatoes are tender with just a little crispness at the center, 1 to 1½ minutes. Transfer to a serving dish and sprinkle with the scallions.

2 tablespoons soy sauce

½ teaspoon five-spice powder

½ teaspoon white sugar

Kosher salt and ground black pepper

3 tablespoons grapeseed or other neutral oil

2 stalks lemon grass, trimmed to the lower 6 inches, dry outer layers discarded, each piece halved crosswise and smashed

4 medium garlic cloves, minced

1 pound cremini mushrooms **OR** oyster mushrooms **OR** shiitake mushrooms (stemmed) **OR** a combination, thinly sliced

8 ounces asparagus **OR** snow peas, trimmed and halved on the diagonal

4 scallions, thinly sliced on the diagonal

1 or 2 serrano **OR** Fresno chilies, stemmed, seeded and thinly sliced

1½ teaspoons unseasoned rice vinegar

Don't choose old or dried-out lemon grass for this stir-fry. Choose stalks that are plump and heavy; once you remove the exterior layers, it should be fragrant and pale. Also, be sure to smash the lemon grass hard enough to flatten the stalks and break up some of the stringy fibers, releasing the flavorful oils within.

1. **In a small bowl** whisk together the soy sauce, five-spice, sugar, ¼ teaspoon pepper and ¼ cup water; set aside.

2. **In a 12-inch skillet** over medium-high, heat the oil until shimmering. Add the lemon grass and garlic; cook, stirring often, until the garlic is lightly browned, 1 to 2 minutes. Add the mushrooms, asparagus and half the scallions, then cook, stirring occasionally, until the mushrooms soften and begin to brown, 5 to 8 minutes.

3. **Stir in the chili(es)** and soy sauce mixture; cook, stirring constantly, until the mushrooms are tender and most of the liquid has evaporated, 2 to 3 minutes. Off heat, remove and discard the lemon grass. Stir in the vinegar and remaining scallions, then taste and season with salt and pepper.

Optional garnish: Chopped fresh cilantro

Stir-Fried Mushrooms and Asparagus with Lemon Grass

In Southeast Asian cooking, herbal, citrusy lemon grass often is used in tandem with strong, salty, umami-rich fish sauce. But for this vegetarian stir-fry, we use soy sauce to achieve bold, deep savoriness and Chinese five-spice powder to add warm, spiced notes. Green, grassy asparagus (or snow peas) offsets the meatiness of the mushrooms and adds another dimension of texture. Use a combination of mushroom varieties for a mixture of flavors and shapes.

Potato, Eggplant and Pepper Stir-Fry

In the classic Chinese dish called di san xian, purple eggplant, yellow potatoes and bell peppers are fried then tossed in a simple, lightly sweetened soy-based glaze-like sauce. The vegetables create an interesting textural combination of silky-soft, dense and starchy, and tender-crisp. Traditionally, each is deep-fried separately and brought together for saucing, but we've sped up and streamlined the cooking process so only the potatoes cook by themselves, and in a minimal amount of oil. If you can't find Shaoxing wine, a type of Chinese rice wine, dry sherry is a fine substitute. Serve with steamed rice.

START TO FINISH: 40 MINUTES
SERVINGS: 4

2 tablespoons soy sauce

1 tablespoon Shaoxing wine **OR** dry sherry

½ teaspoon white sugar

1½ teaspoons cornstarch

6 tablespoons grapeseed or other neutral oil, divided

2 medium Yukon Gold potatoes (12 ounces total), peeled, halved lengthwise, sliced crosswise ¼ inch thick and patted dry

2 Chinese eggplants (12 ounces total), trimmed, sliced into ½-inch rounds and patted dry

1 red **OR** yellow **OR** green bell pepper, stemmed, seeded and cut into thin strips

3 medium garlic cloves, minced

4 scallions, thinly sliced on the diagonal, whites and greens reserved separately

Don't forget to pat the potatoes and eggplant dry before cooking. This helps to prevent the vegetables from sticking to the pan and also helps them brown.

1. **In a small bowl,** stir together ¼ cup water, the soy sauce, Shaoxing wine, sugar and cornstarch; set aside. In a 12-inch nonstick skillet over medium-high, heat 4 tablespoons of oil until shimmering. Add the potatoes and cook, turning occasionally, until browned on all sides, 8 to 10 minutes. Using a slotted spoon, transfer to a medium bowl.

2. **Add the eggplant** to the pan in an even layer and cook without stirring until golden brown on the bottom, about 2 minutes. Flip the slices and add the remaining 2 tablespoons oil and the bell pepper. Cook, stirring often, until the eggplant is tender and the peppers are tender-crisp, about another 3 minutes.

3. **Add the garlic** and scallion whites to the vegetables and cook, stirring, until fragrant, about 30 seconds. Return the potatoes to the pan and toss. Stir the cornstarch mixture to recombine, add to the skillet and cook, stirring constantly with a silicone spatula, until the sauce has thickened and coats the vegetables, about 1 minute. Transfer to a serving dish and sprinkle with the scallion greens.

Sesame-Garlic Stir-Fried Baby Bok Choy

In this simple, speedy stir-fry, garlic and chili complement the bok choy without muddling its fresh, subtly sweet cabbagey notes. Shaoxing wine has a rich, slightly nutty flavor. It's worth searching out in well-stocked supermarkets or at the Asian grocery store, but if not available, dry sherry is a fine substitute. So the bok choy cooks in the right amount of time, look for heads 4 to 5 inches long and 2 to 3 inches in diameter, with bright white stems and deep green leaves. The layers can trap sand at the base; cleaning is easiest after the heads are halved. Plunge them into cold water and swish them about, then drain well and dry thoroughly, as excess water will cause wateriness in the finished dish.

START TO FINISH: 30 MINUTES
SERVINGS: 4

_____

2 tablespoons Shaoxing wine **OR** dry sherry

1 tablespoon soy sauce

1 teaspoon toasted sesame oil, plus more to serve

Ground white pepper **OR** ground black pepper

2 tablespoons grapeseed or other neutral oil

3 medium garlic cloves, smashed and peeled

2 jalapeño chilies, stemmed, halved lengthwise, seeded and sliced lengthwise into strips

12 ounces baby bok choy, halved and patted dry (see headnote)

Don't begin cooking until all your ingredients are prepared and close at hand. From the time the garlic begins heating in the oil to transferring the bok choy to a serving dish is no more than a few minutes.

1. **In a small bowl,** stir together the Shaoxing wine, soy sauce, sesame oil, ¼ teaspoon pepper and 1 tablespoon water; set aside.

2. **In a 12-inch skillet** over medium-high, combine the neutral oil and garlic; cook, occasionally turning the cloves, until the garlic is golden, about 3 minutes. Add the chilies and cook, stirring constantly, until fragrant, about 1 minute. Push the garlic and chilies to the side of the skillet, then add the bok choy to the center. Increase to high and cook, stirring and turning with tongs, until the greens begin to wilt, 1 to 2 minutes.

3. **Add the Shaoxing-soy mixture,** cover and cook until the bok choy stems are tender-crisp and the leaves are bright green, 2 to 3 minutes; stir once about halfway through. Transfer to a serving dish and drizzle with additional sesame oil.

Optional garnish: Toasted sesame seeds **OR** chili oil **OR** both

8

PASTA & GRAIN
DISHES

Zucchini with Tomato, Pearl Couscous and Mint

In this dish, tender, silky slices of zucchini (and/or yellow summer squash) find a delicious partner in satisfyingly chewy pearl couscous coated with a mixture of well browned tomato paste and garlic. Caramelizing the paste enhances its umami and savory-sweet notes for big, bold depth of flavor. Fresh herb(s) and lemon wedges for squeezing bring brightness and balance. Serve this as a side to kebabs, roasts or grilled meats or seafood, or turn it into a light meal by serving a salad alongside.

START TO FINISH: 35 MINUTES
SERVINGS: 4 TO 6

___

¾ cup pearl couscous

Kosher salt and ground black pepper

3 tablespoons extra-virgin olive oil, divided

2 medium (about 1 pound total) zucchini **OR** yellow summer squash **OR** a combination, halved lengthwise, then sliced crosswise ¼ inch thick

3 medium garlic cloves, thinly sliced

3 tablespoons tomato paste

1 cup lightly packed fresh mint

Lemon wedges, to serve

Don't stir the zucchini for the first five minutes after adding the slices to the skillet. Undisturbed cooking allows the zucchini to brown nicely. Thereafter, stir occasionally to facilitate even cooking.

1. **In a medium saucepan,** bring 2 cups water to a boil. Add the couscous and ¼ teaspoon salt, then cook, stirring occasionally, until just shy of al dente, 10 to 15 minutes. Drain in a colander, rinse under running cold water until cool to the touch, then drain again; set aside in the colander.

2. **In a 12-inch nonstick skillet** over medium-high, heat 2 tablespoons of oil until shimmering. Add the zucchini and a pinch of salt, then distribute in an even layer and cook without stirring until the bottom slices are well browned, about 5 minutes. Stir, then cook, now stirring occasionally, until the zucchini is just tender, about 3 minutes. Transfer to a large bowl.

3. **Wipe out the skillet.** Add the remaining 1 tablespoon oil and the garlic, then cook over medium, stirring, until the garlic is lightly browned, about 2 minutes. Stir in the tomato paste and cook, stirring often, until the paste begins to brown, 1 to 3 minutes. Remove the pan from the heat. Stir in the couscous until well combined. Transfer to the bowl with the zucchini, add the mint and fold to combine. Taste and season with salt and pepper. Serve with lemon wedges.

Campanelle Pasta with Asparagus, Lemon and Parmesan

This springtime pasta dish is an elegant supper yet a one-pot affair. The pasta and asparagus start independently but finish together, simmered with half-and-half, so their flavors mix and meld. Be sure to purchase pencil-thin asparagus so the spears cook in the time indicated and are a good size match for the pasta. You will need 2 pounds for this recipe; typically, a bunch weighs about 1 pound. Penne and campanelle are our favored pasta shapes for this, but fusilli and gemelli are good, too.

1 pound campanelle **OR** penne pasta

Kosher salt and ground black pepper

1 tablespoon salted butter

2 pounds asparagus (see headnote), trimmed and cut into 1-inch pieces

2 medium garlic cloves, thinly sliced

1 cup half-and-half

2 ounces finely grated Parmesan cheese **OR** pecorino Romano cheese (1 cup), plus more to serve

2 teaspoons grated lemon zest, plus 2 tablespoons lemon juice

2 tablespoons chopped fresh chives

Don't boil the pasta until al dente. Drain it when it's just shy of al dente, and remember to reserve about ½ cup of the cooking water. The noodles will finish cooking with the ingredients that form the sauce. The starchy reserved cooking water is used to thin the sauce so it lightly coats the pasta.

1. **In a large pot,** bring 4 quarts water to a boil. Stir in the pasta and 1 tablespoon salt and cook, stirring occasionally, until just shy of al dente. Reserve about ½ cup of the cooking water, then drain.

2. **In the same pot** over medium-high, melt the butter. Add the asparagus and ½ teaspoon salt, then cook, stirring often, until tender-crisp, 2 to 4 minutes. Add the garlic and cook, stirring, until fragrant, about 30 seconds. Add the pasta and the half-and-half, then bring to a simmer. Reduce to medium and cook, stirring, until most of the liquid has been absorbed and the pasta is al dente, 2 to 4 minutes.

3. **Off heat,** stir in the Parmesan and lemon zest and juice; add reserved pasta water as needed so the sauce is silky and clings to the noodles. Stir in the chives, then taste and season with salt and pepper. Serve sprinkled with additional cheese.

Broccoli Rabe with White Beans and Ditalini

This simple weeknight pasta features a classic southern Italian combination of ingredients. Each contributes unique character: fruity olive oil, pungent garlic, spicy pepper flakes, bitter broccoli rabe, creamy white beans, wheaty pasta, funky pecorino cheese and tangy lemon juice. For ease, we use canned beans and cook everything together in a single pot—no need to boil the pasta separately.

START TO FINISH: 30 MINUTES
SERVINGS: 4

¼ cup extra-virgin olive oil, plus more to serve

4 medium garlic cloves, minced

½ teaspoon red pepper flakes

1 pound broccoli rabe, trimmed and cut into 2-inch pieces

8 ounces (2 cups) ditalini pasta

15½-ounce can cannellini OR great northern beans, rinsed and drained

Kosher salt and ground black pepper

2 ounces pecorino Romano cheese, finely grated (1 cup)

2 tablespoons lemon juice

Don't discard the leaves from the broccoli rabe unless they're bruised or damaged. The leaves are tender and flavorful, so leave them attached and cut them into 2-inch pieces with the stalks.

1. In a large Dutch oven over medium-high, combine the oil, garlic, pepper flakes and broccoli rabe. Cook, stirring occasionally, until the rabe leaves begin to wilt, about 3 minutes. Stir in 3 cups water and bring to a boil, then stir in the ditalini, beans, ¼ teaspoon salt and ½ teaspoon black pepper. Return to a boil, cover and cook, stirring occasionally, until the ditalini is al dente, 10 to 12 minutes.

2. Remove the pot from the heat and stir in half of the cheese and the lemon juice; if the mixture appears dry, stir in water as needed. Taste and season with salt and black pepper. Serve drizzled with additional oil and sprinkled with the remaining cheese.

Greek-Style Rice with Leeks

Prasorizo, which translates from the Greek as "leek rice," is a homey dish of rice cooked with earthy-sweet leeks. For our take, we use Italian Arborio rice and treat the grains as if making risotto, resulting in a rich, creamy consistency that's a nice match for the tender, silky leeks. As a final flourish and to add some brightness, we garnish the rice with fresh tomato and herb(s), drizzle it with olive oil and serve it with lemon wedges. Be sure to thoroughly rinse the leeks after slicing them in order to wash away the grit trapped in the many layers, then drain well to remove excess moisture. This makes a delicious light main course, or serve it as a side to almost any sort of chicken, pork or seafood.

START TO FINISH: 40 MINUTES
SERVINGS: 4

___

¼ cup extra-virgin olive oil, plus more to serve

2 pounds leeks, white and light green parts halved lengthwise, sliced crosswise ½ inch thick, rinsed and drained (about 8 cups)

2 medium garlic cloves, minced

Kosher salt and ground black pepper

1 ripe tomato, cored and chopped

¼ cup lightly packed fresh dill OR mint OR a combination, roughly chopped

1 cup Arborio rice

Lemon wedges, to serve

Don't forget to cover the leeks and stir them as they cook. While it takes several minutes for the leeks to begin to break down and soften, if left too long undisturbed while covered, they'll brown quickly and burn.

1. **In a 12-inch skillet** over medium, combine the oil, leeks, garlic and 1 teaspoon salt. Cover and cook, stirring occasionally, until the leeks are softened and tender, 12 to 15 minutes. Meanwhile, in a medium microwave-safe bowl, microwave 4½ cups water on high, covered, until hot, about 4 minutes; set aside, covered. In a small bowl, stir together the tomato, dill and ¼ teaspoon each salt and pepper; set aside.

2. **To the softened leeks,** add the rice and ¼ teaspoon pepper; stir until well combined. Add the hot water and bring to a simmer over medium-high. Cook, stirring often and briskly, until the rice is creamy and tender, 12 to 15 minutes; adjust the heat as needed to maintain a vigorous simmer. Taste and season with salt and pepper, then transfer to a wide, shallow serving bowl. Top the rice with the tomato mixture and drizzle with additional oil. Serve with lemon wedges.

Optional garnish: Crumbled feta cheese **OR** toasted sliced almonds **OR** chopped pitted olives **OR** a combination

Rigatoni with Broccoli-Lemon Sauce

This is an adaptation of pasta sauced with a creamy, silky broccoli puree that we tasted in Rome. We use broccoli crowns here and not the lower portion of the stems, which are sometimes tough and fibrous. We start by simmering the broccoli in a large pot of salted boiling water. After removing the pieces, we keep the water at a boil and use it to cook the pasta.

START TO FINISH: 30 MINUTES
SERVINGS: 4 TO 6

Kosher salt and
ground black pepper

1 pound broccoli crowns,
cut into 1-inch pieces

3 medium garlic cloves,
peeled

1 tablespoon drained capers

¼ cup extra-virgin olive oil,
plus more to serve

1 pound rigatoni
OR ziti pasta

2 ounces pecorino Romano
OR Parmesan cheese,
finely grated (1 cup), plus
more to serve

1 tablespoon grated lemon
zest, plus 2 tablespoons
lemon juice

Don't simmer the broccoli until fully tender or its color will turn a dull shade of green. Cooking it only until crisp-tender ensures a vividly hued puree.

1. In a large pot, bring 4 quarts water to a boil. Add 1 tablespoon salt, the broccoli and garlic; cook until the broccoli is crisp-tender, 4 to 6 minutes. Using a slotted spoon, transfer the broccoli and garlic to a blender; keep the water at a boil. Remove about 2 cups of the water; add 1½ cups to the blender (reserve the remainder), along with the capers. Blend until smooth, then, with the machine running, stream in the oil; set aside.

2. Add the pasta to the boiling water and cook, stirring, until al dente. Drain and return to the pot. Add the broccoli puree, the cheese and lemon zest and juice; toss to combine, adding reserved water as needed so the pasta is lightly sauced. Taste and season with salt and pepper. Serve drizzled with additional oil and with additional cheese.

Optional garnish: Chopped or torn fresh basil **OR** chopped toasted walnuts **OR** both

Pasta with Cauliflower, Garlic and Toasted Breadcrumbs

This pasta is a true one-pot dinner. We don't boil the noodles separately—rather, we add them to the pot along with the cauliflower and just enough water to cook both through. Toasted breadcrumbs sprinkled on just before serving offer a welcome textural contrast. We prefer Japanese-style panko over standard dry breadcrumbs for their light, airy texture that, when toasted, takes on a remarkable crispness.

START TO FINISH: 25 MINUTES
SERVINGS: 4

4 tablespoons extra-virgin olive oil, divided

1 cup panko breadcrumbs

4 ounces pancetta, chopped

6 medium garlic cloves, minced

¼ cup tomato paste

1½-pound head cauliflower, trimmed and cut into ½-inch pieces

8 ounces campanelle OR orecchiette pasta

Kosher salt and ground black pepper

1 cup lightly packed fresh basil, chopped

Don't forget to stir the cauliflower-pasta mixture during *cooking to ensure it isn't sticking to the bottom of the pot.*

1. **In a large pot** over medium, heat 2 tablespoons of oil until shimmering. Add the panko and cook, stirring occasionally, until golden brown, about 3 minutes; transfer to a small bowl.

2. **In the same pot** over medium, combine the remaining 2 tablespoons oil, the pancetta and garlic, then cook, stirring, until the garlic is lightly browned about 2 minutes. Add the tomato paste and cook, stirring, until the paste begins to brown, about 2 minutes. Pour in 4 cups water and scrape up any browned bits, then stir in the cauliflower, pasta and 1½ teaspoons salt. Bring to a simmer, then cover and cook, stirring occasionally, until the pasta is al dente and the cauliflower is tender, 10 to 12 minutes. Off heat, taste and season with salt and pepper, then let stand for a few minutes to allow the pasta to absorb some of the sauce. Serve sprinkled with the panko and basil.

Optional garnish: Red pepper flakes **OR** finely grated pecorino Romano cheese **OR** a combination

Broccoli

Broccoli has its haters. George H.W. Bush famously gave it the presidential seal of disapproval, banning it from Air Force One. But treated right with plenty of heat and not too much liquid, it's a delicious and versatile vegetable that pairs excellently with robust spices and crunchy garnishes.

Japanese cooks use goma ae, a sesame seed dressing that often is paired with vegetables (we use it with asparagus, p. 147). For our Broccolini with sesame-miso sauce, p. 164, we mix a white miso into the sauce for added umami.

Broccolini is a cross between broccoli and gai lan, or Chinese broccoli, which has leaves and slender stems, but few florets. Gai lan is often served in dim sum restaurants, steamed or blanched and finished with oyster sauce and other seasonings. In our version, p. 248, we stir-fry the leaves and stem sections separately, starting with the stems so they get a chance to brown. A mix of oyster sauce and soy sauce along with ginger and garlic amp up the flavor.

Scrawny-looking broccoli rabe shows up in all manner of Italian recipes, and for good reason—the deliciously bitter stems, tender leaves and nutty buds are all edible. Our broccoli rabe with beans and pasta, p. 272, features the classic southern Italian combination of olive oil, garlic, pepper flakes, white beans, pecorino and lemon juice. And it's a one-pot dish.

A charred broccoli salad served at New York City's Superiority Burger showed us the power of a good, deep char; it develops nutty, bittersweet flavors while crisping the florets. Our method of choice is a preheated baking sheet in an intensely hot oven; it's easier and more convenient than using the stovetop. The broccoli is great with just a spritz of lemon, but we also offer a quartet of crunchy, flavorful toppings like pistachios and Parmesan, p. 202.

When in Rome, cooks are likely to buy broccoli with leaves attached, which sometimes are pureed into a light and silky sauce. In the U.S., broccoli leaves aren't usually an option but we adapt by pureeing some of the stems for our take, p. 275. We simmer the florets until crisply tender, use the cooking water for our pasta and then toss the pasta and florets with the pureed sauce. A trifecta of broccoli goodness—what's not to love?

1 quart low-sodium vegetable **OR** chicken broth

2 tablespoons salted butter, divided

1 large shallot, minced

Kosher salt and ground black pepper

1 cup Arborio **OR** carnaroli rice

½ cup dry white wine **OR** red wine

1 tablespoon honey, plus more if needed

1 large head radicchio (about 12 ounces), quartered, cored and thinly sliced crosswise

2 ounces Parmesan cheese, finely grated (1 cup)

½ cup walnuts, toasted and chopped

Don't be gentle when stirring the rice. Vigorous stirring helps the starches create a rich, creamy consistency in the risotto, and frequent stirring helps the grains cook evenly.

1. In a 1-quart liquid measuring cup or medium microwave-safe bowl, microwave the broth on high, covered, until hot, about 4 minutes; set aside, covered. In a large saucepan over medium-high, melt 1 tablespoon of butter. Add the shallot and ¼ teaspoon salt, then cook, stirring, until the shallot is translucent, about 1 minute. Add the rice and cook, stirring often, until the rice grains are translucent at the edges, 1 to 2 minutes.

2. Add the wine and honey, then cook, stirring, until mostly evaporated, about 1 minute. Stir in half of the radicchio followed by 2½ cups of broth. Bring to a boil, then reduce to medium and cook, stirring often and briskly, until the grains are almost tender but still quite firm at the core (the consistency will be quite soupy), 6 to 8 minutes; adjust the heat as needed to maintain a vigorous simmer.

3. Stir in 1 cup of the remaining broth and continue to cook, stirring often and briskly, until the rice is al dente, 5 to 7 minutes. Remove the pan from the heat, cover and let stand for 5 minutes.

4. Stir in the remaining radicchio, the remaining 1 tablespoon butter and the Parmesan. The risotto should be loose but not soupy; if it is stiff and dry, stir in additional broth, 1 tablespoon at a time, to achieve the proper consistency. Taste and season with salt and pepper and, if desired, stir in additional honey. Serve sprinkled with the walnuts.

Radicchio Risotto with Parmesan and Walnuts

Risotto al radicchio is a classic Venetian dish. The anthocyanins, or red pigments, in the radicchio give the rice a unique mauve hue, and if you choose to use red wine instead of white, the color is accentuated. We balance radicchio's natural bitterness by adding a little honey, and the sweetness of the shallot and butter as well as of the nuttiness of the Parmesan counter the bitter notes, too. For textural contrast, we add half the radicchio at the same time as the broth so the shreds become meltingly tender, then we stir the remainder in at the very end to only wilt the pieces. Buttery toasted walnuts sprinkled on as a garnish add crispness as well as richness and umami.

Spaghetti with Eggplant, Tomatoes and Gorgonzola

START TO FINISH: 40 MINUTES
SERVINGS: 6

This is our rendition of a pasta dish that we tasted at Antica Osteria Pisano in Naples, Italy. Chunks of eggplant are lightly browned in olive oil, then simmered with cherry (or grape) tomatoes along with some of the starchy pasta-cooking water, forming a simple sauce. But what really pulls the dish together, both in flavor and consistency, is the creamy, savory Gorgonzola cheese tossed in at the end. To be efficient, prep the basil during the five-minute standing time after sprinkling the cheese onto the pasta.

1 pound spaghetti

Kosher salt and ground black pepper

¼ cup extra-virgin olive oil

1-pound eggplant, cut into 1-inch chunks

1 pint cherry **OR** grape tomatoes, halved

2 medium garlic cloves, minced

½ teaspoon red pepper flakes

4 ounces Gorgonzola cheese, crumbled (1 cup)

1 cup lightly packed fresh basil, chopped

Don't discard the remaining pasta water after adding 1½ cups to the eggplant-tomato mixture. You will need some of it to adjust the consistency of the pasta after the cheese is mixed in.

1. **In a large pot,** bring 2 quarts water to a boil over medium high. Stir in the pasta and 1 tablespoon salt, then cook, stirring occasionally, until just shy of al dente. Reserve about 2 cups of the cooking water, then drain; set aside.

2. **In a 12-inch skillet,** heat the oil over medium-high until barely smoking. Add the eggplant and ½ teaspoon salt. Cook, stirring occasionally, until golden brown and starting to soften, 5 to 6 minutes. Add the tomatoes and cook, stirring occasionally, until the tomatoes begin to break down, 3 to 4 minutes. Add the garlic and pepper flakes; cook, stirring, until fragrant, about 30 seconds. Add 1½ cups of the reserved pasta water and bring to a simmer. Add the spaghetti and cook, stirring occasionally, until the pasta is al dente, about 2 minutes.

3. **Remove the pan from the heat.** Scatter the Gorgonzola over the pasta mixture, cover and let stand for 5 minutes to soften the cheese. Toss, adding more reserved water as needed so the noodles are lightly sauced. Add the basil and toss again, then taste and season with salt and black pepper.

Roasted Tomato Risotto with Basil and Parmesan

This dish combines the rich, satisfying starchiness that we crave in the winter with the vibrant flavors and aromas of summer. We roast cherry or grape tomatoes, which tend to be dependably good no matter the season, with garlic, herbs and a little tomato paste in a hot oven to concentrate their flavor and bring out their umami. The tomatoes with juices plus fresh basil and grated Parmesan are stirred into a basic risotto only after the grains have softened to al dente.

START TO FINISH: 1¼ HOURS (30 MINUTES ACTIVE)
SERVINGS: 4

_____

3 tablespoons
extra-virgin olive oil

1 tablespoon tomato paste

2 pints cherry **OR** grape
tomatoes, halved

6 medium garlic cloves,
chopped

½ teaspoon
red pepper flakes

2 thyme sprigs

1 rosemary sprig

Kosher salt and
ground black pepper

2 tablespoons salted butter

1 cup carnaroli
OR Arborio rice

1 medium shallot, minced

½ cup dry vermouth

4 cups boiling water

½ cup chopped fresh basil

2 ounces Parmesan cheese,
finely grated (1 cup)

Don't forget to bring 4 cups water to a boil before starting the risotto. Adding hot liquid to the rice as it cooks maintains the temperature so the grains cook more quickly. (You may not use all of the boiling water; the last ½ cup is for adjusting the consistency of the risotto at the end, if needed.) Don't be afraid to stir vigorously when cooking the risotto. Doing so coaxes starch from the rice for a creamier consistency.

1. **Heat the oven to 450°F** with a rack in the middle position. In a 9-by-13-inch baking pan, mix the oil and tomato paste until homogeneous. Add the tomatoes, garlic, pepper flakes, thyme, rosemary and ½ teaspoon salt. Roast until the tomatoes have softened and begin to char, 35 to 40 minutes, stirring once about halfway through. Remove and discard the thyme and rosemary; set the tomatoes aside.

2. **In a large saucepan** over medium-high, melt the butter. Add the rice, shallot and ½ teaspoon salt, then cook, stirring constantly, until the rice grains are translucent at the edges, 2 to 3 minutes. Add the vermouth and cook, stirring, until mostly evaporated, about 1 minute. Add 2½ cups of boiling water and bring to a boil, then reduce to medium and cook, stirring often and briskly, until the grains are almost tender but still quite firm at the core (the consistency will be quite soupy), 8 to 10 minutes; adjust the heat as needed to maintain a vigorous simmer.

3. **Add 1 cup** of the remaining boiling water and cook, stirring often and briskly, until the rice is al dente, 6 to 8 minutes; the risotto should be loose but not soupy. If it is stiff and dry, stir in additional boiling water 1 tablespoon at a time to achieve the proper consistency.

4. **Off heat,** stir in the tomatoes with juices, the basil and half of the Parmesan. Taste and season with salt and pepper. Serve immediately, sprinkled with the remaining Parmesan and drizzled with additional oil.

Broccoli and Kimchi Fried Rice with "Poached" Eggs

For a twist on standard fried rice, we don't scramble a token egg or two into the mix. Instead, we "poach" a few in hollowed-out areas of the fried rice until the whites are just set but the yolks are deliciously runny. While the eggs cook, the rice forms a golden brown, nicely crisped bottom crust. Fried rice always is best made with cold cooked rice rather than freshly made. To cook enough rice for this recipe, rinse and drain 1½ cups short-grain white rice. In a large saucepan, combine the rice and 1¾ cups water. Bring to boil over medium-high, then reduce to low, cover and cook until tender, 16 to 18 minutes. Remove from the heat and let stand, covered, for 10 minutes. Fluff the grains, transfer to a container, let cool, cover and refrigerate until well chilled. You will need a 12-inch nonstick skillet with a lid for this recipe.

START TO FINISH: 35 MINUTES
SERVINGS: 4

_____

4 tablespoons grapeseed or other neutral oil, divided

1 pound broccoli crowns, cut into ½- to 1-inch florets

1 bunch scallions, thinly sliced, whites and greens reserved separately

4 cups cold cooked short-grain white rice (see headnote)

1 cup cabbage kimchi, roughly chopped, plus 2 tablespoons kimchi juice (or water)

3 tablespoons soy sauce

1 tablespoon toasted sesame oil

Kosher salt and ground black pepper

4 large eggs

Don't forget to create wells in the rice to hold the eggs, and be sure they're deep enough to expose the surface of the skillet. If the wells are too shallow, the eggs will take longer to cook and the bottom of the rice may get too dark.

1. **In a 12-inch nonstick skillet** over medium-high, heat 1 tablespoon of neutral oil until shimmering. Add the broccoli and stir to coat with oil. Cover and cook, stirring occasionally, until well charred and tender-crisp, 7 to 8 minutes. Transfer to a plate and set aside.

2. **In the same skillet** over medium-high, heat the remaining 3 tablespoons neutral oil until shimmering. Add the scallion whites and cook, stirring, until fragrant, 30 to 60 seconds. Stir in the rice, breaking up any clumps, then cook, stirring occasionally, until heated through, 2 to 3 minutes. Return the broccoli to the pan and add the kimchi and juice, soy sauce and sesame oil. Stir, then taste and season with salt and pepper.

3. **Reduce to medium-low.** Using the back of a spoon, form 4 evenly spaced wells in the rice, each about 2 inches wide and deep enough that the pan is visible. Crack 1 egg into each, then sprinkle with salt and pepper. Cover and cook until the egg whites are set but the yolks are still runny, 4 to 5 minutes, rotating the skillet about halfway through for even cooking. Serve sprinkled with the scallion greens.

Sweet Potato Brown Rice with Soy and Scallions

Goguma-bap is a traditional Korean dish of sweet potatoes (goguma) and cooked rice (bap). Our take has a pure sweet potato flavor accented by chewy short-grain rice; we prefer the nuttiness of brown short-grain rice for added complexity. The sweet potatoes and rice usually are steamed together plain, then seasoned at the table with a mixture of soy sauce and chives. We opt to season the sweet potatoes with just a little of this sauce before cooking to make them especially flavorful. Pungent, garlicky Chinese chives resemble thick blades of grass; if you can get them from your local Asian supermarket, use them in place of the scallions. The Korean red pepper flakes commonly used in this dish are called gochugaru, but regular red pepper flakes work perfectly well.

START TO FINISH: 50 MINUTES (10 MINUTES ACTIVE)
SERVINGS: 4

———

1 cup short-grain brown rice, rinsed and drained

½ cup thinly sliced scallions **OR** Chinese chives

⅓ cup low-sodium soy sauce

1 tablespoon unseasoned rice vinegar

1 medium garlic clove, finely grated

1 to 1½ teaspoons Korean red pepper flakes (gochugaru) **OR** red pepper flakes

1 teaspoon honey **OR** white sugar

1 pound orange-flesh sweet potatoes, peeled and cut into ½-inch chunks

Kosher salt and ground black pepper

1 tablespoon white **OR** black sesame seeds **OR** a combination, toasted

Don't cut the sweet potatoes too large or they will not cook in the same time as it takes the rice to soften. Also, be sure to keep an eye on your saucepan as the dish steams; if you see large amounts of steam coming from the lid, quickly uncover to allow the built-up steam to escape, then recover, reduce the heat slightly and continue cooking.

1. **In a large saucepan,** combine the rice and 1¾ cups water. Bring to a simmer over medium, then reduce to low, cover and cook without stirring for 15 minutes.

2. **Meanwhile, in a small bowl,** stir together the scallions, soy sauce, vinegar, garlic, pepper flakes and honey. In a medium bowl, toss the sweet potatoes with 2 tablespoons of the soy sauce mixture and ½ teaspoon black pepper.

3. **After the rice has cooked** for 15 minutes, uncover the pot, scatter the sweet potato mixture over the surface of the rice (without disturbing the grains) and re-cover. Cook over low until both the potatoes and rice are tender, 20 to 25 minutes.

4. **Remove from the heat** and let stand, covered, for 10 minutes. Gently fluff with a fork, trying not to break up the potatoes. Transfer to a serving bowl, sprinkle with the sesame seeds and serve with the remaining soy sauce mixture for drizzling.

Linguine with Artichokes, Lemon and Pancetta

The sauce for this pasta is made by blitzing artichokes in a blender. For ease, we use canned artichokes instead of fresh, but we first brown them in a mixture of olive oil and rendered pancetta fat to build flavor in the sauce. The crisp bits of pancetta lend texture and saltiness, lemon adds brightness and balance, and a generous amount of Parmesan ties all the elements together.

START TO FINISH: 30 MINUTES
SERVINGS: 4 TO 6

---

1 pound linguine **OR** fettuccine

Kosher salt and ground black pepper

1 tablespoon extra-virgin olive oil, plus more to serve

4 ounces pancetta, chopped

14-ounce can artichoke hearts, drained, patted dry and quartered if whole

1 tablespoon grated lemon zest, plus 3 tablespoons lemon juice

2 ounces Parmesan cheese, finely grated (1 cup), plus more to serve

½ cup finely chopped fresh flat-leaf parsley **OR** chives **OR** basil

Don't use marinated artichokes for this recipe, as their flavor is too sharp and tangy. After draining the artichokes, make sure to pat them dry so they caramelize when added to the pot. Don't forget to reserve about 2 cups of the pasta water before draining the noodles. You will need it for pureeing the artichokes and building the sauce.

1. In a large pot, bring 4 quarts water to a boil. Stir in the pasta and 1 tablespoon salt, then cook, stirring occasionally, until al dente. Reserve about 2 cups of the cooking water, then drain.

2. In the same pot over medium, heat the oil until shimmering. Add the pancetta and cook, stirring, until crisp, 3 to 4 minutes. Using a slotted spoon, transfer to a small plate; set aside. Add the artichokes to the pot and cook, stirring, until beginning to brown at the edges, 3 to 4 minutes. Remove the pot from the heat. Transfer half the artichokes to a small bowl; add the remainder to a blender. Reserve the pot.

3. To the artichokes in the blender, add ½ cup cooking water, the lemon juice and ¼ teaspoon each salt and pepper; puree until smooth. In the same pot over medium, bring 1 cup of the remaining cooking water to a simmer, scraping up any browned bits. Add the artichoke puree, the pasta, lemon zest, pancetta, Parmesan and parsley. Cook, tossing to combine, just until the noodles are heated through, 1 to 2 minutes; add more reserved water as needed to make a silky sauce. Taste and season with salt and pepper. Transfer to a serving bowl and top with the reserved artichokes, along with additional oil and Parmesan.

Agrodolce Stewed Peppers with Polenta

Italian peperonata is a stewy mix of silky sweet peppers, with allium(s), olive oil and sometimes tomatoes. How the dish is made and the ingredients that flavor it vary region to region. This version features an agrodolce—or sweet and sour—taste profile that is typical of Sicilian cuisine. We've paired the stewed peppers with polenta to create a dish satisfying enough to be a light main. If you prefer, however, skip the polenta and serve the peperonata as an antipasto, with grilled or pan-seared meaty fish such as tuna, swordfish or salmon, or with grilled or roasted pork.

START TO FINISH: 40 MINUTES
SERVINGS: 6

_____

3 tablespoons extra-virgin olive oil, plus more to serve

¼ cup pine nuts

3 medium bell peppers (a mix of red, yellow or orange), stemmed, seeded and thinly sliced

1 medium red onion, halved and thinly sliced

Kosher salt and ground black pepper

½ cup raisins **OR** golden raisins **OR** currants

¼ cup drained capers

3 tablespoons balsamic vinegar

1 cup instant polenta (see headnote)

2 ounces Parmesan cheese **OR** aged Asiago cheese, finely grated (1 cup), plus shaved cheese to serve

1 tablespoon honey

Don't use regular polenta or quick polenta, as both have different absorption properties and cooking times than instant polenta. Even different brands of instant polenta may vary in thickness once cooked. It should be creamy and spoonable; if yours is too thick, after mixing in the cheese, stir in additional water to thin it to the desired consistency.

1. **In a 12-inch skillet** over medium, heat the oil until shimmering. Add the pine nuts and cook, stirring, until beginning to brown, about 1 minute. Using a slotted spoon, transfer the nuts to a small bowl; set aside. To the skillet, add the bell peppers, onion and ½ teaspoon each salt and pepper. Cook, stirring occasionally, until the vegetables begin to soften, 6 to 8 minutes. Stir in the raisins, capers, vinegar and ¾ cup water. Cover and cook, stirring occasionally, until the peppers are fully softened and most of the liquid has evaporated, 12 to 15 minutes.

2. **Meanwhile, in a large saucepan,** bring 2 cups water and ½ teaspoon salt to a boil. While whisking constantly, gradually add the polenta. Return to a boil, stirring occasionally, and cook, continuing to stir, until thickened, about 1 minute. Remove from the heat, cover and let stand for 2 to 3 minutes. Stir in the cheese and ½ teaspoon pepper, adding more water to thin, if needed. Taste and season with salt and pepper.

3. **When the pepper mixture is done,** remove the skillet from the heat. Stir in the honey, then taste and season with salt and pepper. Stir the polenta to smooth it out and pour the polenta into a serving dish. Top with the stewed peppers and drizzle with additional oil. Scatter on the pine nuts and shaved cheese.

Optional garnish: Chopped fresh mint **OR** fresh basil

Tomatoes

In the Mercado Lonja del Barranco, a produce market turned sleek food hall in Seville, Spain, we encountered what looked like a rainbow of creamy puddings but turned out to be salmorejo, a tomato-based chilled soup. Traditionally, ripe tomatoes are mashed in a mortar and pestle with stale bread, olive oil, garlic and salt. Chopped hard-boiled egg and chunks of cured ham go on top. Our take, p. 95, uses a food processor and a fresh, country-style loaf so the crumbs blend easily into the soup. It's the perfect dish to celebrate the bursting freshness of perfectly ripe summer tomatoes, but it works year-round, too. We've found that when eating tomatoes out of season it's best to go with reliable varieties like grape, cherry and Campari, or cocktail, tomatoes.

Cooks in Provence, France, turn summer vegetables into a tian, which refers to a casserole of sliced vegetables as well as to the shallow dish in which the food is baked. We use just tomatoes for our version, p. 20, baking them with extra-virgin olive oil, garlic and herbs until brown and bubbly. Not sure your tomatoes are at peak ripeness? No worries, the slow bake makes this a forgiving dish.

Cookbook author Marcella Hazan was famous for her simple and superb tomato sauce made with tomatoes, onion and butter. We riff on that in our butter-braised tomato soup, p. 104, which uses fresh tomatoes and adds broth. We top the soup with pesto, toasted baguette slices and shaved Parmesan for a light, flavorful meal.

Panzanella is a classic Italian salad of rustic bread doused in olive oil and the juices of sweetly ripe tomatoes. We use elements of the dish in our tomato, arugula and bread salad, p. 81. Tradition calls for stale bread, but since we don't often have that on hand, we toast crusty bread for crisp-chewy texture. The tomato wedges and onion slices sit briefly in the vinaigrette to mellow the onion's bite. Corn kernels add summery flavor and fresh mozzarella lends substance for a bright and satisfying dish.

Spaghetti Aglio e Olio with Fresh Tomatoes

Classic Italian pasta aglio e olio, or pasta with garlic and oil, is made with those ingredients and little else. This version gets an infusion of bright color and flavor from fresh tomatoes and chopped basil (or parsley). We boil the pasta until just shy of al dente, then reserve about ¾ cup of the cooking water and drain. The noodles will reach al dente when returned to the pot and cooked with half of the wilted tomatoes and some of the cooking water. This technique allows the pasta to absorb the flavors of the sauce and become better integrated with it. The remainder of the tomatoes is piled on top of the pasta just before serving for a bright burst of fresh flavor and color.

START TO FINISH: 25 MINUTES
SERVINGS: 6

_____

1 pound spaghetti

Kosher salt and ground black pepper

⅓ cup extra-virgin olive oil

4 medium garlic cloves, thinly sliced

1 Fresno **OR** jalapeño chili, stemmed, seeded and chopped

1 pound ripe tomatoes, cored and chopped

½ cup chopped fresh basil **OR** flat-leaf parsley

2 ounces finely grated Parmesan **OR** pecorino Romano cheese (1 cup)

Don't use underripe tomatoes. Plump, sweet, full-flavored tomatoes are key. In non-summer months, look for cocktail tomatoes (sometimes sold as Campari tomatoes), as they're dependably good year-round.

1. **In a large pot,** bring 4 quarts water to a boil. Stir in the pasta and 1 tablespoon salt, then cook, stirring occasionally, until just shy of al dente. Reserve about ¾ cup of the cooking water, then drain in a colander.

2. **In the same pot over medium-low,** combine the oil, garlic and chili. Cook, stirring, until the garlic is light golden brown, 1 to 2 minutes. Add the tomatoes and stir to combine. Transfer half of the tomatoes to a small bowl and set aside.

3. **To the pot,** add the cooked spaghetti, ½ cup reserved pasta water and ½ teaspoon each salt and black pepper. Cook, tossing, until the pasta is al dente, 1 to 2 minutes; add more reserved water as needed so the pasta is lightly sauced. Off heat, toss in the basil and half of the cheese, then taste and season with salt and pepper. Transfer to a serving dish and spoon the reserved tomatoes on top. Serve with the remaining cheese on the side.

Scallion Noodles

In this dish, a riff on Chinese scallion noodles called cong you ban mian, just a few simple ingredients provide big, bold flavor. Cutting the scallions into thin strips before cooking requires a little knife work, but allows them to crisp evenly and quickly. Any variety of dried Asian wheat noodles similar in size to thin spaghetti works well in this recipe, but pass on wide, flat shapes. Topped with fried eggs, these noodles are a quick, flavor-packed dinner.

START TO FINISH: 30 MINUTES
SERVINGS: 4

———

2 bunches scallions
(about 12 medium scallions)

10 ounces dried Asian wheat
noodles (see headnote)

⅓ cup grapeseed or other
neutral oil

⅓ cup soy sauce

2 tablespoons white sugar

Kosher salt and
ground black pepper

Don't stir the scallions too frequently as they begin cooking; *this slows the browning and crisping process.*

1. **In a large pot,** bring 4 quarts water to a boil. Meanwhile, cut the scallions into 2- to 3-inch lengths, then slice lengthwise into thin strips, reserving the whites and greens separately.

2. **To the boiling water,** add the noodles and cook, stirring occasionally, until tender (refer to package instructions for cooking times). Drain in a colander and rinse under running cold water until cool. Drain again and set aside.

3. **In a 12-inch skillet** over medium, heat the oil until shimmering. Add the scallion whites and cook, stirring occasionally, until lightly browned, 5 to 7 minutes. Add about half of the scallion greens and cook, stirring occasionally, until well-browned and beginning to crisp, another 3 to 6 minutes. Add the soy sauce and sugar, then bring to a simmer, stirring to combine. Reduce to low and add the noodles. Cook, tossing to combine, until the noodles are heated through, about 1 minute.

4. **Off heat,** taste and season with salt and pepper. Toss in the remaining scallion greens and divide among individual bowls.

Optional garnish: Sriracha sauce **OR** thinly sliced fresh chilies **OR** chopped roasted peanuts

1 navel orange

5 tablespoons extra-virgin olive oil, divided

1 cup short-grain brown rice, rinsed and drained

1 large shallot, minced

Kosher salt and ground black pepper

½ cup dried apricots, chopped

1 pound broccoli crowns, cut into 1-inch florets

½ teaspoon red pepper flakes

2 tablespoons cider vinegar

1 teaspoon honey

½ cup lightly packed fresh tarragon, chopped

Don't purchase regular bunched broccoli for this recipe; look instead for broccoli crowns, which are less stemmy. Lacy florets are a better combination with the grain than dense stem pieces. Be sure to use short-grain brown rice, as its starchiness makes the dish cohesive and satisfying.

1. **Cut two 3-inch-long strips** of zest from the orange; cut the orange into quarters. Set aside. In a medium saucepan over medium, heat 1 tablespoon of oil until shimmering. Add the rice and shallot, then cook, stirring, until some of the grains turn translucent, about 2 minutes. Add 1½ cups water, ½ teaspoon salt and the orange zest strips. Bring to a boil over medium-high, cover and reduce to medium-low. Cook without stirring until the rice is tender-chewy and the water has been absorbed, 35 to 40 minutes. Remove from the heat and let stand, covered, for 10 minutes. Fluff the rice; remove and discard the zest strips. Stir in the apricots, cover and set aside.

2. **While the rice cooks,** heat the oven to 500°F with a rack in the lowest position. Slide a rimmed baking sheet onto the rack to heat. In a large bowl, toss the broccoli, the orange quarters, 2 tablespoons of the remaining oil, the pepper flakes and ½ teaspoon salt. Carefully remove the baking sheet from the oven and distribute the mixture in an even layer; reserve the bowl. Roast without stirring until the broccoli is tender-crisp and lightly charred, 12 to 15 minutes.

3. **Using tongs,** squeeze the juice from the orange quarters into a small bowl. You should have 2 to 3 tablespoons (if needed, supplement with water); discard the rinds. Add the remaining 2 tablespoons oil, the vinegar, honey and ¼ teaspoon each salt and black pepper, then whisk to combine.

4. **Return the broccoli** to the large bowl. Add the rice, dressing and tarragon, then toss. Taste and season with salt and pepper.

Roasted Broccoli with Brown Rice, Tarragon and Cider Vinaigrette

Roasting broccoli on a heated baking sheet in a blistering hot oven gets the vegetable to char, bringing forth deep, nutty, bittersweet flavors. Here, we toss oven-charred broccoli with a brown rice pilaf, dried apricots, a fruity vinaigrette and fresh tarragon to create a warm rice salad. We also roast the orange, cut into quarters, before juicing it to temper its acidity and intensify its flavor. This vegetable-and-grain dish is hearty enough to be the center of a vegetarian meal or serve it as a side to chicken or seafood.

Indonesian-Style Fried Noodles

These savory-sweet noodles are a riff on Indonesian mee goreng. Stir-fried red bell peppers and cabbage add texture and color to the tangle of chewy-tender noodles that get flavorful browning in a hot skillet. Look for fresh yellow Asian wheat noodles, often sold as lo mein or oil noodles, in the refrigerated section of the supermarket near the tofu. For spiciness and a little acidity, offer sambal oelek (or chili-garlic sauce) and lime wedges on the side.

START TO FINISH: 40 MINUTES
SERVINGS: 4 TO 6

1 pound fresh yellow Asian wheat noodles, such as lo mein

Kosher salt and ground black pepper

1 teaspoon plus 3 tablespoons grapeseed or other neutral oil, divided

½ medium head napa cabbage, thinly sliced (about 5 cups)

2 medium bell peppers, stemmed, seeded and thinly sliced

2 large shallots, halved and thinly sliced lengthwise

4 medium garlic cloves, minced

¼ cup low-sodium soy sauce

2 tablespoons oyster sauce

1 tablespoon packed brown sugar

Thinly sliced scallions, to serve

Don't forget to rinse the noodles under running cold water after boiling and draining. This stops the cooking so the noodles don't wind up overdone in the finished dish. After rinsing, be sure to drain the noodles well by shaking the colander and tossing them about.

1. **In a large pot,** bring 2 quarts water to a boil. Add the noodles and cook until just shy of al dente, 2 to 3 minutes. Drain, rinse under running cold water until fully cooled, then drain again. Toss with 1 teaspoon of oil; set aside.

2. **In a 12-inch nonstick skillet** over medium-high, heat 1 tablespoon of the remaining oil until shimmering. Add the cabbage, peppers, shallots and ¼ teaspoon each salt and pepper; cook, stirring occasionally. until well browned, 6 to 7 minutes. Add the garlic and cook, stirring, until fragrant, about 30 seconds. Transfer to a medium bowl.

3. **In the same skillet** over medium-high, heat the remaining 2 tablespoons oil until barely smoking. Distribute the noodles in an even layer and cook without stirring until spotty brown, 2 to 3 minutes. Toss, redistribute in an even layer and cook without stirring for another 2 minutes. Add the soy sauce, oyster sauce and sugar; cook, stirring, until only a small amount of glaze-like liquid remains, 1 to 2 minutes. Add the vegetables and cook, tossing to combine, until the pan is dry, about 2 minutes. Taste and season with salt and pepper. Serve sprinkled with scallions.

Pasta with Tomatoes, Peas and Pancetta

Pasta con piselli e pomodoro, or pasta with peas and tomatoes, is a Neapolitan classic. Our version is based on a recipe taught to us by Antonella Scala, who hosts pop-up dinners in her rooftop kitchen in Naples. Cooked in a single pot, the dish falls somewhere between a thick soup and a saucy pasta. Water is added to a base of cooked onions, pancetta and tomato paste, then the pasta is cooked directly in that mixture. Peas are added at the end of the cooking time, and chopped tomatoes, mint and cheese are stirred in off-heat. To make the dish vegetarian, simply omit the pancetta.

START TO FINISH: 35 MINUTES
SERVINGS: 4 TO 6

1 pound plum tomatoes, cored and chopped

½ cup lightly packed fresh mint **OR** parsley leaves **OR** a combination, chopped

Kosher salt and ground black pepper

3 tablespoons extra-virgin olive oil, plus more to serve

1 medium yellow onion, chopped

4 ounces pancetta, chopped

3 tablespoons tomato paste

½ teaspoon red pepper flakes

1 pound campanelle **OR** orecchiette pasta

2 cups frozen peas

1 ounce pecorino Romano cheese, finely grated (½ cup)

Lemon wedges, to serve (optional)

Don't hesitate to use whatever short pasta shape you have on hand.

1. **In a medium bowl,** stir together the tomatoes, mint and ½ teaspoon salt; set aside. In a large Dutch oven over medium-high, heat the oil until shimmering. Add the onion and pancetta, then cook, stirring, until the onion is softened and the pancetta has rendered its fat, about 5 minutes. Stir in the tomato paste and pepper flakes; cook, stirring, until the paste is incorporated and beginning to brown, about 2 minutes.

2. **Add 6 cups water,** scraping up any browned bits. Stir in the pasta and 1½ teaspoons salt. Bring to a boil, then cover, reduce to medium and simmer vigorously, stirring occasionally, until the pasta is just shy of al dente, 8 to 10 minutes.

3. **Stir in the peas,** then increase the heat to medium-high and cook until the peas are heated through, about 5 minutes. Off heat, stir in 2 tablespoons of cheese along with the tomato-mint mixture. If needed, stir in additional water to achieve a slightly soupy consistency. Taste and season with salt and black pepper. Transfer to a serving bowl, then drizzle with additional oil. Serve with the remaining cheese and, if desired, with lemon wedges.

Pasta with Winter Squash, Kale and Goat Cheese

This hearty, autumnal pasta dish is perfect for cold weather. We use delicata or acorn squash, two thin-skinned varieties that don't require peeling, so prep is that much easier. Thinly slicing the squash ensures it cooks quickly under the broiler, becoming tender and slightly caramelized. Fresh goat cheese is added to the hot pasta, melting into a creamy sauce, while baby kale and toasted walnuts give some additional heft. Ribbon-like pasta shapes, such as pappardelle or tagliatelle, are an especially good match for the thin slices of squash.

START TO FINISH: 40 MINUTES
SERVINGS: 4

———

1½-pound delicata squash **OR** acorn squash, quartered lengthwise, seeded and sliced crosswise about ¼ inch thick

4 tablespoons extra-virgin olive oil, divided

4 medium garlic cloves, minced

¼ teaspoon red pepper flakes

Kosher salt and ground black pepper

8 ounces pappardelle **OR** tagliatelle

2 ounces fresh goat cheese (chèvre), crumbled

2 ounces (4 cups lightly packed) baby kale

⅓ cup walnuts **OR** hazelnuts, toasted and chopped

½ teaspoon white balsamic vinegar

Don't forget to save about 2 cups of the cooking water before draining the pasta. The salty, starchy liquid is a key ingredient, combining with the goat cheese to create a creamy, silky sauce that coats the noodles and squash.

1. **Heat the broiler** with a rack about 8 inches from the element. On a rimmed baking sheet, toss the squash with 2 tablespoons of oil, the garlic, pepper flakes, ½ teaspoon salt and ¼ teaspoon black pepper. Distribute in an even layer and broil, stirring every few minutes, until well browned and a skewer inserted into the largest piece of squash meets no resistance, about 12 minutes. Remove from the oven and set aside.

2. **In a large pot,** bring 2 quarts water to a boil. Add the pasta and 1 tablespoon salt, then cook, stirring occasionally, until just shy of al dente. Reserve 2 cups of the cooking water, then drain. Return the pasta to the pot. Add the squash, the cheese and 1 cup of the reserved pasta water, then cook over medium-high, tossing occasionally with tongs, until the pasta is al dente and creamy, about 3 minutes; adding more reserved cooking water as needed if the mixture looks dry.

3. **Off heat,** toss in the kale, nuts and vinegar, then taste and season with salt and black pepper.

Optional garnish: Finely grated pecorino Romano cheese **OR** toasted walnut oil

4 tablespoons (½ stick) salted butter, cut into 1-tablespoon pieces

1 medium yellow onion, chopped

Kosher salt and ground black pepper

3 medium garlic cloves, thinly sliced

1 cup pearl couscous

⅓ cup dry white wine

1 pound asparagus, trimmed and cut on the diagonal into ½-inch pieces; reserve the stalks and tips separately

1 ounce Parmesan cheese, finely grated (½ cup), plus more to serve

½ cup lightly packed fresh flat-leaf parsley, finely chopped, plus more to serve

Don't use especially thick nor super slender asparagus for this recipe. Choose average, pencil-sized spears so the pieces are perfectly tender when the couscous is done. Make sure to reserve the stalk and tip pieces separately; they're added at different times because they cook at slightly different rates.

1. **In a 12-inch skillet** over medium-high, melt 3 tablespoons of the butter. Add the onion and ½ teaspoon each salt and pepper, then cook, stirring, until it begins to soften, 3 to 5 minutes. Add the garlic and cook, stirring, until fragrant. Add the couscous and cook, stirring often, until it begins to brown.

2. **Pour in the wine and cook,** stirring, until the pan is almost dry, about 1 minute. Add 3 cups water and ½ teaspoon salt, then cook, stirring occasionally, for 5 minutes. Stir in the asparagus stalks and cook, stirring, for 3 minutes, then stir in the asparagus tips. Continue to cook, stirring, until almost all the liquid has been absorbed and the asparagus is tender, about another 2 minutes.

3. **Off heat, add the Parmesan,** parsley and remaining 1 tablespoon butter, then stir until the butter melts. Taste and season with salt and pepper. Serve sprinkled with additional Parmesan and parsley.

Pearl Couscous "Risotto" with Asparagus

Classic risotto is made with starchy medium-grain Italian rice, such as Arborio or carnaroli. This "risotto" uses pearl couscous (which actually is a pasta) and a simplified risotto cooking method to produce "grains" with a rich, creamy consistency. The wheaty flavor of pearl couscous (sometimes called Israeli couscous or ptitim) is a perfect match for grassy, subtly sweet asparagus and the salty, nutty flavor of Parmesan cheese.

Pasta with Pesto Calabrese

Pesto calabrese, from Italy's Calabria region, is a simple puree with a base of sweet red peppers, tomatoes and ricotta cheese. It often includes nuts for richness and, on occasion, cooked eggplant for added creaminess. For our version, we char fresh red bell peppers in a hot skillet to soften their crisp texture and give them a subtle smokiness. We combine them with sun-dried tomatoes for their deep, concentrated, umami-rich flavor. We skip the eggplant but do process toasted sliced almonds into the pesto, then sprinkle some onto the sauced pasta for contrasting texture.

START TO FINISH: 45 MINUTES
SERVINGS: 4 TO 6

½ cup sliced almonds

1 tablespoon grapeseed or other neutral oil

2 medium red bell peppers, stemmed, seeded, and cut into ¼-inch strips

Kosher salt and ground black pepper

4 medium garlic cloves, thinly sliced

¾ teaspoon red pepper flakes

¼ cup whole-milk ricotta cheese

1 ounce Parmesan cheese, finely grated (½ cup)

¼ cup oil-packed sun-dried tomatoes, drained and roughly chopped

¼ cup extra-virgin olive oil

1 pound orecchiette OR campanelle pasta

½ cup lightly packed fresh basil, torn

Don't use extra-virgin olive oil to char the bell peppers. With its low smoke point, olive oil will scorch before the peppers are properly charred. Instead, choose an oil with a high smoke point, such as grapeseed or canola.

1. **In a 12-inch skillet** over medium, toast the almonds, stirring often, until fragrant and light golden brown, 3 to 4 minutes. Transfer to a small bowl and set aside. In the same skillet over medium-high, heat the grapeseed oil until shimmering. Add the bell peppers and ½ teaspoon each salt and black pepper, then cook, stirring occasionally, until lightly charred, 3 to 5 minutes.

2. **Reduce to medium,** stir in the garlic, then cook, stirring, until the peppers are softened and the garlic is golden brown, about 2 minutes. Remove from the heat, then stir in the pepper flakes and ¼ cup of the toasted almonds. Transfer to a food processor and cool to room temperature.

3. **To the pepper mixture** in the food processor, add the ricotta, Parmesan, tomatoes and olive oil. Process until smooth, about 45 seconds, scraping the bowl as needed. Transfer to a large bowl and set aside.

4. **In a large pot,** bring 4 quarts water to a boil. Add 1 tablespoon salt and the pasta, then cook, stirring occasionally, until al dente. Reserve 1 cup of the cooking water, then drain. Add the pasta to the bowl with the pesto, along with ¼ cup of the cooking water. Toss, adding additional cooking water as needed to thin. Taste and season with salt and pepper. Transfer to a serving dish, then sprinkle with basil and the remaining ¼ cup almonds.

Linguine with Artichokes, Asparagus and Lemon-Mint Ricotta

To make this simple one-skillet pasta dish full of bright, spring-time flavors and a pleasing mix of textures, we use store-bought fresh linguine. We cook the pasta in only 3 cups of water; the starch the noodles release as they simmer creates a thickened liquid that's the basis of the sauce. Most jarred marinated artichoke hearts are quartered; if yours are whole or halved, cut them into smaller pieces. Jars come in different sizes, but a 10-ouncer will yield the right amount of drained artichokes for the recipe. Look for asparagus spears that are about as thick as a pencil so they cook to tender-crisp doneness in the right amount of time.

START TO FINISH: 40 MINUTES
SERVINGS: 4

½ cup whole-milk ricotta cheese

½ cup lightly packed fresh mint, finely chopped

2 teaspoons grated lemon zest, plus 1 tablespoon lemon juice

3 tablespoons extra-virgin olive oil, divided

Kosher salt and ground black pepper

4 ounces thinly sliced pancetta, chopped

2 medium shallots, halved and thinly sliced

9-ounce package fresh linguine

1½ cups drained marinated artichoke hearts (see headnote)

1 pound asparagus, trimmed and cut into 1-inch pieces on the diagonal

2 ounces pecorino Romano cheese, finely grated (1 cup)

2 tablespoons salted butter, cut into 2 pieces

Don't forget to cover the skillet after adding the pasta. The lid keeps the heat in the pan so the ingredients cook through properly and without excessive moisture evaporation. After scattering the asparagus over the pasta-artichoke mixture, don't mix it in. It cooks more evenly if left to steam on top.

1. **In a small bowl,** stir together the ricotta, mint, lemon zest and juice, 2 tablespoons oil, ½ teaspoon each salt and pepper; set aside.

2. **In a 12-inch nonstick skillet** over medium, cook the remaining 1 tablespoon oil and the pancetta, stirring, until the pancetta is crisp, 3 to 5 minutes. Add the shallots and cook, stirring, until softened, about 2 minutes. Stir in 3 cups water and bring to a boil over high. Add the linguine, stirring to separate the noodles. Cover and cook, stirring occasionally, until the pasta is just shy of al dente, about 3 minutes.

3. **Stir in the artichoke hearts,** then scatter the asparagus over the top. Cover and cook without stirring until the asparagus is tender-crisp and the pasta is al dente, about 2 minutes. Off heat, add half of the pecorino and the butter, then toss until combined and the butter has melted; add more water as needed so the sauce clings lightly to the pasta. Taste and season with salt and pepper. Serve with the ricotta mixture spooned on top and the remaining pecorino on the side.

1 quart low-sodium vegetable broth **OR** chicken broth

¼ cup extra-virgin olive oil, plus more to serve

1 bunch scallions, thinly sliced, whites and greens reserved separately

1 cup Arborio rice

Kosher salt and ground black pepper

5-ounce container baby spinach

½ cup finely chopped fresh dill **OR** basil **OR** mint **OR** a combination

2 ounces feta cheese, crumbled (½ cup)

Grated lemon zest, plus lemon wedges, to serve

Don't use unheated broth. Warming it helps the rice cook faster. If you prefer, heat it in a saucepan on the stovetop instead of microwaving it.

1. **In a 1-quart liquid measuring cup** or medium microwave-safe bowl, microwave the broth on high until hot, about 4 minutes. Cover to keep warm and set aside.

2. **In a large saucepan** over medium, heat the oil until shimmering. Add the scallion whites and cook, stirring, until wilted, about 2 minutes. Add the rice and stir until the grains are coated in oil. Add 2 cups of the warm broth, a pinch of salt and ½ teaspoon pepper. Cook, stirring often and adjusting the heat as needed to maintain a vigorous simmer, until the liquid is almost absorbed, 7 to 10 minutes. Add another 1½ cups of the broth and cook, stirring often, until the rice is al dente, 5 to 7 minutes.

3. **Reduce to medium-low,** add the spinach and stir until wilted. Cook, stirring and adding more broth about 2 tablespoons at a time as needed, until the grains are tender, about 3 minutes; the rice should be creamy but not soupy.

4. **Off heat,** stir in the dill and scallion greens. Taste and season with salt and pepper. Transfer to a serving bowl and sprinkle with the feta and additional pepper. Drizzle with additional oil, sprinkle with lemon zest and serve with lemon wedges on the side.

Herbed Spinach Rice with Feta and Lemon

This dish melds Greek spanakorizo, or spinach rice, with Italian risotto. We use Arborio rice and add hot broth in stages, as if making risotto, in order to create a dish with a rich, creamy consistency. Added near the end of cooking, the spinach melts into the grains. Herbs, one or more, go in at the end to keep aromas and flavors vibrant. This is an excellent side to grilled or roasted chicken or lamb, or top it with grilled, seared or sautéed shrimp.

Rigatoni with Swiss Chard, White Beans and Rosemary

START TO FINISH: 35 MINUTES
SERVINGS: 6

The deep-green leaves of Swiss chard have a flavor similar to spinach, while the crisp stems have a sweet earthiness that's not unlike beets (the two vegetables are, in fact, related). We use both parts in this hearty one-pot pasta and bean dish, cooking the stems for a few minutes before wilting the leaves. Pasta, greens and beans all are mild-mannered, so for boldness we add garlic, pancetta, pepper flakes, rosemary and pecorino Romano cheese—classic Italian flavors.

1 pound rigatoni

Kosher salt and ground black pepper

1 tablespoon extra-virgin olive oil

4 ounces thinly sliced pancetta, chopped

2 medium garlic cloves, minced

1 bunch Swiss chard, stems chopped, leaves cut into 1-inch pieces, reserved separately

¼ teaspoon red pepper flakes

1 tablespoon minced fresh rosemary

15½-ounce can cannellini beans, drained but not rinsed

1 ounce pecorino Romano cheese, finely grated (½ cup), plus more to serve

Don't rinse the cannellini beans after draining them. The starchy liquid that clings to the beans adds a little body to the sauce. Also, be sure to drain the pasta when it's shy of al dente, not at the ideal degree of doneness. It will finish cooking when it is returned to the pot and simmered for a few minutes with the chard and a little of the pasta cooking water.

1. **In a large pot,** bring 4 quarts water to a boil. Add the pasta and 1 tablespoon salt, then cook, stirring occasionally, until the pasta is just shy of al dente. Reserve about 1 cup of the cooking water, then drain.

2. **In the same pot** over medium, combine the oil and pancetta. Cook, stirring occasionally, until crisp and brown, 2 to 3 minutes. Remove the pot from the heat and, using a slotted spoon, transfer the pancetta to a small bowl.

3. **To the fat remaining in the pot,** add the garlic, chard stems, pepper flakes, rosemary and ½ teaspoon black pepper. Cook over medium, stirring occasionally, until the chard stems begin to soften, 1 to 2 minutes. Add the chard leaves and cook, stirring, until wilted, about 1 minute. Add the beans, pasta, ½ cup of the reserved pasta water and the cheese. Cook, stirring, until the pasta is al dente and lightly sauced, 2 to 3 minutes; add more water as needed if the mixture looks dry. Transfer to a serving bowl, sprinkle with the pancetta and serve with additional cheese.

Penne with Spinach, Raisins and Toasted Garlic

This one-pot pasta dish features a Sicilian combination of salty, sweet and sour elements. It's garnished with slices of crisp, toasted garlic, but the sweet, nutty allium flavor is an undercurrent throughout because the olive oil used for frying the garlic also is used to sauté the spinach. Raisins plumped in wine vinegar dot the pasta, adding bursts of tangy-sweet flavor that complement the savoriness of the cheese.

START TO FINISH: 30 MINUTES
SERVINGS: 4 TO 6

½ cup golden raisins **OR** raisins

2 tablespoons red wine vinegar **OR** white wine vinegar

1 pound penne **OR** ziti pasta

Kosher salt and ground black pepper

¼ cup extra-virgin olive oil, plus more to serve

4 medium garlic cloves, thinly sliced

10 ounces baby spinach

½ teaspoon red pepper flakes

2 ounces pecorino Romano **OR** Parmesan cheese, finely grated (1 cup), divided, plus more to serve

Don't forget to reserve about 1 cup of the cooking water before draining the pasta. You'll need some of the water to toss with the penne, spinach and raisins to loosen up the mixture and lightly sauce the noodles.

1. **In a small microwave-safe bowl,** stir together the raisins and the vinegar. Microwave on high until the raisins are heated through, about 1 minute; set aside.

2. **In a large pot,** bring 2 quarts water to a boil. Add the pasta and 1 tablespoon salt, then cook, stirring occasionally, until the penne is al dente. Reserve about 1 cup of the cooking water, then drain.

3. **In the same pot** over medium, combine the oil and garlic; cook, stirring, until the garlic is golden brown, 3 to 4 minutes. Remove the pot from the heat and, using a slotted spoon, transfer the garlic to a paper towel-lined plate.

4. **To the oil remaining in the pot,** add the spinach and pepper flakes; cook over medium, stirring, just until the spinach is wilted, about 1 minute. Add the pasta, the raisins and any vinegar remaining in the bowl, ½ cup of the reserved pasta water, ½ cup cheese and ½ teaspoon each salt and pepper. Cook, stirring constantly, until the ingredients are well combined and the pasta is very lightly sauced, about 1 minute; add more water as needed if the mixture looks dry. Stir in the remaining cheese.

5. **Off heat,** taste and season with salt and pepper. Transfer to a serving bowl, drizzle with additional oil and sprinkle with the toasted garlic. Serve with the additional cheese on the side.

Optional garnish: Toasted pine nuts **OR** toasted sliced almonds

9

SIMPLY SUPPER

Oaxacan-Style Vegetables in Chili-Garlic Sauce

Some versions of Oaxacan chileajo contain meat, but in chileajo de verduras (also known as chileajo de legumbres), vegetables are the main attraction, along with the earthy, garlicky red chili sauce that coats them (chileajo translates from the Spanish as chili-garlic). Garnet-toned guajillo chilies are mild and fruity; we toast them in a little oil to draw out their rich flavors before softening them in hot water, then we use some of the soaking water when blending the sauce. We especially like the trio of potatoes, cauliflower and green beans, but feel free to substitute your favorites, adjusting for different cooking times. Vegetable chileajo isn't usually served as a main. But sandwiched in telera rolls to make tortas or spooned onto crisp tostadas and topped with a few—or all—of the optional garnishes (see below), we think it's wholly satisfying.

START TO FINISH: 1 HOUR, PLUS RESTING TIME
SERVINGS: 4

___

4 large guajillo chilies, stemmed and seeded

1 tablespoon extra-virgin olive oil

3 medium garlic cloves, smashed and peeled

3 tablespoons cider vinegar

2 teaspoons fresh oregano

¼ teaspoon ground cumin

Kosher salt and ground black pepper

12 ounces Yukon Gold potatoes, peeled and cut into ½-inch pieces

8 ounces cauliflower, cut into 1-inch florets

4 ounces green beans, trimmed and cut into 1-inch pieces

Don't allow the vegetables to cool before adding them to the chili puree. And after saucing, be sure to allow them to rest for at least 15 minutes before serving. The residual heat helps meld and mellow the ingredients in the sauce and, just as importantly, as they cool, the vegetables absorb flavors.

1. **In a small saucepan** over medium-high, combine the chilies and oil; cook, occasionally turning the chilies with tongs, until the oil takes on a reddish hue and the chilies are fragrant, about 3 minutes. Carefully add 2 cups water and bring to a boil. Remove the pan from the heat, cover and let stand until the chilies are softened, 15 to 20 minutes, occasionally pushing the chilies into the water to submerge them.

2. **Using tongs or a slotted spoon,** transfer the chilies to a blender, then add ½ cup of the soaking liquid. Add the garlic, vinegar, oregano, cumin, ½ teaspoon salt and ¼ teaspoon pepper. Blend until smooth, about 1 minute. Transfer to a large bowl.

3. **In a medium saucepan,** combine the potatoes and 1 tablespoon salt, then add water to cover by 2 inches. Bring to a boil over medium-high, reduce to medium and cook, uncovered and stirring occasionally, until the potatoes are just shy of tender, about 3 minutes; adjust the heat as needed to maintain a simmer. Add the cauliflower and beans; cook, stirring occasionally, until the vegetables are just tender, 3 to 5 minutes. Drain in a colander, immediately add to the bowl with the chili puree and toss until well coated.

4. **Let the vegetables stand** for at least 15 minutes or cover and refrigerate for up to 2 days. Taste and season with salt and pepper. Serve warm, room temperature or cold.

Optional garnish: Chopped fresh cilantro **OR** shredded cabbage **OR** crumbled queso fresco **OR** thinly sliced onion **OR** a combination

1 teaspoon cumin seeds, lightly crushed

½ English cucumber, shredded on the large holes of a box grater

1 cup plain whole-milk yogurt

½ cup lightly packed fresh mint, chopped

Kosher salt and ground black pepper

3 tablespoons ghee **OR** neutral oil

2- to 2½-pound head cauliflower, trimmed and cut into 1-inch florets

1 or 2 serrano **OR** jalapeño chilies, stemmed, seeded and thinly sliced

2 teaspoons ground turmeric

¼ cup roasted salted cashews, roughly chopped

Don't be shy about squeezing the water from the shredded cucumber. Removing the excess moisture prevents the raita from becoming watery. Don't stir the cauliflower for the first four to five minutes after adding it to the pan. This allows the florets to brown deeply, which builds flavor.

1. **In a 12-inch skillet** over medium, toast the cumin seeds, stirring often, until fragrant and slightly darker, 2 to 3 to minutes. Transfer to a small bowl; set the skillet aside. Using your hands, squeeze the shredded cucumber to remove excess water, then add to the bowl with the cumin, along with the yogurt, mint and ¼ teaspoon salt, then stir to combine and set aside.

2. **In the same skillet** over medium-high, heat the ghee until barely smoking. Add the cauliflower in an even layer and cook without stirring until well charred on the bottom, 4 to 5 minutes. Stir in the chilies, turmeric, ½ teaspoon salt and 3 tablespoons water, then immediately cover. Reduce to low and cook, stirring once or twice, until the pan is dry and the cauliflower is tender, 15 to 17 minutes. Taste and season with salt and pepper. Transfer to a serving dish, sprinkle with the cashews and serve with the raita.

Turmeric Cauliflower with Cashews and Raita

This cauliflower gets its warm, golden hue from earthy, aromatic and subtly bitter ground turmeric. Raita, a cooling mixture of yogurt, cucumber and mint, is a perfect accompaniment to the skillet-cooked, chili-spiked florets. To lightly crush the cumin seeds before toasting and mixing them into the raita, use a mortar and pestle or pulse them just a few times in an electric spice grinder. And to prevent hot ghee (or oil) from splattering when the cauliflower goes into the pan, be sure the pieces are completely dry. If you like chili heat, leave some or all of the seeds in the serranos or jalapeños.

Asparagus and Herb Pashtida

A pashtida is an Israeli savory quiche-like casserole, usually crustless and often filled with a mixture of vegetables and cheese, sometimes meat. Pencil-sized asparagus works best, but if only fatter spears are available, cut them in half lengthwise so they cook quickly and have good distribution in the baking dish. Serve the pashtida warm or at room temperature with a leafy salad for a light but complete meal.

START TO FINISH: 40 MINUTES
SERVINGS: 4 TO 6

1 tablespoon extra-virgin olive oil, plus more to serve

1 pound asparagus (see headnote), trimmed

6 large eggs

2 tablespoons half-and-half

Kosher salt and ground black pepper

⅓ cup finely chopped fresh dill

4 scallions, thinly sliced

2 ounces sharp white cheddar cheese **OR** Gruyère cheese, shredded (1 cup)

Lemon wedges, to serve

Don't forget to trim the tough bottoms off the asparagus spears. Also, don't forget to coat the baking dish with 1 tablespoon olive oil to help ensure the pashtida will not stick when slices are removed for serving.

1. **Heat the oven to 400°F** with a rack in the upper-middle position. Brush a 9-by-13-inch baking dish with the oil. Place the asparagus in an even layer perpendicular to the length of the dish.

2. **In a large bowl,** whisk together the eggs, half-and-half and ½ teaspoon each salt and pepper. Fold in the dill, scallions and cheese. Pour the mixture evenly over the asparagus. Bake until the eggs are puffed and set, 18 to 20 minutes. Serve warm or at room temperature, cut into squares, drizzled with additional oil and with lemon wedges on the side.

Optional garnish: Finely chopped fresh chives

Persian-Style Swiss Chard and Herb Omelet

Kuku sabzi is a Persian omelet packed with enough herbs—such as cilantro, parsley, dill—and alliums that its color is deep green. This version is baked in the oven instead of cooked on the stovetop as is traditional, and it combines Swiss chard with dill and scallions. You will need 8 ounces of chard, or about half a standard-size bunch, to obtain the correct amount of stemmed and torn leaves. A food processor makes quick work of chopping the chard and herbs. We also include some baking powder to lighten the texture of the omelet and a little flour to bind the eggs. In order to incorporate these ingredients without clumping, we whisk them plus the seasonings with only two of the eggs before beating in the remaining six. The omelet is delicious with warmed flatbread, feta cheese and crisp radishes. Refrigerate leftovers, tightly wrapped, for up to three days.

START TO FINISH: 1 HOUR (25 MINUTES ACTIVE)
SERVINGS: 6

_____

5 tablespoons extra-virgin olive oil, divided

8 ounces Swiss chard, stemmed, leaves roughly torn (4 cups lightly packed)

1 cup lightly packed fresh dill, roughly chopped

1 bunch scallions, roughly chopped

2 tablespoons all-purpose flour

1½ teaspoons baking powder

1 teaspoon ground cumin

Kosher salt and ground black pepper

8 large eggs

Don't use the chard stems in the omelet, as they are too firm and fibrous. When oiling the cake pan, be sure to use the full 2 tablespoons; the oil should pool at the bottom of the pan and generously coat the sides. And be sure to line the bottom with a round of kitchen parchment for guaranteed easy removal.

1. **Heat the oven to 375°F** with a rack in the upper-middle position. Coat the bottom and sides of a 9-inch round cake pan with 2 tablespoons of oil. Line the bottom of the pan with a round of kitchen parchment, then flip the parchment so both sides are oiled.

2. **In a food processor,** combine the chard, dill, scallions and the remaining 3 tablespoons oil. Process until finely chopped, about 10 seconds, scraping the bowl as needed. In a large bowl, whisk together the flour, baking powder, cumin and ¼ teaspoon each salt and pepper. Add 2 of the eggs and whisk until well blended and smooth. Add the remaining 6 eggs and whisk until fully incorporated and no trace of egg whites remains. Add the chard-herb mixture and fold until homogeneous. Pour into the prepared pan and bake until well risen and a toothpick inserted at the center comes out clean, 20 to 25 minutes.

3. **Let the omelet cool in the pan** on a wire rack for about 10 minutes. Run a knife around the edges, then invert the omelet onto a plate. Peel off the parchment, then re-invert onto a cutting board or platter. Serve warm or at room temperature, cut into wedges.

Eggplant "Katsu"

Traditionally made with either pork or chicken cutlets that are breaded and deep-fried until golden brown and perfectly crisp, katsu is a widely popular Japanese meal. For this version, we opted for eggplant cutlets instead of meat. The cutlets typically are coated with flour, egg and breadcrumbs, but we use a cornstarch slurry in place of the egg for an ultra-crispy "cutlet" that also happens to be vegan. We also pan-fry rather than deep-fry, making this a bit more home cook-friendly. Our streamlined recipe for the savory-sweet tonkatsu sauce that typically accompanies katsu is an excellent foil to the rich eggplant. Serve with steamed rice or between slices of white bread and a little sliced green cabbage for a "katsu sando."

¼ cup ketchup

¼ cup Worcestershire sauce

1 tablespoon soy sauce

2 Italian eggplants **OR** small globe eggplants (8 to 10 ounces each), trimmed, peeled and cut lengthwise into ½-inch-thick planks

Kosher salt and ground black pepper

½ cup all-purpose flour

¼ cup cornstarch

1½ cups panko breadcrumbs

1 to 1½ cups grapeseed or other neutral oil, divided

Don't skip salting the eggplant and letting it stand. This removes some of the moisture from the eggplant and also helps prevent it from soaking up all the oil while cooking. And don't substitute conventional breadcrumbs for the panko; the latter are essential for their crisp, light texture.

1. **In a small bowl,** stir together the ketchup, Worcestershire and soy sauces; set aside. Season each eggplant slice lightly on both sides with salt and set aside on paper towels for 5 to 10 minutes.

2. **In a pie plate or wide,** shallow bowl, stir together the flour and ¼ teaspoon each salt and pepper. In a second similar dish, whisk together the cornstarch and ⅓ cup water. To a third dish, add the panko.

3. **Pat the eggplant dry** and, working a slice at a time, dredge through the flour mixture, turning to coat and shaking off any excess. Transfer to the cornstarch slurry and turn to coat on both sides. Finally, coat each slice with panko, pressing so the breadcrumbs adhere. Transfer to a large plate.

4. **Line another large plate** with paper towels. In a 12-inch nonstick skillet over medium, heat ½ cup of oil until shimmering. Add 3 of the eggplant slices and cook, undisturbed, until the bottoms are golden brown, 3 to 4 minutes. Flip the slices and continue to cook until the eggplant is tender and the second sides are golden brown, about another 3 minutes. Transfer to the paper towel-lined plate and sprinkle with salt.

5. **Pour off and discard the oil** and wipe out the skillet. Cook the remaining eggplant in 1 or 2 more batches in the same way, using ½ cup oil for each. Transfer the eggplant to a platter and serve with the sauce.

Roasted Cauliflower with Toasted Bread and Smoked Mozzarella

Tender cauliflower florets, crisp bits of bread, a little melty cheese and leafy fresh basil combine for a dish loaded with contrasting and complementary textures and flavors. Smoked mozzarella or scamorza (which is similar to mozzarella and often is smoked but sometimes not) is especially tasty, but provolone, regular or aged (sometimes called "picante"), also is good.

START TO FINISH: 45 MINUTES (20 MINUTES ACTIVE)
SERVINGS: 4 TO 6

———

⅓ cup extra-virgin olive oil, plus more to serve

6 medium garlic cloves, chopped

1 Fresno OR jalapeño chili, stemmed and chopped OR ¾ teaspoon red pepper flakes

Kosher salt and ground black pepper

2- to 2½-pound head cauliflower, trimmed and cut into 1-inch florets

8 ounces crusty bread, torn or cut into ½-inch pieces (6 to 7 cups)

⅓ cup extra-virgin olive oil, plus more to serve

4 ounces smoked mozzarella cheese OR scarmorza cheese OR provolone cheese OR aged provolone cheese, shredded (1 cup)

1 cup lightly packed fresh basil, torn

½ medium red onion, thinly sliced

¼ cup white balsamic vinegar

Don't prep the basil too far in advance or it will discolor. To make good use of time, wash, dry and tear the leaves while the cauliflower and bread are in the oven. The cheese can be shredded then, too.

1. **Heat the oven to 450°F** with a rack in the middle position. In a large bowl, stir together the oil, garlic, chili, ¾ teaspoon salt and 1 teaspoon pepper. Add the cauliflower and bread, then toss to coat. Distribute in an even layer on a rimmed baking sheet. Roast until the cauliflower is tender and the bread is toasted and crisped, 25 to 30 minutes, stirring once about halfway through.

2. **Scatter the cheese,** basil and onion over the cauliflower-bread mixture, drizzle with the vinegar and toss to combine. Serve drizzled with additional oil.

Baked Zucchini and Gruyère Omelet

This baked zucchini omelet is what Australians refer to as a "slice." Flour and leavener give the eggs sturdiness and a little lift so the finished texture is firm and sliceable. Made with fresh chives (or scallions) and (optional) ham, our recipe comes together quickly and easily and without any ingredients that typically require precooking. Gruyère cheese, mixed into the batter and sprinkled on top just before baking, adds a creamy, subtly nutty flavor. Serve warm or at room temperature, cut into squares.

START TO FINISH: 50 MINUTES (20 MINUTES ACTIVE)
SERVINGS: 4 TO 6

_____

2 tablespoons extra-virgin olive oil, plus more for the baking dish

1 pound zucchini, shredded on the large holes of a box grater (4 cups)

Kosher salt and ground black pepper

5 large eggs

1 cup all-purpose flour

½ teaspoon baking powder

2 tablespoons chopped fresh chives **OR** scallions

2 ounces sliced deli ham, chopped (optional)

4½ ounces Gruyère cheese, shredded (generous 1 cup)

Don't forget to squeeze the zucchini after salting. This step removes excess moisture that otherwise would water down the flavor and texture of the "slice."

1. **Heat the oven to 350°F** with a rack in the middle position. Brush an 8-inch square baking dish with oil. In a medium bowl, toss the zucchini with ½ teaspoon salt; let stand for about 5 minutes. Meanwhile, in a large bowl, whisk the eggs and ½ teaspoon each salt and pepper. Add the flour and baking powder, then whisk until just combined.

2. **Using your hands,** squeeze the zucchini to remove excess moisture, then add to the egg mixture along with the chives, ham (if using) and all but 2 tablespoons of the cheese. Fold with a silicone spatula until well combined, then pour into the prepared dish and spread into an even layer. Sprinkle with the remaining cheese and drizzle with the oil. Bake until golden brown and set, 30 to 35 minutes. Cut into pieces and serve warm or at room temperature.

START TO FINISH: 25 MINUTES
SERVINGS: 4 TO 6

2 tablespoons grapeseed or other neutral oil

1-pound head cauliflower, trimmed and cut into 1-inch florets

8 ounces green beans, trimmed and cut into 1½- to 2-inch lengths

Kosher salt and ground black pepper

2 medium garlic cloves, finely grated

2 Fresno **OR** jalapeño chilies, stemmed, seeded and finely chopped

2 tablespoons lime juice, plus lime wedges to serve

¼ cup unsweetened shredded coconut, lightly toasted

½ cup chopped roasted cashews

Don't seed the chilies before chopping if you're seeking lots of spiciness. Rather, leave in some or all of the seeds. Make sure to use unsweetened shredded coconut; sweetened coconut is too sugary in flavor and too stringy in texture.

1. **In a 12-inch skillet** over medium-high, heat the oil until shimmering. Add the cauliflower, green beans and a pinch each of salt and pepper, then cook, stirring occasionally, until the vegetables are well charred, about 7 minutes. Add the garlic and chilies; cook, stirring, until fragrant, about 30 seconds. Add ¼ cup water, then cover, reduce to low and cook, stirring only once or twice, until the vegetables are tender-crisp, 4 to 5 minutes.

2. **Off heat,** stir in the lime juice and coconut, then taste and season with salt and pepper. Serve sprinkled with the cashews and with lime wedges on the side.

Optional garnish: Chopped fresh cilantro

Spicy Cauliflower and Green Beans with Coconut and Lime

This recipe employs a two-step skillet technique that we often use with vegetables. The cauliflower and green beans first are seared in hot oil, then a little water is poured in and the lid goes on, allowing the vegetables to steam to the finish. Lime juice and shredded coconut stirred in at the end play off the heat and pungency of the garlic and chilies, evoking the flavors of Southeast Asia. This dish is as good at room temperature as it is hot out of the skillet.

Indian-Spiced Spinach
with Tomatoes and Dill

This hearty vegetable dish was inspired by India's dakhni saag—spinach cooked with onions, tomato and dill. Our version is rich with butter, cumin seeds and turmeric. Use as much cayenne as suits your taste for spicy heat. The slightly saucy greens work well as a side for seafood or chicken. Or serve with basmati rice or naan for a flavorful vegetarian main.

START TO FINISH: 30 MINUTES
SERVINGS: 4

4 tablespoons salted butter

1½ teaspoons cumin seeds

1 medium yellow onion, thinly sliced

Kosher salt

1 teaspoon ground turmeric

¼ to ½ teaspoon cayenne pepper

1½ pounds bunch spinach, stems trimmed by 1½ inches, cut crosswise into 1-inch strips, washed and dried well

½ pint grape or cherry tomatoes, halved

½ cup lightly packed fresh dill

Don't use baby spinach. It's too delicate in both flavor and texture. Look for mature bunch spinach that has large, deep-green leaves and crisp stems.

1. **In a large Dutch oven** over medium, melt the butter. Add the cumin and toast, stirring constantly, until fragrant and sizzling, 15 to 30 seconds. Add the onion and ¾ teaspoon salt. Cook, stirring occasionally, until the onion is light golden brown, 6 to 8 minutes.

2. **Stir in the turmeric and cayenne,** then cook until fragrant, about 30 seconds. Add the spinach and tomatoes and combine with tongs, turning to coat with the butter. Cover and cook until the spinach stems are tender, about 4 minutes, stirring once about halfway through. Remove from the heat. Stir in the dill, then taste and season with salt.

Armenian Swiss Chard with Tomatoes and Chickpeas

Greens and chickpeas are a pairing in many cuisines, and this is our version of the Armenian dish called nivik (sometimes spelled "nivig"). Spinach and chard are the typical choices for nivik; we chose the latter, as chard leaves are sturdier and the stems offer added texture, taste and substance. Onion, garlic and tomatoes are trusty flavor accents, and lemon, stirred in at the end, brightens things. For convenience, we use canned chickpeas so the dish can be on the table in well under an hour. It's hearty enough to be a vegetarian main, especially if sprinkled with the optional garnish of toasted almonds, but is equally good as a side to fish, chicken or pork.

START TO FINISH: 35 MINUTES
SERVINGS: 4 TO 6

———

3 tablespoons extra-virgin olive oil

1 bunch Swiss chard (about 1 pound), stems chopped, leaves cut crosswise into rough ¾-inch ribbons, reserved separately

1 medium yellow onion, chopped

Kosher salt and ground black pepper

2 medium garlic cloves, minced

2 ripe tomatoes, cored and chopped

15½-ounce can chickpeas, rinsed and drained

2 tablespoons lemon juice

Don't forget to reserve the chard stems and leaves separately, as they're added to the skillet at different times. Also, be sure to rinse and drain the chickpeas to remove their starchy canning liquid.

1. **In a 12-inch skillet** over medium, heat the oil until shimmering. Add the chard stems, onion and ½ teaspoon each salt and pepper. Cook, stirring occasionally, until softened and golden brown, 10 to 12 minutes. Increase to medium-high, add the garlic and cook, stirring, until fragrant, about 30 seconds. Stir in the tomatoes and chickpeas, then cook, stirring occasionally, until the tomatoes begin to break down, 3 to 4 minutes.

2. **Add the chard leaves and cook,** stirring occasionally, until wilted, 2 to 3 minutes. Off heat, stir in the lemon juice, then taste and season with salt and pepper. Transfer to a serving dish.

Optional garnish: Toasted slivered almonds

Cauliflower-Scallion Frittata with Harissa and Feta

Tunisian tajine (sometimes spelled tajin, and not to be confused with a stewy Moroccan tagine) is similar to a frittata. It's what gave us the idea to season eggs with harissa (a North African spice paste), along with dill and feta before pouring the mixture over a sauté of cauliflower and scallions. This is equally delicious served at room temperature as it is warm, and it makes a good breakfast, lunch or dinner. You will need an oven-safe 12-inch nonstick skillet for this recipe.

START TO FINISH: 45 MINUTES
SERVINGS: 6

_____

10 large eggs

3 tablespoons harissa paste, plus more to serve

4 ounces feta cheese, crumbled (1 cup)

⅔ cup chopped fresh dill

Kosher salt and ground black pepper

2 tablespoons extra-virgin olive oil

2- to 2½-pound head cauliflower, trimmed, cored and cut into ½-inch pieces

1 bunch scallions, thinly sliced

Don't forget to use an oven mitt or potholder when removing the pan from the oven as the handle will be hot.

1. **Heat the oven to 375°F** with a rack in the middle position. In a large bowl, whisk together the eggs, harissa, feta, all but 2 tablespoons of the dill, ⅛ teaspoon salt and ¼ teaspoon pepper. In an oven-safe 12-inch nonstick skillet over medium-high, heat the oil until shimmering. Add the cauliflower and scallions, then cook, stirring occasionally, until the cauliflower is browned and just shy of tender, about 8 minutes. Add the egg mixture and cook, stirring constantly, until large curds begin to form, about 1 minute. Place in the oven and bake until the center of the frittata is set, about 15 minutes.

2. **Run a silicone spatula** around the edges to loosen, then slide the frittata onto a cutting board. Sprinkle with the remaining dill and serve with additional harissa.

Spanish-Style "Poor Man's" Potatoes with Eggs

At its simplest, Spanish patatas a lo pobre, or poor man's potatoes, is, as its name implies, a humble dish of sliced potatoes cooked in olive oil with onions and peppers until all the vegetables are meltingly tender. For our version, we keep the potatoes chunky. We first simmer them in a skillet with a little water. Once they're tender, we flatten them slightly to create more surface area for browning, then we add the peppers and onion and allow the water to cook off so the vegetables begin to caramelize. Eggs sometimes are added to the potatoes; we drop four in at the end to create a one-skillet meal. To serve the potatoes as a side—they're delicious alongside just about any type of grilled or roasted meat or seafood—simply skip the eggs.

START TO FINISH: 50 MINUTES (30 MINUTES ACTIVE)
SERVINGS: 4

1½ pounds small Yukon Gold potatoes (1½ to 2 inches in diameter), halved

⅓ cup extra-virgin olive oil, plus more to serve

1 large sprig rosemary OR 4 sprigs thyme

Kosher salt and ground black pepper

2 medium orange OR red OR yellow bell peppers OR a combination, stemmed, seeded and thinly sliced

1 medium red OR yellow onion, halved and thinly sliced

4 large eggs

Don't stir too often when the peppers and onion are first added to the skillet. Too much stirring may break up the potatoes, causing the mixture to become slightly pasty and thick. When you hear the vegetables begin to sizzle, after most of the water has evaporated, it's fine to stir more often.

1. **In a 12-inch nonstick skillet,** combine the potatoes, oil, rosemary, 1 teaspoon salt and 1 cup water. Bring to a boil over medium-high, then cover, reduce to medium-low and cook, stirring only a few times, until a skewer inserted into the potatoes meets no resistance, about 15 minutes.

2. **Remove the pan from the heat.** Using a potato masher, flatten each potato until it splits open but remains intact. Return to a simmer over medium-high and stir in the peppers, onion and ½ teaspoon pepper. Cook, uncovered and stirring occasionally, until the water evaporates and the vegetables begin to brown, 15 to 20 minutes. Remove and discard the rosemary, then taste and season with salt and pepper.

3. **Using the back** of a large spoon, make 4 evenly spaced indentations in the potatoes, each about 2 inches in diameter. Crack 1 egg into each, then sprinkle with salt and pepper. Cover and cook on low until the egg whites are set but the yolks are still runny, 3 to 5 minutes. Serve drizzled with additional oil.

Optional garnish: Scallions, thinly sliced on the diagonal OR hot sauce OR both

Cauliflower

Cauliflower, according to Mark Twain, is "cabbage with a college education," but we've found it doesn't take advanced study to make the most of this mildly sweet and pleasantly-textured vegetable that is crisply firm when raw, deliciously creamy when cooked.

Chinese cooks use the dry-frying (gan bian) technique in which a protein or vegetable is parcooked in oil until browned, then stir-fried with aromatics and seasonings. The parcooking removes most of the moisture; the seasonings cling to the browned surfaces for a "dry" flavorful finish. We use this technique on cauliflower, p. 253, adding Sichuan peppercorns for a bright jolt of heat that contrasts well with the mild vegetable.

Lebanese shawarma traditionally is lamb seasoned and spit-roasted, but modern, meatless takes often substitute cauliflower, which works well because of its firm texture and ability to take on different types of spices. At the Shawarma Bar in London we had cauliflower brushed with a "shawarma butter" made from butter, lemon juice, garlic, cilantro, cinnamon, sumac, cumin, allspice, nutmeg and cardamom, that was then roasted or grilled. We cut back on the ingredients a bit for our version, p. 194, and added some olive oil for better browning. We do call for sumac, a deep-red spice popular in Middle Eastern cooking. It's not a make-or-break ingredient; lemon zest is a workable substitute, but sumac does add tangy, citrusy flourish and a dash of color.

In Southern Italy, cooks make a dish called cavolfiore affogato, or "drowned cauliflower." For our take, p. 339, we brown cauliflower florets, then braise them with garlic and tomatoes. A minimal amount of liquid keeps the flavors bright and concentrated. Capers, raisins and pine nuts add savory-sweet-nutty impact that is typically Sicilian.

In Lebanon, cauliflower florets are coated, deep-fried and served with a tahini-based sauce for a crisp-creamy snack known as arnabeet mekleh. It's delicious but a bit much for home cooking. For our cauliflower bites, p. 201, we skip the stovetop and instead coat florets with plenty of oil, sprinkle them with a spiced starchy coating and roast them in a hot oven. The crisped florets are flavorful—and splatter-free.

Cauliflower with Eggs, Capers and Lemon

In classic French cooking, "à la polonaise" refers to a garnish of breadcrumbs, chopped hard-cooked egg, butter and parsley; cauliflower commonly receives this treatment. In this recipe, we lighten things up—but retain the essence of chou-fleur à la polonaise—by using fruity olive oil instead of butter and panko breadcrumbs that toast up crisp and airy. Briny capers and lemon also add lots of spark. Serve this as a side or as a light meal with a simple green salad alongside.

START TO FINISH: 45 MINUTES
SERVINGS: 4

———

3-pound head cauliflower, trimmed and cut into 1-inch florets

¼ cup plus 2 tablespoons extra-virgin olive oil, divided, plus more to serve

Kosher salt and ground black pepper

¼ cup panko breadcrumbs

4 large hard-cooked eggs, peeled and chopped

2 tablespoons drained capers

2 tablespoons finely chopped fresh flat-leaf parsley **OR** 1 teaspoon minced fresh thyme **OR** both

1 tablespoon grated lemon zest, plus lemon wedges to serve

Don't stir the cauliflower during the first 20 minutes of roasting. This allows the florets to brown nicely, which develops a rich, nutty flavor.

1. **Heat the oven to 475°F** with a rack in the middle position. On a rimmed baking sheet, drizzle the cauliflower with the ¼ cup oil, sprinkle with salt and pepper, then toss. Roast without stirring until tender and browned, about 20 minutes.

2. **Remove from the oven,** drizzle the cauliflower with the remaining 2 tablespoons oil, sprinkle with the panko and toss. Continue to roast until the panko is golden brown, about another 5 minutes. Sprinkle with the eggs, capers, parsley and lemon zest, then toss. Taste and season with salt and pepper. Serve drizzled with additional oil and with lemon wedges.

Okra Gumbo

Gumbo is the official dish of Louisiana. It's most commonly made with meat or seafood or both, with okra or filé powder (ground dried sassafras leaves) added for flavor as well as for thickening, sometimes in addition to roux. This recipe delivers a flavorful, meat-free stew that's hearty but not heavy, with tangy-sweet tomatoes and a touch of spice and sugar complementing the mild vegetal notes of the okra. Be sure to choose fresh okra that's firm, unblemished and bright green. Serve the gumbo Louisiana style—that is, in individual bowls, spooned around a mound of steamed white rice. And if you like, pair it with shrimp or andouille sausage.

START TO FINISH: 30 MINUTES
SERVINGS: 4

___

1 tablespoon grapeseed or other neutral oil

1 medium yellow onion, chopped

1 poblano chili **OR** 1 small green bell pepper, stemmed, seeded and chopped

2 teaspoons cumin seeds **OR** coriander seeds, lightly crushed

Kosher salt and ground black pepper

28-ounce can whole peeled tomatoes, crushed by hand

1 teaspoon white sugar **OR** packed light brown sugar

1 pound okra, stemmed and sliced into ½-inch rounds

3 scallions, thinly sliced

Hot sauce, to serve

Don't slice the okra too far in advance or it may become slimy. For convenience, you can freeze the cut okra (for up to several months), then thaw it just before use.

1. **In a large Dutch oven** over medium-high, heat the oil until shimmering. Add the onion, chili, cumin and a pinch each of salt and pepper. Cook, stirring occasionally, until the vegetables are lightly browned, about 4 minutes.

2. **Add the tomatoes with juices,** the sugar and 1 cup water. Bring to a boil, then add the okra. Cover, reduce to medium and cook, stirring occasionally, until the okra is tender, 10 to 12 minutes. Taste and season with salt and pepper. Serve sprinkled with the scallions and with hot sauce on the side.

Curried Cauliflower Rice with Peas and Cashews

Cauliflower rice is a popular grain-free alternative to white rice, and it's extremely quick and easy to cook. We've tried both the frozen and fresh uncooked cauliflower rice sold in supermarkets and found that frozen too easily turns to mush and fresh usually is so finely processed that the dish ends up lacking texture. Fortunately, making your own cauliflower rice in a food processor is a breeze. In this recipe, fragrant curry powder and sweet peas add flavor and color, while chopped cashews offer a pleasing contrast in texture along with nutty richness.

START TO FINISH: 40 MINUTES
SERVINGS: 4 TO 6

1½-pound head cauliflower, trimmed and chopped into 1- to 1½-inch chunks

3 tablespoons ghee **OR** coconut oil **OR** neutral oil

2 medium shallots, halved and thinly sliced crosswise

1 or 2 Fresno chilies, stemmed, halved lengthwise, seeded and sliced into thin half rings

1 tablespoon finely grated fresh ginger

Kosher salt and ground black pepper

1 cup frozen peas, thawed and patted dry

1 tablespoon curry powder

½ cup roasted salted cashews, chopped

Lemon wedges, to serve

Don't overprocess the cauliflower. If the "rice" is chopped too finely, it'll cook up soggy and watery. Filling the food processor only halfway will help ensure the cauliflower breaks down into evenly sized bits.

1. **Add enough cauliflower** to fill a food processor about halfway. Pulse until the pieces are smaller than peas but larger than grains of rice, 3 to 5 pulses; do not overprocess (it's fine if the "rice" is somewhat uneven). Transfer to a medium bowl and repeat until all of the cauliflower has been processed; you should have about 4 cups.

2. **In a 12-inch nonstick skillet** over medium-high, heat the ghee until shimmering. Add the shallots and chilies, then cook, stirring occasionally, until softened and beginning to brown, 2 to 3 minutes. Add the ginger and cook, stirring, until fragrant, 30 to 60 seconds. Add the cauliflower rice and ½ teaspoon each salt and pepper, then cook, stirring often, until the "rice" is tender-crisp, 4 to 5 minutes. Add the peas and curry powder, then cook, stirring, until the peas are warmed through, 1 to 2 minutes. Off heat, taste and season with salt and pepper. Transfer to a serving dish, sprinkle with the cashews and serve with lemon wedges.

Optional garnish: Chopped fresh cilantro

Sichuan-Style Eggplant with Scallions

The Sichuan name for this classic dish is yu xiang qie zi, which translates as "fish fragrant eggplant" despite the fact that no seafood of any kind is used in its making. Some sources say it's so called because the eggplant is cooked with ingredients commonly paired with fish in Sichuan cooking. Many versions include ground pork but ours is meat-free, and we pan-fry the eggplant instead of deep-frying it the traditional way, so it's much simpler to prepare. Sichuan chili-bean paste, called toban djan, is salty, spicy and rich in umami. Look for it in the international aisle of the supermarket or in Asian grocery stores. It's worth seeking out, as there's nothing quite like it. And while you're shopping, also try to source Chinese black vinegar, also known as Chinkiang (Zhenjiang) vinegar. If it's unavailable, balsamic, a seemingly peculiar substitution, is the next best option, as its sour-sweet flavor is reminiscent of the malty notes of black vinegar. Serve with steamed rice.

START TO FINISH: 40 MINUTES
SERVINGS: 4

___

1 pound Chinese eggplant, trimmed, cut lengthwise into quarters, then crosswise into 2-inch sections

¼ cup potato starch **OR** cornstarch

½ cup grapeseed or other neutral oil, divided

Kosher salt and ground black pepper

3 to 4 tablespoons chili-bean paste (toban djan)

2 tablespoons minced fresh ginger

1 bunch scallions, thinly sliced

1½ tablespoons white sugar

2 tablespoons Chinese black vinegar **OR** balsamic vinegar

2 tablespoons soy sauce

Don't use regular globe eggplant instead of Chinese eggplant. *Long, slender Chinese eggplants have slightly more tender skin, fewer seeds and a better flesh to skin ratio for this dish.*

1. In a medium bowl, toss the eggplant with the potato starch until evenly coated. In a 12-inch nonstick skillet over medium-high, heat ¼ cup of oil until shimmering. Add half of the eggplant in an even layer and cook, occasionally turning the pieces, until golden brown, 4 to 7 minutes. As the pieces are done, transfer them to a paper towel-lined plate and sprinkle with salt and pepper. Repeat with the remaining ¼ cup oil and the remaining eggplant.

2. Pour off and discard all but 1 teaspoon of the oil in the skillet and add the chili-bean paste. Cook over medium, stirring constantly with a silicone spatula, until slightly thickened and fragrant, about 2 minutes. Add the ginger and all but 1 table-spoon of the scallions, then cook, stirring, until fragrant, about 2 minutes. Add 1 cup water, the sugar, vinegar and soy sauce. Bring to a boil over medium-high, return the eggplant to the skillet, and cook, stirring occasionally, until the eggplant is softened but not falling apart and the sauce has thickened slightly, 2 to 3 minutes. Off heat, stir in the remaining scallions.

Optional garnish: Toasted sesame seeds **OR** chopped fresh cilantro **OR** both

Cauliflower Kati Rolls

A kati roll is a popular type of Indian street food. Kebabs wrapped in paratha flatbread once were the norm, but now the rolls may be filled with ingredients of just about any sort, including paneer (a type of fresh cheese), vegetables and eggs. In this recipe, we roast yogurt-coated, garam masala-spiced cauliflower along with red bell pepper and onion in a hot oven until tender and well-browned. Instead of paratha as a wrapper, we use easier-to-find naan and smear the flatbreads with store-bought cilantro chutney before piling on and wrapping up the veggies. Look for cilantro chutney in the international aisle of the supermarket.

START TO FINISH: 45 MINUTES
SERVINGS: 4

1 medium red bell pepper, stemmed, seeded and thinly sliced

1 medium red onion, halved and thinly sliced

1 tablespoon grapeseed or other neutral oil

Kosher salt and ground black pepper

¼ cup plain whole-milk Greek yogurt

2 teaspoons garam masala

⅛ teaspoon cayenne pepper

1-pound head cauliflower, trimmed and cut into ½- to 1-inch florets

4 tablespoons store-bought cilantro chutney, divided

Four 7- to 8-inch naan, warmed

Don't use regular yogurt. The lower moisture content of Greek yogurt means the cauliflower will brown nicely in the oven. Be sure to put the cauliflower on top of the bell pepper-onion mixture. This not only allows the cauliflower to caramelize, it shields the sliced pepper and onion so they soften without scorching.

1. **Heat the oven to 500°F** with a rack in the middle position. In a medium bowl, toss together the bell pepper, onion, oil, ¼ teaspoon salt and ½ teaspoon black pepper. Transfer to a 9-by-13-inch metal baking pan and distribute in an even layer.

2. **In the same bowl,** stir together the yogurt, garam masala, cayenne and ¼ teaspoon each salt and black pepper. Add the cauliflower and toss to coat, then distribute in an even layer on top of the pepper-onion mixture. Roast without stirring until the cauliflower is well browned and a skewer inserted into the largest piece meets no resistance, 20 to 25 minutes.

3. **Remove the vegetables** from the oven and stir the cauliflower into the bell pepper-onion mixture. Taste and season with salt and black pepper. Spread 1 tablespoon of chutney onto 1 side of each naan. Spoon the vegetables, dividing them evenly, on top of the chutney in the center of the naan, then roll up each naan around the filling.

Eggs with Chickpeas and Spinach

START TO FINISH: 20 MINUTES
SERVINGS: 4 TO 6

To make a super-simple, blazingly fast dinner, Özlem Warren, author of "Özlem's Turkish Table," combines humble chickpeas and hearty greens in a skillet and poaches a few eggs right in the mix. For ease, we use canned chickpeas. Aleppo pepper (or red pepper flakes, if that's what you have in the pantry) and earthy cumin season the dish and add heady aroma. Warren says, "Don't have any chickpeas? Use butter beans or cannellini beans for another delicious variation."

2 tablespoons extra-virgin olive oil, plus more to serve

1 small yellow onion, finely chopped

15½-ounce can chickpeas, rinsed, drained and patted dry

¾ teaspoon Aleppo pepper or ¼ teaspoon red pepper flakes, plus more to serve

½ teaspoon ground cumin

Kosher salt and ground black pepper

Two 5-ounce containers baby spinach

4 large eggs

Plain yogurt, to serve

Crusty bread, to serve

Don't forget to pat the drained chickpeas dry to wick away at least some of the moisture. This will help prevent splattering when the chickpeas are added to the skillet.

1. **In a 12-inch nonstick skillet** over medium-high, heat the oil until shimmering. Add the onion and cook, stirring occasionally, until softened and beginning to brown, 3 to 4 minutes. Add the chickpeas, Aleppo pepper, cumin and ½ teaspoon each salt and black pepper, then cook, stirring, until fragrant, 30 to 60 seconds. Add the spinach and cook, turning and tossing with tongs, until the leaves are fully wilted, 2 to 3 minutes. Taste and season with salt and black pepper.

2. **Reduce to medium-low.** Use the back of a spoon to form 4 evenly spaced wells in the spinach mixture, each about 2 inches wide and deep enough that the bottom of the pan is visible. Crack 1 egg into each, then sprinkle with salt and black pepper. Cover and cook until the egg whites are set but the yolks are still runny, 5 to 8 minutes, rotating the skillet halfway through for even cooking.

3. **Remove the pan from the heat.** Sprinkle with additional Aleppo pepper and drizzle with additional oil. Serve with yogurt and bread.

Indian-Spiced Roasted Potatoes with Quick Pickles

START TO FINISH: 50 MINUTES
SERVINGS: 4 TO 6

Aloo chaat is a South Asian street food that combines potatoes, typically fried, with myriad spices, chutneys and other ingredients, such as fried noodles, for a wide range of flavors and textures. The popular snack inspired this recipe in which we roast rather than fry the potatoes. We make quick-pickled onion and cucumber to pile on top of the potatoes and add a hit of fresh flavor, color and crispness. Tangy-sweet tamarind chutney seasons the potatoes before roasting and also is great for drizzling at the table. Look for it sold in jars or bottles in Indian grocery stores or in the international aisle of the supermarket, but don't mistakenly buy tamarind paste, which is unseasoned tamarind pulp.

1 small red onion, halved and thinly sliced

½ English cucumber, halved lengthwise, seeded and thinly sliced

1 Fresno OR jalapeño chili, stemmed, seeded and thinly sliced

3 tablespoons lime juice, plus lime wedges to serve

Kosher salt and ground black pepper

¼ cup grapeseed or other neutral oil

2 teaspoons ground cumin

1 teaspoon ground turmeric

1 teaspoon ground coriander

1 tablespoon tamarind chutney, plus more to serve

2 pounds Yukon Gold potatoes, peeled and cut into 1-inch chunks

1 cup lightly packed fresh cilantro OR fresh mint OR a combination, chopped

Don't forget to mist the baking sheet with cooking spray. The sugar in the tamarind chutney tends to make the potatoes stick, so oiling the pan helps ensure that they release.

1. Heat the oven to 475°F with a rack in the middle position. Mist a rimmed baking sheet with cooking spray. In a medium bowl, stir together the onion, cucumber, chili, lime juice and a pinch of salt; set aside.

2. In a large bowl, whisk together the oil, cumin, turmeric, coriander, chutney and ½ teaspoon each salt and pepper. Add the potatoes and toss until well coated. Transfer the potato mixture to the prepared baking sheet and distribute in an even layer. Roast until spottily browned and a skewer inserted into the largest piece meets no resistance, 25 to 30 minutes, scraping up and flipping the potatoes once about halfway through.

3. Scatter about half the cilantro over the potatoes and toss. Taste and season with salt and pepper. Transfer to a serving dish, top with the onion-cucumber mixture, including any liquid in the bowl, and the remaining cilantro. Serve with additional chutney and lime wedges.

Optional garnish: Fried wonton strips **OR** chopped roasted peanuts **OR** both

Smothered Cauliflower with Tomatoes, Capers and Raisins

Taking a cue from southern Italian cavolfiore affogato, or "drowned cauliflower," we brown cauliflower florets, then braise them with tomatoes in a minimal amount of liquid and with a few high-impact Mediterranean ingredients. The combination of savory (capers and/or olives) and sweet (raisins) plus the rich, resinous flavor of pine nuts gives this dish a distinct Sicilian flavor profile. Serve this as a vegetarian main with some warm, crusty bread or offer it as a side to grilled pork chops, Italian sausages or meaty, firm fish such as swordfish or tuna.

START TO FINISH: 40 MINUTES
SERVINGS: 4 TO 6

___

3 tablespoons
extra-virgin olive oil

2- to 2½-pound head
cauliflower, trimmed and cut
into 1-inch florets

Kosher salt and ground
black pepper

⅓ cup dry vermouth

4 medium garlic cloves,
smashed, peeled and halved

1 pint cherry **OR** grape
tomatoes, halved

¼ cup drained capers
OR ½ cup pitted Kalamata
olives, chopped **OR** both

½ cup golden raisins
OR regular raisins

⅓ cup pine nuts, toasted

½ cup lightly packed fresh
flat-leaf parsley, chopped

Don't forget to occasionally stir the cauliflower while braising to keep the ingredients from sticking.

1. **In a 12-inch skillet** over medium-high, heat the oil until shimmering. Add the cauliflower and ½ teaspoon each salt and pepper. Cook, stirring occasionally, until charred in spots, about 3 minutes. Add the vermouth and cook, stirring, for about 30 seconds. Stir in the garlic, tomatoes, capers and raisins, then add ⅓ cup water and bring to a simmer.

2. **Cover, reduce to medium and cook,** stirring occasionally and adjusting the heat as needed to maintain a steady simmer, until the cauliflower is tender and most of the liquid has evaporated, 15 to 20 minutes. Remove the pan from the heat. Stir in the pine nuts and parsley, then taste and season with salt and pepper.

Optional garnish: Finely grated pecorino Romano **OR** Parmesan cheese

Spanish Green Beans with Ham, Almonds and Smoked Paprika

4 tablespoons extra-virgin olive oil, divided

¼ cup slivered almonds

2 ounces thinly sliced serrano ham or prosciutto, sliced into ¼-inch-wide ribbons

2 medium garlic cloves, minced

1 pound green beans, trimmed and halved

Kosher salt and ground black pepper

½ teaspoon smoked paprika

Don't stir the beans too often after adding them to the pan. Stirring only a few times allows the beans to take on some char that adds flavor to the finished dish.

1. **In a 12-inch skillet** over medium, heat 2 tablespoons of oil until shimmering. Add the almonds and cook, stirring, until lightly golden, about 2 minutes. Add the ham and garlic and cook, stirring, until the ham crisps and the garlic is fragrant, another 2 minutes. Transfer to a small bowl; set aside.

2. **To the same skillet** over medium-high, add the remaining 2 tablespoons oil and heat until barely smoking. Add the beans, ¼ teaspoon salt and ½ teaspoon pepper. Cook, stirring only a few times, until the beans are lightly charred, about 4 minutes. Return the ham-almond mixture to the pan and add ¼ cup water. Cover, reduce to low and cook, occasionally shaking the pan, until the beans are tender-crisp, about 3 minutes. Taste and season with salt and pepper, then transfer to a serving dish.

3. **Set the skillet** over medium-high and add ¼ cup water. Bring to a simmer and cook, scraping up the browned bits, until the liquid has reduced to about 2 tablespoons, about 2 minutes. Remove from the heat and stir in the paprika. Drizzle the sauce over the beans and serve.

This recipe is our adaptation of the remarkably delicious green beans that we tasted in Extremadura, Spain, home of pimentón, or Spanish smoked paprika. Our method for charring then steaming the vegetables produces perfectly tender-crisp beans. Serrano ham is a Spanish dry-cured ham; if you cannot find it, Italian prosciutto works equally well. The version we had in Spain was topped with a runny-yolked egg that, when broken into, created a velvety, flavorful sauce that coated the beans. If you like, top the beans with a poached egg before drizzling with the paprika-infused sauce.

Potato and Eggplant Tortilla Española

In Spain, a tortilla is a thick, hearty, frittata-like omelet, usually made with potatoes and onion. We make it even more substantial with the addition of eggplant and garlic. Chinese and Japanese eggplants—the varieties called for in this recipe—have thinner skins and fewer seeds than large globe eggplants. If you can't find either, you can substitute Italian or globe, but remove the peel before cutting it into cubes. Aioli is a great accompaniment to any type of tortilla; try our Spanish version, alioli (p. 15).

START TO FINISH: 30 MINUTES
SERVINGS: 4

_____

8 large eggs

Kosher salt and ground black pepper

½ cup roughly chopped fresh flat-leaf parsley

¼ cup extra-virgin olive oil

1 medium yellow onion, chopped

1 pound Yukon Gold potatoes, peeled and cut into ½-inch cubes

8 ounces Chinese or Japanese eggplant, cut into ¾-inch cubes

2 medium garlic cloves, thinly sliced

Don't use a conventional skillet; nonstick is essential for the tortilla to slide easily out of the pan. Also, the skillet must be oven-safe, as the tortilla finishes cooking in a 350°F oven.

1. **Heat the oven to 350°F** with a rack in the middle position. In a large bowl, whisk together the eggs, ½ teaspoon salt and ¼ teaspoon pepper. Stir in the parsley.

2. **In a 12-inch nonstick skillet** over medium-high, heat the oil until shimmering. Stir in the onion, potatoes, eggplant, garlic and ½ teaspoon salt. Cover and cook, stirring occasionally, until the vegetables are browned and tender, about 10 minutes.

3. **Pour the egg mixture** over the vegetables and cook, stirring constantly with a silicone spatula, until almost set, about 2 minutes. Using the spatula, tuck in the eggs around the perimeter to form a neat circle. Transfer the skillet to the oven and bake until set, 5 to 10 minutes.

4. **Run the spatula** around the edge and under the tortilla to loosen, then carefully slide onto a cutting board. Serve warm or at room temperature.

Inverted Pizza with Onions, Potatoes and Thyme

In "Tasting Rome," co-authors Katie Parla and Kristina Gill write about pizza made using an innovative method perfected by Gabriele Bonci of Pizzarium in Rome. Called pizza al contrario, it's pizza turned on its head. The "toppings" are put into a pan, covered with dough and baked. Once out of the oven, the pie is inverted, revealing ingredients that have melded with the dough, and the browned crust that formed on top during baking becomes a wonderfully crisp bottom, no pizza stone required. To keep this recipe for pizza al contrario simple enough for a weeknight, we use store-bought refrigerated pizza dough.

START TO FINISH: 40 MINUTES
SERVINGS: 4 TO 6

2 medium yellow onions, halved and thinly sliced

8 ounces Yukon Gold potatoes, unpeeled, sliced ⅛- to ¼-inch thick

2 tablespoons fresh thyme, roughly chopped

1 tablespoon honey

4 tablespoons extra-virgin olive oil, divided, plus more to serve

Kosher salt and ground black pepper

1½ pounds store-bought refrigerated pizza dough, room temperature

All-purpose flour, for dusting

1 cup whole-milk ricotta cheese

Don't worry if the rolled dough is a little smaller than the dimensions of the baking sheet. When it's laid on top of the hot vegetables, the dough will relax from the warmth, making it easier to stretch.

1. **Heat the oven to 500°F** with a rack in the lowest position. Mist a rimmed baking sheet with cooking spray. In a large bowl, toss together the onions, potato, thyme, honey, 3 tablespoons of oil and ½ teaspoon each salt and pepper. Distribute the mixture in an even layer on the prepared baking sheet and bake without stirring until the onions begin to brown and the potato is softened but not yet fully cooked, about 15 minutes.

2. **Meanwhile, on a well-floured counter,** gently stretch the dough by hand or roll it with a rolling pin into a 12-by-16-inch rectangle (the same dimensions as the baking sheet); work from the center outward to help ensure the dough is of an even thickness. If it is resistant or shrinks after stretching or rolling, wait 5 to 10 minutes before trying again; if it is very elastic, you may need to give it 2 or 3 rests. It's fine if the dough rectangle is a little smaller than the baking sheet.

3. **When the onion-potato mixture is ready,** remove the baking sheet from the oven; leave the oven on. Using both hands and being careful not to touch the hot baking sheet, lay the dough over the vegetables, gently stretching and tucking in the edges as needed so the dough fills the baking sheet and covers the vegetables. Brush the surface with the remaining 1 tablespoon oil, then use a fork to poke holes every 2 to 3 inches all the way through the dough. Bake until the surface is well browned, 15 to 17 minutes.

4. **Remove from the oven** and immediately invert a wire rack onto the baking sheet. Using potholders or oven mitts, hold the baking sheet and rack together and carefully flip to invert. Lift off the baking sheet. Using a metal spatula, scrape up any onion-potato mixture clinging to the baking sheet and replace it on the pizza. Dollop with the ricotta, cut into pieces and drizzle with additional oil.

1½-pound head cauliflower, trimmed and chopped into 1- to 1½-inch chunks

4 tablespoons grapeseed or other neutral oil, divided

8 medium garlic cloves, 6 thinly sliced, 2 minced, reserved separately

1 pound mustard greens, stemmed and roughly chopped

1 bunch scallions, thinly sliced, whites and greens reserved separately

Kosher salt and ground black pepper

Don't overbrown the sliced garlic or it will taste bitter and burnt. Cook it over medium heat, no higher, just until golden brown and take the skillet off the burner when transferring the garlic to a plate.

1. **Add enough cauliflower** to fill a food processor about halfway. Pulse until the pieces are smaller than peas but larger than grains of rice, 3 to 5 pulses; do not overprocess (it's fine if the "rice" is somewhat uneven). Transfer to a medium bowl and repeat until all of the cauliflower has been processed; you should have about 4 cups.

2. **In a 12-inch nonstick skillet** over medium, heat 3 table-spoons of oil until shimmering. Add the sliced garlic and cook, stirring, until golden brown and crisp, 4 to 5 minutes. Remove the pan from the heat and, using a slotted spoon, transfer the garlic to a small plate. Set the pan over medium-high, add the greens and cook, stirring, until wilted, 2 to 3 minutes. Add the minced garlic and the scallion whites, then cook, stirring, until fragrant, about 30 seconds; transfer the mixture to a bowl.

3. **In the same skillet** over medium-high, heat the remaining 1 tablespoon oil until shimmering. Add the cauliflower and ½ teaspoon each salt and pepper, then cook, stirring often, until crisp-tender, 4 to 5 minutes. Return the greens to the pan and, cook, stirring, just until heated through, 1 to 2 minutes. Taste and season with salt and pepper. Transfer to a serving dish and sprinkle with the fried garlic and scallion greens.

Optional garnish: Hot sauce

Garlicky Cauliflower Rice with Mustard Greens and Scallions

The idea for this cauliflower rice comes from sinangag, or Filipino garlic fried rice. We add peppery mustard greens and a generous amount of scallions to ratchet up the flavors and give the dish vibrant color. The garlic in classic sinangag is chopped and fried until toasty and brown, but here we slice the cloves so they fry up into crisp garlic chips; we also cook minced garlic with the greens. Pass on store-bought cauli-flower rice; we've tried both frozen and fresh but neither is nearly as good as homemade. Fortunately, making your own in a food processor is easy. To turn this into a light main, serve it topped with runny-yolked fried eggs.

Indian-Style Scrambled Eggs with Tomatoes and Chilies

START TO FINISH: 25 MINUTES
SERVINGS: 4

The Indian dish called anda bhurji consists of eggs scrambled with spices and aromatics. We include fresh green chilies and tomatoes in this version, and also mix in some garam masala for warm, subtly sweet spiciness. Ghee, a type of clarified butter with rich, nutty notes, adds to the flavor of the eggs, but neutral oil works, too. For a milder version, remove the seeds from the chilies before chopping. In India, anda bhurji often is sold by street vendors as a late-night snack, piled on a piece of warm naan or rolled in a paratha, but these eggs are good any time of day.

8 large eggs

2 tablespoons ghee or neutral oil

½ small red onion, thinly sliced

1 tablespoon finely grated fresh ginger

1 or 2 jalapeño chilies, stemmed, halved lengthwise, seeded, and thinly sliced crosswise

2 ripe medium tomatoes, cored, seeded and roughly chopped

1 teaspoon garam masala

Kosher salt and ground black pepper

Chopped fresh cilantro, to serve

Don't forget to seed the tomatoes or their moisture will make the eggs too wet. Also, be sure to use a nonstick skillet or the eggs will stick to the surface.

1. **In a medium bowl,** whisk the eggs until well combined. In a 12-inch nonstick skillet over medium-high, heat the ghee until barely smoking. Add the onion and ginger, then cook, stirring often, until golden brown, about 3 minutes. Add the jalapeño(s), tomatoes, garam masala and ¼ teaspoon salt; cook, stirring, until fragrant, about 2 minutes.

2. **Pour the eggs** into the center of the pan. Using a silicone spatula, continuously stir the eggs, pushing them toward the middle as they begin to set at the edges and folding the cooked egg onto itself. Cook until just set, 45 to 60 seconds. Remove the pan from the heat, then taste and season with salt and pepper. Serve sprinkled with cilantro.

Hoisin Broccoli and Tofu Traybake

In British parlance, a classic traybake is a sweet, such as a cake, that's oven-baked in a wide, shallow baking pan or tray. But the term has also come to refer to savory, one-pan meals cooked on a baking sheet or in a baking dish in the oven. This simple vegetarian traybake combines several pantry staples—hoisin, soy sauce and garlic—with broccoli and tofu and yields a hearty, satisfying main. A 475°F oven develops the right amount of flavorful char on the broccoli and cooks the florets to a pleasing tender-crisp texture. Serve with steamed rice.

START TO FINISH: 40 MINUTES
SERVINGS: 4 TO 6

___

¾ cup hoisin sauce

3 tablespoons soy sauce

3 medium garlic cloves, finely chopped

1 tablespoon toasted sesame oil

1 pound broccoli crowns, cut into 1½-inch florets

14-ounce container firm OR extra-firm tofu, drained, halved lengthwise, cut crosswise into ½-inch-thick slices and pressed dry

Toasted sesame seeds, to serve

Don't skip the baking-sheet prep. Be sure to line it with foil and mist it with cooking spray. The sugar in the hoisin makes things a little sticky in the oven. The foil and cooking spray help ensure the broccoli and especially the more fragile tofu release from the baking sheet.

1. **Heat the oven to 475°F** with a rack in the middle position. Line a rimmed baking sheet with foil and mist with cooking spray.

2. **In a small bowl,** stir together the hoisin, soy sauce, garlic and sesame oil. In a medium bowl, toss the broccoli with half of the hoisin mixture until evenly coated. Distribute in an even layer on the prepared baking sheet. Transfer the remaining hoisin mixture to the now-empty bowl, add the tofu and gently toss to coat. Place the tofu on the baking sheet, arranging it in a single layer, being sure that all the slices lay flat against the baking sheet.

3. **Roast the broccoli and tofu** without stirring until the broccoli is charred and tender-crisp, about 25 minutes. Using a wide metal spatula, transfer to a platter. Sprinkle with sesame seeds.

Optional garnish: Chopped fresh cilantro

10

HEARTY MAINS

Roasted Potatoes and Zucchini with Tomatoes and Feta

The Greek dish called briam is a medley of vegetables roasted with a generous amount of olive oil. This recipe is a twist on classic briam. It roasts sliced potatoes, zucchini and onion on a baking sheet, then finishes them with fresh tomatoes, herbs and feta cheese (or fresh goat cheese). The result is a combination of deep, rich, caramelized flavors and tender, yielding textures, plus the bright pop of juicy tomatoes, verdant herbs and briny feta. This is excellent warm, but also is delicious at room temperature.

START TO FINISH: 50 MINUTES (25 MINUTES ACTIVE)
SERVINGS: 6

8 ounces plum tomatoes, cored and sliced crosswise into ¼-inch rounds

Kosher salt and ground black pepper

1½ pounds medium Yukon Gold potatoes, unpeeled, halved lengthwise and sliced ⅛ inch thick

¼ cup plus 2 tablespoons extra-virgin olive oil, divided, plus more to serve

2 medium zucchini (about 1 pound total), halved lengthwise and sliced crosswise ¼ inch thick

1 medium red onion, halved and thinly sliced

½ cup lightly packed fresh oregano OR roughly chopped fresh dill OR torn fresh basil, divided

2 ounces feta cheese OR fresh goat cheese (chèvre), crumbled (1 cup)

Don't skip the step of salting the tomatoes, and be sure to allow them to drain in a colander as you roast the other vegetables. This removes some of the tomatoes' juices that would otherwise cause sogginess.

1. **Heat the oven to 500°F** with a rack in the middle position. Mist a rimmed baking sheet with cooking spray. In a colander set over a medium bowl, toss the tomatoes with ¼ teaspoon salt; set aside. In a large bowl, toss the potatoes with the ¼ cup oil and ½ teaspoon each salt and pepper. Distribute in an even layer on the prepared baking sheet; reserve the bowl. Roast until lightly browned, about 15 minutes. Meanwhile, in the reserved bowl, toss together the zucchini, onion, ¼ cup of oregano, the remaining 2 tablespoons oil, ¼ teaspoon salt and ½ teaspoon pepper.

2. **When the potatoes are ready,** remove the baking sheet from the oven. Using a wide metal spatula, scrape up the potatoes and push them to the edges. Add the zucchini-onion mixture in an even layer to the center of the baking sheet. Roast until a skewer inserted into the zucchini meets no resistance, 10 to 15 minutes.

3. **Transfer the vegetables** to a serving dish. Scatter the tomatoes on top; discard the juices. Drizzle with additional oil, then top with the cheese and the remaining ¼ cup oregano.

Pipian Verde with Potatoes, Green Beans and Zucchini

Pipian verde is a type of green mole originating from Oaxaca, Mexico. It's similar to a salsa verde, with its combination of tomatillos, chilies and cilantro, but the addition of toasted pumpkin seeds differentiates pipian verde and gives the sauce wonderful body and a subtle nutty flavor. To toast the pumpkin seeds, simply heat in a skillet over medium-high, stirring often, until light golden brown, about 3 minutes.

START TO FINISH: 35 MINUTES
SERVINGS: 4 TO 6

_____

2 ounces baby spinach (about 2 cups lightly packed)

3 medium tomatillos, husked and roughly chopped

2 serrano chilies, stemmed, seeded and roughly chopped

½ cup pumpkin seeds, toasted, plus more to serve (see headnote)

½ cup lightly packed fresh cilantro, plus more to serve

3 medium garlic cloves

1 teaspoon ground cumin

Kosher salt and ground black pepper

8 ounces Yukon Gold potatoes, peeled and cut into 1-inch pieces

8 ounces green beans, trimmed and halved

1 medium zucchini OR summer squash (about 8 ounces), trimmed and cut into 1-inch chunks

Don't forget to cover the Dutch oven during the first part of cooking. Uncovered, the sauce will reduce too much and start to burn.

1. **In a blender,** combine 1½ cups water, the spinach, tomatillos, chilies, pumpkin seeds, cilantro, garlic, cumin, ½ teaspoon salt and ¼ teaspoon pepper. Blend until smooth, 15 to 25 seconds, scraping down the jar as needed. Transfer to a large Dutch oven and add the potatoes, green beans and zucchini.

2. **Bring to a simmer** over medium-high. Cover, reduce to medium-low and simmer, stirring occasionally, until a skewer inserted in a potato meets little resistance, 10 to 12 minutes. Uncover and cook, stirring often, until the sauce has thickened and clings to the vegetables and the potatoes are fully tender, 5 to 7 minutes. Transfer to a large shallow bowl, top with cilantro leaves and pumpkin seeds.

Callaloo

START TO FINISH: 35 MINUTES
SERVINGS: 4

Made throughout the Caribbean and with many regional versions, callaloo is, in most basic terms, a dish of spicy stewed greens. Depending on the place of origin, the star ingredient might be taro greens, water spinach or amaranth greens. If those aren't available, recipes may call for kale, spinach or, as in our version, Swiss chard. Cured meat, salted fish or shellfish are common, but we forgo these and focus on building bold flavor with chilies, thyme, scallions and allspice. With both tomatoes and coconut milk, our recipe is hearty and stewy but is not true to any particular regional version of callaloo. The optional okra thickens the consistency, but if you're not a fan, simply omit it; the flavor of the dish won't suffer. Serve as a side or as a main with rice, and offer hot sauce if the fresh chilies don't supply enough heat for your taste.

2 tablespoons grapeseed or other neutral oil

1 bunch scallions, thinly sliced, whites and greens reserved separately

4 large thyme sprigs

Kosher salt and ground black pepper

2 bunches (about 2 pounds total) Swiss chard, stemmed and roughly chopped

1 cup cherry **OR** grape tomatoes, halved

1 cup coconut milk

1 or 2 habanero **OR** Scotch bonnet chilies, stemmed, seeded and thinly sliced

4 ounces okra, stemmed and cut into 1-inch pieces (optional)

1 teaspoon ground allspice

2 teaspoons lime juice, plus lime wedges to serve

Don't use the chard stems. *This dish should be all about the silky, supple greens. If you have rubber gloves, you may want to wear them when handling the chilies to prevent the capsaicin, the heat-containing compound, from getting onto your hands.*

1. In a large pot over medium, heat the oil until shimmering. Add the scallion whites, thyme and ½ teaspoon salt. Cook, stirring often, until the scallions are translucent, about 3 minutes. Add the chard in batches, stirring to help the leaves wilt, then add half of the scallion greens, the tomatoes, coconut milk, chilies, okra (if using), allspice and ½ teaspoon pepper. Bring to a simmer over medium-high, then cover, reduce to medium and cook, stirring occasionally, until the chard is just tender, about 10 minutes.

2. Uncover and cook, stirring only a few times, until the mixture has thickened slightly and the chard is completely tender, 4 to 6 minutes. Off heat, remove and discard the thyme. Stir in the lime juice and the remaining scallion greens, then taste and season with salt and pepper.

Cauliflower Steaks with Chipotle-Cashew Sauce

This chunky, flavor-packed sauce gets brightness from lime zest and juice, smoky heat from chipotle chilies, and buttery crunch from chopped roasted cashews. It's a perfect pairing with tender, well-caramelized roasted cauliflower "steaks" (thick planks cut from a whole head). Cutting the steaks will leave you with bits of cauliflower that can be reserved for another use (roasting, steaming, stir-frying or making cauliflower "rice"). If you'd like to keep the sauce on the mild side, use only one chili and remove the seeds, but don't reduce the amount of adobo sauce. This dish is substantial enough to be a vegetarian main.

START TO FINISH: 45 MINUTES
SERVINGS: 4

Two 2-pound cauliflower heads, trimmed

6 tablespoons grapeseed or other neutral oil, divided

1 teaspoon sweet paprika

Kosher salt and ground black pepper

½ teaspoon grated lime zest, plus 2 tablespoons lime juice, plus lime wedges to serve

1 medium garlic clove, finely grated

¾ cup roasted cashews, chopped (salted or unsalted)

1 or 2 chipotle chilies in adobo sauce, minced, plus 2 tablespoons adobo sauce

½ cup lightly packed fresh cilantro, finely chopped, plus more to serve

Don't use raw cashews. Roasted cashews have a deeper, more complex flavor. Either salted or unsalted works in this recipe.

1. Heat the oven to 450°F with the rack in the middle position. Line a rimmed baking sheet with kitchen parchment. Cut each cauliflower in half from top to bottom. From the cut side of each half, slice off a 1½-inch-thick slab, creating 4 cauliflower "steaks." Reserve the ends for another use. Liberally brush all sides of each steak with 2 tablespoons oil, then arrange in a single layer on the prepared baking sheet.

2. In a small bowl, stir together the paprika, 1½ teaspoons salt and ½ teaspoon pepper. Sprinkle the spice mix on all sides of each steak, including the edges. Roast the cauliflower until well-browned and a skewer inserted into the cores meets no resistance, 25 to 30 minutes, flipping once halfway through. Cool for 5 minutes, then transfer to serving plates.

3. Meanwhile, in a small bowl stir together the lime zest and juice and the garlic; let stand for 5 minutes to mellow the garlic. Stir in the cashews, chipotle chilies and adobo sauce, cilantro, the remaining 4 tablespoons oil and ¼ teaspoon salt. Taste and season with salt. When the cauliflower is done, spoon the sauce over it, sprinkle with additional cilantro and serve with lime wedges.

Sweet Potato and Black-Eyed Pea Stew

Ndambe (pronounced NAM-bay), a stew of black-eyed peas, tomatoes and onion, is found throughout Senegal, often with bits of lamb or beef added. We speed cooking time by using canned black-eyed peas in place of dried, making it an option for a weeknight dinner. Serve with rice or fonio, or do as they do in Senegal, mashed slightly and spread over a split baguette.

START TO FINISH: 45 MINUTES
SERVINGS: 6

_____

2 tablespoons coconut oil, preferably unrefined

1 large yellow onion, chopped

Kosher salt and ground black pepper

4 medium garlic cloves, minced

1 or 2 Fresno **OR** jalapeño chilies, stemmed and sliced into thin rings

15½-ounce can black-eyed peas, rinsed and drained

1 bay leaf

1 pound sweet potatoes, peeled and cut into ½-inch cubes

1 pound ripe tomatoes, cored and chopped

½ cup chopped fresh flat-leaf parsley

1 tablespoon lemon juice, plus lemon wedges, to serve

Don't use neutral-flavored oil in place of the coconut oil. Coconut oil, particularly unrefined coconut oil, infuses the stew with a sweet aroma and distinctive flavor.

1. **In a large pot over medium,** heat the coconut oil until shimmering. Add the onion and ¼ teaspoon each salt and pepper, then cook, stirring occasionally, until softened and light golden brown, 7 to 10 minutes. Stir in the garlic and chilies, then cook until fragrant, about 30 seconds. Add the black-eyed peas, bay leaf and 4 cups water. Bring to a simmer over medium-high, then reduce to medium and cook, uncovered and stirring occasionally, until the flavors meld, about 15 minutes.

2. **Stir in the sweet potatoes** and ½ teaspoon salt. Cover, reduce to medium-low and cook until the sweet potatoes are tender, about 10 minutes. Off heat, remove the bay, then stir in the tomatoes, parsley and lemon juice. Taste and season with salt and pepper. Serve with lemon wedges alongside.

Curried Eggplant
and Chickpea Stew

This stew is a much-simplified version of Indian chole baigan, an eggplant and chickpea curry. Instead of using a slew of spices, we reach for only curry powder, but we build depth of flavor by cooking the tomato paste and curry in oil until the mixture begins to brown. And to speed along the cooking, we make the sauce on the stovetop while browning the eggplant and onion under the broiler. Canned chickpeas also make the stew a breeze to prepare. The best tool for shaving wide zest strips from the lemon is a Y-style peeler, but try to remove only the colored skin without taking much of the bitter white pith just underneath. Serve the curry with warmed naan and basmati rice.

START TO FINISH: 40 MINUTES
SERVINGS: 4 TO 6

_____

1-pound eggplant, trimmed
and cut into 1-inch cubes

1 medium red onion, halved
and thinly sliced

4 tablespoons grapeseed
or other neutral oil, divided

2 tablespoons curry powder,
divided

Kosher salt and
ground black pepper

¼ cup tomato paste

15½-ounce can chickpeas
(do not drain)

Three 3-inch-long strips
lemon zest, plus
2 tablespoons lemon juice

½ cup lightly packed fresh
cilantro, chopped

Don't drain the chickpeas of their liquid. We add the starchy liquid to the skillet along with the chickpeas to create a rich, stewy consistency.

1. **Heat the broiler** with a rack about 6 inches from the element. In a large bowl, toss together the eggplant, onion, 3 tablespoons of oil, 1 tablespoon of curry powder and ½ teaspoon each salt and pepper. Distribute in an even layer on a rimmed baking sheet and broil until the eggplant is softened and spotty brown, 12 to 15 minutes, stirring once about halfway through.

2. **Meanwhile, in a 12-inch skillet** over medium, heat the remaining 1 tablespoon oil until shimmering. Add the remaining curry powder and the tomato paste, then cook, stirring, until the paste begins to brown, 1 to 3 minutes. Stir in the chickpeas with their liquid, ¾ cup water and the lemon zest. Bring to a simmer and cook, uncovered and stirring occasionally, until the liquid has reduced slightly and a spoon drawn through the mixture leaves a trail, about 10 minutes; if the mixture becomes dry and thick as it cooks, stir in a few tablespoons additional water.

3. **Off heat,** remove and discard the lemon zest. Stir the eggplant-onion mixture and the lemon juice into the chickpea mixture. Taste and season with salt and pepper. Transfer to a serving dish and sprinkle with the cilantro.

¼ cup smoked almonds

½ cup panko breadcrumbs

½ teaspoon fresh thyme

Kosher salt and ground black pepper

5 tablespoons extra-virgin olive oil, divided

2½ teaspoons smoked paprika, divided

Three 15½-ounce cans chickpeas, 2 cans rinsed and drained

5 medium garlic cloves, minced

1 teaspoon finely chopped fresh rosemary

14½-ounce can diced fire-roasted tomatoes

⅛ teaspoon cayenne pepper

10-ounce bunch spinach, stemmed

Braised Chickpeas and Spinach with Smoked Paprika and Garlic

This Spanish-inspired chickpea stew gets deep flavor from fire-roasted tomatoes and a good dose of smoked paprika and garlic. Toasted panko and chopped smoked almonds sprinkled on just before serving adds textural contrast.

Don't use baby spinach in place of mature bunch spinach. We found that bunch spinach became tender when wilted, but baby spinach turned mushy in the stew. Don't drain all three cans of chickpeas. One is used with its liquid.

1. **In a food processor,** pulse the almonds until coarsely chopped, about 8 pulses. Transfer to a small bowl. In the food processor, process the panko until slightly finer in texture, about 10 seconds, then add the thyme, ¼ teaspoon each salt and black pepper, 1 tablespoon of the oil and ¾ teaspoon of the paprika. Process until well combined, about 10 seconds. Transfer the panko mixture to a 12-inch skillet and set aside. Pulse 1 cup of the drained chickpeas until coarsely ground, about 5 pulses, then transfer to another small bowl.

2. **Set the skillet** with the panko mixture over medium and cook, stirring, until crisp and browned, 4 to 5 minutes. Stir in the chopped almonds, then scrape the mixture onto a plate; set aside.

3. **In a large saucepan** over medium low, heat 3 tablespoons of the remaining oil until shimmering. Add the garlic and cook, stirring occasionally, until pale golden, about 2 minutes. Stir in the remaining 1¾ teaspoons paprika and the rosemary; cook until fragrant, about 1 minute. Add the tomatoes with their liquid and cook, stirring occasionally, until slightly thickened, about 3 minutes. Stir in the ground chickpeas, the remaining drained chickpeas, the remaining 1 can chickpeas (with its liquid), ½ teaspoon salt and the cayenne. Bring to a simmer over medium-high, then reduce to low, cover and cook, stirring occasionally, until the flavors have melded, about 10 minutes.

4. **Stir in the spinach,** then cover and cook until wilted, about 1 minute. Taste and season with salt and black pepper. Transfer to a serving bowl, sprinkle with the panko-almond mixture and drizzle with the remaining 1 tablespoon oil.

Leek, Kale and Emmentaler Panade

START TO FINISH: 1¼ HOURS
(30 MINUTES ACTIVE), PLUS COOLING
SERVINGS: 6

"Panade" has a few culinary meanings, but in this context, it's a way to turn stale bread into a rustic, casserole-like dish made by baking the bread with cooked vegetables, cheese and broth and/or dairy. Some versions are quite soupy, while others, like ours, are a bit drier. We skip the cream and milk, preferring the lightness of a broth-only panade. Leeks take the lead role and baby kale, hearty and deep green, is a nice add-in that doesn't require any knifework (baby spinach is great, too, if that's your preference). Make as a side for a simple roasted chicken, or serve it as a main, with a green salad alongside.

12 ounces crusty white bread **OR** whole-wheat bread, torn into rough 2-inch pieces (about 8 cups)

6 tablespoons extra-virgin olive oil, divided

2 pounds leeks, white and light green parts, quartered lengthwise, cut into 3-inch lengths, rinsed and drained

4 medium garlic cloves, minced

Kosher salt and ground black pepper

10 ounces baby kale **OR** baby spinach (about 12 cups)

1 teaspoon grated lemon zest, plus 2 teaspoons lemon juice

½ teaspoon grated nutmeg

4 ounces Emmentaler cheese **OR** Gruyère cheese, shredded (1 cup)

3 cups low-sodium chicken broth

Don't forget to let the panade rest after it comes out of the oven and before serving. This allows it to cool slightly and the bread to re-absorb the broth for even moistness throughout.

1. **Heat the oven to 375°F** with a rack in the lower-middle position. Place the bread on a rimmed baking sheet and toss with 3 tablespoons oil. Bake, stirring once or twice, until light golden brown, 10 to 14 minutes; set aside.

2. **In a large Dutch oven** over medium-high, combine the remaining 3 tablespoons oil, the leeks, garlic and ½ teaspoon salt. Cover and cook, stirring occasionally, until the leeks are softened and lightly browned, 9 to 12 minutes. Add the kale and stir just until wilted. Remove the pot from the heat and stir in the lemon zest and juice, nutmeg and ½ teaspoon pepper. Distribute the mixture in an even layer.

3. **Nestle about half** of the toasted bread into the leek-kale mixture. Sprinkle half of the cheese over the top, then add the remaining bread in an even layer. Pour the broth around the edges of the pot, pressing on the layers to compact slightly. Top with the remaining cheese. Bake, uncovered, until golden brown and bubbling, 35 to 40 minutes. Cool on a wire rack and for about 20 minutes before serving.

Optional garnish: Red pepper flakes **OR** hot sauce

Cauliflower and Chickpea Tagine

A tagine is a shallow Moroccan earthenware pot with a conical lid. The term also refers to the stew cooked in the vessel. Here, however, we use a more common Dutch oven to simmer a cauliflower and chickpea "tagine," and we season it with ras el hanout, a complex Moroccan blend of warm and pungent spices. If ras el hanout isn't available, a simple mixture of ground cumin and cinnamon also delivers a delicious, richly aromatic dish. Serve with couscous or flatbread.

START TO FINISH: 30 MINUTES
SERVINGS: 4 TO 6

_____

2 tablespoons extra-virgin olive oil, plus more to serve

1 medium yellow onion, chopped

¼ cup tomato paste

2- to 2½-pound head cauliflower, trimmed and cut into ½- to 1-inch florets

2 tablespoons ras el hanout OR 1 tablespoon ground cumin, plus ½ teaspoon ground cinnamon

Kosher salt and ground black pepper

15½-ounce can chickpeas, rinsed and drained

2 tablespoons lemon juice

Chopped fresh mint, to serve

Don't be shy about cooking the tomato paste until it browns. The caramelization develops compounds that help build a solid flavor base for the stew.

1. In a large Dutch oven over medium-high, heat the oil until shimmering. Add the onion and cook, stirring occasionally, until softened and beginning to brown, 5 to 7 minutes. Add the tomato paste and cook, stirring, until beginning to brown, about 1 minute. Pour in 2 cups water and scrape up the browned bits, then stir in the cauliflower, ras el hanout and ½ teaspoon each salt and pepper. Bring to a simmer, cover and cook, stirring occasionally, until the cauliflower is crisp-tender, 5 to 6 minutes.

2. Stir in the chickpeas, re-cover and cook until the cauliflower is fully tender, about another 5 minutes. Off heat, stir in the lemon juice, then taste and season with salt and pepper. Serve drizzled with additional oil and sprinkled with mint.

Potatoes and Sweet Potatoes

Potatoes are culinary chameleons, morphing from a fistful of fries to the elegant spirals of Parisian pommes Anna. With their versatile texture and mild taste it's no surprise cooks around the world have put their own spin on spuds.

In Spain, patatas bravas are tapas bar staples, fried until crisp and served punishingly hot with creamy alioli or mildly spicy smoked paprika sauce. For our patatas bravas, p. 15, we skip the hassle of deep-frying and get our potato chunks crisp-tender by parcooking them in the microwave, tossing them in cornstarch, then finishing them in a hot oven. Also from Spain comes patatas a lo pobre, or poor man's potatoes—sliced potatoes cooked in oil with onions and peppers. We simmer our potatoes, p. 325, then flatten them for more surface browning. Four eggs added at the end make this a simple and delicious skillet supper.

From the Shandong province of China, comes di san xian, which more or less translates to three treasures from the ground. The treasures are eggplant, yellow potatoes and green bell peppers. We make ours, p. 265, by shallow-frying the potatoes and stir-frying the other ingredients for convenience.

Aloo chaat is a street food snack popular in South Asia. Typically, it consists of potatoes fried with lots of spices, chutneys and other ingredients such as fried noodles. Our version, p. 337, roasts the potatoes rather than fries them; we season the potatoes with tangy tamarind chutney before they go into the oven. For color and crisp contrast we pile quick-pickled onions and cucumbers on top.

Like potatoes, sweet potatoes are tubers. They can be pale yellow or deep orange, and the darker versions sometimes are mislabeled as yams, though a true yam has dry flesh and a bark-like skin. Candied sweet potatoes are an American Thanksgiving classic, but they're popular elsewhere, too. Japanese cooks make a dish called daigaku imo, or "university potatoes," due to their popularity as a student snack. Traditionally, the potatoes are deep-fried, coated in caramel and finished with sesame seeds. For our version, p. 158, we cook the potatoes in a syrupy mixture and turn up the heat at the end until the potatoes are glazed and sizzling.

For a savory version of sweet potatoes, we borrow the French concept of a tian, slicing vegetables into thin rounds arranging them in a shallow baking dish and baking them in the oven. We toss our sliced sweet potatoes, p. 235, with vinegar, spices and red pepper flakes to keep the dish from being one-note sweet and tuck herbs and shallots between the slices. Elegant yet earthy, sweet and savory, it's a dish that would be at home on the Thanksgiving table—but would do just as well for any old Thursday.

Lemony Wine-Braised Artichokes

Preparing fresh artichokes requires time and patience, so to keep this stovetop braise quick and easy, we use frozen artichoke hearts. They simmer in white wine infused with aromatics and a little chicken broth, with a few strips of lemon zest to provide citrusy essential oils. Lemon juice and butter added at the very end round out and brighten the dish. A Y-style vegetable peeler is the best tool for removing zest in strips from the fruit, but try to take only the yellow peel, as the white pith underneath is bitter. Serve with warm, crusty bread.

START TO FINISH: 25 MINUTES
SERVINGS: 4

___

3 tablespoons salted butter, cut into 1-tablespoon pieces, divided

1 tablespoon extra-virgin olive oil

2 medium carrots, peeled, halved lengthwise and cut crosswise into ¼-inch pieces

1 medium yellow onion, halved and thinly sliced

Kosher salt and ground black pepper

4 medium garlic cloves, minced

1 cup dry white wine

12-ounce bag frozen artichoke hearts, thawed, quartered if whole

Three 3-inch strips lemon zest, plus 2 tablespoons lemon juice

1 cup low-sodium chicken broth

½ cup lightly packed fresh flat-leaf parsley **OR** mint, finely chopped

Don't use canned or marinated artichoke hearts for this recipe. Frozen artichokes have a fresher, cleaner flavor that's a better partner for the butter, wine and lemon.

1. **In a 12-inch skillet** over medium, heat 1 tablespoon of butter and the oil until the butter melts. Add the carrots, onion and ½ teaspoon each salt and pepper, then cook, stirring occasionally, until the onion is translucent, 3 to 5 minutes. Add the garlic and cook, stirring, until fragrant, about 30 seconds. Add the wine, bring to a simmer and cook, scraping up any browned bits, until the liquid is reduced by about half, 2 to 4 minutes.

2. **Stir in the artichokes,** lemon zest and broth. Bring to a simmer over medium-high and cook, uncovered and stirring occasionally, until the carrots are tender and the liquid is slightly reduced, 4 to 5 minutes.

3. **Remove and discard** the lemon zest. Off heat, stir in the remaining 2 tablespoons butter until melted, then stir in the lemon juice and parsley. Taste and season with salt and pepper.

Braised Potatoes and Green Beans with Olive Oil and Toasted Garlic

Hearty with chunks of potatoes and tender green beans, this is a comforting, stew-like dish. Sliced garlic cloves become deliciously crisp garlic chips that are sprinkled on as a garnish, and the heady garlic-infused oil that remains is stirred into the vegetables at the very end along with a couple tablespoons of woodsy sherry vinegar, suffusing the vegetables with rich flavor. This is hearty enough to be a vegetarian main though it also could be a side to roasted or seared meat, chicken or fish.

START TO FINISH: 30 MINUTES
SERVINGS: 4 TO 6

1 pound Yukon Gold potatoes, unpeeled, cut into 1-inch chunks

2 bay leaves

Kosher salt and ground black pepper

12 ounces green beans, trimmed and halved

¼ cup extra-virgin olive oil, plus more to serve

6 medium garlic cloves, thinly sliced

2 tablespoons sherry vinegar

½ cup finely chopped fresh flat-leaf parsley

Don't use waxy potatoes, such as red or white varieties, as they lack the starch to lightly thicken the cooking liquid. Also, don't worry if the potatoes begin to break apart as they simmer; you'll be mashing some of the pieces anyway.

1. **In a large saucepan,** combine the potatoes, bay, 1 teaspoon salt and 3 cups water. Bring to a simmer over medium-high, then reduce to medium and simmer, stirring occasionally, for 10 minutes. Add the beans and cook, stirring occasionally, until a skewer inserted into the potatoes meets no resistance and the pieces just begin to fall apart, another 10 to 12 minutes.

2. **While the vegetables cook,** in an 8-inch skillet over medium, cook the oil and garlic, stirring occasionally, until the garlic is golden brown, 2 to 3 minutes. Remove from the heat and, using a slotted spoon, transfer the garlic to a small plate; reserve the oil in the pan. To the skillet, whisk in the vinegar, ¼ teaspoon salt and ½ teaspoon pepper.

3. **When the vegetables are done,** remove the saucepan from the heat. Remove and discard the bay, then, using a wooden spoon, gently mash several chunks of potatoes against the side of the pan to lightly thicken the liquid. Stir in the vinegar, parsley and the garlic-infused oil. Taste and season with salt and pepper. Transfer to a serving dish, drizzle with additional oil and sprinkle with the toasted garlic.

Greek Peas with Potatoes and Herbs (Arakas Kokkinistos)

The Greek name for this dish, arakas kokkinistos, translates as "reddened peas." The version taught to us by Greek cooking instructor Argiro Barbarigou included tomato paste, and that's what we call for here. Whereas traditional arakas kokkinistos is pea-centric, we've included a generous amount of potatoes and some carrots to give the stew-like dish enough substance and heft that it can be served as a vegetarian main. Lemon zest and juice added at the end, along with a generous dose of fresh herbs, brightens the flavors.

START TO FINISH: 35 MINUTES
SERVINGS: 4

---

6 tablespoons extra-virgin olive oil, divided, plus more to serve

1 medium red onion, finely chopped

4 medium garlic cloves, minced

2 tablespoons tomato paste

2 medium carrots, peeled, halved lengthwise and cut into ½-inch pieces

1½ pounds Yukon Gold potatoes, unpeeled, cut into ½-inch pieces

Kosher salt and ground black pepper

2½ cups (12 ounces) frozen peas

1 tablespoon finely grated lemon zest, plus 1 tablespoon lemon juice

¾ cup chopped fresh dill

½ cup chopped fresh mint

3 ounces feta cheese, crumbled (¾ cup)

Don't allow the onion and garlic to brown. Cook only until the onion has softened so the flavors remain light and without any caramelized notes. Don't thaw the peas before use; they can be added frozen to the pot.

1. In a large Dutch oven over medium-high, heat 3 tablespoons of the oil until shimmering. Add the onion and garlic, then cook, stirring occasionally, until the onion begins to turn translucent, about 3 minutes. Add the tomato paste and cook, stirring constantly, until the onion is well coated and the tomato paste is fragrant, 1 to 2 minutes. Add the carrots, potatoes, 2½ cups water, 1½ teaspoons salt and ¾ teaspoon pepper, then bring to a simmer. Cover, reduce to medium and cook until a knife inserted into a potato meets no resistance, 15 to 18 minutes.

2. Off heat, stir in the peas. Cover and let stand until the peas are warmed through, about 2 minutes. Stir in the remaining 3 tablespoons oil and the lemon zest and juice. Taste and season with salt and pepper. Stir in ½ of the dill and mint. Transfer to a serving bowl, sprinkle with the remaining herbs and feta, then drizzle with additional oil.

Coconut Curry with Carrots and Broccoli

Kerala, India, is home to ishtoo, a curry awash in coconut broth. The dish gave us the idea for this bright, gently spiced vegetable curry. Carrots and broccoli are the featured vegetables here, but you could substitute others with similar cooking times. For instance, diced potatoes or winter squash could take the place of the carrots; cauliflower florets or asparagus or green beans cut into 2-inch lengths could stand in for the broccoli; and thawed green peas could be stirred in near the end of cooking. Curry leaves have a distinctive flavor, at once lemony and nutty. You can find them at most Indian grocery stores; any surplus can be stored in the freezer for several months. If you can't find curry leaves, not to worry—the dish is plenty flavorful without. Serve basmati rice alongside to soak up the broth.

START TO FINISH: 45 MINUTES
SERVINGS: 4

2 tablespoons coconut oil **OR** neutral oil

12 curry leaves (optional; see headnote)

1 cinnamon stick

⅛ teaspoon ground cloves

Kosher salt and ground black pepper

1 medium yellow onion, finely chopped

2 tablespoons minced fresh ginger

1 jalapeño **OR** Fresno chili, stemmed and sliced into thin rings

¼ teaspoon ground turmeric

14-ounce can coconut milk (see headnote)

12 ounces medium carrots (about 4), peeled and sliced ½ inch thick on the diagonal

8 ounces broccoli crowns, cut into 1-inch florets

Don't use light coconut milk. The flavor and consistency of the curry is best when made with regular full-fat coconut milk. Also, look for a brand that does not contain guar gum or other stabilizers, which affect the texture and color of the dish.

1. **In a large pot over medium,** heat the coconut oil until shimmering. Add the curry leaves (if using), cinnamon, cloves and ¼ teaspoon pepper. Cook, stirring constantly, until fragrant and sizzling, 1 to 2 minutes. Add the onion and cook, stirring occasionally, until softened, 5 to 8 minutes.

2. **Add the ginger,** chili and turmeric; cook, stirring, until fragrant and the mixture begins to stick to the bottom of the pot, 1 to 2 minutes. Stir in the coconut milk, then add the carrots, ½ cup water and ¾ teaspoon salt. Bring to a boil over medium-high, then reduce to medium-low, cover and cook until the carrots begin to soften, about 4 minutes.

3. **Add the broccoli,** cover and cook, stirring occasionally, until the vegetables are tender but not falling apart, 10 to 14 minutes. Remove and discard the cinnamon, then taste and season with salt and pepper.

Optional garnish: Lime wedges **OR** finely chopped fresh chives

Yukon Gold and Artichoke Hash

Fresh artichoke hearts would undoubtedly be delicious for this chunky hash, but being pragmatists, we use frozen because they don't require time-consuming prep. Thaw them, pat them dry and halve them (quartered artichokes can be used as is) and they're ready for the skillet. This hash is great with eggs as a main or served alongside just about any type of roast or braise.

START TO FINISH: 35 MINUTES
SERVINGS: 4 TO 6

1 pound Yukon Gold potatoes, peeled and cut into 1-inch chunks

Kosher salt and ground black pepper

2 tablespoons salted butter

1 tablespoon extra-virgin olive oil

1 medium yellow onion, chopped

12-ounce bag frozen whole artichoke hearts, thawed, halved and patted dry **OR** frozen quartered artichokes, thawed and patted dry

1 medium garlic clove, minced

3 tablespoons finely chopped fresh flat-leaf parsley, divided

Lemon wedges, to serve

Don't forget to pat the artichokes dry after thawing to remove excess moisture. They'll brown more quickly and deeply if excess moisture has been wicked away.

1. **In a 12-inch nonstick skillet,** combine the potatoes, ¼ teaspoon salt and 2 cups water. Bring to a simmer over medium-high, then cover and cook, stirring occasionally, until a skewer inserted into the potatoes meets a little resistance, 8 to 9 minutes. Drain in a colander and set the potatoes aside; wipe the skillet clean.

2. **In the same skillet** over medium-high, combine the butter and oil; heat until the butter begins to foam. Add the onion and cook, stirring occasionally, until softened and beginning to brown, 5 to 6 minutes. Add the cooked potatoes, the artichokes, and ¼ teaspoon each salt and pepper. Cook, stirring occasionally, until the vegetables are well browned, 8 to 10 minutes.

3. **Off heat, stir in the garlic** and 2 tablespoons of parsley, then taste and season with salt and pepper. Transfer to a serving dish and sprinkle with the remaining parsley. Serve with lemon wedges.

Potato Curry with Tomatoes and Yogurt

Korma, sometimes spelled qorma, is a South Asian meat or vegetable braise typically made with yogurt or cream, which yields a rich, velvety sauce. For this potato korma, we use russets for their satisfying starchiness and we keep them chunky so the curry is hearty and substantial. Just the right amount of yogurt, added at the end, enriches the curry without making it unctuous. With steamed basmati rice on the side, this is a perfect vegetarian main.

START TO FINISH: 50 MINUTES
SERVINGS: 4 TO 6

2 tablespoons grapeseed or other neutral oil

1 medium yellow onion, chopped

Kosher salt and ground black pepper

3 medium garlic cloves, minced

1 tablespoon finely grated fresh ginger

1 tablespoon cumin seeds

2 teaspoons ground coriander

2 teaspoons Aleppo pepper OR ½ teaspoon cayenne pepper

1 teaspoon ground turmeric

½ teaspoon ground cinnamon

2 tablespoons tomato paste

2 pounds medium russet potatoes, peeled, halved crosswise, then cut into ½-inch wedges

1 pound ripe tomatoes, cored and chopped

½ cup plain whole-milk yogurt, plus more to serve

Don't use low-fat or nonfat yogurt, which are more likely to separate because of their leanness. Even if using whole-milk yogurt, don't stir it in until the curry has cooled for about five minutes as added insurance against separation.

1. **In a large Dutch oven** over medium, heat the oil until shimmering. Add the onion and ½ teaspoon salt, then cook, stirring occasionally, until the onion begins to soften, about 5 minutes. Add the garlic, ginger, cumin, coriander, Aleppo pepper, turmeric, cinnamon, 1 teaspoon of salt and ½ teaspoon black pepper; cook, stirring, until fragrant, about 30 seconds.

2. **Add the tomato paste and cook,** stirring, until the paste begins to stick to the pot, 1 to 2 minutes. Add 2½ cups water, the potatoes and half of the tomatoes. Bring to a simmer, scraping up any browned bits, and cook, uncovered and stirring occasionally, until a skewer inserted into the potatoes meets no resistance, 30 to 35 minutes.

3. **Remove the pot** from the heat and cool for 5 minutes. Stir in the yogurt and the remaining tomatoes. Taste and season with salt and pepper. Serve with additional yogurt on the side.

Optional garnish: Chopped fresh cilantro

Winter Squash

Roasted, pureed or braised, spiked with savory or spicy flavorings, or mellowed to earthy sweetness, winter squash are good any way and most any time of year.

Japanese cooks make a simple dish out of kabocha, a variety of winter squash that is green with stripes, braising it with soy sauce and a sweetener. In our version, p. 160, we add a little spice by way of toban djan, a fiery chili-bean sauce popular in Asian cooking.

In Afghanistan, cooks braise pumpkin with ginger and onions and serve it with a yogurt sauce. We substitute easier-to-find butternut squash for our take, p. 381, and use tomato paste instead of fresh tomatoes, called for in some versions. We don't skip the yogurt sauce, which gets punch from garlic and mint, and really finishes the dish.

Butter-drenched and roasted winter squash is an American fall classic, but it can be a bit on the fatty side. For our acorn squash, p. 226, we use browned butter and add tangy orange juice and white wine vinegar to balance the richness of the butter. A salad of greens tossed with orange segments and toasted hazelnuts complements the sweet and earthy squash.

Butternut squash lives up to its name, buttery and nutty, which makes it a great partner to lively seasonings. Our spiced soup, p. 112, is made with fresh ginger, cumin and coriander, and we add carrots for an extra layer of flavor and color. We use water instead of stock, which lets the flavors of the vegetables shine through more clearly. The result is a soup that would be fine on an autumn night—or a cool summer evening.

Spicy Peanut and Vegetable Stew

Maafe (also spelled mafe or mafé) is a spicy West African stew made rich with peanut butter. It typically contains meat, but we make a vegetarian version that's hearty with sweet potatoes (or butternut squash) and turnip (or carrot). We like the color and tender-crisp texture that sliced okra adds to the dish, but it's an optional ingredient. If you do add it, stir it into the stew with only about five minutes of simmering left so it doesn't overcook. Serve with steamed rice for a satisfying meat-free meal.

START TO FINISH: 1 HOUR (20 MINUTES ACTIVE)
SERVINGS: 4

⅓ cup smooth peanut butter

2 tablespoons grapeseed or other neutral oil

1 medium yellow **OR** red onion, chopped

3 medium garlic cloves, minced

Kosher salt and ground black pepper

2 tablespoons tomato paste

14½-ounce can diced tomatoes

1½ pounds sweet potatoes, peeled and cut into 1-inch chunks **OR** 1¼ pounds butternut squash, peeled, seeded and cut into 1-inch chunks

1 medium turnip **OR** carrot, peeled and cut into ½-inch cubes

2 habanero chilies, each slit a couple times with a paring knife

4 ounces okra, stemmed and thinly sliced (optional)

2 teaspoons lime juice, plus lime wedges to serve

Don't be afraid of the habanero chilies. *They're whole but slit with a paring knife, so they add fruity flavor and just a little heat. For a really spicy stew, cut the chilies in half to expose the ribs where fiery capsaicin resides, but remember to remove and discard all the halves before serving.*

1. **In a medium bowl,** whisk the peanut butter and 2 cups water until no lumps remain; set aside. In a large pot over medium, heat the oil until shimmering. Add the onion, garlic and ¾ teaspoon salt, then cook, stirring occasionally, until the onion is translucent, 3 to 5 minutes. Stir in the tomato paste and cook, stirring often, until the paste begins to stick to the bottom of the pot, about 2 minutes. Add the tomatoes with juice, scraping up any browned bits. Bring to a simmer and cook, stirring occasionally, until slightly thickened, 3 to 5 minutes.

2. **Stir in the peanut butter mixture.** Bring to a simmer, then add the sweet potatoes, turnip and habaneros. Return to a simmer and simmer, uncovered and stirring occasionally, until the vegetables are tender but not falling apart, about 35 minutes; if using okra, add it after 30 minutes of simmering.

3. **Remove the pot from the heat,** then remove and discard the chilies. Stir in the lime juice, then taste and season with salt and pepper. Serve with lime wedges.

Optional garnish: Chopped roasted peanuts **OR** thinly sliced fresh chilies **OR** chopped fresh cilantro **OR** flat-leaf parsley **OR** a combination

Chilaquiles Verdes

Chilaquiles are a popular Mexican breakfast dish of fried tortillas mixed with salsa, topped with garnishes and often accompanied by eggs. With the sauced tortilla's chewy-crunchy texture and salty, creamy cheese melting on top, the dish is delicious and satisfying. For our version, we use tomatillos rather than red salsa, hence the name chilaquiles verdes (verde means "green" in Spanish). We char tomatillos, chopped onion, garlic and chili; recipes often blend the ingredients to make a smooth salsa, but we skip that step and make a chunkier sauce. And instead of deep-frying the tortillas, we simply toss them with oil then toast them in the oven until crisped and brown. Serve directly from the skillet.

START TO FINISH: 50 MINUTES
SERVINGS: 4 TO 6

Twelve 6-inch corn tortillas, each cut into 8 wedges

6 tablespoons extra-virgin olive oil, divided

Kosher salt and ground black pepper

1 pound tomatillos, husked and quartered

1 medium red onion, chopped

1 jalapeño chili, stemmed and chopped

2 medium garlic cloves, smashed and peeled

1 teaspoon ground cumin

1 cup lightly packed fresh cilantro, roughly chopped

4 ounces queso fresco, crumbled (1 cup) OR sharp white cheddar cheese, shredded (1 cup)

Don't let the chilaquiles sit for too long after you've stirred the tortillas into the sauce, or they'll get uniformly soft and soggy. The dish is best as soon as it's made.

1. Heat the oven to 450°F with a rack in the middle position. On a rimmed baking sheet, toss the tortillas with 3 tablespoons of oil, then sprinkle with salt and pepper. Distribute in an even layer and bake until browned and crisped, 8 to 10 minutes, tossing once about halfway through. Transfer to a large plate; reserve the baking sheet and leave the oven on.

2. On the same baking sheet, combine the tomatillos, onion, jalapeño and garlic. Drizzle with 2 tablespoons of the remaining oil and sprinkle with the cumin and ½ teaspoon each salt and pepper. Toss, then roast until the vegetables are softened and lightly charred, 15 to 18 minutes, stirring once about halfway through. Remove from the oven.

3. In a 12-inch skillet over medium-high, heat the remaining 1 tablespoon oil until shimmering. Scrape in the tomatillo-onion mixture, mashing any large pieces of tomatillo with a wooden spoon. Add ½ cup water, bring to a simmer and cook, uncovered and stirring occasionally, until slightly thickened, about 5 minutes. Stir in the cilantro, then taste and season with salt and pepper.

4. Add the tortillas and carefully toss to coat with the sauce. Remove from the heat and sprinkle with the cheese. Serve directly from the skillet.

Optional garnish: Fried eggs **OR** chopped tomato **OR** peeled, pitted and diced avocado **OR** sour cream **OR** finely chopped white onion **OR** a combination

Ligurian Potato, Green Bean and Mushroom Gratin

Polpettone alla Ligure is the Italian name for this rustic dish. The term polpettone translates as "meatloaf," but in this case, it refers to a mashup of vegetables baked into a casserole. Before baking, we top the vegetables with a mixture of panko and Parmesan for toasty crispness; after baking, the vegetables are set enough to be cut into neat squares. The gratin can be assembled, covered and refrigerated for up to six hours before baking, but keep the panko mixture separate. Just before baking, sprinkle with the topping and extend the cooking time by about 15 minutes. With a salad alongside, this dish is a satisfying vegetarian main, or offer it as a side to braises or roasts.

START TO FINISH: 1 HOUR 20 MINUTES
(50 MINUTES ACTIVE), PLUS COOLING
SERVINGS: 8

———

4 tablespoons salted butter, plus 2 tablespoons salted butter, melted

1 pound Yukon Gold potatoes, peeled and sliced ¼ inch thick

Kosher salt and ground black pepper

3 tablespoons extra-virgin olive oil

2 medium shallots, finely chopped

1 pound green beans, trimmed and cut into ¼-inch pieces

8 ounces cremini mushrooms, trimmed and sliced about ¼ inch thick

1 tablespoon minced fresh marjoram **OR** oregano

2 large eggs

3 ounces Parmesan cheese, finely grated (1½ cups), divided

½ cup panko breadcrumbs

Don't overcook the mushrooms and beans when sautéing them, as they will continue to cook in the oven. Cook until the mushrooms give up their moisture and the beans are bright green but still quite crisp; they should not be browned.

1. Heat the oven to 400°F with a rack in the middle position. Mist a 9-by-13-inch baking dish with cooking spray and set aside. In a 12-inch skillet over medium, melt 4 tablespoons butter. Add the potatoes and ½ teaspoon salt, then stir to coat. Add ½ cup water, then distribute the potatoes evenly. Cover and cook until a skewer inserted into the potatoes meets no resistance, 15 to 20 minutes, stirring once about halfway through. Transfer the potatoes and any liquid in the pan to a large bowl, then use a fork to mash to the consistency of chunky mashed potatoes; set aside.

2. Wipe out the skillet and set it over medium. Add the oil, shallots and ¼ teaspoon salt. Cook, stirring occasionally, until the shallots are softened but not browned, 5 to 6 minutes. Add the beans and mushrooms, then increase to medium-high. Cook, stirring occasionally, until most of the liquid released by the mushrooms has evaporated and the beans are bright green but still crisp, about 5 minutes; the vegetables should not begin to brown. Stir in the marjoram and cook until fragrant, about 30 seconds. Transfer to the bowl with the potatoes and cool for about 10 minutes.

3. In a medium bowl, whisk the eggs, 2 ounces (1 cup) of Parmesan, and ½ teaspoon each salt and pepper. Add the egg mixture to the vegetable mixture and fold with a silicone spatula until combined. Transfer to the prepared baking dish and spread evenly.

4. In a small bowl, combine the panko, the melted butter and the remaining 1 ounce (½ cup) Parmesan, then stir until the panko is evenly moistened. Sprinkle evenly over the vegetables. Bake until golden brown and bubbling at the edges, about 30 minutes. Cool for about 15 minutes before serving.

START TO FINISH: 35 MINUTES
SERVINGS: 4

3 tablespoons grapeseed or other neutral oil

½ teaspoon ground turmeric

3 large shallots, halved and thinly sliced

3 medium garlic cloves, minced

2 tablespoons minced fresh cilantro stems, plus ½ cup lightly packed fresh cilantro leaves, roughly chopped, reserved separately

12 ounces cremini mushrooms **OR** oyster mushrooms **OR** maitake mushrooms **OR** a combination, cut or torn into rough 1-inch pieces

Kosher salt and ground black pepper

1 pint cherry **OR** grape tomatoes, halved

1 or 2 jalapeño chilies, stemmed and sliced into thin rings

2 teaspoons fish sauce **OR** soy sauce

Lime wedges, to serve

Mushrooms, Tomatoes and Shallots with Turmeric and Green Chili

Sautéed shallots, garlic and cilantro stems lend backbone to this vegetable curry, and the commingling of softened mushrooms and tomatoes creates a simple but flavorful sauce. Sliced green chilies add spicy kick and a little fish sauce stirred in to finish provides deep savoriness and additional umami (you can substitute soy sauce if you want to keep it vegetarian). Serve with rice.

Don't forget to salt the mushrooms as soon they hit the skillet. This helps draw out their liquid, serving the dual purpose of softening them and infusing the dish with their flavor.

1. **In a 12-inch skillet** over medium, heat the oil until shimmering. Add the turmeric and cook, stirring, until the oil takes on a yellow hue, about 15 seconds. Add the shallots and cook, stirring occasionally, until softened but not brown, 2 to 4 minutes. Add the garlic and cilantro stems, then cook, stirring, until fragrant, about 30 seconds. Add the mushrooms and ¼ teaspoon each salt and pepper. Cook, stirring often, until the mushrooms release some of their liquid, 3 to 5 minutes.

2. **Stir in the tomatoes,** chili(es) and ½ cup water. Bring to a simmer over medium-high and cook, uncovered and stirring occasionally, until the tomatoes have broken down and the mushrooms are tender, 5 to 8 minutes.

3. **Add the fish sauce** and cook, stirring, until well combined, about 30 seconds. Off heat, stir in the cilantro leaves, then taste and season with salt and pepper. Serve with lime wedges.

Afghan-Style Braised Butternut Squash with Garlic-Mint Yogurt

START TO FINISH: 50 MINUTES (25 MINUTES ACTIVE)
SERVINGS: 4 TO 6

This is our version of the Afghan pumpkin dish called borani kadoo. We use butternut squash instead of pumpkin since it is readily available throughout the year, and swap tomato paste for the fresh tomatoes called for in many versions. The garlicky, minty yogurt is an excellent foil for the stewed squash—don't omit it, as it really elevates and completes the dish.

4 tablespoons grapeseed or other neutral oil, divided

2-pound butternut squash, peeled, seeded and cut into 1½-inch chunks

1 medium yellow onion, chopped

Kosher salt and ground black pepper

2 medium garlic cloves, minced

1¼ teaspoons ground coriander

½ teaspoon ground turmeric

½ teaspoon ground cinnamon

1 tablespoon tomato paste

1 tablespoon white sugar

1 cup plain whole-milk yogurt

¼ cup lightly packed fresh mint, chopped

Don't allow the moisture to cook off as the squash braises. Add water 2 tablespoons at a time as needed to ensure the sauce remains loose, not thick and concentrated.

1. **In a large Dutch oven** over medium-high, heat 2 tablespoons oil until shimmering. Add the squash and cook, stirring often, until golden brown, 6 to 8 minutes. Transfer to a medium bowl.

2. **To the pot,** add the remaining 2 tablespoons oil along with the onion and ½ teaspoon salt. Cook over medium-high, stirring often, until lightly browned, about 3 minutes. Add half of the garlic, the coriander, turmeric and cinnamon; cook, stirring, until fragrant, about 30 seconds. Stir in the tomato paste and return the squash to the pot. Add the sugar and 1 cup water, then bring to a simmer, scraping up any browned bits. Cover, reduce to medium-low and cook, stirring occasionally and adding water 2 tablespoons at a time as needed if the mixture looks dry, until a skewer inserted into the squash meets no resistance, 25 to 30 minutes; there should be a little lightly thickened liquid remaining in the pot.

3. **While the squash cooks,** in a small bowl, stir together the yogurt, mint, the remaining garlic and ¼ teaspoon salt and pepper; set aside until ready to serve. When the squash is done, taste and season with salt and pepper. Transfer to a serving dish and serve with the yogurt mixture.

Tuscan Braised Potatoes (Patate in Umido)

This hearty vegetable stew is based on a recipe by Rolando Beramendi. The potatoes are cooked using a technique that's often employed with risotto: the liquid is incorporated in multiple additions. This concentrates flavors while using the potatoes' natural starch to create a sauce that clings lightly to the chunks. We like the flavor backbone of chicken broth, but you could make this dish vegetarian by substituting vegetable broth. Patate in umido is an excellent accompaniment to roasted chicken, pork or seafood.

START TO FINISH: 1 HOUR
SERVINGS: 4

_____

¼ cup extra-virgin olive oil, plus more to serve

2 small red onions, quartered lengthwise and thinly sliced crosswise

3 medium garlic cloves, smashed and peeled

2 pounds russet potatoes, peeled and cut into 1-inch chunks

14½-ounce can whole peeled tomatoes, crushed by hand

2½ cups low-sodium chicken broth, divided

½ teaspoon red pepper flakes

8-inch sprig fresh rosemary

Kosher salt and ground black pepper

½ cup lightly packed fresh basil leaves, roughly chopped

Don't use a narrow pot; the wide diameter of a Dutch oven allows for more rapid evaporation of liquid. Also, don't use lower-starch potatoes, such as red, white or Yukon Gold potatoes. Russets are the best choice, as their starchiness gives them a light, tender texture when cooked and lends the sauce a velvety quality.

1. **In a large Dutch oven** over medium, combine the oil, onions and garlic. Cook, stirring occasionally, until the onions just begin to brown, 8 to 10 minutes. Add the potatoes and stir to coat with the oil. Cook, stirring occasionally, until the potato starch that coats the bottom of the pot starts to brown, about 5 minutes.

2. **Stir in the tomatoes,** 1 cup of broth, the pepper flakes, rosemary and ¼ teaspoon salt. Bring to a simmer over medium-high, then distribute the potatoes in an even layer. Cook, occasionally scraping along the bottom of the pot with a silicone spatula and gently folding the mixture, for 10 minutes; adjust the heat as needed to maintain a steady simmer

3. **Add ½ cup of the remaining broth** and cook, occasionally scraping and folding, for another 10 minutes. Add the remaining 1 cup broth in 2 additions in the same way, cooking for only 5 minutes after the final addition and stirring gently so the potatoes don't break up. Cover the pot, remove from the heat and let stand for 5 minutes.

4. **Stir in half the basil,** then taste and season with salt and black pepper. Remove and discard the rosemary, then transfer the potatoes to a bowl, drizzle with additional oil and sprinkle with the remaining basil.

Greek Baked Vegetables (Briam)

START TO FINISH: 50 MINUTES
SERVINGS: 6

The Greek baked vegetable dish known as briam is an example of lathera (also spelled ladera), vegetable-centric dishes that feature a generous amount of olive oil (lath in Greek). In briam, potatoes give the dish weight and substance, but it's the summer produce—such as zucchini, tomatoes, garlic and herbs—that are the main attraction. Because potatoes take longer to cook than juicier, less starchy vegetables, we give them a head start by parcooking them in the microwave. Crumbled feta cheese scattered on after baking provides salty, briny notes that play off the sweetness of the tender, sweet vegetables. Briam is excellent warm but also is delicious at room temperature.

2 pounds Yukon Gold potatoes, unpeeled, sliced ¼ inch thick

2 medium zucchini (about 8 ounces each), sliced into ½-inch-thick rounds

1 medium red onion, halved and thinly sliced

4 medium garlic cloves, thinly sliced

6 ripe plum tomatoes, 4 cored and chopped, 2 cored and sliced crosswise into ¼-inch-thick rounds

1 tablespoon plus ½ teaspoon dried oregano

¼ cup plus 2 teaspoons extra-virgin olive oil, plus more to serve

Kosher salt and ground black pepper

2 ounces feta cheese, crumbled (½ cup)

¼ cup lightly packed fresh basil, torn, or 3 tablespoons chopped fresh flat-leaf parsley or dill (or a combination)

Don't use round tomatoes for this recipe. Because plum tomatoes are relatively dry, their juices won't turn the dish watery as they soften during baking. Also, don't use a glass baking dish or a baking dish that's not broiler-safe. The vegetables are finished under the broiler to caramelize the surface, so it's essential to use a baking vessel that can withstand the heat.

1. **Heat the oven to 475°F** with a rack in the middle position. In a large microwave-safe bowl, combine the potatoes and ¼ cup water. Cover and microwave on high until the potatoes are just shy of tender, about 10 minutes, stirring once halfway through.

2. **Pour off and discard** any liquid in the bottom of the bowl. Add the zucchini, onion, garlic, the chopped tomatoes, the 1 tablespoon oregano, ¼ cup of the oil, 1½ teaspoons salt and 1 teaspoon pepper. Toss well, then distribute evenly in a 9-by-13-inch broiler-safe baking pan. Lay the tomato slices on top, spacing them evenly. Drizzle with the remaining 2 teaspoons oil, then sprinkle with the remaining ½ teaspoon oregano and ¼ teaspoon each salt and pepper. Bake until a skewer inserted into the vegetables meets no resistance, about 25 minutes.

3. **Turn the oven to broil** and broil until well browned, about 5 minutes. Remove from the oven and sprinkle with the feta. Let rest for about 10 minutes, then sprinkle with the basil and drizzle with additional oil.

Fingerling Potato Curry with Fire-Roasted Tomatoes

This fragrant vegetable curry gets its big, bold flavor from spices that are freshly ground plus a good amount of garlic and ginger. We like to use fingerling potatoes, which hold their shape well, and canned fire-roasted tomatoes which have a subdued smokiness. Fresh mint lightens and brightens the assertive flavors, but it's not added until the end, so a good time to prep it is while the curry simmers. This is hearty enough to be a vegetarian main, with basmati rice or warm naan served alongside.

START TO FINISH: 1¼ HOURS
SERVINGS: 4 TO 6

1 tablespoon coriander seeds

1 tablespoon fennel seeds

1 teaspoon black peppercorns

½ teaspoon red pepper flakes, plus more to serve

2 tablespoons coconut oil, preferably unrefined

1 medium yellow onion, finely chopped

3 medium garlic cloves, thinly sliced

2-inch piece fresh ginger, peeled and sliced into thin coins

1½ pounds fingerling potatoes, halved lengthwise

28-ounce can fire-roasted diced tomatoes

Kosher salt and ground black pepper

½ cup lightly packed fresh mint, torn

Plain whole-milk yogurt, to serve (optional)

Don't overprocess the spices. Pulse them in a spice grinder or pound them in a mortar with a pestle until they're coarsely ground, not pulverized to a fine powder, so they add textural interest to the curry.

1. **In a spice grinder,** pulse the coriander, fennel, peppercorns and red pepper flakes until coarsely ground. Alternatively, combine the spices in a mortar and pound with a pestle until coarsely ground.

2. **In a large Dutch oven** over medium, heat the oil until shimmering. Add the onion and cook, stirring occasionally, until softened, 5 to 7 minutes. Add the spice mix and cook, stirring, until fragrant, about 1 minute. Add the garlic and ginger; cook, stirring, for about 1 minute. Stir in the potatoes, the tomatoes with juices, 1 cup water and ½ teaspoon salt. Bring to a simmer over medium-high, then cover, reduce to medium and cook, stirring occasionally and adjusting the heat as needed to maintain a simmer, until the potatoes begin to soften, about 20 minutes.

3. **Uncover and cook,** stirring occasionally, until the liquid has thickened and a skewer inserted into potatoes meets no resistance, 20 to 25 minutes. Off heat, stir in half of the mint, then taste and season with salt. Transfer to a serving bowl and sprinkle with the remaining mint. If desired, drizzle with yogurt or offer it alongside.

Spanish Summer Vegetable Stew (Pisto Manchego)

Pisto manchego is the Spanish equivalent of French ratatouille. The hearty, colorful vegetarian stew can be served as a tapa (small plate), as a side dish or topped with a fried egg as a meal in itself. To achieve just the right texture and flavor, we add the vegetables to the pot in stages so each cooks for just the right amount of time and retains its character in the finished dish. This pisto does not contain eggplant, a common addition in many versions. And for flavor and color balance, we like to use one green bell pepper and one red, but if you like, replace the green with a yellow or orange pepper. Serve with crusty bread to soak up the juices.

START TO FINISH: 50 MINUTES
SERVINGS: 4 TO 6

⅓ cup extra-virgin olive oil, plus more to serve

2 medium yellow onions, chopped

Kosher salt and ground black pepper

1 medium zucchini **OR** yellow summer squash (about 8 ounces), quartered lengthwise and cut crosswise into ½-inch pieces

4 medium garlic cloves, thinly sliced

1 medium green bell pepper, stemmed, seeded and cut into ½-inch pieces

1 medium red bell pepper, stemmed, seeded and cut into ½-inch pieces

1 pound ripe tomatoes, cored and finely chopped

Don't brown the vegetables. Though we often cook ingredients until well browned to develop flavor, for this dish we cook the vegetables more gently so they retain their freshness, character and color. Don't use plum tomatoes here. Because they are drier and firmer than round tomatoes, they won't meld well with the other ingredients.

1. **In a large pot over medium,** heat the oil until shimmering. Add the onions and ¼ teaspoon salt, then cover and cook, stirring occasionally, until softened but not browned, 8 to 10 minutes. Add the zucchini and garlic. Increase to medium-high and cook, uncovered and stirring occasionally, until the zucchini is beginning to soften, about 7 minutes.

2. **Stir in both bell peppers** and cook, stirring occasionally, until the peppers are softened, about 7 minutes. Add the tomatoes, ½ teaspoon each salt and pepper, then cook, stirring occasionally, until the tomatoes have softened and the mixture is stewy, about 5 minutes. Taste and season with salt and pepper. Serve drizzled with additional oil.

INDEX

olive oil
    Greek baked vegetables with, 384
    potatoes and green beans with, 367
    potatoes and zucchini with, 351
    spaghetti aglio e olio with, 292
    tomato and bread soup with, 95
    tomato and onion salad with, 31
    tuna packed in, 75, 89
olives
    carrots and leeks with, 155
    celery and avocado salad with, 54
    fennel-orange salad with, 50
    Greek cabbage salad with, 58
    kale salad with, 29
    potato salad with, 82, 89
    romaine and radicchio salad with, 66
    tomato tart with, 2
    watercress salad with, 61
omelets
    Swiss chard and herb, 314
    zucchini and Gruyère, 318
onions, 103
    agrodolce stewed peppers with, 289
    artichokes braised with, 364
    cabbage stir-fried with, 252
    cauliflower kati rolls with, 335
    with cilantro yogurt, 207
    fennel slow-roasted with, 233
    Indian-spiced potatoes with, 337
    Indian-spiced spinach with, 320
    inverted pizza with, 342
    Lebanese-style greens with, 185
    mashed vegetable curry with, 144
    potatoes and zucchini with, 351
    salads with, 31, 32, 73, 81
    Sicilian caponata with, 10
    soups with, 104, 113
    Spanish-style potatoes with, 325
    Spanish-style roasted, 208
    Spanish vegetable stew with, 387
    sunchokes with, 85
    tomato tart with, 2
    tortilla Española with, 341
    Tuscan braised potatoes with, 383
    zucchini fritters with, 11
    See also leeks; scallions; shallots
orange
    broccoli with, 135, 295
    carrots and parsnips with, 189
    radishes and snap peas with, 131
    salads with, 47, 50, 226
oyster sauce
    carrots and bok choy with, 259
    Chinese broccoli with, 248

Indonesian-style noodles with, 296

P

panade, leek, kale, and Emmentaler, 359
pancakes, savory fresh corn, 3
pancetta, pasta with
    campanelle or orecchiette, 276, 297
    linguine, 286
    rigatoni, 305
paprika
    bravas sauce with, 15
    broccoli with, 176
    chickpeas and spinach with, 358
    romanesco with, 191
    soups with, 120, 123
    Spanish green beans with, 340
Parmesan cheese
    agrodolce stewed peppers with, 289
    artichoke tart with, 22
    broccoli with, 202
    Ligurian gratin with, 379
    pasta with, 271, 286, 292
    risotto with, 280, 283, 300
    salads with, 68, 86
    soups with, 104, 127
    zucchini and fennel with, 215
parsley
    habanero-onion soup with, 113
    mushrooms with, 205
    salads with, 31, 41, 59, 66, 86
    tomatoey tabbouleh with, 67
parsnips
    Basque-style soup with, 101
    carrots and, 189
    curried, 150
pashtida, asparagus and herb, 313
pasta
    with artichokes, asparagus, and ricotta, 303
    with artichokes, lemon, and pancetta, 286
    with asparagus, lemon, and Parmesan, 271
    with broccoli-lemon sauce, 275
    broccoli rabe with, 272
    with cauliflower, garlic, and breadcrumbs, 276
    with eggplant, tomatoes, and Gorgonzola, 281
    with pesto calabrese, 301
    spaghetti aglio e olio, 292
    with spinach, raisins, and garlic, 307
    with squash, kale, and goat cheese, 299
    with Swiss chard, white beans, and rosemary, 305
    with tomatoes, peas, and pancetta, 297

    See also noodles
pastry, tart, 2, 22, 23
patatas bravas, 15
patate in umido (Tuscan braised potatoes), 383
pav bhaji (mashed vegetable curry with buns), 144
peanuts
    broccoli with, 202
    salads with, 26, 91
    vegetable stew with, 376
    Vietnamese-style eggplant with, 200
pears
    radicchio salad with, 68
    rutabaga and, 237
peas
    cabbage stir-fried with, 252
    curried cauliflower rice with, 331
    Greek, with potatoes and herbs, 369
    mashed vegetable curry with, 144
    pasta with, 297
    potato salad with pigeon, 82
    radishes and snap, 131
    salads with snap or snow, 46, 73, 75
    stew with black-eyed, 355
    stir-fried snap or snow, 251, 258, 261
    See also chickpeas
pecans
    salad with, 79
    squash soup with, 115
pecorino Romano cheese
    broccoli rabe with, 272
    kale salad with, 29
    pasta with, 275, 297, 303, 305, 307
peperoncini, salad with, 86
pepper, Aleppo
    eggplant and peppers with, 213
    Lebanese-style potatoes with, 171
    muhammara (dip) with, 6
    eggs with, 336
    vegetables roasted with, 207
pepper, black
    carrots and bok choy with, 259
    Thai-style stir-fry with, 261
pepper, red, flaked
    Brussels sprouts with, 174
    gochugaru, 16, 28, 285
peppercorns, Sichuan
    cauliflower dry-fried with, 253
    mushrooms braised with, 172
    potatoes stir-fried with, 263
    snow peas stir-fried with, 251
peppers, bell, 13
    agrodolce-stewed, 289
    cauliflower kati rolls with, 335

ACKNOWLEDGMENTS

Milk Street is aptly named for its address, 177 Milk Street in Boston. But we also are a group of people who work all over the world, from Australia to Los Angeles, from San Francisco to Barcelona. This global community of like-minded cooks, editors and designers has brought you the book that you are holding in your hands and they deserve a kindly mention.

In particular, I want to acknowledge J.M. Hirsch, our tireless editorial director, Matthew Card, food editor, Michelle Locke, books editor, Dawn Yanagihara, recipe editor, Bianca Borges, contributing food editor, and Shaula Clark, managing editor, for leading the charge on conceiving, developing and editing all of this. Also, Jennifer Baldino Cox, our art director, and the entire design team who deftly captured the look, feel and energy of the recipes. Special thanks to Brianna Coleman, art director of photography, Connie Miller, photographer, Christine Tobin, stylist, and Gary Tooth, book designer.

Our team of production cooks who have been showing up at Milk Street for most of the last year did yeoman's work including Diane Unger, Courtney Hill, Rebecca Richmond, Calvin Cox, Rose Hattabaugh and Elizabeth Mindreau. Deborah Broide, Milk Street director of media relations, has done a spectacular job of sharing with the world all we do at Milk Street. Wes Martin, who runs our kitchen, deserves a special mention; he shopped and personally delivered ingredients to our cooks who were safe at home during the height of the pandemic.

We also have a couple of folks to thank who work outside of 177 Milk Street.

Michael Szczerban, editor, and everyone at Little, Brown and Company have been superb and inspired partners in this project. And my long-standing book agent, David Black, has been instrumental in bringing this project to life both with his knowledge of publishing and his friendship and support. Thank you, David!

Finally, a sincere thank you to my business partner and wife, Melissa, who manages our media department, from television to radio. Melissa has nurtured the Milk Street brand from the beginning so that we ended up where we thought we were going in the first place.

And, last but not least, to all of you who have supported the Milk Street project. Each and every one of you has a seat at the Milk Street table.

Christopher Kimball

ABOUT THE AUTHOR

Christopher Kimball is founder of Christopher Kimball's Milk Street, a food media company dedicated to learning and sharing bold, easy cooking from around the world. It produces the bimonthly *Christopher Kimball's Milk Street Magazine*, as well as *Christopher Kimball's Milk Street Radio*, a weekly public radio show and podcast heard on more than 220 stations nationwide, and the public television show *Christopher Kimball's Milk Street*. He founded *Cook's Magazine* in 1980 and served as publisher and editorial director through 1989. He re-launched it as *Cook's Illustrated* in 1993. Through 2016, Kimball was host and executive producer of *America's Test Kitchen* and *Cook's Country*. He also hosted *America's Test Kitchen* radio show on public radio. Kimball is the author of several books, including *Fannie's Last Supper*.

Christopher Kimball's Milk Street is changing how we cook by searching the world for bold, simple recipes and techniques. Adapted and tested for home cooks everywhere, these lessons are the backbone of what we call the new home cooking. We are located at 177 Milk Street in downtown Boston, site of our editorial offices and cooking school. It also is where we record *Christopher Kimball's Milk Street* television and radio shows and is home to our online store, which curates craft food and cookware products from around the world. Visit 177milkstreet.com to shop and for more information.